Richard Overstreet

ROBERT GOTTLIEB is the former president, publisher, and editor-in-chief of Alfred A. Knopf and the former editor of *The New Yorker*. He has contributed to *The New York Review of Books, The New York Times Book Review, The New Yorker*, and *The New York Observer*, where he has been the dance critic for many years. He is the author of *Sarah: The Life of Sarah Bernhardt, George Balanchine: The Ballet Maker, Lives and Letters*, and *Great Expectations: The Sons and Daughters of Charles Dickens*. In 2015, he received the annual Award for Distinguished Service to the Arts from the American Academy of Arts and Sciences.

ALSO BY ROBERT GOTTLIEB

Great Expectations: The Sons and Daughters of Charles Dickens

Lives and Letters

Sarah: The Life of Sarah Bernhardt

George Balanchine: The Ballet Maker

Reading Dance (editor)

Reading Lyrics (editor, with Robert Kimball)

Reading Jazz (editor)

Everyman's Library *Collected Stories* of Rudyard Kipling (editor)

The Journals of John Cheever (editor)

A Certain Style: The Art of the Plastic Handbag, 1949–59

Avid Reader

A LIFE

Robert Gottlieb

PICADOR

FARRAR, STRAUS AND GIROUX

NEW YORK

AVID READER. Copyright © 2016 by Robert Gottlieb. All rights reserved.
For information, address Picador,
175 Fifth Avenue, New York, N.Y. 10010.

picadorusa.com • picadorbookroom.tumblr.com
twitter.com/picadorusa • facebook.com/picadorusa

Picador® is a U.S. registered trademark and is used by Macmillan Publishing Group,
LLC, under license from Pan Books Limited.

For book club information, please visit facebook.com/picadorbookclub or
email marketing@picadorusa.com.

Designed by Abby Kagan

The Library of Congress has cataloged the Farrar, Straus and Giroux edition as follows:

Names: Gottlieb, Robert, 1931– author.
Title: Avid reader : a life / Robert Gottlieb.
Description: First edition. | New York : Farrar, Straus and Giroux, 2016. |
Includes index.
Identifiers: LCCN 2015048673 | ISBN 9780374279929 (hardcover) |
ISBN 9780374713904 (ebook)
Subjects: LCSH: Gottlieb, Robert, 1931– | Book editors—United States—
Biography. | Periodical editors—United States—Biography. | Publishers and
publishing—United States—Biography. | Publishers and publishing—United
States—History—20th century.
Classification: LCC PN149.9.G68 A3 2016 | DDC 070.5'1092—dc23
LC record available at http://lccn.loc.gov/2015048673

Picador Paperback ISBN 978-1-250-14105-7

Our books may be purchased in bulk for promotional, educational, or
business use. Please contact your local bookseller or the Macmillan Corporate
and Premium Sales Department at 1-800-221-7945, extension 5442, or by
email at MacmillanSpecialMarkets@macmillan.com.

First published by Farrar, Straus and Giroux

First Picador Edition: September 2017

P1

To my grandsons, Oliver and Jacob Young,
in case they're ever curious about how their grandfather spent his life

And to the memories of Nina Bourne and Deborah Rogers

By the employment of methods amounting almost to the so-called third degree, the heads of the publishers syndicate who I am under contract has finally got me to write my autobiography, a task which I shrink from it like Pola [Negri] from a camera, yet which the doing of which I feel I owe it to my public.

—from the introduction to *The Story of a Wonder Man, Being the Autobiography of Ring Lardner*

CONTENTS

NOTE
xiii

READING
3

LEARNING
12

WORKING
Simon and Schuster
36

WORKING
Alfred A. Knopf
101

WORKING
The New Yorker
198

WORKING
Knopf Redux
237

DANCING
261

WRITING
290

LIVING
306

ACKNOWLEDGMENTS
325

INDEX
329

NOTE

For a long time when people asked me whether I was ever going to write a memoir or autobiography, I answered that all editors' memoirs basically come down to the same thing: "So I said to him, 'Leo! Don't just do war! Do peace too!'" For various reasons—I wanted to set bits of the record straight; I wanted to say some things about editing and publishing and even myself—I eventually changed my mind and have, to my chagrin, discovered the inevitability of the Tolstoy syndrome. There was no way I could talk about editing and publishing except in terms of the books I myself had worked on. So it all comes down to "I did this" and "I did that," and naturally it's one's successes one tends to remember—as with Leo.

Avid Reader

READING

I BEGAN AS I WOULD GO ON—reading. By the time I was four, my grandfather had shown me how to do it, mostly by having me follow along as he read to me. My mother, a New York City public school teacher, left for work early every morning, but Grampa, her father, who lived with us until he died when I was nine, was always there, and after breakfast I would climb into his bed and he would tell me stories, teach me chess, and read aloud. Most important were Kipling's *Jungle Books*, and I still have the two volumes—one bound in mustard, one in green—that he read from, and which thrilled me. But before that was Dorothy Kunhardt's *Junket Is Nice*, which came into the world in 1933, two years after I did, and which I couldn't get enough of. (Later, she would write the indispensable *Pat the Bunny*.) Although it was a success, *Junket Is Nice* disappeared—not just my copy, but altogether. Apparently there were legal problems with the Junket people, and only recently has it been restored to us. Going back to it after more than seventy-five years, I discovered that it's about a little boy who turns out to be smarter than anyone else in the world. What a surprise that I needed constant access to it!

The next book to seize me totally was read to our fourth-grade class by nice, motherly Mrs. Hurst. It was *Lad: A Dog*, by Albert Payson Terhune, and dogs were my passion. But Lad was not a dog like my cute little Waggie; Lad was a collie, and—a recurrent Terhune theme—a *thoroughbred.* Albert Payson Terhune did not care for "mongrels," in fact was a devoted eugenicist—the burglar whom Lad routs in the middle of the night is, unsurprisingly, a "negro." But what did I know about eugenics? Lad was noble, Lad was true. As I discovered on a recent rereading, among his many exploits Lad saved the life of a five-year-old paralyzed girl by flinging himself between her and a striking copperhead, not only almost dying from snake venom but somehow prompting the child to walk. I already loved dogs—so much easier to deal with than other children—and Lad was not just any dog, as we learn in the first paragraph: "He had the gay courage of d'Artagnan, and an uncanny wisdom. Also—who could doubt it, after a look into his mournful brown eyes—he had a soul." I tried not to show I was crying during Mrs. Hurst's read-alouds.

Lad: A Dog went through seventy printings in its original edition, and Terhune went on to write at least thirty other dog books, many of which I read and all of which I assume displayed the mawkish Terhune style and reflected the repulsive Terhune beliefs. But it was *Lad* that revealed to me the amazing power of books to arouse feelings—and therefore to change lives. I was emotionally prepared when Eric Knight's *Lassie Come-Home* (the movie dropped the hyphen) came my way, an infinitely better book than *Lad*, which I think I recognized even then. Horse books didn't get to me, not even *Black Beauty*, although I liked and still like Mary O'Hara's *Flicka* trilogy. But it was their boy hero, Ken, with whom I identified, not the horses.

Of course I also read the established children's classics—*Alice, The Wind in the Willows, Tom Sawyer*, Jules Verne, all the Oz books and Dr. Dolittle books—as well as the more recent ones, especially the inevitable Winnie-the-Poohs. There were also adventure series, which I could take out from the public library in batches of three or four: Tarzan, naturally, and a successful rip-off series I liked even more, the only title of which I remember being *Bomba the Jungle Boy in the Swamp of Death*, which I haven't revisited.

The key books of my childhood, though—and sometimes, I think, of my entire life—were the twelve novels by Arthur Ransome, beginning with *Swallows and Amazons*, published in 1930, just in time for me. The

Swallows were the four Walker children, the Amazons were the two Blackett girls, and they took their aliases from the two little boats they sailed in the summers on the author's reimagining of Lake Windermere in England's Lake District. In the fourth book, *Winter Holiday*, they're joined by the two Callum children, Dick (a budding scientist) and Dorothea (a novelist-in-waiting). These two were the characters I felt closest to: Bookish, shy loners, they were the outsiders who were swept up by the Swallows and Amazons and joined in their adventures. I was certainly not an adventurer, and didn't want to be one, so it wasn't the sailing, the camping out, the racing, or the gentle plots that called to me. It was that community of decent, independent youngsters, superbly individualized by Ransome, trusted by their parents, enjoying a healthy childhood, having fun. If the Walkers and the Blacketts could adopt the Callums, they might have made room for me.

Over a period of four or five years I read and reread and re-reread the Ransome books—my favorites as many as fifty times each. They were the counterpoint to school, homework, playing cards with my parents and occasionally chess with my father (the only activity we shared), typical nighttime phone calls with classmates, and radio—the essential entertainment of the period. Since I was sickly (though not as sickly as I made myself out to be), I was home from school a lot, caught up in radio soap operas—*Our Gal Sunday* (the story of an orphaned mountain girl married to Lord Henry Brinthrope, England's "richest, most handsome Lord"); *Life Can Be Beautiful* (the story of the waif Chichi Conrad, who one day stumbles into benign Papa David Solomon's Slightly Read Bookshop, where she takes up permanent residence along with the embittered cripple Stephen); *Mary Marlin* (theme song: "Clair de Lune"), in which the heroine, when her husband, Senator Joe Marlin, disappears while on a secret mission to Siberia, becomes senator in his stead. And let's not forget *Ma Perkins, Stella Dallas* ("based on the immortal novel by Olive Higgins Prouty"), and the quintessential *Romance of Helen Trent*, "who, when life mocks her, breaks her hopes, dashes her against the rocks of despair, fights back bravely, successfully, to prove what so many women long to prove, that because a woman is thirty-five or more, romance in life need not be over." (*Helen Trent* broadcast for twenty-seven years.) I assume that all this sentimental radio melodrama helped prepare me for my later immersion, both as reader and as editor, in genre fiction. It was certainly harmless stuff, since nothing bad or nasty ever really happened, except for the offstage disappearance of Senator Joe and the inevitable episodes involving either amnesia or trial for murder (or both) that punctuated the lives of Sunday, Chichi, and the rest. When in the early 1950s, home from Cambridge, I dropped back in on soap opera—just in time to hear the final episode of *Life Can Be Beautiful*—everything had changed: Alcoholism, abortion, and adultery had barged in, the charm was gone, and the soaps were migrating to TV.

Soap opera was a special taste. Nighttime radio was for everyone. Jack Benny, Bob Hope, Red Skelton, Fibber McGee and Molly, George Burns and Gracie Allen, Eddie Cantor, Fred Allen, Bing Crosby, Lucky Strike's *Your Hit Parade, Information Please,* Fanny Brice as Baby Snooks, were as pervasive as today's top TV shows—more so, since there were fewer options. The big fight with your parents was whether you could have the radio on while you were doing your homework. They didn't realize that you were also doing your homework in the late afternoons while tuned in to the kid shows: *Captain Midnight, Little Orphan Annie,* and my special passion, *Jack Armstrong* ("all-American boy"), another adventurer, often to be found deep in the Amazon jungles and also embedded in a family not his own (his sidekicks Billy and Betty and their Uncle Jim). Annie was by definition an orphan, as were Tarzan and Kipling's Mowgli. More deracinated than any of these was my hero of heroes, the Lone Ranger, who not only needed no one in his life other than the faithful Tonto and the "great horse Silver" but was hidden behind a mask. I was also lucky enough to have been in on the birth and early exploits of the comic-book heroes Superman and Batman—also more or less loners, also masked, and also omnipotent. Comic books were anathema to parents, their brutality ("POW!" "Wham!"), and the desperate struggles of their heroes with avatars of Evil, presumably luring us middle-class kids into lives of violence if not crime.

All in all, it was a sweet popular culture, from the anodyne pop music to the daily "funnies," which I didn't get to see since *The New*

York Times didn't run any, and it was the only paper we got. So no Popeye, no Dick Tracy, no Li'l Abner. And almost no movies, although Disney's *Snow White and the Seven Dwarfs*, released when I was seven, was traumatic for me: I lay awake at night, terrified by the ravishingly beautiful—and murderous—Queen. There were also our household's two essential magazines: *Life* and *The New Yorker.*

Even the "national sport," baseball, which I followed eagerly, was benign. New York had three teams, and I was crazy about the Yankees (maybe because they usually won) and the Brooklyn Dodgers (maybe because they were so raffish). I loathed the Giants—who knows why? My family was utterly unaware of sports, although my father occasionally played golf; once and only once he made me walk around a golf course with him—the most boring afternoon I ever spent. My parents went to the theater occasionally, the movies rarely, out to dinner never. Sometimes we played gin rummy, but mostly, like me, my mother and father read.

My mother had had a genteel upbringing in Boston and New York on no money, her favorite novel George Eliot's *The Mill on the Floss.* As a girl, she worked hard at the piano (Czerny exercises, the easier Beethoven sonatas), and she and her family loved going to the Met (Caruso, Farrar, Ponselle), sitting way up in the family circle. Because Grampa was an artist (unsuccessful), there were etchings and drawings and reproductions of paintings in our home, and as I grew older my mother took me to museums occasionally, and we went to hear the most famous musicians of the day—once each: Vladimir Horowitz, Arthur Rubinstein, Jascha Heifetz, Marian Anderson, Toscanini. By the time I was in high school I had my own records—78s, back in those days. Most important were the famous Glyndebourne recordings of the Mozart operas, Wanda Landowska playing Bach's *Italian Concerto* and *The Goldberg Variations*, and Caruso. And the big Romantic piano concertos—Grieg, Rachmaninoff, Tchaikovsky. As for my own piano playing, I just didn't practice enough—my ear was good, I was "musical," I picked my way through simple Beethoven and Mozart, but alas I never applied myself seriously.

And there was Gilbert and Sullivan, whom we sang at home, my mother at the piano, and in three of whose works I drew attention to myself in summer camp: as Ko-Ko in *The Mikado*, Bunthorne in *Patience*, the Sergeant of the Police in *The Pirates of Penzance*. They had to let me play leads since I couldn't or wouldn't do much in the sports line except for Ping-Pong, which required agility, not strength. Awards were given out at the end of the summer, and there was nothing I could win an award for except acting, although one year I did get one for volleyball (which I had never once played). The last of my four years at Meadowbrook Lodge (in the Berkshires), I never once went down to the lake but lay on a blanket outside our bunk reading Norman Douglas's scandalous *South Wind*—not that I understood what made it scandalous. Obviously, I was not made for summer camp, but what were my parents to do with me? My bunkmates, among them Eddie (later E. L.) Doctorow, seemed to be enjoying themselves.

I spent a lot of time during the early forties tracking the progress of the war on the huge fold-out maps that came with the *National Geographic* and that I taped to the walls of my bedroom. Somehow, in the summer of 1945, when I was fourteen, I arranged to have *The New York Times* delivered to me every day at camp and was jolted out of my self-absorption by the terrifying news of Hiroshima. Earlier that year, and even more frightening, had appeared pictures of the newly liberated death camps. For American kids with no relatives fighting, the war was essentially offstage, except for mild rationing and collecting silver foil and rubber bands for the war effort; for me, I suppose, it was a different kind of serial drama. Like the rest of the world, though, I was filled with anticipation about the Allied invasion of France, and when the news of D-day came over the radio on the morning of June 6, 1944, I rushed outside to buy all the morning papers. It was one of the most exciting moments of my life.

My mother's cultured background must have been a major draw to my father, who came from a more typical immigrant family, with an Orthodox father who barely spoke English and spent his life studying the Talmud and with whom he did not get along. My father (Charles) made his own way out of Lower East Side poverty, going (the story persisted) to one high school by day and another by night so that he could start college (City College) sooner. Then on to NYU law school with the help of scholarships and what he could earn on the side. At college he fell in love with philosophy and poetry, founding a Thomas Gray society and determinedly shedding his Lower East Side speech and manner. He was hungry and driven (and good-looking), and my gentle and impressionable mother (Martha) was drawn to him like Desdemona to Othello. He didn't, however, end up strangling her; stifling her naturally gregarious nature was as far as things went. Except for his mother, who had died well before I was born, he had little interest in or sympathy for his family, a family caught up in feuds and resentments. And my mother had no family on the scene either, except for her father. Nor did I have brothers or sisters—whatever money was available in the thirties was to be spent on little Bobby. We were an isolated group of three.

Even during Depression and post-Depression times, when funds were low, my father's great extravagance was going to Brentano's, America's premier bookstore, across the street from his law office on Fifth Avenue, and indulging himself with half a dozen books, all nonfiction: the Holmes-Laski correspondence, Bertrand Russell, George Santayana, Karen Horney (whose theories appealed to him more than Freud's), the writings of the famous CCNY philosopher Morris Raphael Cohen. Although we didn't agree about much, he completely understood when one day when I was in college I called him in his office, a rare event, to say that I'd just seen a Brentano's ad offering a two-volume boxed set of Proust for six dollars, and petitioning him to go across the street and acquire it for me. It was waiting for me the next time I came home from my dorm.

My mother, true to form, was always reading—old familiar books, books from the public library, and also books from what were known as lending libraries, usually located in stationery stores or drugstores, where for a dime or fifteen cents you could borrow the latest in fiction and nonfiction for three days. I myself, when I was in high school, belonged to three of them, and would read at least one new book a night in my obsessive need to have devoured every bestseller or potential bestseller within days of its publication. (Key to this obsession was my addiction to bestseller lists, which I followed fanatically, and which was due more, I think, to my obsession with statistics than to the books themselves.) I remember a crisis moment when two new novels—one the new Book-of-the-Month, the other the new Literary Guild selection—became available for borrowing the day before I was leaving for summer camp. (One was Margery Sharp's *Brittania Mews*, the other, I think, by Daphne du Maurier.) I was up all night, leaving them for my mother to return the next day.

Given that books were the natural order of things in our family, it seemed reasonable to me that often the three of us would sit reading at the dinner table; only later did it occur to me that this was not normal, but a symptom of our particular brand of dysfunction. The way I read was odd, too: I more or less *devoured* books—skimming them rather than bringing them into focus line by line. (One particular attack of showing off, when I was fifteen or sixteen, involved "reading" *War and Peace* in a single marathon fourteen-hour session.) This kind of browsing was a habit I had to break when I became an editor: It was very useful for judging manuscripts quickly, but editing itself is a slow and laborious process, and in order to go at it properly, I had to change the way I read.

When I was ten or eleven, my parents decided I needed more fresh air than I was getting on the ninth floor of our apartment building on West Ninety-sixth Street, and I was commanded to spend at least one hour a day outside. We were only a few yards from Central Park, but nature had no appeal for me—it still doesn't have much. There were a few kids on the block I could and sometimes did play cops and robbers with, but what was the point? I usually spent the prescribed hour standing next to the doorman, practicing with my yo-yo, until I could get back upstairs to my books and my radio. From the start, words were more real to me than real life, and certainly more interesting.

As I was steeping myself in the art of the popular genre writers of the day—Thomas B. Costain (*The Black Rose, The Silver Chalice*), Frances Parkinson Keyes (*Dinner at Antoine's, Came a Cavalier*), Samuel Shellabarger (*Captain from Castile, Prince of Foxes*), Frank Yerby (*The Foxes of Harrow, A Woman Called Fancy*)—I was also marching through the middlebrow writers (John P. Marquand, Pearl S. Buck, John O'Hara), the current literary heroes (Waugh, Orwell, Faulkner), and the classics: Balzac, Dickens, Hardy, Twain. My crucial literary experience of these pre-college years was my first reading of *Emma*, when I was sixteen. When Emma behaves so rudely to poor, harmless, talkative Miss Bates in the famous scene of the picnic on Box Hill, I was suffused with mortification: I had been forced to look at my own acts of carelessness and unkindness. Jane Austen had pinned me to the wall. It was the first time I really made the connection between what I was reading and my inner self. There was no religious instruction in my life, no guiding principles other than to work hard, and my mind was not a philosophical one. It was in the novel, beginning with *Emma*, that I would discover some kind of moral compass.

LEARNING

MY FIRST SCHOOL was a tiny affair called the Dunham Day School. It was in the Bronx, somewhere in our solid, prosperous neighborhood close to Yankee Stadium and the imposing Bronx County Courthouse. I was one of five kids in my class, and in my final year the five of us shared a classroom with the next highest class—of ten. It was like a one-room prairie schoolhouse, and the methods of teaching were just as old-fashioned, complete with blackboard, chalk, rulers, and inkwells.

And learning by rote. Most important: the multiplication tables. "Two times two is four," we chanted day in, day out, "two times three is six," and up through the tricky twelves. Then the five of us stood in a line and were grilled. If you got the answer right, you stayed where you were; if you got it wrong, you went to the foot of the line. There was no way I was going to the foot of a line, so I mastered my multiplication tables. After months of this, I could more or less intone the tables in my sleep: If on my deathbed someone says, "Six times seven," I'll mutter, "Forty-two." The same methods were applied to spelling, with the same results. This approach was rigorous, it was mindless, and it worked. I didn't need to understand the principles, I needed to know that six times seven is forty-two.

The only exciting thing about the Dunham Day School was that while my class was reciting the tables, the kids in the next grade up were reciting the names of the forty-eight states, their capitals, and their largest cities. "Maine: largest city, Portland; capital, Augusta. New Hampshire: largest city, Manchester; capital, Concord." I soaked up this data, and at the prompting of my parents would recite the list to anyone who came to our house who was willing to listen. (Though what choice did they have?) It was marginally less embarrassing than playing the piano—badly—for them.

When we moved to Manhattan, I was sent for fourth grade to a small and somewhat precious private school in the West Nineties which still exists, though it crossed the park many years ago. It was called Birch-Wathen, having been founded by two ladies: Miss Birch, who presided over the high school, and Mrs. Wathen, who oversaw the lower school. Tiny Mrs. Wathen was a benevolent spirit, somewhat ethereal—she had white hair piled high, wore hand-knitted suits in grays and greens, and in her cozy office kept a pair of canaries (or were they doves?). Every Friday she gave a poetry class during which we recited and memorized such sweetly pretty verses as "Ann, Ann! Come quick as you can! / There's a fish that talks in the frying pan!" (Walter de la Mare) and "Up the airy mountain / Down the rushy glen / We daren't go a-hunting / For fear of little men" (William Allingham). At our grade-school graduation ceremony she crooned, "You are the fairy children." As for schoolwork, my favorite occupation was making maps to scale—my "Africa" was a masterpiece—and I liked arithmetic because it was so logical and trustworthy.

Whereas Mrs. Wathen was comforting, Miss Birch was tough: a round, hard woman with no charm. Or maybe I just thought that because she made it clear that she didn't like me—I was restless and a smart aleck. She was determined to run her school as if it were Protestant and English: We sang hymns, and had "chapel" once a week. This was pure self-delusion on her part, since more than three-quarters of the students were Jewish. On the High Holy Days, out of my class of thirty-nine only the four Gentiles and atheistical me would be present. (My parents were confirmed atheists.) One of my few friends among the teachers confided in me that on one Yom Kippur Miss Birch asked the faculty why there were so many absences. "Because it's Yom Kippur,

Miss Birch," someone said. "Ridiculous," she said. "This isn't a Jewish school."

Certainly none of the teachers was Jewish. Definitely not Mademoiselle Gallairand, a severely unattractive woman with (I think) a good heart. "Robaire," she said to me more than once, "at the teachers' meetings I am the only one who defends you, and now you haven't done your homework!" Defend me against what charges? I never knew. I suppose I just didn't fit in, either with the faux-genteel pretensions of Birch-Wathen or with the majority of my schoolmates, who tended to live on ritzy Central Park West or Park Avenue and whose families belonged to country clubs.

My one great friend on the faculty was the math teacher, Miss Lewis—Mary-Jean Lewis—from Winnetka, Illinois, a sweet, nervous woman whom everyone liked and no one took seriously. I think she was fond of me because I was the only one of her students who really loved her subject. On the other hand, I was a problem in class. Algebra in particular was so easy that I went crazy trying to stay quiet while most of the others struggled to comprehend what seemed to me so obvious. Every math class was an hour of torture; there were days when I would just have to get up and wander around the room. Finally, to settle me down, Mary-Jean would have me teach the class—frustrating in a different way.

One day she asked me what a Jewish service was like. She had asked the wrong boy—given the fact of my parents' atheism, I'd never been to one. We decided to investigate, and a classmate who belonged to an Orthodox synagogue invited the two of us to attend one Friday evening. It was not a success. The congregation was segregated by gender, so she and I were separated—even more bewildered than we would have been sitting together. To make things worse, when she tried to light a cigarette outside on the street, she was told by an official to stop.

This was my last venture into a synagogue until, a dozen years later, I found myself walking down Fifth Avenue past the fancy Reform Temple Emanu-El and decided that since I had explored churches and cathedrals all over Europe, I should see what a great synagogue was like. As I entered, a guard came up to me and said, "I'm sorry, we don't allow tourists here." So ended my experiments with Jewish places of worship. But my problem with religion didn't stem from these misadventures. I've simply always lacked even the slightest religious impulse—when people talk about their faith, I can't connect with what they're talking about. This isn't a decision I came to, or a deep belief or principle; I'm just religion-deaf, the way tone-deaf people hear sounds but not music. I suppose my religion is reading.

Our assigned reading through high school veered from *Julius Caesar*, *A Tale of Two Cities*, *Silas Marner*, *Ivanhoe*, and the Romantic poets to *Lost Horizon* and *The Bridge of San Luis Rey*. It could have been worse. Luckily, we also had to memorize some poetry: one sonnet each by Shakespeare, Wordsworth, and Keats, Falstaff's great speech about honor in *Henry IV, Part One*, and the opening passage of *The Canterbury Tales* ("Whan that Aprille with his shoures soote / The droghte of March hath perced to the roote . . ."). I can still summon up most of these selections—maybe the happiest residue of my Birch-Wathen education. And I can't get "Ann, Ann! Come quick as you can!" out of my head.

It was, all in all, an education that kept me unchallenged and unstimulated. I hated Latin because I hated the Latin teacher, and I got straight A's in physics and chemistry, subjects in which I had no interest and of which I had no understanding, by memorizing the textbook the night before big tests. Twenty-four hours later I had forgotten everything I had memorized, but I had learned how to take tests. If I did any sports, I don't remember them. The one distinguished thing Birch-Wathen offered was that our glee club was led, once a week, by the esteemed Hugh Ross, head of the famous Schola Cantorum, friend and colleague of Toscanini, Stravinsky, Boulez, et al., for decades chorus master at Tanglewood. I can only imagine what this important musician made of having to train a bunch of mostly unmusical and uninterested schoolkids to sing songs like "Columbia, the Gem of the Ocean." Although I loved music, I was too ignorant or too self-absorbed to notice the distinction Mr. Ross offered us.

My nine-year stretch at Birch-Wathen was interrupted when I spent the winter of seventh grade with my mother in Tucson, Arizona. The ostensible reason was my erratic health (sinusitis, general debility), and at the time I didn't question it. Only decades later, when my mother was dying, did she tell me that the real reason was a crisis in my parents' marriage. My father wanted a divorce (for the usual reasons), my mother refused ("for the sake of the child"—me), and they compromised on this period apart. I barely remember Tucson or the large, agreeable public school, the only one I ever attended. It was wartime, and Tucson was the major Air Force base in the Southwest, but the swarms of airmen barely impinged on our tidy, eventless existence. The entire episode isn't worth recalling except for an extraordinary reminder that came along almost twenty years later. I was at a small dinner party being given by my friend Richard Howard and was seated next to the emerging literary celebrity Susan Sontag. We'd never met but were happily chatting away (Susan was always easy to talk to) when somehow the subject of Tucson came up—I don't think I'd mentioned my stay there to anyone in all the intervening years. It turned out that she had been there, too—her stepfather one of those Air Force officers—and she too had been at Mansfield Junior High in 1943. And in the seventh grade. We had been classmates. A bizarre coincidence, but more bizarre was the fact that it had surfaced.

Back in New York, when I was thirteen or so, I was struck by a passion for the theater. When I was five, I had been taken to my first show, the spectacular Rodgers and Hart musical *Jumbo*, in the even more spectacular newly renovated Hippodrome, the largest theater in America. *Jumbo* itself was best known for Jimmy Durante and a live elephant. All I remember is the vastness of the auditorium and, just maybe, the elephant. Next came *Life with Father*, which ran for eight years and was seen by every middle-class child in New York—an essential rite of passage, like *The Nutcracker* today. More musicals—*Oklahoma!*, of course; Oscar Hammerstein's *Carmen Jones*; Mary Martin in *One Touch of Venus*—and several hailed dramatic events: the visit of the Old Vic with Laurence Olivier and Ralph Richardson in *Henry IV*, parts one and two, *Uncle Vanya*, *Oedipus Rex*, and *The Critic*; the Paul Robeson–José Ferrer *Othello* for my graduation from junior high (I was disgruntled because it wasn't a musical); and—bless my parents—Laurette

Taylor in *The Glass Menagerie*. By then I was old enough to realize how beautiful the play was and how great her performance—I still think the greatest I've ever seen; it wasn't acting, it was real life, but transcendent.

By the time I was fourteen I was on my own. Most Saturdays I would take the subway down to the theater district and stand in line to buy a single ticket for whatever shows had opened to good reviews that week. That's how I spent my allowance, buying $1.20 or $1.80 seats in the upper balcony. It was a heyday for Broadway hits—*Harvey*, *I Remember Mama* (the young brother Nels was played by Marlon Brando), *Carousel*, the thrillingly sophisticated *On the Town*, *The Madwoman of Chaillot*, dozens more. These solo ventures were daring for me: I was an overprotected boy who had hardly ever done anything on his own. The climax was Eugene O'Neill's *The Iceman Cometh*, which was so long it played no matinees—it was the first time I had ever gone alone to the theater at night. This was the height of worldliness for a fearful fifteen-year-old. (I would have been more fearful if I had realized at the time that the nice man sitting next to me was trying to pick me up.) Theater opened up my life. I was still in thrall to reading, but even more exciting were those anguished moments of anticipation alone in a theater (having arrived half an hour early), waiting feverishly for the curtain to go up.

Even so, the most decisive cultural event of my high-school years followed the arrival at Birch-Wathen in my senior year of a young, lively English teacher named Kay Muhs (pronounced "mews"). She was as out of place there as I was, and we hit it off—more like co-conspirators than teacher and student. A month or so before graduation, Kay invited me and my close friend Joan to a Saturday matinee at the City Center of something called Ballet Society. I had never heard of it, but I went—what could be more glamorous than going to the theater with a *teacher*? What proved to be far more glamorous, more moving, more earth-shattering was the performance of George Balanchine's latest masterpiece, *Orpheus*, just one week old. I was overwhelmed. Here was a reward for the years of dullness at school; here was a release of feelings and imagination that only certain books, and occasionally theater, had previously provided. It was May 1948, and within months Lincoln Kirstein's Ballet Society would morph into the New York City Ballet and I would begin my undergraduate life at Columbia College, a quick subway ride to the City Center, where I would obsess over Balanchine and his dancers for the next four years. One day, against all odds, they would become an essential part of my life.

In those days Birch-Wathen imposed on all the seniors an aptitude test administered by some outside agency, to help steer us along appropriate career paths. The school official whose job it was to discuss the results with each of us was openly unhappy about mine, making it clear to me that the preferred outcome was one that identified a single strong predilection—Bob would be a terrific accountant; Joan would be an excellent English teacher. My results were weighted too heavily at both ends of the spectrum. I would be a good match for half a dozen or so professions (confusing and counterproductive), and there were all too many professions for which I would be a disaster. I remember that I was the only one in the class who scored two zeroes: one for forest ranger, one for undertaker. (I could have identified a third: lawyer. I had spent too many years observing my father.)

One of the benefits meant to accrue from this test was a hint about the colleges we should consider applying to. In my case, however, there was only one choice. For my mother, born in Boston and proud of her Boston roots, Harvard was the Great Good Place, and I think my father felt the same way. This was at a time when Harvard was the accepted summit of American education, with Yale and Princeton slightly behind and such places as Stanford or Berkeley nonexistent. There were the huge state universities—Michigan, Wisconsin, Ohio; there was the radical University of Chicago, with its tantalizing "Great Books" program; and there were the "experimental" little places like Swarthmore and Oberlin. None of these fell within the expectations of my parents, whose only snobberies were educational. So for me it was Harvard or . . . nothing.

My marks were fine, but my Harvard interview was a disaster—I was tense, scruffy, showing off—and the interviewer was actively unsympathetic. In addition, there was the notorious Jewish quota, and I was the worst kind of Jew (because there were so many of us hoping to get in): a New York Jew. When I was rejected I was humiliated but not surprised.

I had been told that you had to apply to at least two colleges, and I had no second choice, so arbitrarily I put down Columbia; I didn't know much about it, but at least it was in New York. This interview was almost farcically opposite to the Harvard one. I was still scruffy, but I wasn't tense and I wasn't showing off because I wasn't invested in the outcome. The interviewer—he must have been about forty—was a Mr. Alexander, and almost from the first moment, he was explicit: I was exactly the kind of boy he wanted at Columbia. I told him I hoped for Harvard, but that didn't put him off. When I heard that the dorms didn't accept students who had homes in New York, and told him I couldn't go on living with my family, he said he would make certain that an exception was made for me. Of course I was flattered, but I wasn't grateful—or convinced. I might not be good enough for Harvard, but I was certainly too good for Columbia! As it turned out, I had no choice.

Mr. Alexander, whom I never saw again, was the second person, after Kay Muhs, to radically change my life for the better. Harvard in all its self-satisfaction would have been a calamity for me, as I realized later when I became somewhat familiar with it. And Columbia in the late forties and early fifties was exactly right. It wasn't so much the actual (strong) education it offered, it was the place itself—the atmosphere, the intellectual challenge. And it afforded me the excitements of New York in those heady post-war years—a golden age for theater, dance, "foreign" film. Birch-Wathen had been a lethargic backwater; the energy of Columbia and New York helped release my own energy. Many young people find college a place where they can reinvent themselves. For me, it was the place where my true self could begin to emerge.

That meant, primarily, that I found a literary world I could happily swim in. There were famous teachers—Lionel Trilling, Mark Van Doren, and others—who together constituted what was considered by many the country's finest English department, but they were not central to my college experience. Rather, I had blundered into a group of fellow students who were as obsessed with books as I was. There were compulsory courses outside my interests, but I dealt with them the way I'd dealt with physics and chemistry in high school—score A's on tests and papers and forget everything. (Worst was economics, which I took at my father's insistence—almost as boring as golf.) We also had compulsory athletics. I survived fencing; bowling (in the basement of Riverside Church, which sported Gothic phone booths)—I could barely pick up the ball, let alone send it down the lane; my nemesis, volleyball, which I attended with a friend who, like me, was blind without his glasses (we stood in the back row and flinched when the ball came our way); track (I'd go to the gym, sign in, change, sit in the locker room reading, change back, sign out). The year I entered Columbia, 1948, was also the year Dwight Eisenhower became president of the university, a prestigious stopgap on his way to NATO and the White House. He spoke to our incoming class of '52. "We're all freshmen together," he said with the famous twinkle. And, later, "I hope to see all-round young men here. We don't want greasy grinds at Columbia." But there I was—inevitably a grind, if not greasy.

Ike's thinking was typical of the post-war moment, and so were the rules regarding social and sexual conduct. Central was the ban against any female other than your mother entering your dorm room, and she was welcome only on Friday afternoons. Who could have guessed that by my daughter's college years young men and women would be sharing the showers? But these rules in no way affected the way we conducted ourselves. As ever and always, young people found each other and did what young (and older) people do. By my junior year I was living outside the dorm with the girl who would become my first wife, and everyone I knew was in perpetual heat, and acting on it. (Was that what constituted being all-round men?) Sex, as others have remarked, wasn't invented in the sixties.

In fact, in the late forties and early fifties New York was enjoying a new "bohemian" moment—which, as it had decades earlier, flourished in the Village. It was there you found the new artists, the jazz clubs, the rather tamely louche bars—most startlingly, the gay and lesbian bars.

None of it was for me, though: I was far too timid, repressed, and naïve for anything even tamely louche. Even the Museum of Modern Art, a famously convenient pick-up venue, was a place I went to see movies like Carl Dreyer's *The Passion of Joan of Arc* and to experience Picasso's *Guernica* rather than to encounter girls.

Real life was at Columbia, not in the classrooms but in the surround, as I started meeting people I could talk to. The crucial encounter was with Dick Howard (now Richard, but never to me). He was a year older and a year ahead, but that never really registered. Someone took me to his dorm room and there was instant and total connection. He was infinitely more sophisticated than I was, but not intellectually, the way that mattered; there we were on even terms, our interests coinciding and our literary excitements mutual. Immediately that afternoon we set off together for the Gotham Book Mart, the West Forty-seventh Street bookstore of legend ("Wise Men Fish Here") reigned over by the formidable Miss Frances Steloff, always in her electric-blue smock and with her indispensable pencil poked through her white hair. ("*You*," she once snapped at me when there was no one else in the store. "Go to the corner and bring me a hot dog and an orange drink!" It was the only one of the dozens of times I was in her store that she acknowledged my existence.)

From the start, then, Dick and I were bound together by books. But also by other things—mostly, I suppose, by shared tastes and interests (and snobberies). There's a need, when you're young, to announce your standards, your preferences; to identify yourself through your choices. They can be political, sports-related, dress-related (that's usually high school). In our case, they were cultural. Shakespeare, yes; Milton, no. Bach and Mozart, yes; Tchaikovsky, no (that would change). Henry James, yes; Stendhal, yes; Balzac, yes. *Les Misérables*, no (that would change, too). Jane Austen, George Eliot, Chekhov, yes; Tennessee Williams, yes; Arthur Miller, no. Abstract art, yes; realism, no. Balanchine and Martha Graham, yes; Fred Astaire, yes; Gene Kelly, no. Metaphysical poetry, yes; Faulkner, yes; Hemingway, no. Eliot and Pound and Yeats, of course. Proust, yes—the most emphatic yes. But Gide yes, too. Movies, yes; television, no. And on and on. In other words, we shared an aristocracy of taste that was acute, impassioned, and snobbish—perfect glue for a young friendship.

All this was outside our academic work, which was mainly geared, sensibly enough, to kids who had read less than we had. A general course on American poetry was taught by Mark Van Doren and attended by boys who had not only never read Emily Dickinson but had never heard of her; Van Doren didn't seem to mind. Dick and I took a seminar on Chaucer's *Troilus and Criseyde*, taught by an elderly genial professor out of a distant past. There were six of us, only two of whom ever said anything. (Guess which two.) For a happy term we did nothing but read this great poem aloud, which was certainly more educational and satisfying than any discussion among this group would have been. The prominent literary critic F. W. Dupee—also genial but smart as well—was stuck with the two of us in the front row of his class on contemporary literature (Joyce, Eliot, Kafka, Woolf, Proust, et al.). We wouldn't stop talking (well, *somebody* had to talk), until he kept us after class one day and guaranteed us A's if we would just stay away—an offer we couldn't refuse.

The major disappointment for me was Trilling's nineteenth-century English literature course, the third and final year of the prescribed three-year sequence for English majors. I had read and absorbed his famous book *The Liberal Imagination* (what English major hadn't?), but my burning interest was text, not imagination; the severe and indignant judgments of Cambridge's F. R. Leavis were my touchstones, and his magazine *Scrutiny* my bible. I felt that the graying Trilling wasn't really interested in undergraduates, that his prime concern was with his postgraduate seminars with their historical/sociological emphasis. When he asked us to vote in class on which we preferred, *Jane Eyre* or *Wuthering Heights*, I was offended at being used as a sociological guinea pig and mortified because in my certainty there was no choice—Emily was so clearly the *only* Brontë. (There's always something for a snob to be snobbish about.) I recently came upon a letter to me from Cynthia Ozick dated 1998, in which she quotes an interview with John Hollander that she had just read: "[After] Trilling published 'Wordsworth and the Rabbis,' some of us felt a little funny about it ... It caused one man, Robert Gottlieb ... to come in the next day and just before Trilling came to class, post himself outside the room and recite 'Tintern Abbey' with a Yiddish accent.'" I did? I guess so, if John says I did.

Among Trilling's prize students just before my day had been Allen Ginsberg, Norman Podhoretz, and Jason Epstein. Jason and I got to know each other years later when I was at Knopf and he was running Random House, Knopf's sister publishing house, and we've had a collegial relationship ever since, not, however, based on college. Podhoretz I never knew. But I was friendly with, though not close to, Ginsberg, who was an agreeable and unassuming young guy—I knew nothing about his poetry. My most pronounced memory of him was of my surprise when he came to see me off when I sailed for Europe on a freighter in 1951. I was even more surprised when my mother mentioned in a letter that a very nice, polite boy named Allen had gone out of his way to see her home.

As I've suggested, it wasn't the classes at Columbia that I found nourishing but the surround—the intense atmosphere of seriousness about literature. I read and read, usually all night (since I didn't bother to get up for most morning classes), devouring everything by everybody. All of Shakespeare, naturally, especially because the most brilliant of our teachers was a short, chubby man—caponesque, really—named Andrew Chiappe, whose intense lectures, punctuated by his blazing readings from the texts, were utterly thrilling. His were the only morning classes I would drag myself out of bed to attend. Jason would later employ Chiappe as his chief adviser when he was founding Anchor Books at Doubleday, the first and most influential of the trade paperback lines.

I also read my way through the great Russians and the major French novelists; all of Austen (of course), Dickens, Thackeray, Eliot, Hardy, Fielding, Richardson, and the other important English novelists; Melville and Hawthorne; plus the moderns—Lawrence, Woolf, Forster, Joyce, etc. What was the point of reading only *some* of a writer's work? In the summers I would sweep straight through a writer chronologically— one year, Conrad; the next, Cather. But the writer who meant most to me was Henry James. This was at the height of the James revival, though it wasn't his emergence as a great figure that propelled me; it was the way he thought and the glory of his style. More important, the moral issues he probed reflected my own inner life more closely than those of any other writer except perhaps Proust. For me, James was not just a writer but an issue: Anyone who didn't appreciate him (my father, for instance) was outside my universe and worthy of contempt. One of the great days of my early life was the morning after I saw an ad in the Sunday *Times Book Review* for the complete New York Edition of James's work. Where I found the hundred dollars to buy it I don't know—probably borrowed it from Dick, whose background was far more affluent than mine—but I was outside the bookstore when it opened that Monday morning, and I carried the prize home. I'm looking at it as I write.

My close high-school friend Liz Lahm (her father—a founder of the Lamston five-and-dime store chain—was another older person who was endlessly generous to me) had gone to Connecticut College for Women, where she grew close to a girl from Wellesley, Massachusetts, named Muriel Higgins and decided we were meant for each other. As it turned out, we both were and weren't. Muriel had an original mind, strong opinions, and sultry looks, and we had a good time together. Apart from anything else, she was a voracious reader, and a very intelligent one. She was also considerably more worldly than I was— by the time she was sixteen she was drinking martinis when she went out to dinner with her parents! I didn't even drink beer. I thought she was the Scarlet Woman. By our third year of college she had transferred to Columbia and we were living together off-campus. Her roofing-contractor father didn't approve of me—I believe his verdict was "If I had a son like that, I'd take him out and drown him like a sick kitten." In return, my father loathed Muriel: She was too assertive, and "Catholics all revert in the end." (She was about as Catholic as I was Jewish.)

So I was part of a couple, which often became a threesome, since my friendship with Dick was never diluted, and luckily he and Muriel interested and amused each other: He respected her strong mind and her tough humor. We had other friends, too—Dick was particularly gregarious. For one thing, he collected young men whom he would fascinate, seduce, and grow bored with; from the beginning he was totally out. (No, it didn't all start with Stonewall.) Like Queen Victoria, I did not approve—no problem with his being gay, but I deplored his casual treatment of these bedazzled and bewildered boys. I had inherited not only my mother's naïveté but my father's puritanism.

Dick had a close friend from his childhood in Cleveland, Anne Loesser, niece of the songwriter Frank Loesser, who had entered Barnard when I entered Columbia and who had dated another friend of mine. Now she was half of a couple with John Hollander, and they were part of our extended group—endless late-night talk at the Bickford's coffee shop on Broadway over toasted English muffins and tea. (We were devils.) Anne was clever, with a touch of malice, and John was smart, if a little goofy. Their eventual marriage would produce two daughters, while John went on to his exemplary career as poet and pedagogue and Anne to her distinguished work on the history and importance of clothes. Anne died very recently, but not before Dick was able to bring her in the hospital a finished copy of his latest book of poems, *A Progressive Education*, about their school, dedicated to her and with a snapshot of her very young self on the cover.

By my junior year, Dick and I were editing the college's literary magazine, *The Columbia Review*, and we collaborated on a short story for it called "The Way We Live Now—A Tale for Christmas." The story was very much *à clef*, focusing on a dazzling and highly identifiable young couple who among other things stole money in order to acquire a copy of Villiers de l'Isle-Adam's *Contes cruels* bound in human skin— we must have been reading too much early Waugh. John took this story badly, and one wintry day he came up to Dick and me, nodded, asked Dick to hand him his glasses, carefully took them, slapped Dick in the face, said "Merry Christmas," politely handed the glasses back, and passed on. I was both insulted and relieved that I was exempted from punishment. Perhaps John suspected that I might slap him back? This incident—surely a supreme moment in the history of literary duels—

was never mentioned again, and we all went on at Bickford's as before, and Dick and John to a lifelong friendship.

A more distinguished use of the *Review*, perhaps, was our decision to devote an entire issue to André Gide, who had recently been awarded the Nobel Prize. Together Dick and I translated a short play of his which had never appeared in English, and we nervously wrote him a letter explaining the project and inviting him to say something to Columbia (perhaps exaggerating the degree of interest the college as a whole had in modern French literature). He replied quickly and generously, but of what he specifically said I have no memory. We definitely had the sense of having scored a coup.

Whereas I very much admired Gide—*The Immoralist, The Counterfeiters, Lafcadio's Adventures, Strait Is the Gate*, were central modernist texts at that time—my whole being responded to Proust, whom I had decided to read in an unorthodox way. The seven novels of *Remembrance of Things Past* (this was decades before it became *In Search of Lost Time*) were mostly encountered back then in seven Modern Library volumes— the two-volume boxed set my father had procured for me was too awkward for actual reading. Seven volumes, seven days. I cut myself off from the outside world for an entire week, never once leaving the room Muriel and I were living in, consuming a volume a day. Friends stopped in, food was provided, and I read and read. It wasn't a struggle—you can read six or seven hundred galvanizing pages in fifteen hours if that's all you're doing—and the result was overpowering: Total immersion proved to be an extraordinary way of experiencing and absorbing that great mind and style. I emerged feeling that Proust was mine—or I was his. It was a personal relationship, of the kind I already felt with Henry James, whose final and most knotty novel, *The Golden Bowl*, was my holy of holies.

In the summer of 1951—I was twenty—I set out alone on a freighter for a not-so-grand tour of Europe. Dick and I were supposed to go together, but there was some glitch related to his graduation and he had to stay behind. I was scared, my parents were opposed to my going alone, and money was short, but I cashed in some war bonds (they had matured just in time) and I had won some literary prizes. On this trip—a month each in France, Italy, and England—I did all the usual things, guidebooks anxiously in hand, barely holding my own in high-school French and pidgin Italian. But the self-sufficiency I mustered for the adventure as a whole (for instance, my first stab at hitchhiking) suggested that I might actually be growing up.

This trip confirmed my fantasy that England—Dickens's England, Austen's England, James's England, Dr. Leavis's England—was the place I had to be. The physical beauty and charm of Cambridge were especially seductive. My last year at Columbia was spent reading (needless to say), publishing in *The Columbia Review* a long, fierce review of new books by Trilling and Leavis, much to the advantage of the latter, and, as a senior-year project, working alone for a term on Hawthorne's notebooks with the daunting, enigmatic Quentin Anderson (son of the playwright Maxwell Anderson), whose silences were as profound as his discourse. That was rewarding, but essentially I was treading water until I would be chosen as one of the two English majors whose superior academic performance would be rewarded with a Kellett Fellowship to Cambridge.

When the fellowships in my year were awarded to two boys whose claim to them was considerably inferior to mine—at least in my opinion—I seethed with resentment at the injustice of it and confronted Trilling in his office (the only meeting I ever had with him). How could he and his colleagues ignore my qualifications in favor of these two chumps? Far from being defensive or outraged, as a lesser man might have been, he was courteous and responsive, explaining that the judges felt that the "chumps" were in much greater need than I was of the polish Cambridge would afford. When I protested that I hadn't realized the Kellett was given in response to need rather than performance, he asked whether I really wanted to go to Cambridge. That was easy to answer, and he immediately offered to write to Basil Willey, Cambridge's Professor of English Literature, recommending me to him. In a stunning (to me) illustration of how the Old Boy network operated, ten days later I received not an application form but an acceptance letter from Pembroke, Willey's college at Cambridge. In my view, justice had been done, but even in my self-congratulation I was aware of Trilling's generosity in the face of my public dismissal of him in *The Columbia Review.*

There was a hitch: In the spring of 1952 we had discovered that Muriel was pregnant. She certainly didn't want a baby—she was meant to be attending an important acting school in London while I was at Cambridge—and I barely knew what a baby was; I had literally never seen one close-up. Abortion was a possibility, since we all were aware of the doctor operating out of a clinic in a small Pennsylvania coal town who was known as "the Ivy League abortionist." But although a baby was a practical impossibility, both of us shrank from the idea of abortion. How to proceed? Our parents wouldn't have helped, since they disapproved so violently of our relationship, and I couldn't imagine giving up Cambridge. I certainly wasn't prepared to find a job in New York and take responsibility.

We got married surreptitiously, our only witnesses Liz Lahm and her father. (It had never occurred to us that we could produce a baby without being married.) I was not romantic in the least about my sneaky behavior, but I was so romantic about my reading that I decided we should be married on the porch of the justice of the peace in Rye, New York—because Henry James had lived in Rye, England. Then, through a skein of lies and half-lies, we got through the summer undetected by our parents and decamped to London. The baby, our son Roger, was born by Caesarian section in a nursing home there in mid-October. The matron of the home made it known that she strongly disapproved of three things—Americans, Jews, and men—and I qualified on all three counts. She advised us to take the baby home (we had rented a flat in West Hampstead) and start toilet training. When I suggested nervously that in America we didn't believe in such early measures, she said, stonily, "You're the ones who have to wash the nappies."

I had already begun at Cambridge, living in Pembroke and coming down to London every other weekend, leaving Muriel alone most of the time attending to an infant she didn't know what to do with. Roger flourished, but we didn't, although I was off at Cambridge more or less enjoying myself. Muriel was the victim: She was in a strange city, without the support of family or friends, unable to attend school, unprepared to be a mother, and half-abandoned by her husband. This was not my finest hour.

Making matters worse was the ongoing deception of our parents, since our funds would have been cut off if they had known the reality. It was more than a year before we revealed our duplicity, with predictable results: My mother was horrified but indulgent, my father didn't speak to me for four years. Muriel's father was equally angry, but to her anguish he died suddenly of a heart attack while we were still at Cambridge—she had joined me there after five months alone in London. There's only one cheerful memory of the London days: The charwoman who came in once a week happened to mention that she had once worked for the Freuds (!), who had lived a few doors down from our flat. I was desperate for details, and when I persisted in interrogating her, she declared, in her sublime cockney accent, "Well, they were terribly clean—for foreigners."

This kind of parochial reaction to foreigners—and Jews—was one of the surprises England had for me. Although I was very aware of the casual anti-Semitism that punctuated English literature, I wasn't aware of how compartmentalized middle-class Jews and Gentiles were in their lives. Or to put it another way, it was strange to discover that most British Jews felt themselves to be *other*, and that they were perceived that way: The English Jews I met in both London and Cambridge to a large degree *defined* themselves as being Jews, in a way I had never encountered in New York. New York, everyone at home joked, was a Jewish city, and indeed in all my years there I never came up against anti-Semitism. And at Cambridge it was my being American, not Jewish, that identified me. Being American in the early fifties was on the one hand a handicap, since resentment of, and condescension to, America still ran deep, while on the other hand it was a plus, since everything about America—its movies, its music, its clothes, its new situation as the world's dominant country—had glamour and excitement, especially for young people. I was so inescapably American that, given my other particularities—my being married, having a baby, having a house—there was no room left for my totally secular Judaism to make an impression.

Cambridge at that moment was a peculiar place, the new students being a mixture of eighteen- and nineteen-year-olds, fresh from school, and armed-forces veterans, well into their twenties. I was an anomaly, a married American with an American bachelor of arts degree, for which the university didn't have much respect: Four years at Columbia (or Harvard or anywhere else) was considered the equivalent of only one of the three years that constituted the Oxbridge undergraduate program. But I knew that I wasn't at Cambridge to further my education; I was there to be there. I went to a few lectures—one of Professor Willey's out of politeness; one of Leavis's out of loyalty—but there was nothing in them for me. Leavis, already in his semi-paranoid mode, spent most of the time fulminating against the forces he saw as lined up against him: the "Bloomsbury crowd," *The Times Literary Supplement*, everyone else at Cambridge.

Attending lectures was voluntary. Writing weekly essays for a college supervisor was not. I was fortunate that at Pembroke I found a youngish and up-to-date supervisor named Matthew Hodgart, whose interests lay in writers like James Joyce rather than the author of *Beowulf.* With my all too typical cockiness, I told him at our first meeting that I had spent four years at Columbia writing papers and didn't need that kind of preparation for the tripos exams that were the climax of the Cambridge educational process. When he asked to see an example of my work, I slyly gave him the results of my Hawthorne project, aware that he knew far less about Hawthorne than I did. But he was delighted to have someone to talk to who had extensive reading behind him, and we settled into cordial weekly chats about books, none of which related to the tripos. (Pembroke was not a very literary college. Its typical undergraduate owned three books—the Bible, *Brideshead Revisited*, and *The Collected Stories of Somerset Maugham*—and had heard of a French writer named Marcel Prowst.) And I was reading compulsively, usually until five or six in the morning—a month's worth of such nights, for instance, carrying me through the exhilarations of Gibbon.

Reading, however, wasn't enough to keep me busy. The dominant undergraduate cultural activity in Cambridge was theater—there were two main groups of actors, plus a fistful of splinter groups putting on plays all the time, as well as the famous Cambridge Footlights, which presented sophisticated revues (in my time it spawned Jonathan Miller). Late one night, sitting around my room with three or four other bored young men and antsy with unused energy, it occurred to me that I too could direct a play. But what play? And where? The college boasted a lovely early Wren chapel, and at two in the morning we sneaked down into it, confirming my notion that it would be a perfect setting for T. S. Eliot's *Murder in the Cathedral*. Pembroke was totally out of the cultural swim, which may be why when I approached the dean, who administered the chapel, he nervously gave permission. Since he was an earnest Anglican minister with serious doubts about both Americans and married undergraduates—he was far from married himself—this was a notable act of bravery on his part.

Posting notices in the two women's colleges, Newnham and Girton, I held auditions for the ten women I needed for the Chorus, and had the luck to find in Pembroke an extraordinarily handsome young man to play Thomas Becket—his air of saintliness (genuine) must have been inherited from his father, who was an Anglican missionary bishop in Africa. Over the protracted Christmas recess in London I worked long hours with Muriel, breaking up the lines for the Chorus so that every syllable had its own inflection and emphasis. Then, for a month, rehearsals of three or four hours a day with the Chorus, until they were syllable-perfect (and exhausted). The result was a tremendous success, the stars being the Thomas, the Chorus, and Christopher Wren. The dean was ecstatic. Every performance was sold out. And, to our amazement, Stephen Spender reviewed us in the Manchester *Guardian*, though how he knew about the production I have no idea. The gist of his review was that it was the finest performance he'd ever seen of *Murder in the Cathedral*. This was not only intoxicating in itself but a justification for the dean in the stuffy world of Pembroke College.

Since I wasn't studying, I just kept directing plays. There was still official censorship of the theater in England, and on the proscribed list was Sartre's *No Exit*, not because it involved prostitution and lesbianism but because it was considered blasphemous. But such plays could be performed in private homes, or anywhere else that didn't charge for admission. Casting Muriel and two graduates of the cast of *Murder in the Cathedral*, I put together a persuasive version, which we circulated among half a dozen venues, including professors' homes, and which became one of those chic events that small communities thrive on. (One of the oddities for me after working so intensely on these two plays is that I ended up with a far higher opinion of Eliot's than I'd started with, and a far lower one of Sartre's.)

As a result of having produced two such visible events, I was offered the direction of both the leading theater groups for the following year when Peter Hall, the leading director of his years at Cambridge, went down to London to triumph with the first British production of *Waiting for Godot*. And so more Sartre, *The House of Bernarda Alba*, *Heartbreak House*, and *The Master Builder*, all efficient and even worthwhile but none as strong or individual as *Murder in the Cathedral*. It occurred to me that Eliot's play was literary, which is why I understood how to stage it, whereas I didn't really know how to help actors in realistic plays. I also came to understand that I didn't want theater to be my life, just as this second exposure to a university made it clear to me that I would dislike even more a life spent in the academic world. Unfortunately, I had no alternative ideas of what to do with myself when I got home.

On the surface, our Cambridge life was stimulating and satisfying— we lived in a big, pleasant house; baby Roger was a calm, undemanding presence; Muriel was acting and directing; and our finances, although funds from our families had vanished, were holding up, since I had no scruples about accepting money from Dick Howard to help us out. (His generosity and my ability to take advantage of it were obviously made for each other.)

But I wasn't happy with myself or in myself. My romance of Cambridge and England had faded in the face of the depressed realities of the post-war world there; everything seemed bleak, the country's energies depleted. I suspect, though, that this take on things was to a large degree a symptom of a suppressed depression of my own. The realities of being married, being a father, and being unanchored in a place that I no longer saw through rose-colored glasses were sapping my buoyancy. Now, suddenly, I felt a strong need to get back to America.

Muriel was there already, having rushed home with year-old Roger when her father suddenly died. (When Roger was born, we had registered him as an American at the embassy, but he had no passport. The embassy would grant him one overnight in this emergency, but there was no time to procure a standard passport photo. Aha! A local photographer sold me a photo of some other baby. Even we couldn't tell which baby was which.) I was staying on to finish up my last production ("The show must go on"), to close down our house, and—in a final burst of self-indulgence—to hitchhike to Italy with a close friend, Jane Llewellyn, from the *Murder in the Cathedral* Chorus. (Later she would join us in New York.) The most useful aspect of the trip was memorizing the first act of *King Lear* while waiting for rides. The most ridiculous was attempting an homage to a writer I loved by visiting his grave. Stopping a peasant on a road in the south of France, I blurted out something like "*Où se trouve le tombeau du grand écrivain anglais D. H. Lawrence?*" No surprise that he seemed stunned: I'm sure he couldn't understand a word of my pathetic French, and in any case he wasn't likely to know anything about *le grand écrivain*, who had died twenty-five years earlier. Later that day I found out in a local bookstore that whereas Lawrence had indeed died in Vence, his wife, Frieda, had eventually transported his ashes to Taos, New Mexico, for interment. Another romance shattered.

In Rome I met up with my one close American friend from Cambridge, Meg Greenfield. She was in Cambridge, having graduated from Smith, on a two-year Fulbright, but she hated everything about it, from the weather to the regulations—she simply ignored the injunction against undergraduates owning cars—to the spiders in her landlady's house. The final straw: She sent a favorite coat to the only good dry cleaner in town, part of a national chain called Pullars of Perth, and when it came back a week later, it had been tightly folded into a small square. Meg, who was not only rich but finicky, was out of there.

After some years in Rome, where apart from everything else the coffee was great, she arrived back home, and I was able to point her to her first job—working for the 1956 Adlai Stevenson campaign. As long as she lived in New York she was at our house for Christmas every year, at which occasions we developed a "Meg & Bob" routine that predated Nichols and May but alas was heard only by Muriel, little Roger, and a few close friends. (Is it possible that it wasn't as witty as we thought it was?)

Meg was funny and caustic, and she grew increasingly political. Her writing talents led her first to the *Reporter* magazine and then to her job of twenty years as the director of the editorial page of *The Washington Post* and a columnist for *Newsweek*; in other words, she became an ultimate Washington insider. Yet she remained a relentless bullshit detector, sort of the Maureen Dowd or Gail Collins of her day. She also became Katharine Graham's closest friend and adviser—when she got cancer, Kay drove her every week from Washington to Johns Hopkins in Baltimore for treatment—and when I was editing Kay's autobiography in the mid-1990s, she was an invaluable support, pulling no punches with Kay so that I could afford to be more tactful. Meg's death, in 1998, was devastating—she was the first close friend of my age to die. When I spoke at her memorial service in Washington Cathedral, I realized I must have been the oldest of her friends there—and the only observer of her Pullars of Perth era. The "Meg & Bob" days were over.

Meg's joy at having scrubbed the second year of her grant and at getting out of Cambridge only confirmed my sense that I had to get out too. The Italy jaunt was my last possible excuse for not going home to America—and real life. I had come to realize that even apart from shirking the responsibilities I had incurred, I had become someone I didn't like, arrogant and all too comfortable as a local celebrity. When I actually departed, in the middle of a term, the Cambridge under-

graduate newspaper ran a front-page story headlined "Gottlieb Goes."
So Gottlieb went—or more accurately, slunk away. I was demoralized,
angry, ashamed of having let Muriel go home alone, not knowing what
I wanted to be or do, and pretending to myself that I wasn't scared—
scared, mostly, of work. I couldn't know that, as would be the case my
entire life, it was work that would save me.

WORKING

Simon and Schuster

FOR MORE THAN A YEAR, while Muriel waitressed, I sporadically looked for a job—answering the few ads in the *Times* that seemed plausible, then some that looked less plausible. The one that came through was for Macy's, where I was hired as a temp to work in the huge greeting-cards department on the ground floor—greeting cards in the fall meaning Christmas cards. Because I was good with numbers (those days at the Dunham Day School were paying off), I was soon at one of the two central cash registers, racking up sales so swiftly that the very nice if somewhat flustered woman who was head of the department would come and stand behind me, muttering, "Robert, you really don't have to go so fast." But I *did* have to go so fast. This was my first experience of a working-class environment, and I enjoyed the work and liked my colleagues. Maybe the regulars were used to the seasonal appearance of nerdy college grads; certainly, they were friendly and helpful, most crucially when in an emergency I was plucked from my cash register to help dip scented candles.

My salary was forty-five dollars a week, but it *was* a salary, and I was excited about it. With my first paycheck, and knowing that all employees had a discount on anything in the store (fifteen percent, I think), I went to the book department and, after a crisis of indecision, bought two Little Golden Books for two-year-old Roger—a book of nursery rhymes, and what was to become one of the bestselling children's books of all time, *The Poky Little Puppy*. I think the total expense, including tax, was sixty-nine cents, which was something of an assault on our budget, but I was inordinately proud of having ventured out of the cave and brought home the essential bacon for my child. (Muriel was bringing home the rent money from her waitressing tips.)

Before I got back from Cambridge she had found a very agreeable apartment on the top floor of a brownstone on St. Mark's Place, when it was still mostly Polish and Ukrainian, long before it became the East Village. There was us, W. H. Auden across the street (not that I would have known him if I'd seen him), a strip club down the block (which later became the Theatre 80 St. Marks), and a few Abstract Expressionist artists, among them Joan Mitchell, who shared our top floor and was a great neighbor, finding tactful ways to help feed us, snaking in an electric line when Con Ed did its worst, and when she moved out, leaving us a superb "Joan Mitchell" as a parting gift. It looked exactly right in our place, which we had furnished in the standard décor of young intellectual New Yorkers in the fifties—bamboo blinds, Indian cotton bedspreads, bookcases made by stacking pine boards on bricks liberated from the street, and of course the famous Noguchi lamp, with its crinkly white paper globe. Our rent was ninety-six dollars a month, and we were usually on time with it—particularly after two, then three, close friends from Cambridge joined us: We were a commune *avant la lettre*. I think the subway still cost a dime, phone calls the same; the *Times* was a nickel. Cigarettes, which I'm afraid we still smoked, were something like fifteen cents. Life was affordable.

But hardly happy. I was drifting. Somehow I met a sympathetic, rather vague woman named Evelyn Shrifte who ran a small publishing house called the Vanguard Press. It had published early Dr. Seuss, early Joyce Carol Oates, early Saul Bellow, and it was about to launch *Auntie Mame*, but it was hardly flush. Evelyn took to me—or, rather, felt sorry for me—and she gave me occasional French books to read and report on, at something like fifteen dollars a go. Then I translated a very bad French-Canadian novel for her, its name, author, and content having fled from my memory. To get away from the distractions of our toddler, I would take my French novel over to Dick Howard's apartment while he was out at his job working for a dictionary publisher. I've never hated any work so much as I hated translating—not even dipping candles—whereas Dick went on to become America's leading translator from the French (as well as a superb critic, teacher, and Pulitzer Prize–winning poet).

I still didn't know what I wanted to do or *could* do, and found myself answering ads and undergoing uncomfortable interviews for jobs at advertising agencies, magazines (*The New Yorker* personnel person was particularly frosty), even banks. And publishing houses, which my background seemed most appropriate for. Though Macy's disagreed. At the end of my predetermined stint there, I was one of two temps out of several hundred to be invited to stay and train for a management job. Naturally, my vanity was gratified, but I was self-aware enough to know that the retail business was not for me any more than the academic world was. That didn't leave many alternatives for a young man with a degree in English literature. So as the months crawled by, I decided to focus more on publishing—a world in which I knew nobody. But if you keep going, eventually you meet someone who sends you to someone else. And someone sent me to Harper's.

There's a tradition in publishing that old hands faced with young hopefuls pass them along to other old hands in other houses, both in a genuine attempt to help and as a way of getting them out of their hair. Which is why the pleasant but tough-minded Joan Kahn, who ran Harper's mystery-novel line, passed me on to her friend Nina Bourne, the advertising director of Simon and Schuster. I had read novels about the advertising world, beginning with the big bestseller *The Hucksters*, so I knew what to expect: a hard-bitten, competitive bitch. Bourne didn't disappoint, although when she came out to the reception desk to get rid of me, she wasn't actually bitchy, she just didn't register my existence. There were no jobs at S & S, she said distractedly, and was gone. Later I understood that this was Nina in her work mode—there was nothing in her head but the ad copy she was writing—but at the time I was sure she had sized me up and found me both irrelevant and irritating. Certainly my look couldn't have impressed her: My wardrobe consisted of a pair of corduroys, two or three Shetland wool sweaters acquired in England, and heavy English brogues. Also my hair was long and messy, and at twenty-four I looked five years younger. This, remember, was the mid-fifties, the era of the well-groomed *Man in the Gray Flannel Suit* (Sloan Wilson's novel that S & S was about to launch). I didn't even own a pair of gray flannel pants.

A few months later I found myself at yet another employment agency—over the months I'd been to half a dozen—hoping to interest a friendly, focused woman who didn't seem to notice my scruffiness and asked a few sensible questions. "There's only one publishing house I can see you at," she then said firmly but without explanation, "Simon and Schuster," and she made an appointment for me to meet its personnel director. I was not encouraged, since the only people who had shown less interest in me than employment agents were personnel directors. And in any case, I knew that even if anyone there wanted to hire me, the ruthless Nina Bourne would block it, since I had snuck back in after she had dismissed me. Finally, I had no interest in the books Simon and Schuster published: They just didn't live up to my exquisite literary standards.

Even so, to prove to myself (and Muriel) that I was trying hard, I kept my appointment at Simon and Schuster, where a youngish man named Jerry Morse spent half an hour with me, told me to sit and wait, and eventually came back with the news that on Thursday afternoon, at four p.m., I had an appointment with Jack Goodman. He uttered this name with awe, but since I had never heard it, I was unimpressed, even when Jerry explained that Jack was the company's editorial director. (Max Schuster clung to the formal title of editor-in-chief, but no one took that seriously—except Max.) So when I turned up in Mr. Goodman's office I was in no way anxious. But then he turned out to be not the old fart I had expected but a humorous, charming, provocative man in his mid-forties who looked tired but ready to be amused. His interviewing technique was simple and to the point: "Tell me about yourself."

This was a subject on which I could talk endlessly and without restraint, and for a full hour I *did* tell him about myself—far more than anyone could possibly have wanted to know. He listened to it all: my obsessive reading, my academic achievements (Cambridge on top of Columbia!), my passion for bestseller lists and publishing history, my tastes, my habits, my childhood, my marriage, my child, my dog. Whether out of amusement or exhaustion, he gamely heard me out and then said he would like to hire me but had to get the approval of the treasurer, who wouldn't be back until Monday. Would I meanwhile write him a letter setting forth why I wanted to be in publishing? That was too ludicrous. "Something like 'How I Spent My Summer Vacation'?" "Exactly."

By then I felt I had some grasp of this eccentric man's nature—that he would respond better to impertinence than to solemnity—so that night I typed out my letter and in the morning left it for him at the front desk. "Dear Mr. Goodman," I wrote, "You asked me to tell you why I want to be in publishing. I find that impossible to do, since it has never occurred to me to be in anything else." It was not only cheeky, it was a lie, but trotting out a lot of platitudes would have been a worse crime. On Monday morning I got a call summoning me back to his office. By now I *was* nervous, but it no longer mattered: I was hired. Jack tried to explain what the job would be—I'd be his personal editorial assistant—but since he'd never had one, he couldn't really tell me what my duties would be: more or less everything that needed doing is about as far as he could get. Certainly reading manuscripts, making editorial suggestions, writing jacket copy, anticipating his needs. The one thing he didn't mention was salary. He had never hired anyone directly, I had never been hired for this kind of job, and we were both too embarrassed to raise the subject. Finally, at the end of an hour, he managed to blurt out that I'd be getting seventy-five dollars a week—so much more than I had ever earned before, or expected, that I was actually rendered speechless.

Months later I pieced together what had happened, and why. Jack was not only vastly overworked, but his health was precarious (blood pressure, heart), and his colleagues were worried—*for* him and *by* him. He wasn't getting things done on time, his attention was fractured, and since he was not only the top editor but in charge of the whole publishing program (famous for coming up with provocative campaigns like the one that declared, "Before they made S. J. Perelman, they broke the mold"), he was indispensable. When Jerry Morse interviewed me, he thought I might be the answer and went to Lee Wright, the formidable editor of S & S's Inner Sanctum mystery line (I learned later that she was much more), who was determined to find a way to shore Jack up and who more or less bludgeoned him into seeing me.

It was, then, a series of flukes that got me into publishing: A clever woman in an employment agency spotted something in me that she was certain matched something at Simon and Schuster; a sympathetic personnel director (whose career at S & S didn't last very long) who was under pressure to solve a problem; a woman who, without even meeting me, decided I might be the answer to the problem (we would become good friends); and a critical moment in the firm's life. Typically, I took it all for granted—at last, I assumed, my specialness was being acknowledged. But the deeper reality was that I was both elated and scared.

Simon and Schuster's offices were then at 630 Fifth Avenue—the famous Rockefeller Center building in front of which looms the famous statue of Atlas holding up the world. This was true glamour in the mid-fifties, and it still has glamour, at least for me. The company's offices were on the twenty-eighth floor, and Jack had a big office overlooking Fifth. I was parked at a desk outside his door. And at the desk just across from mine when I turned up on July 5, 1955, was Phyllis Levy, a gorgeous, snappy brunette exactly my age, whose first day at S & S this also was. She was out of Scarsdale, she was out of Radcliffe, she had worked for a Broadway producer. She was Herman Wouk's Marjorie Morningstar, except smarter. She was an untarnished Holly Golightly—in fact, you could say she was a Jewish Audrey Hepburn: stylish, funny, adorable. And she was Jack's new secretary. Within days, maybe even hours, we were best pals.

Phyl liked to predict that one day she and I would find ourselves alone in a mountain cabin during a blizzard with a single pair of pajamas between us and would whisper to each other, "It's you!" It not only never happened, it never really occurred to either of us. (Apart from everything else, neither of us would have been caught dead in a mountain cabin.) Anyway, her taste was for much older, distinguished, married men, and although I was married, I was neither older nor distinguished, and was far too puritanical to even think of having an affair. Which may be why we were able to stay close friends, with complete confidence in each other, until her death in 2001.

In fact, from the start our relationship, far from being romantic, was conspiratorial, its goal to keep Jack going, to make life easier for him, to make him proud of us. It didn't worry me that although I had the impressive title (boys were "assistants," girls were "secretaries"), Phyllis was earning ten dollars a week more than I was: She not only took perfect shorthand, she kept Jack's checkbook for him. On top of that, every one of Jack's (male) authors was crazy about her: It quickly became obvious that Sid Perelman, Romain Gary, Chas Addams, et al., would much rather have lunch with her than with Jack—and what's more, they paid.

Maybe because from the start Phyllis and I were having so much fun with each other and with our quizzical, teasing, and dazzling boss, my first weeks on the job were utterly wonderful. But a dark cloud hung over them. Early on I had learned that the alarming Nina Bourne was on an unprecedented extended holiday in Europe and would be gone for another six weeks. Which meant that I had six weeks in which to ingratiate myself, since I knew that the moment she spotted me on the premises, she would do her best to have me fired. Where this paranoid fantasy came from I don't know, but it was real, and the more I fell in love with my job, the more distressed I became. When the day of her return arrived and we were introduced, she cunningly acted as if we had never met. Within days we were having lunch together. Within weeks she was coming home with me to meet Muriel. Within months, she was part of our family, and stayed there—an older sister to me, and later to my second wife, Maria, and a beloved babysitter, aunt, fairy godmother to our children; a life partner as well as a work partner. For many years we shared rented summer houses in the Hamptons (eventually she bought her own), with Maria broiling bluefish, Nina practicing her recorder and teaching our little Lizzie how to break eggs into a bowl while keeping the yolks whole, and me reading aloud (*Our Mutual Friend*, *The Woman in White*).

We were all together until she died, at ninety-three, in an apartment we found for her around the corner from us. Although she was a New Yorker since childhood, her immediate family didn't live in New York, so it was up to us, her other family, to see her through her death—in fact, through her final hours. Youthful, energetic, Nina never seemed to age; she said she felt thirty-five until she was eighty-five. And she was still coming into work, carefully decanted into and out of hired cars, until six months before she died, a legend, an inspiration, and most of all, a delight. As for our brief encounter at the reception desk, Nina simply denied that it had ever taken place—she could never have been so brusque with a young job-seeker, and she could never have forgotten *me*. About five years after I got to S & S there was a shout from her office and she rushed into mine. "Look!" She was cleaning out a crammed desk drawer and had come upon a scribbled note to herself: "Interview Robert Gottlieb, Joan Kahn," and a date in early 1955. I was vindicated!

Jack didn't really know what to do with me, apart from having me read manuscripts. My first two specific jobs were writing captions for *The Jerome Kern Song Book* and clearing permissions for *The Ladies' Home Journal Treasury*—no one explained what kind of captions were wanted or what you did to clear permissions, so I just got down to it. Then he sent me to Washington to pry a book out of the famous political cartoonist Herblock, who had signed a contract but seemed to have forgotten that he had to come up with a manuscript. Herblock was a hero, but not to me; he obviously didn't enjoy having a nagging kid around. Still, the book got written. So did a gigantic picture-and-text book called *The Movies*, involving three prima donnas—the two authors and the designer—and me: Jack never looked at what I was doing.

One day, when I'd been at S & S about a year, he decided that I should have an expense account, and when I said that I didn't have any-one to spend it on, he found me someone to wine and dine: the young agent Georges Borchardt, who at that time was handling only French books from his one-room apartment. (Georges had arrived in New York from France after the war and, with his consummate profession-alism, impeccable taste, and appealing, wry manner—and in eventual partnership with his striking American wife, Anne—became a major literary agent here. We're still on the best of terms today, sixty years after our first encounter, and we suspect we're the oldest members of our publishing generation still at it.) I was only the second editor he had ever met, so we had lunch again and again, a pleasure in itself and productive for the firm, since I acquired from him a series of interesting if hardly profitable French writers. Meanwhile, I was cursing my (limited) French when I found myself slowly and painfully rewriting a terrible translation of a book already in the works. It was my first step toward the humbling realization—after struggling with books poorly converted from Italian, German, Spanish, and Japanese as well as French—that no matter how assiduous you are, you can't turn a bad translation into a good one: You can only make it less bad.

I was sticking my nose into everything, because everything fascinated me. I loved scanning the daily sales reports: *The Man in the Gray Flannel Suit* was riding high; Jack's beloved *Pogo* books (Walt Kelly's wildly popular comic strip) were running away; and James Newman's *The World of Mathematics*—four volumes, boxed, at twenty dollars!—was an astonishing popular success. Nina, whose grasp of mathematics was nonexistent, had come up with one of the most imposing selling tools I've ever seen: an eight-page (I think) brochure that filleted the contents, quoted seductively, and presented the whole thing with an urgent sense of excitement and importance that made it irresistible. Our mail-order campaign was a tremendous triumph: Every day coupons and checks flooded in, and Nina and I were there counting them first thing in the morning—and gloating. It wasn't our business to be counting them, but who could resist? Quickly, we sold more than a hundred thousand sets.

This kind of cultural popularizing was one strong element in the Simon and Schuster repertory, perhaps seen at its most typical in *A Treasury of Art Masterpieces*, by Thomas Craven, which—astutely marketed by Richard Simon—sold hundreds of thousands of copies following its publication in 1939. It was from Dick Simon that first Jack, then Nina, learned how to market books. The more pretentious side of the operation was the province of Max (M. Lincoln) Schuster, who championed, among other things, the Durants' eternal series, *The Story of Civilization*, which over forty years (1935–1975) and in eleven volumes and millions of words indeed gave us . . . the story of civilization, at least up to Napoleon. (The Durants died before they could bring civilization up to date.) This is certainly the most successful history series ever published, winning the authors the Pulitzer Prize, the Medal of Freedom, and immense profits for them and for us. Max kept tight control of books like these, coddling the "geniuses"—Nikos Kazantzakis was another—who produced them, and himself composing and signing what the rest of us enjoyed calling "windswept ads": "Last night I dined with Rembrandt . . ." Although I coincided at S & S with the self-important and demanding Durants for a dozen years, several of them as editor-in-chief, I managed never to meet them.

In my first years, when I had almost no books of my own to work on, other, busier editors generously brought me in to help with some of their projects, one of them Niccolò Tucci's remarkable memoir/novel called *Before My Time*. Tucci was a political exile from Italy. In the mid-thirties he had been working for Mussolini's foreign office in Rome and was sent to America as part of a cultural exchange. What he saw here and the people he met helped him understand that he was far more of an anarchist than a Fascist, and when the war began, he realized he had to get out of Italy fast. He made a beeline for New York, where he became part of a group of young political firebrands including Mary McCarthy, Saul Steinberg, Dorothy Thompson, and Dwight Macdonald. A few months later, in 1940, he was able to import his new wife and infant son from Florence, in time for his second child, Maria, to be born in New York a year later. When, in 1959, he insisted that I come to see this daughter, now an actress, in a Soviet play called *Five Evenings* that ran Off-Broadway for four, I obeyed. The play was a zero, but Maria (known to family and friends as Bimba—"little girl") was ravishing: a dark-eyed, dark-haired, slender beauty with a combination of an almost childlike innocent charm and a rich, sensual voice. She was eighteen but looked sixteen, and to me she seemed an enchanting kid. (I was ten years older.) Five years later, my marriage to Muriel in the dust—it had never been much of a marriage—Maria and I fell for each other (over margaritas at the Spanish Pavilion at the 1964 World's Fair), and after more than fifty years, we're still together. I think that may have been the last strong drink she's ever had (wine is her thing), but it proved to be the right one.

As it happens, I had encountered her long before we ever met—in a series of beguiling short stories Tucci wrote for *The New Yorker* about her and her brother, Vieri, including an account of his taking them as young children to Princeton to visit Albert Einstein, a close family connection. When Einstein died, Tucci dragged shy Maria, then thirteen, to a TV station late at night to be interviewed about the great man. She was, she says, tongue-tied and mortified, but it never occurred to the Italo-Russian Tucci to modify his behavior in any way. And his behavior was strikingly unlike anything I had ever encountered: the European dash, the dandyish look yet virile manner, the outrageous but enthralling storytelling. He spoke six languages fluently and had been an acclaimed young writer in Italy before immigrating here and, like Conrad and Nabokov, mastering a dazzling English literary style. He had a series of impossibly elegant aristocratic mistresses, although he never could entirely distance himself from his wife, the long-suffering Laura, who was forced to be the practical one in the family. (One of those women—brilliant, witty, sardonic Mimi Gnoli—would become Maria's closest and lifelong friend; in fact, family.) With Tucci, everything was intense, charged, dramatic. Maria was inured to receiving letters proclaiming "You are no longer my daughter" followed immediately by communications ignoring, or forgetting, the Lear-like condemnations. No wonder that after she and I had been together for six months or so, I started referring to myself as an Ibsen character who had wandered into a Chekhov play.

When *Before My Time* was published, Dorothy Parker acclaimed it in a three-page review in *Esquire*. It's unexpected things like that which publishers live for—and pray for. I was just barely beginning to understand my trade. The first book Nina and I collaborated on, back in the late fifties, was Sybille Bedford's magnificent novel *A Legacy*, which had arrived at S & S via two different editors, neither of whom really liked it. But they asked me to read it, and when I found it extraordinary, I gave it to Muriel, who liked it even more, and she pressed it on Nina, who fell in love, and our seniors graciously allowed us to take it over. Impressively, the British edition came with blurbs from Evelyn Waugh, Nancy Mitford, Aldous Huxley, Janet Flanner, and other notables, and we broke with standard practice and placed these quotes on the front of our dust jacket. The first printing must have been five thousand, and we probably sent out three or four hundred copies to critics, writers, buyers in carriage-trade stores like Brentano's and Scribner's—to anyone who might be remotely sympathetic. Each copy went with a personal letter from Nina—convincing, intelligent, inviting, because, like all her letters, it stemmed from her deep understanding of the book and her excited personal reaction to it. The most amazing response she ever received was from André Malraux, to whom she had sent a novel about the Communist insurgency in Malaysia. He never blurbed books, he wrote back, but for the first time in his life was so impressed by the quality of a letter accompanying a set of galleys that he felt impelled to congratulate the writer of the letter on her acuity and elegance.

We were so caught up in the excitement of launching *A Legacy* that we decided we couldn't trust the shipping room (in another building) to match the right letter to the right shipping label, so to the astonishment of the busy mailroom workers we invaded their space and did the job ourselves. And to the astonishment of our colleagues, all our frenzied activity made an impression on the public and we ended up selling twenty thousand copies of this very European, very distinguished, and definitely elitist novel about an aristocratic German family (Sybille's). This was a highly unlikely success back in the fifties, and even more unlikely was *A Legacy*'s spending a few weeks at the bottom of the *Times* bestseller list. For me, apart from the obvious satisfaction and my pleasure in Sybille's pleasure, this was a milestone in my education about publishing—grasping the fact that the act of publishing is essentially the act of making public one's own enthusiasm. Whenever I deviated from that principle over the following half-century and published halfheartedly, things did not go well.

My relationship with Sybille, that dry, intense, sharp, elitist, yet enchanting woman with a slight stutter, maintained itself through half a dozen books over forty-odd years, years that were remarkably free of disagreement. Like many English writers of her era, she did not believe in editing, although she did allow me to make suggestions about her vast biography of Huxley, whom she had known from girlhood and whom she revered. Sybille was an impassioned, and snobbish, food person. About Julia Child she once said to Maria and me, "You must understand that Julia's cooking is very good—very good hotel cooking, mind you."

In a burst of spousal sadism I invited Sybille to dinner at our house. Poor Maria. With the help of Manhattan's finest butcher she came through and produced a filet de boeuf that passed muster. (Years later, when I was at Knopf, I repeated the offense by asking Julia herself to lunch. This time Maria came up with a cheese soufflé. Another success. "I didn't think Julia would be so easy," Maria recently recalled. "She was delightful, and clearly would have cheerfully eaten the wallpaper left over from the original tenants. Ah, the fear, and then actually the simple pleasure with both of the ladies.")

Sybille was even more impassioned and knowledgeable about wine than about food, with a French certificate to prove it. Editors and publishers, to Sybille, were essentially glorified tradesmen, privileged to treat her to expensive and elaborate meals. Once, at one of New York's most highly esteemed French restaurants, to which she had insisted I take her, I suggested that we share the rack of lamb. "Yes, my dear Bob," she stammered, "but you must remember that lamb is nothing but the vehicle for a good claret!" She chose it, and it *was* good. Her intimates (of whom I was far from being one) called her Bunny.

In 1957, while *A Legacy* was making its way, a series of cataclysms hit S & S. First, suddenly, Jack died. It was a terrible blow to all of us, or almost all—Max Schuster and the behind-the-scenes business Machiavelli, Leon Shimkin, did not seem felled by grief. (One wit had rechristened the firm Simon and Schuster but Shimkin.) The worst hit was Nina, who worshipped Jack, and who liked to think she still worked for him, even though he had stepped back, in awe like everyone else of her talents. It took her a long time to recover from his death. But already by the time he died, she and I were consulting with each other on every ad and piece of copy, and we went on doing it for thirty years, for the sheer joy of collaboration. Jack had acquired Kay Thompson and Hilary Knight's *Eloise*, and Nina more or less kidnapped it—she obviously felt some kind of identification with the naughty child of the Plaza, although no one was ever less naughty than Nina. Until the week of her death, more than fifty years later, Nina enjoyed reminding me that as we hunched over her typewriter composing the jacket copy for *Eloise*, it was she, not I—who had brought her around to my love of Henry James—who had injected his name into the copy.

Phyllis and I were also devastated by Jack's death, although I remember thinking it was not really a surprise that he had died—after all, he *was* forty-seven. (I was twenty-six.) But his death also left us dementedly busy. Apart from everything else, his authors needed caring and feeding, and there was no one on hand but me equipped to deal with James Thurber and Sid Perelman and the others, including Meyer Levin, whose *Compulsion* we were about to publish. I had given Jack countless editorial notes on the manuscript, but now I was left to deal with the jacket, the jacket copy, and the author himself, who was notoriously not easy to deal with. He was already in the grip of his war with the Anne Frank people over the dramatic rights to her famous Diary, of which he had been one of the earliest and most ardent champions. The great success of *Compulsion*, a novel based on the Leopold and Loeb murder, did nothing to alleviate his fury at the injustices done him and his scorching sense of grievance. Watching him suffer, I felt a good deal of sympathy for him. We worked together on half a dozen more books, two of which—*The Fanatic* and *The Obsession*—were about his endless and bitter search for justice in regard to "the Anne Frank case."

Jack's death was only the first of the disasters that struck the firm that year. Another changed its history. In 1944, Simon and Schuster had been sold by the original owners to the department store magnate Marshall Field, and when he died, the lawyers who controlled his estate had no interest in keeping it: It was too small, it was always getting into hot water, and its politics (like Field's) were decidedly pink. Dick

Simon had previously cashed in his chips, and a buy-back agreement led to Max and Leon re-acquiring the company. Since they loathed each other and were barely on speaking terms, they agreed to divide up the responsibilities: Max would preside over the trade house, and Leon would control Golden Books, the children's line, and Pocket Books, the first major mass-market paperback line, which he had helped launch in 1939. Its first ten titles included James Hilton's *Lost Horizon*, Agatha Christie's *The Murder of Roger Ackroyd*, *Wuthering Heights* (just in time for the Laurence Olivier movie—the first tie-in?), Thornton Wilder's *The Bridge of San Luis Rey*, Thorne Smith's *Topper*, and Shakespeare's *Five Great Tragedies*.

This division of the realm made for an uncomfortable situation on the highest level, but not for us in the trade division, since the highly idiosyncratic Max essentially hid out in his gloomy office, holding occasional editorial meetings while digging his ballpoint pen into the arm of his chair. People made him nervous. As a result, his favored mode of communication was through memos, usually with a straight pin attaching them to whatever it was he wanted to bring to our attention. "PAAIIMA," he would scrawl on them: Please Answer As If In My Absence; "DTN" (Do The Necessary). He was not allowed by his dreadful and demanding wife, Ray, to have female secretaries, lest one of them tempt the owlish little Max from the straight and narrow. One of the unfortunate young men who held this post—his chief occupation seemed to be filing stories that Max would carefully scissor from newspapers—famously lost his equanimity one day and rushed out to exhibit to everyone a photo his boss had torn from one of the tabloids showing a mother weeping over the body of her little child, who had been run over. "File under grief," the accompanying memo instructed. For years Nina and I fantasized about using "File Under Grief" as the title of the novel we would someday write about S & S and its somewhat peculiar and incestuous history. (Among the peculiarities: People were frequently hired because of their bridge game. What was incestuous was that the men had a tendency to marry each other's mistresses.)

One of my treasures is a tattered copy of something called "Home

Thoughts From Abroad: An Informal Travel Journal in the form of some short sentences and long memories of Ray and MLS"—nineteen mimeographed pages of snobbery and self-flattery that in 1954 the Schusters had concocted and shared with the world. A typical jotting from Max's memos back to the office: "Both Beerbohm [Sir Max] and Berenson [Bernard] embraced and kissed Ray with uninhibited joy, and thus confirmed their reservations for rooms-with-bath in the Hall of Fame." And an excerpt from a letter of Ray's: "B.B. [Berenson] was simply marvelous. He said, Ray darling, I never met anyone like you. You are delightfully tender, how I wish you would come here, near me, I want to see you all the time." For years a little cult of worshippers would gather together for read-alouds. A wicked rumor persisted that when the Schusters sent copies of these typed pages around town, they received a formal rejection letter from Knopf. Can it possibly be true?

In the wake of Jack's death and the resurgence of Max and Leon, just about every key executive in the trade division abruptly departed—the heads of sales, of production, of design, of marketing—as well as a few editors. The decks were cleared, but Max couldn't or wouldn't bring in new people, and he certainly didn't want to oversee matters himself. As a result, six of us, of whom I was by far the youngest, just started running things. No one told us to, and no one told us not to.

By this time I was getting to meet a few people in the business, among them the formidable Lillian Friedman, head buyer for Brentano's, who took me under her capacious wing. One day she said to me emphatically, "Bob, you have to tell them who you are!" "But I'm not anyone, Lillian," I said. "That makes no difference," she said. "Tell them who you are." But how? Getting to know people in the profession wasn't easy—raffish Simon and Schuster was really a world apart from the more buttoned-down Doubleday, Harper's, Harcourt Brace, Houghton Mifflin, Holt, Lippincott, and Little, Brown. It had always been an exciting house, but one somewhat looked down on by the establishment publishers—those crossword puzzle books! those cartoon books! Founded in 1924, we were also one of the first of the "Jewish" publishers in what had been a very Gentile profession. Alfred Knopf, a pioneer, was acceptable: German-Jewish, a gentleman (didn't he know all about wine?), coming from the ultra-respectable Doubleday, with high literary tastes and connections, *and* with that ultra-elegant dog as his colophon! Bennett Cerf was not exactly a gentleman, but he was well liked, and his partner at Random House, Donald Klopfer, was unquestionably patrician. The Ginsburg family, of Viking, were also socially acceptable. Whereas Dick Simon was first and foremost a promoter—practically a huckster! Max Schuster was *hors de catégorie.* And Leon Shimkin was... Leon Shimkin. During my time more or less at the helm, the ship seemed to be steering into more respectable waters, though let's not forget the abominable *Calories Don't Count*—one of history's most irresistible titles—of which in 1961 we sold more than two million copies in a few months before the FDA got after the author for his involvement in pushing a particular kind of safflower oil in his masterpiece.

So we were generally considered eccentric (we were) and outrageous (maybe that too). Because none of us had ever worked anywhere else, there was very little connection with the rest of the publishing world. And despite the Durants' and many other highly reputable books— nonfiction successes like Wendell Willkie's *One World* and Margaret Halsey's *With Malice Toward Some,* and hit novels like *Kings Row, Father of the Bride, The Cardinal,* and *Gentleman's Agreement,* even Proust's early *Jean Santeuil*—we were still most closely identified with humorists like Thurber and Perelman and Bob Hope, cartoonists like Chas Addams and Peter Arno: all Jack territory. He was superbly connected on Broadway and in Hollywood and at *The New Yorker,* but he wasn't "literary"; he knew Marilyn Monroe, but he didn't know Willa Cather.

And then there were the self-help books, such as the biggest nonfiction success of the thirties, Dale Carnegie's *How to Win Friends and Influence People.* It's never stopped selling: In 2013, according to *Publishers Weekly,* a trade paperback edition sold more than 150,000 copies. (When Nina began at her job—on what she liked to call "the first working day of 1939"—one of her early responsibilities was answering the flood of Dale Carnegie mail, letters saying, "It was a revelation when you wrote that if I smiled at the man in the post office, he might smile back. I tried it and it worked!") Carnegie was a Shimkin discovery, as were the annually bestselling Lasser Tax Guides. It was Dick Simon, however, who was responsible for our next great inspirational bestseller, (Rabbi) Joshua Loth Liebman's *Peace of Mind*, which in the late forties spent more than a year as number one on the *Times* bestseller list.

Jack Goodman had always needed money, given a highly complicated domestic situation: divorce, kids, and a luscious and funny girlfriend, along Marilyn lines, aptly named Blossom Plum. (Blossom loved to tell the story of a date she once had with the famous Hollywood lawyer and cocksman Greg Bautzer—Joan Crawford, Lana Turner, Dorothy Lamour. She and Bautzer were in a nightclub, she went to the ladies' room, and while she was there an orchid was delivered to her accompanied by a note saying, "Hurry back! I miss you already.") Jack made a lucrative arrangement with the top movie producer Jerry Wald (*Mildred Pierce, An Affair to Remember, Peyton Place*), to act as a kind of glorified scout, alerting Wald to upcoming major book properties. And Jack hired me (for a badly needed hundred dollars a month) to write synopses of a series of mostly dreary books—though writing a synopsis of *any* book is dreary work. His one big score was Edwin O'Connor's *The Last Hurrah*, which he spotted, Jerry acquired, John Ford directed, and Spencer Tracy starred in. And then Wald came up with the idea of *commissioning* novels he could then turn into movies. Early in 1957 he put it into practice.

Phyllis had had a close friend at Radcliffe, an ambitious, well-heeled girl named Rona Jaffe, who was now working at Fawcett, one of the leading mass-market paperback houses. Rona wanted to write, and the rest was history, of a sort. She brought the outline of *The Best of Everything* to Phyllis and me, we showed it to Jack, Jack took it to Jerry, we were in business. Here was a story right up Hollywood's alley, since by then it had been the source of hit movies for more than thirty years. Three (or four, or five) young women land up in New York, trying to find their way. Will it be career? Marriage? Will they find Mr. Right or Mr. Wrong or no Mister at all? Inevitably, one will rise to the professional top, having sacrificed True Love; one will marry the nice-guy-next-door and settle down to happy domesticity; and the one who Goes Bad will die tragically. In *Ladies in Love* (1936), for instance, Constance

Bennett marries big money but misses out on love; Janet Gaynor finds love and doctor Don Ameche; and Loretta Young, dumped by gorgeous Tyrone Power, attempts suicide. (She does, however, end up with her own little hat shop.) In *Sally, Irene and Mary* (1925) it's Joan Crawford who dies the death, mourned by Constance Bennett and Sally O'Neil. In *Three on a Match* (1932)—the other two are Joan Blondell and Bette Davis—it's Ann Dvorak who flings herself from the window to save her kidnapped little boy from gangsters, having used her lipstick to scrawl his whereabouts on her nightgown.

What was different about *The Best of Everything* was that a lot of it wasn't just Hollywood hokum but was taken from life. Two of the central characters were partially inspired by Phyllis herself—Caroline, who loses her fiancé to a rich Dallas girl and goes on to replace her boss (Joan Crawford, still at it, in Jerry's film), and Gregg, who, obsessed with her theatrical-producer boss and ex-lover, ransacks his garbage and falls to her death down a handy fire escape. (Phyl was definitely not a source for the girl from the sticks who can't take the New York fast life and ends up going back to Colorado with a nice, simple fellow who adores her.) Also, Rona had worked in a publishing house suspiciously like the one in her novel, and she had the ambience down cold.

This, to say the least, was a different kind of challenge from *A Legacy*, and we improvised, hiring the famous photographer Philippe Halsman to shoot Rona on Fifth Avenue (we had recently published his intriguing *Jump Book*). The image he came up with became the cover of the book—certainly the first time a staged color photo of an author was used to sell a novel. Then we decided to do a pre-publication paperback promotional edition, Halsman photo and all, to stir up excitement. My memory is that this now de rigueur sales tool was also a first, and we deployed it with considerable effect at the ABA convention at Atlantic City in June 1958. (At that time, the American Booksellers convention was a venue for sales departments to push their upcoming lists to booksellers; it hadn't yet turned into the international trading post for agents, editors, and foreign publishers it's become since.) The crowning though unplanned stroke of publicity was provided by Rona herself at a nightclub where she, her current boyfriend Prince Serge Obolensky, Phyllis, and I were at a ringside table, in the midst of hundreds of other publishing types. The emcee was getting swishier and swishier, Rona was getting drunker and drunker, and then—never the most delicate of girls—she abruptly stood up, swayed, and shouted wildly at him, "Go suck a cock, I'm going to the john." *The Best of Everything* was launched.

Almost fifty-five years later, a slick yet touching stage version of it opened to excellent reviews at a small downtown theater in New York. Part of its charm lay in the pre–*Mad Men* retro effect—the up-to-the-moment fifties typewriters and telephones of the "girls" at the publishing house, their little hats and white gloves, their worries over their virginity. But it also worked because of its basic irresistible situation—those confused young women trying to find their way. (They're still doing it here in the twenty-first century—think *Girls.*) Rona dedicated her book to "Phyllis, Bob, Jay [her agent], Jerry, and Jack." Of them all, I'm the only survivor, although the book survives too, repackaged most recently in 2005 and selling away. It was unsettling to watch Phyllis being impersonated up on the stage by an attractive young actress who got so much right and who even resembled her. All I could think of was how unfair it was that Phyl wasn't there sitting next to me.

During the month in 1958 that *The Best of Everything* was published, I took a radical step in my private life, beginning an eight-year stretch of psychoanalysis: four mornings a week, on my back on the couch. It was a very difficult and painful process—people who think that talking about oneself is necessarily a joyride or a self-indulgence haven't experienced the rigors of strict Freudian therapy.

There were two reasons I decided to do this. One was physical—I had begun to experience numbing sensations in my hands and feet which I realized were psychosomatic. The other was more serious. I could sense myself behaving more and more like my father, feeling and expressing more and more anger, and though I rationalized that Muriel had known what she was getting into when she chose me, little Roger had had no choice. The New York Psychoanalytic Institute, to which I applied for financial help, confirmed that I was a reasonable candidate for analysis and found me a doctor I could afford. His fee was fifteen dollars a visit, which was sixty dollars a week—a tremendous expense for us. (I was probably earning about twelve thousand dollars a year at this point.) But I saw no choice. I was certain that this was the only therapy that could help me—a puritanical Central European Jewish therapy for a puritanical Central European Jewish cast of mind.

I wasn't very good at analysis, finding it almost impossible to relax my controls well enough to free-associate, which made working with dreams almost impossible. But the essential thing happened: the "transference" to the analyst, so that the process could take hold. My resistance to authority, my resentment of it, were so strong that I fought the analyst and the analysis until, at the end of our seventh year, my patient doctor calmly suggested that perhaps we should consider "terminating"—at the end of the following year, perhaps? A deadline! I ceased resisting, threw myself into the work, and a year later was able to stop rushing up by subway from where we lived in midtown to East Ninety-sixth Street ("Analysts' Row") four mornings a week.

Those eight years had seen me through the extinction of my marriage, as well as my mother's long and painful death, which I dealt with methodically, step by step, visiting her every day, not permitting myself any emotion. And then a year of lying on the couch often unable to speak but weeping, the tears trickling down into my ears—that's what happens when you cry lying on your back. There were no Eureka! moments of revelation during my therapy, but by the end I knew that I had managed to reverse course, and was no longer spiraling down into the worst of myself and was clambering up toward what I hoped to become—less possessive, less competitive, less angry, less needy for approval, more open.

Psychoanalysis rescued me, but I don't recommend it (not that it's in fashion any longer); it takes someone as moralistic and severe as I was even to be able to stand it, let alone benefit from it. When, for instance, Phyllis tried it to see whether she could break her pattern of relationships with older, married men, she and her doctor after a couple of years agreed that since she was obviously content living within this pattern, it didn't make sense for them to go on trying to disrupt it.

Phyllis was now officially my assistant, which was a joke between us. I would arrive at the office from Ninety-sixth Street at about ten-fifteen, and she would be leaving for *her* daily session, and then on to lunch. By then I was at lunch too—these were the days of long publishing lunches—and we rarely got to sit down together to get things done until mid-afternoon. But that's all the time we needed: Phyl was as efficient as she was glamorous. We sailed along blissfully together until Ray Schuster discovered that Phyl was having a serious affair with her son-in-law, the highly regarded civil rights lawyer Ephraim London, and forced Max to have her fired. It sounds like a plot from one of Rona's novels, and in fact her best piece of fiction, *Mr. Right Is Dead*, tracks this fraught romance, which continued on for decades.

My favorite memory of Ray, who liked referring to me as "my Max's young genius," was of standing next to her on the receiving line at a reception she gave to celebrate Jessica (Decca) Mitford's *The American Way of Death*. "Balenciaga!" she exclaimed to the guests as they filed past, whipping open the jacket of her elegant suit: "Fully lined!"

Ray would have been a great target for Decca Mitford (one of the six notorious Mitford sisters—Nancy was the oldest), who loved most of all to puncture the ridiculous. Yes, she had been a fierce Commie; yes, she was a savage fighter for equal rights—for everyone's rights; yes, she loved to expose chicanery; but I think what she loved most of all was revealing the idiocies of the foolish, the greedy, and the pompous. Certainly she went to town on them in *AWOD*, as we referred to her book. It wasn't just the machinations of the funeral people that called to her, it was their language, their posturing. The more she tormented them, the dopier they became—it wasn't a fair fight because she was so much smarter than they were, and so much more ruthless.

At our first meeting Dec and I bonded over trocars, those neat little instruments used in funeral parlors to extract what needs to be extracted so that embalming can follow. (Actually, we bonded over Bloody Marys at the Italian Pavilion, the then-trendy publishing lunch hangout, where at that point in my life I was pretentious enough to be proud of having "my" table. Vodka was always the way to Decca's heart.) Candida Donadio, the young, extraordinarily gifted literary agent who had become my closest friend and ally in the publishing world, brought us together, to see if we would get along. Late one night a year or so earlier I had been whining to Candida over the phone that if I was supposed to be such a hotshot editor, why didn't I ever think up good ideas for commissioned books? The only subject I'd ever come up with, I said, was the world of funeral parlors, and needless to say I hadn't done anything about it. "Too bad," she said. "My client Jessica Mitford is under contract for that very book with Houghton Mifflin."

This was a blow. I had read Mitford's first book, the hilarious memoir *Daughters and Rebels* (*Hons and Rebels* in Britain), and loved it. Well, I said, if the funeral book ever comes free, let me know and I'll pay twice whatever they paid. When Decca delivered most of the manuscript, to Candida's amazement Houghton wanted out of the deal—their top editors were horrified by the embalming chapter, and their lawyers were worried, too. Like Yossarian at the very end of *Catch-22*, I jumped. And when Decca and I met—again like Yossarian, this time at the very start of *Catch*—it was love at first sight, though anyone less like a Chaplain than Decca would be hard to imagine.

Everything about the publication of *AWOD* went flawlessly. There were no editorial conflicts because we saw everything the same way—gleefully. The title was perfect. The ingenious designer Janet Halverson—she had created a new look with her rebus-like jacket for *Born Free*—came up with the single best symbol for a book I've ever seen: a funeral wreath in the shape of a dollar sign. It told the whole story. And Decca turned out to be a fabulous promoter. She was completely prepared, she had that enchanting upper-class English accent, she was funny, and when she was confronted by funeral industry spokesmen who made the mistake of challenging her, she slaughtered them. The book leaped up the bestseller list to number one, and Decca was declared the Queen of the Muckrakers. For all of us who were involved, there was the double satisfaction of having such a good time while doing so much good: Legislation was passed that at least for a while made the funeral directors pull in their horns. (When thirty years later we went back to the subject in *The American Way of Death Revisited*, things had reverted—in fact, were worse than they had ever been.) Typical of Decca: In my copy of *AWOD*, she wrote, "Thank you for making me richer than the undertakers."

When in 1963 Nina's mother died while Decca's book was still in galleys, I got a firsthand lesson in funeral practices. I went with Nina to Riverside, the West Side (Jewish) "memorial chapel," where she asked to see a traditional plain pine coffin. The solemn salesman led us through acres of elaborate, glistening sarcophaguses (sarcophagi?), one more hideous than the next. Nina showed her true strength. After a good deal of disagreeable back and forth, he very reluctantly unlocked an obscure door behind which, in the dark, were two pine coffins— exactly what she knew her intelligent and refined mother would have preferred. The one she chose had a wooden Star of David glued to its top, and she asked to have it removed, because, as she explained, her mother was completely unreligious and would have been distressed by it. Our man had a final arrow in his quiver. This coffin, he explained, was made by a religious community in New Jersey, who wouldn't allow it to be sold unadorned. Perhaps if we paid a little extra, I suggested? Seventy-five dollars did the trick. Without having read *AWOD*, we would have been lost.

Decca and I soldiered on together through half a dozen more books, including her autobiographical *A Fine Old Conflict*. But the two of us *had* no conflicts, because even if she grumbled when I pulled her back from the brink of overstating her case, she would acknowledge that she needed pulling. My favorite exchange with her over the years was about a number of things she wrote about me in a memoir. "Dec," I told her, "this is all lots of fun and I have no personal objections, but I've got to point out that every single fact is wrong." "Have it your way," she said. "Make it accurate—if you have to." (I did have to.) The reality, as I often rubbed it in, was that she was a total gutter fighter who would go for broke and then see what she could get away with, and we both enjoyed our forty-year-long routine of bickering over which of us was the Biter and which the Bitten. (Most of her letters to me begin "Dear Bites.") You can take it from me that she did plenty of biting, but then, she's not here to state her side of the story.

Needless to say, Decca Mitford was honest in the important things, true blue, generous, deeply private, and endlessly, gloriously funny. I'm still friends with her daughter, Constancia Romilly (Dinky to everyone). Dinky's two boys are the sons of James Forman, a leading black figure in the civil rights movement, who for political reasons couldn't marry a white woman. Decca's most famous bon mot was her response to a Southerner who demanded to know how she would feel if her daughter were to marry one of *them*. "Oh," said Dec, "if only she *would*!"

Decca was only one of many authors who came to me through Candida. (Among the others were Joseph Heller, Bruce Jay Friedman, Wallace Markfield, William Gaddis, Robert Stone, and John Cheever.) Candida and I were only about a year apart in age, and almost instantly we became close, despite the radical difference in our backgrounds and temperaments. Candida was Sicilian, as she liked to boast—particularly about her taste for Sicilian cold revenge. She was short, plump, matronly, and always swathed in black—a figure from post-war Italian neo-realist film. Her deep voice was often filled with doom and anguish— "The children! The children!" she liked to cry, literally thumping her ample bosom. She herself had no children, but as Michael Korda was to write, "All writers were like children, but her writers *were* her children. She felt about them as if she were their mother." She did have marriages, two of them, both disasters. For one of them, Muriel and I gave the wedding dinner in our apartment, and within weeks the bridegroom was gone to L.A., never to return. (I was reminded of how George Eliot's husband, John Cross, twenty years her junior, flung himself into the Grand Canal from a window in the hotel in Venice where they were spending their honeymoon.)

Our alliance, as it was thought of in our little world, would in the mid-sixties be officially cemented by *Esquire*, which named the two of us the "red-hot center" of the publishing world—momentarily satisfying but far from the way we saw ourselves. What connected us wasn't ambition or the hope of public notice but the fact that we were obsessive readers whose tastes were highly similar, and our bedrock belief that writers came first. Candida lived in a tiny apartment a few blocks from our floor-through in a dilapidated brownstone on Second Avenue in the Fifties—we had a blue-painted floor and there were old-fashioned fire escapes front and back. If she was sick, either Muriel or I would carry over homemade chicken soup, while if we had an emergency babysitting crisis, she would pad over in her sneakers and take care of little Roger. We shared our problems, or as my great friend Irene Mayer Selznick liked to say, we "took in each other's washing."

On August 29, 1957, Candida sent me a note that read, "Here is the 'script of CATCH 18 by Joseph Heller about which we talked yesterday. I've been watching Heller ever since the publication of Chapter 1 in New World Writing about a year ago. He's published a good bit in The Atlantic Monthly, Esquire, etc. I'll tell you more about him when I see you at lunch next week. As ever, Candida." About seventy-five pages of manuscript came with it, and I was knocked out by the voice, the humor, the anger. We offered Joe five hundred dollars as an option payment. This was only months after Jack Goodman's death, and the editorial department had developed no real modus operandi; I suppose I just said "I want to do this" and there was nobody interested enough to say no. Joe and Candida decided to wait until there was enough of a manuscript to warrant an actual contract.

When I met Joe for the first time, for lunch at a hearty restaurant near our offices, he came as a big surprise. I expected a funny guy full of spark and ginger, but what I got was more or less a man in a gray flannel suit—he was working as an ad executive at McCall's, and he looked it. And sounded it. I found him wary (which shouldn't have been a surprise, given the paranoid slant of much of his book), noncommittal, clearly giving me the once-over. He told me later he found me nervous and ridiculously young. I was only eight years younger than he was, but he was a mature ex-vet, a former college teacher, and a successful business executive. I was twenty-six, still looking much younger than I was, and with no track record as an editor or publisher—this was well before Mitford, et al.

So it wasn't love at first sight. But it proved to be something a lot more substantial: a professional and personal relationship that never faltered, despite gaps in our publishing together, and despite (or because of?) the fact that through the more than forty years we worked with each other on and off, we rarely saw each other socially. As with Decca Mitford, there was never a disagreeable word between us, and there was always complete trust. I certainly always knew that I could turn to him in need, and I know he felt the same way about me. Indeed, there would be dark moments ahead in our personal lives—usually involving our children—which proved it.

The most significant trust was editorial. Once his book was completed, three or so years after we first met, I tore into it—relaxed about doing so because I had no notion that I was dealing with what would turn out to be sacred text. Or that Joe would turn out to be as talented an editor as he was a writer, and absolutely without writer ego. On *Catch*, as on all the other books we worked on together, he was sharp, tireless, and ruthless (with himself), whether we were dealing with a word, a sentence, a passage of dialogue, or a scene. We labored like two surgeons poised over a patient under anesthesia. "This isn't working here." "What if we move it *there*?" "No, better to cut." "Yes, but then we have to change *this*." "Like this?" "No, like *that*." "Perfect!" Either of us could have been either voice in this exchange. I wasn't experienced enough back then to realize how rare his total lack of defensiveness was, particularly since there was never a doubt in his mind of how extraordinary his book was, and that we were making literary history. Even when at the last minute, shortly before we went to press, I told him I had always disliked an entire phantasmagorical chapter—for me, it was a bravura piece of writing that broke the book's tone—and wanted to drop it, he agreed without a moment's hesitation. (Years later, he published it in *Esquire*.) Where my certainty came from I don't know, but although I mistrusted myself in many areas of life, I never mistrusted my judgment as a reader.

Joe was so eager to give me credit that I had to call him one morning, after reading an interview he had given to the *Times*, to tell him to cut it out. I felt then, and still do, that readers shouldn't be made aware of editorial interventions; they have a right to feel that what they're reading comes direct from the author to them. But enough time has gone by that I don't think any harm will be done if I indulge myself by repeating what Joe's daughter, Erica, wrote in her uncompromising memoir, *Yossarian Slept Here*: "My father and Bob had real camaraderie and shared an almost mystical respect. No ego was involved, regardless of where Bob's pencil flew or what he suggested deleting, moving, rewriting. To Dad, every word or stroke of this editor's pencil was sacrosanct." Even if this is friendly overstatement, and it is, it reflects the reality of our dealings with each other.

Not that there weren't stumbling blocks along *Catch*'s path to publication. First of all, when the finished manuscript came in there were colleagues who disliked it intensely—they found it coarse, and they saw the repetitions in the text as carelessness rather than as a central aspect of what Joe was trying to do. Then we had a copy editor who was literal-minded and tone-deaf. Her many serious transgressions included the strong exception she took to Joe's frequent, and very deliberate, use of a string of three adjectives to qualify a noun. Without asking me, she struck out every third adjective throughout. Yes, everything she did was undone, but those were pre-computer days: It all had to be undone by hand, and it wasted weeks.

And then when the book was ready to be launched, at the meeting to decide the size of our fall-list printings the naysayers came up with the figure of five thousand. This roused the tiger in Nina, whom everyone had always thought of as a genius, yes, but also as an adorable little bunny. Suddenly she stood up, glared around, and spoke: "If after all these years my total belief in a book doesn't warrant a printing of seventy-five hundred, what's the point of my being here?" Stunned silence. This was not the Nina people knew and loved. "Of course, Nina!" "Yes, Nina!" "Seventy-five hundred if you think that's the right number, Nina!" It was completely hilarious, and especially satisfying to me, who enjoyed taking credit (privately) for what she and I called the "de-bunnying of Nina Bourne." Later, when she had become slightly more assertive and I might occasionally push back, she would say, "You can take the bunny out of someone, but you can't put it back in."

In the famous campaign to sell *Catch-22* to the world, Nina—more fervent about it than about any other book in her seventy-year career—was the secret, and deadly, weapon.

But the biggest catch on the way to *Catch*'s publication was the title. Through the seven or so years that Joe worked on his book, including the four during which he and Candida and Nina and I grew more and more attached to it, its name was *Catch-18*. Then, in the spring 1961 issue of *Publishers Weekly* that announced each publisher's fall books, we saw that the new novel by Leon Uris, whose *Exodus* had recently been a phenomenal success, was titled *Mila 18*. They had stolen our number! Today, it sounds far from traumatic, but in that moment it was beyond trauma, it was tragedy. Obviously, "18" had to go. But what could replace it?

There was a moment when "11" was seriously considered, but it was turned down because of the current movie *Ocean's 11*. Then Joe came up with "14," but I thought it was flavorless and rejected it. And time was growing short. One night lying in bed, gnawing at the problem, I had a revelation. Early the next morning I called Joe and burst out, "Joe, I've got it! Twenty-two! It's even funnier than eighteen!" Obviously the notion that one number was funnier than another number was a classic example of self-delusion, but we wanted to be deluded.

Over the years, Candida, whose relationship to mere data had begun fraying as her health and self-esteem declined, started telling interviewers that we had settled on "22" because October 22 was her birthday and thus the title was a tribute to her. I found it very distressing that someone so talented and wise was reduced to what you might generously call fantasy or, less generously, lying. Joe, who was both fond of her and grateful to her but understood the fragility of her relationship to strict truth, eventually decided that he had to give his fiction to another agent to handle. (So as not to humiliate her, he allowed her to go on representing his nonfiction.) Candida, whose amazing list of clients had at one time or another included Philip Roth, Saul Bellow, Mario Puzo, Bernard Malamud, and Thomas Pynchon, among many others, lived to watch just about all of them leave her. I concluded that like most boys, these "children" of hers wanted to get away from Mom.

My own relationship with Candida came to an ugly end decades after *Catch-22* when I discovered that she had told me a far more serious lie in a negotiation involving millions of dollars and a very famous writer. Very little lying goes on in publishing, and when she finally acknowledged that she had, indeed, lied to me, I was so angry and hurt that I could never bring myself to speak to her again. A sad ending for a "red-hot center."

But in the glory days, we were bound together not only by our personal friendship but by the excitement of *Catch-22*. To talk of a "campaign" is to put a label on something that didn't exist. There was no marketing plan, no budget: Nina and I just did what occurred to us from day to day, spending our energies (and S & S's money) with happy abandon. We began with little teaser ads in the daily *Times* featuring the crooked little dangling airman that the most accomplished designer of his time, Paul Bacon, had come up with as the logo for the jacket. We had sent out scores of advance copies of the book, accompanied by what Nina called her "demented governess letters"—as in, "the demented governess who believes the baby is her own." Almost at once, excited praise started pouring in. Particularly gratifying to Joe was a telegram from Art Buchwald in Paris:

PLEASE CONGRATULATE JOSEPH HELLER ON MASTER-PIECE CATCH 22 STOP I THINK IT IS ONE OF THE GREATEST WAR BOOKS STOP SO DO IRWIN SHAW AND JAMES JONES.

The range of early admirers was astonishingly broad, from Nelson Algren ("The best American novel that has come out of anywhere in years") to Harper Lee ("*Catch-22* is the only war novel I've ever read that makes any sense") to Norman Podhoretz (!). There were at least a score of letters from notable writers, but, perversely, the one we most enjoyed was from Evelyn Waugh:

Dear Miss Bourne:

Thank you for sending me *Catch-22*. I am sorry that the book fascinates you so much. It has many passages quite unsuitable to a lady's reading. It suffers not only from indelicacy but from prolixity. It should be cut by about a half. In particular the activities of 'Milo' should be eliminated or greatly reduced.

You are mistaken in calling it a novel. It is a collection of sketches—often repetitive—totally without structure.

Much of the dialogue is funny.

You may quote me as saying: "This exposure of the corruption, cowardice and incivility of American officers will outrage all friends of your country (such as myself) and greatly comfort your enemies."

Yours truly, Evelyn Waugh

We didn't take him up on his offer, though we probably should have.

Reviews were mixed, veering from ecstatic to vicious, but the success of the book built and built. It was slow, though—never strong enough at any one moment to place it on the bestseller list, yet sending us back to press again and again for modest printings. Meanwhile, Nina and I unleashed a series of ads that just occurred to us as things happened, all of them rehearsing the ever-swelling praise from critics, booksellers, academics, and just plain book-buyers: We had enclosed postage-paid cards in thousands of copies and got hundreds of responses, positive ("Hilarious"; "Zany") and negative ("A complete waste of time"; "If everyone in Air Force was crazy—How did we win war?"). Many of those who loved it were demented governesses in the Nina mold, like the college instructor who wrote,

At first I wouldn't go into the next room without it. Then I wouldn't go outside without it. I read it everywhere—on the buses, subways, grocery lines. If I did leave it out of my sight for a moment, I panicked . . . until last night I finally finished it and burst out crying. I don't think I'll ever recover . . . But before

I die of *Catch-22*, I will do everything to keep it alive. I will change ads on subways to "Promise her anything but give her *Catch-22*." I'll write *Catch-22* on every surface I can find. I'll pirate and organize a *Catch-22* Freedom Bus ... I'm a happier person today for *Catch-22*. Happier, sadder, crazier, saner, better, wiser, braver. Just for knowing it exists. Thank you.

Comparable if less rhapsodic communications arrived for Joe or for us from a put-and-call broker, a New Jersey die-casting manufacturer, a New York grandmother, a fifteen-year-old boy from Eugene, Oregon, a housewife ("I am now getting phone calls in the middle of the night from people I've given the book to who want to read him aloud to me!")

It was this kind of unbridled enthusiasm that sealed Joe's success— the impulse of his readers to keep the ball rolling. (A well-known example was the concocting of thousands of "Yossarian Lives" stickers by the NBC anchorman John Chancellor, which blossomed on campuses and public buildings everywhere. Another fan came up with, and widely distributed, "Better Yossarian than Rotarian" stickers.) *Catch*, indeed, swept college students up with its challenges to authority and the establishment; again and again commentators compared its influence on young people to that of *The Catcher in the Rye* and *Lord of the Flies*.

All these phenomena were grist for the giant ads we went on devising. For its six-month anniversary, a huge "REPORT ON CATCH-22." For its hitting the number-one spot on the British bestseller lists (it had been greeted with exorbitant praise by Kenneth Tynan, Graham Greene, Philip Toynbee), another full-page ad in the *Times*. Finally, a page shouting, "HAPPY BIRTHDAY, CATCH-22!" By then we had managed to sell about thirty-five thousand hardcover copies, but the great commercial success was to come when Dell released its mass-market edition and millions of copies were sold. (It was the largest-selling paperback book of its first year.) As was widely recognized at the time, it was being read as a scathing assault on our war in Vietnam, a place I'm sure Joe was barely aware of when he first sat down to write.

My own reading of the book was somewhat different from that of most of its enthusiasts: I read it as tragedy, not comedy, its humor painful rather than rib-tickling. What helped me understand it better was the movie Mike Nichols made out of it—clever, unstinting, with riveting performances, but somehow unsatisfactory. I thought I saw why. *Catch-22*, even as it reflected realities of war, was above all surreal. When everything was made literal by the camera, its essential nature disappeared.

Because *Catch* became such a phenomenon, because the work Nina and I did to sell it was so highly visible and remarked upon in the publishing world, and because Joe never stopped talking about what he saw as my crucial role in editing it, I became highly visible myself—it's still the book I'm most closely associated with among the kind of people who think about such things. But in the years that followed its publication, I more or less put it out of my mind. I certainly never re-read it—I was afraid I wouldn't love it as much as I once had. When in 2011 its fiftieth anniversary was being widely celebrated, I agreed to take part in the celebrations. But there was a catch: *Catch-22*. There was no way I could talk about it without reading it again. It was a big relief to find that I still did love it, that Nina and Candida and I—and Joe—and the world—hadn't been misguided in our passion for it. I was knocked out all over again by the brilliance of the construction, the exhilaration of the writing, the pathos *and* the humor.

I was, though, brought up short by coming upon a two-page sequence that I felt was overextended and not very funny, and then remembering that I had had the exact same reaction half a century earlier. Why didn't I excise it back then? Was Joe for once being defensive? Were we just too tired after the endless cutting and revising to take yet another look? No way to know. I did, though, find it comforting that my editorial impulses, whether right or wrong, were at least consistent.

Beginning during the long-drawn-out *Catch* experience (and continuing long after it), I was caught up in an entirely different intense editorial relationship with a New Zealand woman named Sylvia Ashton-Warner (not to be confused with the English novelist Sylvia Townsend-Warner). At the height of a typical Meyer Levin crisis, this one about the Broadway production of *Compulsion*, I took his play agent out to lunch to see if we could help calm Meyer down. We couldn't—no one could have—but she and I took to each other right away. She was a doughty Scottish woman named Monica McCall, well into middle age, with a sparkling eye, a tart tongue, and total integrity. (Years later, well into her seventies, she took herself to Washington, on her own in her wheelchair, to participate in the great "I Have a Dream" march.) Casually she asked me as we were leaving the restaurant whether I'd be interested in a novel about a New Zealand schoolteacher who had invented a radical way of teaching reading to Maori children. This was hardly an ideal subject for American fiction readers, but I had realized that the subject of a novel didn't matter if the writing and feeling were strong and persuasive enough. The book was called *Spinster*, and I read it that weekend and bought it on the Monday.

This was a few years after our success with *A Legacy*, and Nina and I went into *Legacy* mode, spreading the word and spending recklessly. *Spinster*, too, became a minor bestseller, as well as a terrible Hollywood movie. (It was called *Two Loves*, and Sylvia's heroine, Anna Vorontsov, was transformed into a Pennsylvania schoolmarm played, dreadfully, by Shirley MacLaine.) Sylvia herself, a woman of many talents and a passionate temperament, with an adoring husband but unappreciated by her country's education establishment and everyone else except a coterie of like-minded "artistic" friends, felt trapped in a small community in a country she despised: Her letters to me, on flimsy blue stationery, were all headed "From Behind the Woolen Curtain." Over the years we published five or six novels together, but her great success was a work of nonfiction called *Teacher*.

In about 1961 she wrote to tell me that she had bundled up her papers and snapshots and scrapbooks and letters and diaries—some of them had been lying around for years in an unused shed—and was shipping them to me, to do with whatever I wanted: turn them into a book, throw them out, just get them out of her life. Well, I wasn't going to throw them out, and I started trying to decipher and organize them. It became hideously obvious that over the years she had produced many versions of everything she had written—versions of versions of versions—and that what pagination existed was, to say the least, volatile. There were many hundreds, perhaps thousands, of pieces of paper in almost no discernible order, and very little indication of what was meant to go with what.

The important thing, though, was faintly visible: It was just possible to trace and track her educational ideas, the organic method she had invented over the years for teaching the "native" children. (She may have invented this usage of the word "organic.") Since the Maori kids were making no progress with the alien world of "Dick and Jane," she substituted what she called a Key Vocabulary of words they *could* relate to—including ghosts and witches, even murder. Almost overnight they were reading.

Her scrapbooks might include pretty magazine color illustrations of leaves or cats (teaching tools) side by side with furious letters to New Zealand's educational authorities, who were clearly terrified of her and resistant to her revolutionary methods, and poems (hers), and recipes, and love letters. Here were accounts of her fervent friendships with other women, her loving but fraught marriage, her three children, her forays into painting, into music—she was a dedicated pianist—all this creative and emotional force lived out in a little seaside outpost of a school. My job was to pick up the pieces and knit them together into . . . something.

I spread everything out on our long blue-painted floor, and for a couple of months I spent all my spare time sorting, comparing, adjusting, jettisoning, simplifying, until I had a body of text that I could try to find a structure for. Eventually it all came together, helped by the sometimes water-stained snapshots that had got the roughest treatment in the shed. When I had what I thought was a book I gave it the title *Teacher* and sent it off to Sylvia, for an introduction and her approval. She provided the one and offered the other, but I felt she did it reluctantly—her life's work was no longer her own, it was something a stranger had stitched together.

Teacher had an astounding career. Reviewed ecstatically on the front cover of *The New York Times Book Review*, it became a bible in America for young teachers and parents (and some older ones) who were hoping to make drastic changes in the way we educated our children. This was the sixties—*Teacher* was published in 1963, just as the Montessori method was making a comeback, and it quickly gathered admirers and disciples here and around the world. By the time Sylvia's husband died, in 1969, she was famous, and quickly she burst through the woolen curtain, hightailing it out of New Zealand and spending a number of years teaching and demonstrating her methods in the United States, India, England, and elsewhere: always on the move and on the go. Her long and eloquent and intense (she was always intense) autobiography, *I Passed This Way*, was published in 1979, but not until I again had to rein in an author's imaginative notions about me. I had been her lifeline to the big world, and she had invested me with qualities that, alas, I lacked.

Sylvia and I worked together for a quarter of a century, linked by our endless airmail correspondence. When her husband died, I tried to call her, but she wouldn't come to the phone. Years later—not long before she herself died, at a moment when we both happened to be in England—we might actually have come together, but she decided that it was too late, and that it would be too emotional for her. So just as we never spoke to each other, we never met. Even so, it was an epic love affair.

Monica McCall brought another extraordinary writer and person into my life, the Canadian novelist Mordecai Richler, who had recently had a conspicuous success with *The Apprenticeship of Duddy Kravitz*. We would work together until he died, in 2001—six novels, plus assorted nonfiction, much of it savagely funny commentary on his native country in general and the Quebec separatists in particular. Unlike novelists who start strong and fade out, Mordecai got better and better: His final book, *Barney's Version*, was in my view his richest and finest, and the critics more or less agreed.

Our editing process was easy, direct, frictionless. Occasionally I had something substantial to suggest, but usually it was just standard cosmetic work—repetitions, questionable punctuation, matters of tone. In all this I was helped immensely by the fact that Mordecai's wife, Florence, was always his first reader and first editor. He had absolute faith in her judgment, and so did I—since I almost invariably agreed with it.

Florence and the five Richler children were the great bonus of my relationship with Mordecai. Not that he and I didn't get along swimmingly, but his talent was for chumming around—jokeyness, ribbing, shop talk; a drink, a pastrami sandwich, a cigar (though not for me). Florence and I, though, almost from the start, shared an intimacy that's lasted from our early days into our mid-eighties. She was a great beauty—a model when she first took herself to London in the fifties—as well as a superb cook, homemaker, mother, and most of all, helpmeet. She was there for Mordecai morning, noon, and night, and he was as besotted with her almost fifty years after they met as he had been at the start. (According to an amused Doris Lessing, who had palled around with them in their early London years, tough Mordecai followed cool, elegant Florence around like a moonstruck calf.) I've never known a more uxorious husband. When they were in New York together—which was often, since for years he was a Book-of-the-Month Club judge and they would turn up in town for the club's semi-monthly meetings, almost always staying with us—he would grow increasingly anxious unless he heard from her every few hours. He always behaved like a suitor: "I'm taking Florence out to dinner tonight," he'd say proudly, and I'd counter, "Why don't you just say 'Florence and I are going out to dinner tonight?' You're married, you're not on a date." But he was always on a date with her—except when he was as grumpy, selfish, and demanding as all male writers can be. (All males?)

After twenty fulfilling years in London, the Richler clan decamped to their native Montreal. Mordecai knew that for the sake of his work he had to get back to his Canadian roots, but Florence was not amused by *her* Canadian roots and she did very much like her English life. Maria and I happened to be in London and were at their house out in Richmond the night before the family was to sail home with all its household goods—on a Russian freighter, as I remember it. Pandemonium: harassed Mordecai, steely Florence, five over-excited kids, and—am I embellishing?—an over-excited dog. It was *The Cherry Orchard*, only more manic than mournful.

Over the decades we watched those children grow up, and Florence kept a keen eye on ours. It was, and is, a family affair. All five of the junior Richlers are bright, interesting, charming. I've always been close to Jake, the youngest, our lovely godchild, now a lovely man deep in his forties. (I can't claim, alas, that I've been much use to him as a spiritual guide.) And very close to Emma, the older daughter, who's become a novelist with a remarkable and original voice. We bonded once and forever on a long, long walk on the beach in the Hamptons when she was twelve and I about forty-five. By the time we got back to Nina's house, we were doting friends. I used to make up stories for my own daughter, Lizzie, about two puppies called Brownie and Blackie, and ever since those beach days Emma and I have been Brownie and Blackie. So we had dogs as well as books in common. But that doesn't explain the mystery of what Goethe called elective affinities, and the joy she and I have had in our friendship all these years.

Mordecai and I were born within months of each other, in 1931, and by a strange coincidence, within a twelve-month span three other writers were also born whom I would work with for years: Edna O'Brien, Toni Morrison, and John le Carré. The latter two came into my life after my S & S days, but Edna went way back. We got together soon after her breakthrough book, *The Country Girls*, made her a star in England and a scandal in her native Ireland, and we worked on at least half a dozen books together. Our professional relationship was always pleasant and serene, but the real relationship was personal—both between her and me and even more between her and Maria. Edna, too, often stayed with us in New York, coming home late at night from her adventures, plopping down on the side of our bed, and recounting all—such as her *shock* when her handsome taxi driver, after she had persuaded him to let her ride with him in the front of his cab, suggested that he in turn might accompany her home.

She was a glory—so stunningly handsome and sexy, with her pale white skin, spectacular red hair, and exotic outfits: ankle-length gossamer skirts, vivid antique-lace blouses, and layers of baubles, bangles, and beads. She dangled and wafted. (One entranced six-year-old girl we knew stared at her and asked, "Are you from India?" and when

Edna crooned, "No, darlin'," followed up with, "Well, at least you're from Hawaii!") But her mind wasn't exotic. She was an acute reader, an acute observer, and a lot of fun. "Arms in the night!" she would sigh dramatically during our pajama parties, and we would chime in: *"Arms in the night!"*

Edna was, and is, an extravagant woman—that's what I would title a biography of her—but her extravagance was always generous. She was a wonderful single mother to her two boys (they stayed with us too), a superb cook, and an irrepressible gift-giver. And brave: It wasn't easy being on her own, particularly before her unique talents were properly celebrated in the literary world. How could she be that gifted a writer if she was that glamorous a personality? Once I moved to *The New Yorker* we gently drifted apart professionally, but the friendship endured—Maria was recently with Edna in London, and soon after, she sent us her latest (and finest) novel, *The Little Red Chairs.*

As the fifties passed into the sixties, the composition of S & S's staff began to alter. When clever young Richard Grossman—a favorite of Dick Simon's and Jack's, and now a key member of our publishing cabal—left to go into business for himself, to replace him as a kind of assistant publisher and liaison to the sales department the management brought in from the road a young salesman named Tony Schulte. We would become unofficial partners, first at S & S, then at Knopf, when he, Nina, and I moved there in 1968. When Tony died, the *Times* with rare acumen remarked on his "patrician manner" and his "kindly presence." The patrician manner no doubt came from his background—his father a partner at Lehman Brothers, his grandfather a great business success, his education at Deerfield, Yale, and Harvard—but the kindliness came from Tony himself. He was almost painfully generous to anyone needing help, support, or advice, he was implacably loyal, and he was amazingly tolerant of the less than perfect behavior of others. Nina, needless to say, required no tolerance, but I know that what was too often my own willful and careless manner must have distressed him. He managed not to show his dismay, though I could sense it. What I never sensed, however, was the slightest resentment of the fact that with my more flamboyant style I was the more visible member of the partnership. Envy and resentment were simply absent from Tony's makeup, and I know he understood how much I respected him and how deeply fond of him I was.

At work Tony was practical, smart, and a model of probity. And although he was officially on the business side, he had excellent editorial impulses, bringing in such authors as Alistair Cooke (*Alistair Cooke's America* was one of the great publishing successes of the seventies) and Walter Cronkite. Eventually he ascended from Knopf into the upper reaches of Random House, but our friendship never wavered; only months before his death, in 2012, I had a last lunch with him and his wife, the agent Liz Darhansoff, and nothing had changed—except that we were more than fifty years older.

At about the time Tony arrived, along came Michael Korda—so close to me in age, but from such a different world. He was one of *the* Kordas: his uncle the British-Hungarian film mogul Alexander Korda; his father, Vincent, a superb film designer; his other uncle, Zoltan, an accomplished director (*The Four Feathers*). Michael (only a very few people called him Miki) had gone to Oxford, been in the RAF, immigrated to New York in his early twenties, and eventually found himself in publishing. His first job was as assistant to Henry Simon, one of Dick's brothers—more of an academic, really, than a publisher, and narrow in his tastes and interests. He was the most vociferous of those who tried to drive a stake through the heart of *Catch-22*.

For a while Henry kept Michael busy with his own projects, and Michael's behavior was exemplary, but mine wasn't. I hated seeing this obviously clever and capable young guy trapped in what seemed to me a backwater of the firm—you could see in his eyes that he was observing and noting everything, but from a distance; he was decisively outside the group that was getting things done. I didn't know him well, but one day, as he's written in his immensely readable *Another Life: A Memoir of Other People*, I walked into his office and said something like "You've got to get out of this situation. I'd like you to work on some things with me when Henry doesn't have your nose to his grindstone. But first of all we have to fix your office—help me turn your desk the other way so it's facing the door and your back isn't to everyone passing by." We heaved it up and switched it around. My irrepressible need to edit everything that crossed my path apparently extended to other people's furniture.

The most bizarre (and fruitful) project Michael and I shared over the years was editing a far-from-distinguished but potentially commercial novel that had come to him from a notoriously shady agent named Jacques Chambrun who had famously ripped off clients ranging from Somerset Maugham and Grace Metalious (*Peyton Place*) to the young and penniless Mavis Gallant. The writer, Dariel Telfer, turned out to be a genial middle-aged woman from Colorado who had worked in a big mental hospital and been seared by what she had observed there. Her plot was over-the-top, her writing was sub-par, but she had conviction and the need to tell the world what she had witnessed. There was also a lot of (for then) steamy sex, always a problem for the S & S elders. Michael gave me the manuscript, and the next morning I told him I thought we could make something out of it—if he could deal with the awful Chambrun and I could get it past Max & Co. We coped with the awful Chambrun by inventing a contract under which we sent the author her ninety percent share directly—unheard of then and now. And I bullied the official editorial board—Max, Henry, and Peter Schwed—into resentful compliance.

Then we got to work, pulling the thing apart, gluing it back together, gouging whole characters and subplots out of the text, rewriting, and—achievable only because of Michael's extraordinary talent for pastiche—writing new paragraphs, pages, scenes. (He was a born writer, as the future would prove.) When we were done, we *had* made something out of it. Nina came up with the title *The Caretakers*, we created a big fuss, and, since I was now in charge of the extra-rights department, I auctioned the paperback rights and sold it to NAL (New American Library) for the amazing sum of ninety thousand dollars, a record amount for a first novel in 1959. The book did modestly well, but the movie made a splash—with (of course) Joan Crawford as the wicked head nurse—and the paperback was a big hit. Dariel was tickled pink and, in her understated way, wholeheartedly appreciative of what we had accomplished for her. And to thank us properly, she shipped us an outsize crate of celery—a first! Who knew that Arvada, Colorado, was the Celery Capital of the World?

Michael and I grew close through the years, both professionally and personally—I was especially fond of his little boy, Christopher. But although his career was expanding rapidly, and he was being well rewarded, he was caught between his connection to me and my closest colleagues and his obligations to Henry and to Max. S & S was peculiarly divided. Not as in a civil war—there were no surface struggles— but as if there were two different publishing houses under a single roof. The well-meaning if prickly Peter Schwed—about twenty years older than I was—edited P. G. Wodehouse, sports books, and general nonfiction (like Cornelius Ryan's *The Longest Day*) and we got along well, I thought, although Michael in his memoir reported Peter's resentment of me, as though we were rivals. If we were, I didn't know it, because I just didn't think that way. In fact, I enthusiastically handed over to him his most successful writer, the unique memoirist-raconteur Alexander King, whose first book—*Mine Enemy Grows Older* (his Enemy was Himself)—ratcheted up to number one on all bestseller lists, spurred on by Alex's many appearances on the Jack Paar show. His second book, *May This House Be Safe from Tigers*, did just as well. Alex had been introduced to me by his old friend Sid Perelman, and we got along extremely well, but Peter was so mad about his work that I gladly turned the two men over to each other, and it was a perfect marriage.

My "rivalry" with Peter was a symptom of Michael's view of the world, or at least of the Simon and Schuster world. The thing that perplexed me most about his book was his take on my "ambition" and his general view of things as a struggle for power, which was certainly valid on the highest level: Leon Shimkin's resentment of Dick and Max fueled his decades-long ascent to total dominance of the company. But it was Michael himself, not I, who wrote a book called *Power*. What I was determined to achieve was *autonomy*—it was really irksome having to deal with the elders. I was especially irked when Max questioned my decision to publish John Lennon's *In His Own Write*. This was just before Beatlemania hit America, but with my fervent interest in pop music, I was aware of what was taking place in Britain.

Tom Maschler, the brilliant Young Turk of Jonathan Cape, was urging me to import fifteen thousand copies of this odd, charming item and I was very keen to do it. Max, who had never heard of the Beatles (how would he have?), turned up his nose, which made me even more determined than I already was, and again I bullied the elders into acquiescence. Tom had airmailed me two copies (an extravagance for an English publisher) of his finished book, and by this time excitement over the Beatles was escalating. The production department was able to tear apart one of our two copies, photograph it, and rush our book into existence well before the fifteen thousand copies from England were due to arrive, so that we were in the unique situation of selling the second printing before we had the first.

Nina and Tony and I tried to be inventive, organizing promotions with disk jockeys, deploying bus cards, running clever ads. Meanwhile—this was January 1964—"I Want to Hold Your Hand" and "She Loves You" were at the top of the charts and the boys had invaded America. (At their famous appearance at Carnegie Hall, to which I took young Roger, you couldn't hear a word they were singing over the screams of the young fans, but on our way out onto Fifty-seventh Street I did overhear one obviously private-school teenybopper gush to another, "Sylvia, this is the greatest catharsis I've ever had!") No wonder we were printing and reprinting the book in quantities of fifty thousand as it swarmed out of the stores. One morning I said to Nina, "Stop everything! We're in the grip of delusion! It's as if we were standing on the shoreline saying to the waves, 'Come in, go out,' and thinking we were accomplishing something." We stopped on a dime, but the world didn't notice our stopping any more than it had noticed our starting, and we just went on shipping books.

I don't mean to complain of Michael's treatment of me in *Another Life*—in fact, when it was published, in 1999, and I was asked to review it, I wrote that the book was so generous to me that I would have recused myself from writing about it if it hadn't been so crammed with factual errors. Typical of Michael's generosity and sense of humor is that the day the review ran, he called me, laughing, and asked, "How could I have said all those things?" "Because," I said to him, "as a writer you're first and foremost a fabulist." That would change as he turned himself into a responsible and admired biographer.

It would be nice to think that I had lived up to Michael's loving view of me, but at the time I was aware only of wanting everything to go our way and to go our authors' way; to make things work. My passions were for books, for publishing, and for people, not for money or position—in all my career I only once asked for a raise, and that was out of pique, not hunger for money.

When *Another Life* was published more than fifteen years ago, I was startled and nettled by Michael's analysis of me: that I had a need to dominate which was hidden deeply, even unconsciously, beneath my need to see myself as someone totally without ambition, interested only in fulfilling responsibilities and being collegial. Me? I recognized that I resented and fought authority, but as far as I knew, I just wanted to be left alone so I could get things done. Let's face it, though, Bob: Unless you inherit the company, you don't get to run things unless you want to run them. Michael may have had a point.

When I was named editor-in-chief, I certainly wasn't going to do anything more than expand what we published by following my own inclinations and by encouraging our other editors to follow theirs. Every editor has to follow his or her own tastes and instincts within the general boundaries of the house's sense of itself, and S & S had always had very spacious boundaries. The more, the merrier. I myself as an editor seemed to gravitate toward a kind of superior popular fiction that we hadn't really published before, but my obsessive reading stretched very wide, from Racine to nurse romances, and carrying a large umbrella is a healthy modus operandi for the chief editor of a general trade publisher. Not that I had the sole authority to acquire books: There was still an editorial board, on which I was now the loudest voice.

A writer I was pleased to acquire was Ray Bradbury, who came to us mid-career looking for more publishing energy than he thought he was getting at Doubleday. It happens: A publisher begins to take for granted an acclaimed writer whose audience isn't expanding, and the acclaimed writer grows itchy. Bradbury was the most admired of all science-fiction writers, but he was artistically ambitious and not willing to settle for being a superior master of genre. And why should he have limited himself? After all, his god was Shakespeare.

Our first venture together was the full-length novel *Something Wicked This Way Comes*—a mix of horror, fantasy, nostalgia, without a trace of his most famous book, *The Martian Chronicles*. We tried hard to deliver on our promises to him and his agent and to break him out into a wider readership, but succeeded only to a modest degree: What his readers wanted was *The Martian Chronicles*.

And then there was an intense youngish novelist named J. R. (Jack) Salamanca, whose first novel, *The Lost Country*, was a Thomas Wolfe-ian explosion of raw feeling and somewhat fancy writing about a high-school boy in love with his schoolteacher. The book got some attention, and Jack made a good deal of money from it because I managed to sell the film rights to my old friend Jerry Wald—the deal was clinched while I was having lunch at a Rockefeller Center restaurant called the Forum of the Twelve Caesars (the staff were dressed like ancient Romans, sort of, and everything came to you flaming, including the salad). On this occasion a telephone was brought to my table—the only time this ever happened to me—and it was Jerry, laying out his terms. I demanded a bonus if the book won the Pulitzer Prize—a delusionary suggestion that clinched the deal. Jerry went on to make the movie, called *Wild in the Country*, as a vehicle for Elvis Presley. And Elvis was very good in it.

It was Jack's second novel, *Lilith*, that achieved real réclame and even minor bestsellerdom. It revolved around a fascinating schizo-phrenic girl and a young man's obsession with her (Warren Beatty and Jean Seberg in the movie), but the girl didn't enter the book for many chapters, and I felt readers needed a signal that she was on her way. Her enticing name was Lilith, so we made her name the title. And Gray Foy's exquisite rendering of her for the jacket promised readers that something—someone—remarkable was coming their way. Titles and jackets can make all the difference.

Because I wasn't only interested in the books I edited but in all S & S books, I flung myself into the marketing of the whole list—getting involved in jacket art, jacket copy, pricing, size of printings, titles, anything that caught my attention and I thought could be done better. Nina and I went on working on all ads together—the joy of it! Nina curled up in her desk chair, pecking away at her typewriter, a cigarette dangling from her fingers or burning out in her ashtray—she rarely took more than a puff or two—while I paced around, urging her on, laying down the law (well before I *knew* the law). Proofs would stream in from our ad agency, Sussman and Sugar: "Nina, the Suss messenger is here!" Then rip it up, redesign, add a blurb, goose up the headline, fix the margins, relocate the image—it drove Suss crazy, but our ads, everyone acknowledged, were the best in the business. (We took our style to Knopf when we moved there, in 1968, and Knopf ads are *still* the best in the business.) All this, remember, was decades before you could do all the fine-tuning, in seconds, at your computer. It was also before copy machines (forget Xeroxes) and e-mail—it was a world of phones, pencils, and, worst of all, carbon paper.

Probably my favorite moments of the week were the promotion meetings, at which the publishing gang got together to decide on strategies and tactics. I chimed in on everything, sometimes to no effect, sometimes to considerable effect. A vital intervention took place in 1960 as we were preparing to publish William Shirer's *The Rise and Fall of the Third Reich*, which he had been working on for years (and which Shimkin kept trying to scuttle because of its long-standing twenty-five-thousand-dollar contract). Shirer's editor, Joe Barnes, was a distinguished old-time journalist whom everyone respected but whom I hardly knew and who kept the lowest possible profile. I hadn't read the book until late in the day, when Michael alerted me to its potential and I took a set of galleys home. The next day I roared around the office insisting that the ugly jacket be scrapped and the title changed: Shirer had called it *Hitler's Nightmare Empire*. Nina solved the title problem by suggesting we use the very underplayed subtitle, and the art department, under protest, came up with the striking and controversial swastika design.

Even more crucial, at the next publishing meeting I found out that someone had decided to issue it as a two-volume set for fifteen dollars. That way lay madness for a book with this much potential, and not very tactfully I forced through the decision to publish it in one mammoth volume at the unheard-of high price of ten dollars. The original designated printing of five thousand copies was abandoned and the book went on to gigantic success—number one for six months, acclaim, prizes. (To demonstrate the diversity of the S & S list: Our four number-one nonfiction titles between 1960 and 1963 were Shirer, Alex King, *Calories Don't Count*, and *The American Way of Death*.)

My only other connection to Shirer's book was selling the paperback rights. Tony, who was on an extended sabbatical to work in the newly formed Peace Corps, had been selling our subsidiary rights, and I had taken over. Auctions had now become the standard method of dealing with what had become the cash cow of the industry, but a zillion-page history of Nazi Germany wasn't standard mass-market fare. I decided to wait until the book was securely the top-selling book in America and then I sent it out to the paperback houses—but with the stipulation that everyone would have only one chance to place a bid, there would be no back-and-forth auction (too vulgar for Shirer), and don't bother offering less than three hundred thousand dollars. Not only was this arrogant scenario unique, but no one had paid anything like that amount of money for *any* book. I didn't care if we ended up with no bids, though, since I was certain that the hardcover would make a fortune for us on the backlist if there were no paperback edition at all. Even so, I was a nervous cat as the hours went by on the day of the sale.

Bantam didn't bid, Dell didn't bid, NAL didn't bid. Pocket Books (our own paperback house) didn't bid. But my good friend Leona Nevler, editorial director of Fawcett, called and plunked down four hundred thousand dollars. Graciously, I accepted. Leona was a little embarrassed when, later, she found out that she had been the only bidder, but she had the last laugh: The Fawcett edition was so successful that within a year, it had earned out the entire amount and Fawcett was home free.

Indicative of how S & S was organized at this time—and perhaps of how cocky I had become—is that it never occurred to me to let anyone know what I was doing, and no one asked. Who *would* ask? There was no one in charge. (It was the same dynamic as still prevailed a year later when

Nina and I spent the bank on *Catch-22* ads.) This may have been a helluva way to run a railroad, but the trains ran on time. I don't remember Peter Schwed, whose official title was publisher, commenting on the Shirer paperback coup. Joe Barnes took the news of it lethargically. As for Shirer, I have no idea what he thought, since I never met him.

I found office life—collaborating, negotiating, pressure—totally enjoyable; I even enjoyed meetings, which so many people dread. I didn't take vacations, I hated long weekends, I couldn't wait to get to work. Yet it was at home that the real work, the real job, got done— that is, the job of reading and editing manuscripts. I've never been able to do any of that in the frenzied atmosphere of the office. Just about every workday for many decades I got home, ate dinner, and began turning manuscript pages, usually with a pencil in my hand. Luckily, I was still a very fast reader, so could make judgments about new manuscripts quickly: Was it worth publishing? If yes, what kind of basic revision might it need: Rethinking? Restructuring? Mere cosmetic work? Or best of all, *none*! (That, alas, was rarely the case.) Actual editing was naturally a much more protracted process and sometimes it was maddening, but it was the heart of the matter, and writers deserved their editors' full attention. Besides, it was so interesting.

The only advantage to weekends and holidays was that they gave me more time to work, but I never felt that this was a hardship or a sacrifice; it was what I wanted to be doing. (It was more of a hardship for my family.) I went fairly often to dance events, but almost never to movies or plays, unless Maria was in them. We saw close friends, but no dinner parties, no publishing parties, no television, certainly no sports. And if I left town, it was to London for business reasons— acquiring books, seeing writers and publishers and agents—though there was pleasure, too, with a bunch of English friends accumulated over the years.

Through my Simon and Schuster days I was mostly editing fiction— purely commercial novels like *The Best of Everything* and *The Caretakers*; the Candida writers: Bruce Jay Friedman's brilliant *Stern* and *A Mother's Kisses* and Wallace Markfield's *To an Early Grave*; James Leo Herlihy's *Midnight Cowboy* (curiously, the two stars of the movie John

Schlesinger made from it, Dustin Hoffman and Jon Voight, were both nominated for Oscars but lost to John Wayne in the first filmed version of another novel I had edited, *True Grit*); new-wave French fiction, like the work of Michel Butor; established writers I was thrilled to be able to accommodate, Ivy Compton-Burnett for one—the day I got a cordial postcard from her was a red-postcard day. And dearest to my heart, a series of conventional novels that had nothing in common except highly original stories and immense readability, and all of which found large readerships. (A comparable book today: *All the Light We Cannot See.*)

The first was *The Moonflower Vine*, which I inherited from an odd-ball with an oddball name—Rudo Globus—who had been working with Dick Simon and who when he departed for greener fields bequeathed me not only this book but his exceptionally neurotic poodle, Hooper (né Pooper), who had been raised like a child and who was made redundant, as they say in Britain, when the Globuses produced a real one. (Among Hooper's salient characteristics were his ferocious intelligence and his utter lack of interest in any human being.)

The author of *The Moonflower Vine* was Jetta Carleton, a former modern dancer and now a successful advertising executive, who lived with her amiable husband across the river in Hoboken. With her bright red curls and dramatic jewelry and garments (to call them clothes doesn't quite do them justice), Jetta was an enchanting and very smart bohemian, and Hoboken was at that time an outpost of New York bohemia. She had been working on this complicated and moving novel for a number of years, piecing together the life of a Missouri farming family with a secret at its heart. I fell in love with it, and with her.

The Moonflower Vine became a Literary Guild selection, a Reader's Digest Book Club selection, a bestseller, a paperback (Fawcett again), and earned enough money for Jetta and her husband to buy their dream ranch outside Santa Fe (named, I say proudly, El Rancho Gottlieb). This novel has been rediscovered—and republished—three times since its initial commercial success in the early sixties, most recently after Jane Smiley made it one of her hundred choices in her 2005 book *13 Ways of Looking at the Novel.*

A few years later, along came a far bigger, though equally unlikely, hit, Robert Crichton's *The Secret of Santa Vittoria*. This long, funny, exciting story involved the peasants of an Italian village during the German occupation who decide that they're going to outwit the enemy by hiding a huge store of the excellent local wine. Crichton was a master narrator, a natural tale-spinner—I liked to say that he could go down to the corner to buy a cigar and come back with a saga on the scale of the *Odyssey*. I did the usual amount of standard editing, and Nina and I did our usual drum-beating, but even I was surprised by *Santa Vittoria*'s tremendous success—fifty weeks on the *Times* bestseller list, eighteen of them at the top. One delicious touch: The week it first hit number one, replacing the long run of *Valley of the Dolls*, Crichton received a telegram from the ever-gracious Jacqueline Susann saying that if she had to be knocked off the pedestal, she was glad it was by him.

Long before *Santa Vittoria* had peaked, Maria and I had been more or less absorbed into the Crichton family—Bob, his wife, Judy, and their four children. For many years we spent evenings and holidays together—more than ready to become part of such a large, rambunctious, and apparently contented family. (Freud's term for this kind of attachment was "a family romance.")

It was through Judy's lifetime friendship with Tony Schulte that *Santa Vittoria* had come to us. A niece of Richard Rodgers, Judy was a strikingly tall and handsome woman—all the Crichtons were giants—with an outstanding career as a documentary television producer, at a time when such success was rare for women. Her own childhood had not been a happy one, and she had a deep need to create a secure and wholesome surround for her own brood. Maria and I, neither of whom had enjoyed a generous family situation, fitted right in as Bob and Judy's . . . what? Somewhat younger siblings? Cousins? Certainly as loving ringside witnesses to the Bob-and-Judy show. None of this affected the very different kind of relationship Bob and I had as author and editor, in which I guess I was the heavy. Many years later our relationship suffered an unhappy break, but not before Bob had written his second fiction bestseller, *The Camerons*, a multi-generational chronicle based on his own Scottish family history.

Nothing, however, could disturb our friendship with the two older Crichton girls, which began when Sarah was twelve and Jenny nine or ten. (Just last year I was at Sarah's sixtieth birthday party.) The connections multiply. Sarah is now an important publisher, with her own line of Sarah Crichton Books, an imprint of FSG (the publisher of *this* book); Jenny is a star teacher at the first-rate middle school our grand-twins go to in Park Slope, Brooklyn—this year she's Oliver's English teacher. Both girls have done their parents proud.

And then came *The Chosen*, Chaim Potok's remarkable novel about two Jewish boys in Brooklyn during and immediately after World War II. It's a story of deep-rooted friendship, of traumatic divisions between fathers and sons, of the clash between modern Orthodox Judaism and Hasidism and the clash between religion in general and secularism. And one of its driving metaphors is baseball. An unlikely prescription for a major bestseller.

Its start with us had been rocky. An agent I had never worked with sent over the manuscript, which was seriously dog-eared—a sign, in those pre-Xerox days, that this was a single copy that had already been turned down by a series of publishers. Ordinarily I would have read it that night, but I wasn't free to and so asked my astute assistant, Toinette Rees, to do a first reading. Toinette was a young Englishwoman of very firm opinions, and my interest was piqued when I read her long report that said it was utterly wonderful but a hopeless publishing possibility. Toinette ambivalent? When I rushed through the manuscript that night after work I saw how right she was: It *was* wonderful, but it was certainly unpublishable—as it stood. The next morning I called the agent and told her I would publish it in a flash if Mr. Potok could agree with me that his very long novel actually ended midway through his manuscript, at which point he had tacked on an entire second novel. Mr. Potok agreed, we met to discuss it, and a partnership was launched that flourished for more than thirty affectionate and unclouded years.

Chaim was a dedicated writer, his literary idol Hemingway, whose work, fortunately, his own didn't resemble. He was an ordained rabbi, a student of religions with a PhD in philosophy, the editor-in-chief of the Jewish Publication Society of America, and—key to his success—a happy family man, whose warm but formidable wife, Adena, a psychiatric social worker, effortlessly managed their three children, their large house in Philadelphia, and Chaim.

After the two novels he had written were reduced to one and the usual editorial work was accomplished, there remained a major problem: the title. I can't remember what the original one was, but it was hopelessly fancy. Some books arrive with perfect titles, others don't, and this was a severe example of the latter kind. No one could come up with anything plausible: The book had so many aspects that it seemed impossible to find something that reflected the whole. Very late in the day we still had no title, and a jacket had to be designed and the book announced. What happened was one of the very few miracles I've ever stumbled into—maybe the only one. I was brooding on the problem as I was walking down the hall from my office to the men's room when I ran into a man named Arthur Sheekman, to whom I had given an office when Groucho Marx, his closest friend, asked him to come east and lend a hand in putting together *The Groucho Letters*, which I was overseeing at the time. Arthur was a screenwriter—he had written a bunch of Marx Brothers movies, starting with *Monkey Business*, as well as movies for Eddie Cantor, Danny Kaye, and others—and he possessed a friendly elegance and refinement that made him a favorite on our floor. "You look worried," he said to me as we passed each other in the hall. "What's the problem?" So I told him I was going nuts trying to find a title for a book about boys in wartime Brooklyn, Hasidism, and baseball. "Call it *The Chosen*," he said casually, and walked on. Literary history was made because I had to take a leak.

The book took off like a missile after the *Chicago Tribune Book Review* plastered the kind of review on its cover that we all dream about: "Let there be dancing in the streets," it began; and in essence, "Run, do not walk, to your nearest bookstore." Nina and I and Toinette *were* dancing in the streets, or at least in our office hallways. *The Chosen* made its way to the top of the fiction bestseller list—that, I suppose, was the *true* miracle, and the kind that makes publishing so fulfilling. It was impossible that a novel by a complete unknown, on so obscure and parochial a subject, should win such a large audience. But it happened. And *The Chosen* is still selling and being celebrated fifty years later.

How did it happen? First and foremost, naturally, through its large merits. And the fact that it revealed to readers an exotic world they didn't know—something I've seen happen again and again. Other examples: Maxine Hong Kingston's *The Woman Warrior*, and in a very different way, *The Spy Who Came in from the Cold*. But there was also our unanimous belief that Potok's novel was not only excellent but *could* achieve a popular success. When I lecture about publishing and the personal conviction that motors it, I tell this story: When the manuscript was completely ready, I gave it to Nina—I hadn't wanted her to see it before I was one hundred percent satisfied. The next morning she rushed into my office and said, "When I finished it last night I loved it so much that I needed to tell someone about it, but it was too late to call you. So I made myself a cup of tea, sat down, and told myself!"

A year later it happened again—with Charles Portis's *True Grit*. I had published Charlie's *Norwood* a few years earlier, charmed by its pitch-perfect voice and hilarious and poignant characters (among them, Grady Fring, the Kredit King, and Joann the Wonder Hen—the College Educated Chicken). *Norwood* was perfect but slight. *True Grit* was perfect but more substantial. If we did any editorial work on it I can't imagine what it could have been. Certainly I never dreamed of touching Mattie Ross, its fourteen-year-old heroine. Talk about pitch-perfect voice! From first to last her relentless determination to avenge her father's murder is conveyed through the utterly humorless tone of the much older Mattie, whose memories make up the first-person narrative. Her cohorts—the not-quite-over-the-hill marshal, Rooster Cogburn, and LaBoeuf, the keen young Texas Ranger—are no match for her single-minded tenacity: They can't shake her. Alas, neither of the movie Matties does her justice, but how could they? The fun, the edge, the quality of her one-track mind, are conveyed in the texture of her speech, not in her actions. John Wayne, though, is a glorious

Rooster in the first film version, and his performance won him his only Oscar. For me, the later Coen brothers version was pallid compared with the original.

I went on working with Charlie after *True Grit*, but to say "working with" is not exactly accurate. I hardly knew him. He was famously reclusive, or at the least, private; uninterested in celebrity, hunkered down in Little Rock—a very likable man, but in my case likable from a distance. And since so little editing was involved, the traffic between us was limited. But I was mad about his work, and amused by the contrast between the semi-parodied Old West of *True Grit* and the wildly different worlds of *The Moonflower Vine*, *Santa Vittoria*, and *The Chosen*.

Hard to believe, no doubt, but there were failures along the way— failed relationships, unsuccessful publishing ventures, lost opportunities. Every editor turns down books someone else snaps up and triumphs with. I try to forget these blunders, but all too clearly remember saying no to John Fowles's first novel, *The Collector*, which didn't seem to me as original and clever as everyone else found it to be. Years later, I foolishly resisted Larry McMurtry's *Lonesome Dove*. And no doubt on and on. But my most conspicuous failure was over John Kennedy Toole's *A Confederacy of Dunces*.

He sent the original manuscript to me out of the blue in 1964 because, he later told me, displaying his excellent taste, he had been so impressed by Bruce Friedman's *Stern*. There followed several years of back-and-forth, since I was very taken with his energy and originality and wanted to help him make *Confederacy* the best book he had it in him to write (that's what editors do).

But I couldn't convince myself that I'd succeeded. The sad story of his subsequent life, climaxed by his suicide three years after my final rejection of the book, has been told a number of times, as has the inspiring story of the eventual championship of the manuscript by Walker Percy after its rejection by Percy's own publisher (and mine), Farrar, Straus; its publication by the Louisiana State University Press; its Pulitzer Prize. Reading over what remains of our correspondence, as quoted *in extenso* in several biographies, I'm surprised both at how likable and rational, how willing, he appears in it, and how lavish with time and patience I was with a writer I didn't know and wasn't committed to publishing. As time passed, though, I began to sense that his mind, or psyche, was beginning to fray, and after he made an ill-considered (and unannounced) visit to our office, creating an irrational and unnerving scene, I decided that I had to end our affair. Ken's horrifying mother, Thelma, deciding that I was responsible for her beloved son's death, began a campaign of vilification of me that climaxed with her suggestions that it was an East Coast Jewish elite who had deliberately destroyed Ken. I thought about suing her, or at least responding to her deranged outbursts, but came to feel that if such inflamed delusions were helping to assuage the grief of an unhinged mother whose son had killed himself, I could afford to swallow my outrage.

I knew that Ken had done a good deal of rewriting of his book before he died, but I had no notion as to whether the book as published was the result of this work or was more or less the book I had first seen. When recently I read that the latter was the case, I decided to go back to it—and found that my reactions were almost exactly the same as they had been fifty years earlier. There was the explosive energy I remembered, the prodigious imagination, the heady humor—and the overload, the strain, the sophomoric take on life. I guess I was both sorry and relieved that my opinion hadn't changed.

Through all the time I was shepherding new authors into the firm, I was still working with an assortment of writers Jack had been responsible for, among them the two great humorists whose *New Yorker* pieces I was mad about in my early teens: James Thurber and S. J. Perelman. Thurber's highly successful collection *The Thurber Carnival*—published in 1945, when I was fourteen—was my favorite book for a year or two, and when I found myself with the responsibility of watching over his S & S catalogue, I was excited. There was no work to be done—he was no longer producing new books; it was a matter of being the person he or his wife, Helen, could touch base with at S & S. (Thurber, who generally despised publishers, had liked Jack—as who did not?)

My stewardship lasted the four years until he died, in 1961, but the

Thurbers by this point were rarely in New York, never came to the office, and grumbled from afar. He was by now just about totally blind, and convinced that *The New Yorker* was no longer welcoming. Those were the days when I thought I had to entertain writers at expensive meals, and nervously Muriel and I took the Thurbers out to dinner, not knowing what to expect. I've described what it was like in a long piece I wrote about him for *The New Yorker* more than forty years after the event. "He was incoherent with rage against the magazine in general and Shawn in particular . . . Faced at dinner with a drunken, abusive Thurber—and his somewhat less drunk but equally abusive wife—I was totally thrown; whatever I had expected, it wasn't King Lear at the Italian Pavilion spouting invective about a publication and an editor I so admired." We got through the evening somehow; I bundled the Thurbers into a cab and never saw them again.

Perelman was a very different kind of customer. If Thurber was filled with wrath, Sid was filled with bitterness. Thurber was a physical mess; Perelman was trim and dapper, in his bespoke English suits and exquisite shoes. His behavior was unexceptionable, and for ten years we got along very well—the Perelmans were constantly throwing parties and we were occasionally going to them. We once went down to stay with them in their handsome Bucks County home, a pleasure for me because I so much liked Laura Perelman, a large, once-beautiful woman with, I thought, a tragic countenance. (She had a lot to be tragic about. I doubt that she ever fully recovered from the early death of her brother, Nathanael West; the Perelman son and daughter had serious problems—Nina remembered observing them years earlier on Martha's Vineyard, utterly unattended; Sid was not the faithful type; and she had a ruinous history with liquor. I saw her as a noble wounded bird.)

I steered a number of Perelman collections through their publication, but of course there was no editing to be done. My only contribution to his professional life was dreaming up a fat collection of his best work and giving it a fortunate title: *The Most of S. J. Perelman.* (We used that format again with *The Most of P. G. Wodehouse* and *The Most of Ray Bradbury*—and more than half a century later, *The Most of Nora*

Ephron.) Through the sixties, Sid's disaffection with *The New Yorker* grew more severe—like Thurber, he intensely resented William Shawn, who dared to reject some of his work. He did a lot of lucrative writing for other magazines and for the movies, and his books sold, but his tastes were expensive. I'm quoted in a Perelman biography as saying, "He was very charming and very affable and a wonderful raconteur, a very amusing man, fun to be with, but in my view, a deeply self-involved, selfish and angry person . . . He ran away from trouble. He ran away from real emotional or psychic engagement. He was impeccable, but he was not generous." He was also a funny, funny writer, though as his resentments mounted, the fun could be forced, even rancorous. When I left S & S, our professional relationship broke off and I was not sorry. I didn't think it was a good idea—either for him or for us—for him to switch publishers so late in his career.

A far more lovable writer, a great favorite of Jack's, was Cynthia Lindsay, the Connecticut WASP daughter of a movie director, who grew up in Hollywood, becoming among other things a stuntwoman. (You can catch a glimpse of her in Busby Berkeley's famous "By a Waterfall" sequence in *Footlight Parade.*) When stunting palled, she became a screenwriter, sponsored by her great friend Boris Karloff—she and I would work together, many years later, on her fond, perceptive biography of him. Cynthia was the best kind of sophisticated good ol' gal. The first time she came east to New York after Jack's death I took her out to lunch at one of the fancy restaurants that looked down on the Rockefeller Center skating rink, and practically before she sat down she ordered a dry martini. (These were the fifties, remember.) Out of politeness I ordered one too—a first for me. Soon she was on her second, and I felt I had to join her. She ordered a third round. The next thing I remember was waking up the next morning. I must have gone back to the office, got home, made it to bed, but those hours were lost to me forever.

Early on, Cynthia used to trek down to St. Mark's Place in the East Village to see Muriel and Roger and me, gamely mounting the three flights of what she called our melted staircase (it wasn't melted, only tilted). I never visited her in Malibu, where she lived in a showplace beach house with whatever husband or kid was in residence, together with Gottlieb, her large cat, but Maria stayed with her when she was out there making a movie.

One of Cynthia's freelance experiences provided us with a family mantra. She had been commissioned by the *Ladies' Home Journal* to write a Christmas story about Lassie, and she did all the necessary— interviewed Pal, the collie who for years played Lassie (he lived to be eighteen); interviewed Pal's famous trainer, Rudd Weatherwax; soaked up their home atmosphere. Her piece was rejected, she was content with her kill fee, and the next time she was in town, having lunch with her *LHJ* editor, she asked where she had gone wrong. "Oh no, Cynthia," she was told, "you didn't do anything wrong. Your piece was thoroughly researched, really well written, and very interesting." "But?" "It lacked only one thing: The element of greatness."

That was a professional highlight. In the realm of sociology and/or psychopathology, Cynthia made a unique contribution to the study of anti-Semitism. She had an elderly Connecticut aunt of whom she was very fond but who was unyieldingly disagreeable about Jews. (Cynthia was married to one.) Twice she tried to get her aunt to explain her prejudice. The first time, Auntie snapped, "They dart out of alleys!" The next time, "They cluster on lawns!" Auntie could have been a character out of Thurber's *My Life and Hard Times,* except that Thurber's family, however eccentric, wasn't demented.

Books by these and a number of other writers I was editing were thought of as "my" books—that's the way self-deluded editors refer to books by writers whom they're there to serve. But of course Nina and Tony and I were overseeing the publication of the entire list, and though it was mostly enjoyable, it was also harrowing, since we were ridicu- lously short-handed. Luckily, in September 1957, just weeks after the convulsions that had shaken the company from top to bottom, Kay Hartell came aboard as Nina's new assistant. Calm, capable, and ador- able, she was got up in proper young *Best of Everything* style—the kind of girl who in fifties movies starts off in seemly librarian mode and then, when she takes off her glasses and lets down her hair, turns out to be Doris Day. (She's as beautiful today, at eighty, as she was back then.)

Yet again, elective affinity struck. Within weeks, she and Nina had bonded—Kay turned out to be a superb copywriter, completely tuned in to Nina's way of thinking and writing—and she and I had begun a lifelong friendship. A couple of days a week we'd scoot downstairs at lunchtime to the International Pharmacy (for me, a peanut-butter-and-bacon sandwich on rye toast and a malted; Kay's tastes were more refined). It was immediate intimacy, sealed by our love for Nina. During the next half-dozen years at S & S, Kay was an essential part of our publishing team. For instance: Twice a year we had to write the catalogue that presented our upcoming list to the world—fifty or sixty pieces of copy meant to be descriptive, alluring, and (the hard part) not too clichéd. It was hellish work, but we turned it into a party. On two consecutive nights the three of us and Tony would stay on in the office, fortified by pizza and Cokes, and churn it all out, darting in and out of each other's offices for assistance and, sometimes, approbation.

Soon after Kay arrived, she married her boyfriend, Elliot Cattarulla, whose job took him and Kay to London in late 1963—he was to run Esso's (later Exxon's) British operations. (Eventually he would become Secretary of the corporation.) Muriel and I threw a farewell party for him and Kay on the night of November 22, hours after President Kennedy was assassinated. All the people we called to say that they certainly didn't have to come decided there would be comfort in company, so we gathered in desolation, and there *was* comfort in company.

In London, Kay worked for Jonathan Cape, Britain's most exciting publishing house, until the Catts were on the move again: to Saudi Arabia, to Miami, to Lima, back to London, to Athens, and finally, in 1973, after ten years in various wildernesses, back to New York, when they and their two-year-old son, John, moved in with Maria and me and *our* two-year-old, Lizzie, for six months while they found and fixed up an apartment. In other words, we were another extended family, and still are.

Maria and I were married in 1969. We had been living together for four years, and since we wanted children, marriage seemed appropriate—we certainly hadn't been making a statement by *not* getting married. Besides, Laura—Maria's devout mother, "the most beautiful girl in Florence"—was distressed about her daughter's living in sin with a divorced Jew. Not that she was anti-Semitic; in fact, she herself was half-Jewish, although her own mother, an heiress from Trieste, had become more Catholic than the Pope after marrying her Florentine count. What was really wrong with me was that I wasn't a Roman prince. But Laura and I got along well; it was Maria she maddened. Maria, by the way, had been educated at the Convent of the Sacred Heart, where she too appeared to be devout—until the day she graduated, from school and from the Church. In her mind, she was already onstage. And, in fact, she already *was* onstage—she started working for Joseph Papp's Shakespeare in the Park when she was sixteen, a year after it opened for business.

We were married in the Provensens' backyard in Dutchess County—Alice and Martin Provensen, whom Nina had brought me and Muriel and Baby Roger to visit soon after I arrived at Simon and Schuster. The Provensens were among the leading children's book illustrators of the day, though perhaps best known for the *Fireside Book of Folk Songs*, which was on the piano bench of every self-respecting musical middlebrow family in America and is still in print, almost seventy years after its publication. They did more than forty books together, winning the Caldecott Medal and being named eight times to the *New York Times* annual list of the ten best illustrated children's books; after Martin died, Alice went on alone, masterfully.

To me from the start, and later to Maria and our children, the Provensens on their fairy-book farm were magical, and we found another family romance (that endures). Maple Hill Farm was so simple, so perfect—nature gently improved on by true artists—with its red barn, beautiful allée of trees, geese-populated pond, and assortment of picturesque animals (at one time featuring goats, horses, a parrot, a bloodhound, and the most exotic fowl you ever saw, until the foxes got them). We spent countless weekends there, and many Christmases, with Alice and Martin and their beloved daughter, Karen. For years I loved the look of the land adjacent to theirs, almost glimpsable over the fields and through the trees, and one day I was able to buy it, although it would be many more years before nature-besotted Maria built our roomy, airy house on it and turned herself into a gardener—not quite Vita Sackville-West, but impressive.

Present at our very small wedding in the Provensens' garden were most of our nearest and dearest—Nina and the Crichtons, among others. Solemn Roger, now sixteen, was my best man. A local justice of the peace presided. Chickens and dogs were in attendance. Maria's parents, who couldn't live together but were in daily communication, circled each other like wary tropical birds. And also there, to our joy, was my beloved Deborah Rogers, already on her way to becoming the most admired and cherished literary agent in London. A lifetime went by and she was with me in Paris to celebrate the forty-fifth anniversary of this auspicious occasion (Maria was in America, but sent her warmest congratulations).

The half-dozen years from the mid-sixties to the early seventies were the great hinge in my life: the deaths of my parents; a new and happy marriage; a new baby—Lizzie, in 1971; a new way of living, in a brownstone I was able to buy when my father died; and the traumatic (for me) move from Simon and Schuster to Alfred A. Knopf.

Michael Korda in *Another Life* ascribes my decision to abandon S & S as the result of my chafing under Leon Shimkin's refusal to put me in total charge of the trade division. But it wasn't like that—I had plenty of responsibility. Simon and Schuster was the only professional home I'd ever had, and I was contented there from my first day to my last, and had been treated with extraordinary generosity. It was a place where when you started out as cabin boy, everybody seemed to be standing around cheering you on to become admiral. (Well, maybe not everybody.) And due to Jack's devastating death and the changes in ownership, I had been in on running things long before it could otherwise have happened—I didn't have to change jobs, as so many people do, in order to move up the ladder: There *wasn't* a ladder.

The simple truth was that as time passed, everything had become all too easy and comfortable for me—life in the office was like a daily party—and I was growing restive. This was hardly a tragedy, and certainly not a serious enough reason for departing, but it affected my state of mind. The real issue was trying to anticipate what further, and direr, corporate changes were up ahead for S & S. (How right we were: Gulf & Western and Viacom were over the horizon.) Nina and Tony and I started discussing our future, but without any serious intention of doing anything about it. Then one day, after Max had permanently retired from the field and Leon had become sole owner, he called together all the executives of what was now a very large company and made a gloating little after-lunch speech. Well oiled by his daily dose of martinis, and with a flushed face, he celebrated his own ascendancy, saying, "Years ago I had a vision of bringing together all the different parts of S and S. It took me all this time to make it happen—there were so many people in the way!" Nina and I were sitting across from each other, and as so many bad novelists have put it, "Our eyes met in the middle of the room." A future of Leon wasn't a future we could look forward to.

Within a couple of weeks I was having another of my late-night phone calls with Candida and casually mentioned that I had actually begun contemplating changing jobs but had no notion of what to do about it. (Tony had been talking about buying a firm—it seemed that Dutton might be available—but that didn't interest me at all: I didn't want any of the risks or rewards of ownership, and I certainly didn't want us distracted from what we really knew how to do.) Instantly, Candida said, "There's only one other place you could work, and that's Random House," a place I had no particular interest in. It didn't seem all that different from S and S. Without telling me she was going to, the next morning she called Joe Fox, a very well-liked editor at Random House, and told him of our conversation.

Within hours, I had a call from Bob Bernstein, then president of Random, speaking for himself and Bennett Cerf, the founder. He got right to the point: Would I consider leaving S & S to run Knopf, which Random had acquired but didn't know what to do with? If I did, I told him, it wouldn't be just me, it would be Nina too. He had assumed that, he said, knowing that we were the closest of teams—besides, he knew Nina from early in his career when he too was at S & S, had actually worked for her for a while, and adored her the way everyone did. And it would be Tony Schulte as well, I added. Bob and Bennett didn't know Tony but had heard great things about him. "Any one, two, or three of you," he said.

Suddenly it was becoming real. I never would have considered just another publishing house, but Knopf! It was the great literary house of the century, and the one I had grown up on: Mann, Gide, Kafka, Undset, Hamsun, Cather, Camus, Sartre, de Beauvoir, E. M. Forster, D. H. Lawrence, H. L. Mencken, Elizabeth Bowen, Max Beerbohm, Wallace Stevens, Elinor Wylie, Langston Hughes . . .

Within days the three of us began surreptitiously meeting with Bob and Bennett in our various homes and we started negotiating, even though we hadn't yet decided we wanted to do this terrifying thing of leaving the home planet. (As Nina once put it, being at S & S was like having one family more than you needed—and *it* was the family I needed.) To speak of negotiations isn't accurate, though. The usual key issue of recompense didn't come up: I said at once that I didn't want to be paid more money than I was then making (I think it was forty thousand dollars a year, a lot in those days); this was a life decision, not a financial one, and I didn't want to confuse the two things. Nina and Tony felt the same way. There *was* a problem, however. Yes, we would have complete authority at Knopf, but when I asked how this would be explained to Alfred Knopf himself, who having sold his company to Random House had no say in the management but was still there on the premises, and—more important—to the staff, the answer was that no one would explain it; it would just happen. This seemed so loony that we balked, and balked. I remember Nina saying, "Do you mean that one day those poor Knopfies are just going to wake up and find that the three bears have landed on their heads from outer space?"

The discussions had begun in June 1967. Six months later we were still discussing. When the whole thing began, I had dutifully gone to Peter Schwed and Seymour Turk, the treasurer, and told them that for the first time I was considering the possibility of leaving. I was thanked, with a pat on the head. After the first three months of dithering, I went back and warned them that our departure might actually become a reality. More thanks. By December, Bennett—a loose talker, to put it mildly—was beginning to leak hints around the industry. We three were emotionally exhausted, and one day just decided that if we could trust Bennett and Bob with our futures, we might as well trust their view of what would work best at Knopf. And so we slid into saying yes: There would be a formal announcement that we were coming and one day we'd just turn up and take charge.

On the last working day of 1967, Friday, December 29, Tony and I went into Peter's office to break the news. I was on the verge of crying, Tony was on the verge of throwing up. Peter's reaction was typical of his delicacy: First, he complained that we had spoiled his New Year's weekend—couldn't we have waited till Monday? His next complaint: "I let you do my job. Now I'm going to have to do it myself."

Before the news became public, our colleagues at S & S had to be informed. Peter wanted to hold a big meeting at which everyone would be told at once. I insisted that everyone be told individually, which, since Nina was away for the holidays with her brother's family in Texas and Tony had left for a skiing vacation, left it to me to make the rounds. It was awful—like Alice and the pool of tears, many of them mine. The hardest hit were Michael Korda and Dick Snyder—Leon's very clever protégé who was ambitious in a way no one at S & S had ever been . . . except Leon himself. But Dick, like Michael, was hurt and bewildered that he was being left behind. There was no way, however, for us to take along anybody at all, except invaluable Toinette, since we didn't know who was who or what was what at Knopf.

Since we didn't want to leave Simon and Schuster high and dry, we decided we'd stagger our departures. I had to be the first to go since authors and agents needed immediate reassurance. Nina would follow three weeks later and Tony three weeks after that, so that current books could be published smoothly. I drew up a list of all "my" authors— forty or fifty of them—and divided it into three columns: those who would definitely come with me, those who would be better off staying where they were, and those who didn't have to make a decision since they had no book in the works or coming up soon. By contract, Joe Heller had the right to leave if I was gone, and so did several others. S & S could have made difficulties about some of the rest, but chose not to—it wanted an amicable transition as badly as we did. There were a few books—*True Grit* and Mordecai's *Cocksure* among them—that were already in the pipeline, and I felt it would be too confusing to shift them, but we worked things out so that Nina and I were allowed to do the actual publishing from Knopf: commission the jacket art, write the jacket copy and ads, coordinate the publicity, sell the paperback rights.

I spent some time in January inviting key people from Knopf to my office so that we could begin to get a sense of each other—senior editors like Ash Green, Judith Jones, and Angus Cameron; lovable Bill Koshland, officially president of the company but more the lifelong slave of Alfred and Blanche Knopf. (I didn't meet Alfred until we actually went to work.) Right away I began vetting jackets and jacket copy—I remember all too well being shown copy for a biography of the great Italian historian Guicciardini that went out of its way to underline what an unattractive person he was, and not very interesting, either. For a grim moment Nina and I were afraid we had made a terrible mistake, but she cheerfully fixed it up and made it presentable. I raised the price of a new Julia Child book by a dollar. I vetoed the hideous Knopf practice of casting a tone of color over author pictures on the backs of jackets—a green novelist here, a purple poet there. And then I got out of town.

Yes, I was impatient to dig in and face the music at Knopf, but I also needed to recuperate from the awful strain of the preceding months, so before I started my new job, Maria and I went down to Miami to stay with the Cattarullas for a week. It was during this week that I was carded in a liquor store for the last time. I was thirty-six.

WORKING

Alfred A. Knopf

W E PLUNGED INTO WORK. Knopf was by no means dead, but it was moribund, and it was challenging to try to re-energize it. Not that I thought about it that abstractly—I've always just gone from one task (one detail) to the next, with not much of a long view—but the increased responsibility and visibility drove my energy into even higher gear than usual. I just loved it all, even learning to deal gently with some of the older generation who couldn't help viewing our arrival with trepidation. And even if there were those who resisted my manic enthusiasm, they couldn't—no one ever could—resist Nina's captivating life-force, or Tony's probity. The old team soldiered on, somewhat relieved when things started quickly to go well, and a new group was coming together, either up from the ranks (Kathy Hourigan, Jane Friedman) or imported as they happened to turn up and strike my fancy (Vicky Wilson, Carol Janeway, Alice Quinn)—all women, as it happens. But not that many young guys in the 1970s were trying to claw their way into publishing: they wanted to get into "film."

It's easy to romanticize the past, but I'm not much of a romantic, and I feel secure in remembering my Knopf years as a period of accomplishment, fulfillment, and, most of all, a good time. It really was one for all and all for one—a comfortable place where people could work productively. That's something I'm as proud of as any particular success or our consistent profitability. I mean, why not have a good time at work if you can? Yet why preside over a for-profit operation that doesn't make a profit? The trick lay in doing well without compromising Knopf's deserved reputation for quality.

Whether we could accomplish that was certainly a question in the publishing world. The headline of one story about our change of jobs had been "Avid Reader to Head Knopf," and it was accurate as far as it went, but the story quite appropriately was focused on Knopf, not the Avid Reader. If we had moved to Doubleday or Little, Brown or Macmillan it would have been a business story; the fate of Alfred A. Knopf, Publishers, was treated as a matter of cultural significance. Despite the gentle desuetude into which the firm had fallen, the name of Knopf still stood above all others for quality—the quality of the books it published and the quality of how they were designed and produced. One of Alfred's masterstrokes had been the way that, over the decades since the firm's founding in 1915 (when he was twenty-three), he had convinced the literary world—and the public—that his books were superior; that the Borzoi logo on the spine of a book, on its title page, and in the company's ads was a guarantee of distinction.

It was a claim that had merit. No firm equaled Alfred's record of Nobels and Pulitzers. My bookshelves had always been crowded not only with the great literary names he had published but with his superior entertainments—Raymond Chandler, Dashiell Hammett, James M. Cain, Eric Ambler, Roald Dahl. He had established an important list of American historians (Richard Hofstadter, among many others), another of South American writers (his favorite: Jorge Amado), another of Japanese writers (Kawabata, Tanizaki, Mishima, Abe). His list of food writers—the star, of course, was Julia Child—was without rival. He published at least one of America's leading contemporary writers of fiction, John Updike.

And he had a secret weapon: Kahlil Gibran's *The Prophet*, published almost by accident in 1923, which has sold well over ten million copies without benefit of advertisement or promotion. Its sales peaked in the 1970s—no thanks to anything we were doing to help them along—at about four hundred thousand copies a year. Neither Nina nor Tony nor I had ever read a word of Gibran, or attended one of the multitude of weddings at which he was solemnly intoned, and we decided to grit our teeth and see just how embarrassing he was: After all, he was paying our salaries. One summer weekend out in the Hamptons we took turns reading aloud from *The Prophet* and were relieved that though its flowery ersatz-mystical language was every bit as overblown as we knew it would be, the actual sentiments were harmless and even naïvely touching: "You are the bows from which your children as living arrows are sent forth." We could eat our bluefish and corn and strawberry-rhubarb pie without too much guilt.

Knopf had been the private domain—and the battleground—of Alfred and Blanche Knopf until she died, in 1966; she had been there, a formidable force on her own, since the creation. For many years they more or less lived separate lives, she (with her poodles—not borzois; she despised them) in their Manhattan apartment, he in their grand Westchester house. Blanche had among other things exercised the European side of the editorial impulse, reeling in a Gide here, a Camus there. (She paid $250 for the American rights to Camus' *The Stranger*.) I never met her, but once I was having lunch with my old friend Georges Borchardt and he pointed her out to me as she came into the restaurant—a tiny woman who looked as if she had gone straight from Dachau to Elizabeth Arden. No wonder everyone was scared of her.

Everyone was scared of Alfred, too, because he was a famous bully, frequently humiliating his staff with insulting outbursts of displeasure, and so distancing himself from his son, Pat (officially, Alfred, Jr.), that Pat—the presumed heir—left the company to help found Atheneum. All you need to know about the family dynamic is that at an ABA convention in Washington, just after the news had gone round that Blanche had died, I ran into Pat, whom I knew only slightly, and stopped to say how sorry I was about his mother. When I asked when he was leaving for New York, he snapped at me, "Why would I leave for New York because *she* died?" I had no answer.

It was when Pat jumped ship that the Knopfs sold the firm to Bennett Cerf and Donald Klopfer at Random House, but Alfred stayed on in an ambiguous capacity, no longer in charge but very much a presence. Once a week an executive from Random came over to the Knopf offices a few blocks away to check in and check up, but he was as wary of the great panjandrum as everyone else was. And since over the decades every talented young editor who had come to work at Knopf with high hopes had either been fired or had quit in indignation at the way he was treated, there was no strong editorial personality leading the way into the future. The distinguished older editors had made their peace with the situation and were working skillfully but without a great deal of zest. You could say the whole place was suffering from low-level depression.

Alfred—he insisted that we use his first name—was extremely gracious and welcoming; he had, of course, been alerted that the three of us were taking over. Even so, it was nervous-making not only taking over his firm, even though it was no longer actually his, but having him there in the office every day, with his secretary, doing . . . what? Observing? The happy circumstance for him, and therefore for everyone connected to him, was that his second wife, Helen, whom he had married less than a year after Blanche died, was her opposite in every way: warm, lively, and devoted to him. They had met years before, in the early forties, when he had published her only novel. Helen understood him, cherished him, and did her best to take the edge off him, even effecting some kind of rapprochement between him and Pat. She was a strong-minded, independent woman from the Northwest, a part of America to which Alfred was particularly drawn. We thought of her as an apple from Oregon, and she was certainly instrumental in helping him accept us as the guardians of his legacy.

At once she and Alfred invited the three of us to lunch at his favorite restaurant, the Pool Room at the Four Seasons, and we had a jolly time—especially tickled because the maître d' (or for all I know, the owner) kept rushing up to our table not only to make sure that all was to Alfred's satisfaction but to inform him of certain specialties not available to just anyone. "Mr. Knopf," he enthused at one point, "we've just received an air shipment of a small supply of fiddlehead ferns from Ireland. I think you'll like them!" Alfred let him know that they passed muster.

Even so, Alfred's presence in the office produced some strain, at least in me. Tony, always generous and particularly patient with father figures, spent a good deal of time with him. I, not only less generous and less patient but particularly antagonistic to father figures, was always polite (I hope) but kept as much distance as I could between my corner of the office and his. There was only one "incident," but it might have escalated badly if not for Nina's wisdom. We had decided that "our" first book would be Joe Heller's play *We Bombed in New Haven*, which we rushed into print in the early fall of 1968. Paul Bacon had created a bomb logo for the book, and in the big ad we ran in the *Times*, we playfully substituted the bomb for the standard Borzoi. The morning the ad ran, a shaken Nina came into my office to show me a furious memo she had just received from Alfred, blasting her for daring to deface the Knopf name, history, aesthetic, that he had spent a lifetime establishing. No one—not even Leon Shimkin (who actually treated her with atypical delicacy)—had ever addressed her that way. I was beyond incensed, not only outraged for Nina but because I took this as interference with our autonomy and was itching to storm into Alfred's office and tell him to fuck off. No, Nina said; she wanted to deal with this her own way.

Her way was to dispatch a return memo to Alfred saying, in essence: "Dear Alfred, I'm returning the note you just sent me, since I'm sure that when you calm down, you'll be embarrassed at having such a rude communication from you left in other hands. This way you can destroy it together with your carbon copy. Best, Nina." Within minutes Alfred was in her doorway, spouting apologies. "Nina, Nina, I'm so sorry—I didn't realize this was rude." Apparently, no one had ever told him that he couldn't behave this way. I began to see him differently—not as a brutal tyrant but as a spoiled baby who flew into tantrums when the nipple was plucked from his mouth. The "incident" ended benignly—Alfred chastened, me curbed, World War III averted. And there would be no further incidents of this kind. Indeed, over the next years Alfred became our number-one fan, sending me little scrawled congratulatory notes torn from his magenta notepad when he felt that something had gone especially well. The bottom line is that he was first and foremost a publisher, and recognized and appreciated good publishing when he saw it. Of course, I was pleased. As the famous phrase (from an early nineteenth-century play) has it, "Praise from Sir Hubert is praise indeed."

On one occasion when I badly needed his help he rose vigorously to the occasion. Willa Cather, probably the writer Alfred was proudest of having captured, had insisted on legal protection in her contracts against her books ever being issued in paperback format. She had died in 1947, when "paperback" meant mass market, but by the close of the 1960s it was crucial for her backlist to appear in what we then called "quality" paperbacks—the form of publishing Jason Epstein had developed at Anchor Books and Knopf had imitated with Vintage. Bookstores could no longer stock most of the literary backlist in hardcover, so the only Cather books widely available were the four that Houghton Mifflin had published before she moved to Alfred. Having been abandoned, Houghton quite sensibly saw no reason to obey her preferences, which meant that although *My Ántonia* and *O Pioneers!* were on sale everywhere, later works like *Death Comes for the Archbishop* were not. Alfred grasped this problem at once when I approached him for help in dealing with it and he appealed so effectively to the lawyers of Cather's now defunct heirs that they quickly granted us the permission we needed, and her eight later books re-entered the mainstream. The Cather people would never have listened to an upstart like me.

My sharpest memory of Alfred is of a moment at a Knopf lunch binge. Once or twice a year we'd have a picnic in the park with everyone proudly bringing in something home-cooked or baked—it was an office of foodies—or in the winter we'd mill around in the reception area, pigging out and gossiping. (Actually, not everyone cooked. Some people had secret weapons; mine was Maria.) On this occasion we had decided to try something different: the famous six-foot-long hero sandwiches from Manganaro's, a popular Italian market and deli, and vast tubs of Baskin-Robbins ice cream. Naturally we had invited the Knopfs, and they seemed pleased to be part of it all. I was in the manic mood that comes over me at moments like these and was behind the reception desk scooping ice cream into cones. People were rushing around on the kind of sugar high that only great junk food can trigger. When I went over to Alfred and Helen to ask what flavor of ice cream they wanted, Alfred looked up at me and said quietly, "I didn't know it could be like this." Helen reached over and touched his hand.

I knew it would take time to develop a solid new list, although a number of our writers from S & S would soon be delivering manuscripts. One thing we could do right away was to disencumber the office of a number of pointless routines that had proliferated through the years. For every new book signed on, for instance, Blanche and Alfred had each demanded a long, insanely detailed form to be filled out and filed—the green form, the pink form. Blanche's forms were still being churned out two years after her death: No one had said to stop. Alfred's were hardly more to the point. A good deal of unnecessary make-work was being ground out daily. We had an "office manageress" who walked around the office hectoring the secretaries: "Type faster, girls. Type faster." There was a weekly meeting at which the elders discussed reprints of the backlist: The cost of manufacturing, say, 750 copies of an academic book on American history from 1938 was announced, the book in question was handed around, the discussion went on until a consensus was achieved. It had to be a consensus because no one was in charge, and since time immemorial, one of the chief activities of the browbeaten Knopfies had been to dodge direct responsibility lest the wrath of the gods descend.

Tony and I went to two of these meetings, at which I tried very hard to be well behaved and almost succeeded. The meetings had to come to an end, but I didn't want simply to decree their demise. Then it occurred to me that since we were now the ones with the responsibility for decisions of this kind, there couldn't be a meeting if we didn't show up. The point was made, the point was taken, and face was saved. After we had been at Knopf for about a month I asked Kathy Hourigan, the young assistant managing editor (today, after close to fifty years, still a dear friend and indispensable colleague), to post a notice announcing a systems-destruction meeting for anyone interested. We had a full house, and a bunch of systems—the green cards, the pink cards, among them—were shut down that day. The secretaries could type more slowly.

It was at one of those soul-battering reprint meetings that I took the full measure of the Knopf dynamic. As we emerged from our internal meeting room, we became aware that there was almost no one in the halls or offices. One brave person had stayed behind to tell us that the building had been evacuated in the wake of an explosion on the roof that had rocketed a steel beam across Madison Avenue, killing a man sitting in a coffee-shop window. Apparently it was felt that our meeting was too sacred to interrupt, even for a matter of life and death.

But while we were grappling with the bizarreries of the old Knopf regime, we were also going about our primary consideration: invigorating the list. No one was more helpful than Lynn Nesbit, who had succeeded Candida as New York's leading young literary agent. And no one was less like Candida than Lynn. Candida was soulful, dramatic, oracular, and sneaky—she would have added "Sicilian." Lynn was—and is—sensible, realistic, and honest; she would add "Midwestern." We've been doing business together for well over forty-five years without a disagreeable moment or even a disagreement, because we see negotiating the same way: as solving a problem rather than fighting a battle. "Here are the things crucial to the writer; here are the things crucial to the publisher. Who gives up *this* in order to achieve *that*?" No ego at work, just the determination to leave both parties satisfied, so that the *real* work—writing, editing, publishing—can proceed smoothly.

And Lynn has another gift: an almost infallible instinct for knowing which editor will work best with what writer. There was very little in common among the many writers she pointed my way except that the relationships always worked—she understood what I would be good at and what I wouldn't, and she wasn't going to waste her time or mine by offering me something inappropriate. So I understood that if she sent me a manuscript or a project it would almost certainly be right for me. I can't remember saying no to any submission from Lynn except once when she called to say, "I'm sending you this manuscript because the author insisted." Paul Revere couldn't have warned me more clearly.

Two completely unknown writers she sent my way early in my Knopf years were Michael Crichton (no connection to Robert Crichton, apart from their great height) and Robert A. Caro. Michael was in his mid-twenties, at Harvard Medical School, and had published several novels under pseudonyms. His new book, *The Andromeda Strain*, would be the first "Michael Crichton," and it would launch an armada of what came to be called techno-thrillers, a genre more or less invented by H. G. Wells in the 1890s, though let's not forget Mary Shelley's *Frankenstein* and Conan Doyle's *The Lost World* (a title Michael would one day appropriate). Unlike his predecessors, however, Michael had a strong background in science. And he had a keen eye, or nose, for cutting-edge areas of science—and, later, sociology—that could be used as material for thrillers while cleverly popularizing the hard stuff for the general public. You got a lesson while you were being scared.

What Michael wasn't was a very good writer. *The Andromeda Strain* was a terrific concept, but it was a mess—sloppily plotted, underwritten, and worst of all, with no characterization whatsoever. His scientists were beyond generic—they lacked all human specificity; the only thing that distinguished some of them from the others was that some died and some didn't. I realized right away that with his quick mind, swift embrace of editorial input, and extraordinary work habits he could patch the plot, sharpen the suspense, clarify the science—in fact, do everything necessary except create convincing human beings. (He never did manage to; eventually I concluded that he couldn't write about people because they just didn't interest him.) It occurred to me that instead of trying to help him strengthen the human element, we could make a virtue of necessity by stripping it away entirely; by turning *The Andromeda Strain* from a documentary novel into a fictionalized documentary. Michael was all for it—I think he felt relieved.

The editorial process went on through draft after draft—but at lightning speed. I'd read the newest text overnight, call Michael with suggestions, and within forty-eight hours I'd have a new version. It was editorial Ping-Pong. At times I sensed that his patience was wearing thin, and certainly mine was. But so what? We both had the same goal and we both had endless energy. Since I have as little background in science and technology as I do in religion, I never questioned where Michael was leading us in those areas, which must be why the thing I was proudest of in my editing of *The Andromeda Strain* was my single contribution to the actual workings of the plot. Michael would years later recall it this way in *The Paris Review*: at the climax of the action, he said, "I had it so that one of the characters was supposed to turn on a nuclear device, and there was suspense about whether or not that would happen. Bob said, No, no, the switch has to turn *itself* on automatically, and the character has to turn it *off.* He was absolutely right." It proves that even when you're out of your depth you can get lucky.

Andromeda was a big bestseller, helped yet again by an ingenious and original Paul Bacon jacket design as well as by its faux-documentary you-are-there excitement. The movie, directed by Robert Wise, was equally successful, and Michael was on his way to becoming one of the very top genre novelists of his era. We worked together productively on half a dozen more novels, including the original and entertaining *The Great Train Robbery*, and several interesting nonfiction books before I left Knopf for *The New Yorker*, my last go-round with him being the first draft of *Jurassic Park*. He had not grown more sophisticated as a writer over these years—both *Sphere* and *Congo* were essentially YA (young adult) novels, and this early version of *Jurassic Park* was even more juvenile in tone. I told him what I felt, and we signed off on each other, he to be edited by someone else at Knopf. It was a relief: I was increasingly uneasy editing books I didn't think were very good, and although our personal interactions remained cordial, I found him—all six feet, nine inches of him—very uncomfortable within his skin and particularly ill at ease with me as a somewhat older man who was a kind of authority figure.

One thing I began to understand more fully from working with Michael was how genre works, and how a given writer can *become* a genre. Detective novels are a genre, but so is Agatha Christie on her own. Spy novels are a genre, but so is John le Carré. And something I've always found heartening is that the reading public usually gets things right. Yes, there are inferior genre writers who become highly popular, but on the whole the most popular ones are the ones who are the best at what they do. I tested this notion a few years ago in a field I had no experience of—the romance novel. Browsing through Barnes & Noble's vast array of romance literature, I picked three writers at the absolute top of the field—Nora Roberts, Jude Deveraux, and Sandra Brown—and took home three novels by each. What a ride! But worth it to me, because it turned out that Roberts, by far the biggest seller of them all, was by far the best writer of them all. Nor does she write down to her public. She also had, at least in these books, the most healthy and appealing message: Yes, Ms. Reader, you *can* have it all—a productive professional life (and a sexual one) of your own *and* Mr. Right. No either/or. (What an ocean of difference from the ubiquitous Harlequin Romance novels, which for a while we distributed at Simon and Schuster, and about which Nina once said, "They're all stories about Monte Carlo and Bombay by Canadian ladies who never got as far as Toronto.") In the long run, the public knows: Stephen King, John Grisham, Danielle Steel do what they do better than anyone else does.

Michael, for all his weaknesses as a writer, was unquestionably the best of his techno breed, and easily deserved his tremendous success. After *Jurassic Park* he went on and on writing hit novels, including the highly disagreeable *Rising Sun* (anti-Japanese) and *Disclosure* (anti-feminist), neither of which I could imagine editing. It was lucky for both of us that when I left Knopf, the cup passed from me in a seemly way.

My life with Bob Caro has been a very different story—and a very long one. It was in 1971 that I first saw the manuscript of *The Power Broker*, and as I write today, in 2016, Bob is working on (and I'm waiting for) the manuscript of volume five of his life of Lyndon Johnson. No doubt it will be a long wait, because we published volume four only four years ago.

Our life together has been a blessed one—except when it's been thorny. On a personal level we get along very well, although to use the word "personal" in relation to Bob is a stretch: He's private to an extraordinary degree. I used to joke that he would flinch at a remark as invasive as "How are you feeling?" I suppose I should say instead that there's a strong bond between us that over the decades has grown from professional respect to trust and fondness. Like Lynn he's utterly upstanding.

Like Michael he's a compulsive worker. Like me he's an obsessive perfectionist. Not always, however, have our ideas of perfection been totally in sync.

I was surprised when Lynn suggested *The Power Broker* to me. I had brought the editor of the *Herald Tribune*'s Book Week, Richard Kluger, to S & S to commission nonfiction books, something I felt I was never going to be good at and which was becoming an important aspect of publishing. Among the books he proposed was a biography of Robert Moses, New York City's "master builder," by a young *Newsday* reporter. Although I was a lifelong New Yorker, my interest in Moses was nonexistent, and I couldn't imagine a readership for such a book. But why hire someone to do a job and then not let him do it? Kluger acquired the book for a very modest advance, and when he left S & S a few years later to take a better job at Atheneum, the Caro contract went with him. And then when he left Atheneum to become a writer, Lynn took charge and brought it to me at Knopf—all million-plus words of it. I only had to read a few pages to realize what an amazing book it was and to rush to take it on, but it had to be cut—or shortened, or compressed, or reduced, or whatever euphemism you choose to employ. Apart from everything else, there was no way we could print and bind a physical book large enough to contain the whole thing—the manuscript stacked up almost three feet high in my office. And a multivolume publication wasn't a practical possibility: As I said to Caro, we can get people interested in Robert Moses once, but not twice.

It took an entire year to edit *The Power Broker*, and I'm a fast worker. Cutting isn't just a matter of snipping here and snipping there—you have to grasp a book as a whole in order to judge what there's too much of (and also what there's too little of, though that's never a problem with Caro). Part of the difficulty was that it wasn't only Bob who agonized over having to lose some of the material. I loved it, too. I could have read twice as much, but I couldn't print twice as much. We now more or less agree that we shrank *The Power Broker* by three hundred thousand words, give or take a hundred thousand—not a pleasant experience. We also battled—hour after hour—over language, punctuation, repetition. (Bob is often concerned that readers may not get something the first time; I'm often concerned that they'll be annoyed at being told something more than once.) At times our exchanges grew heated, and one or the other of us would stomp out of my office to cool down. He felt I was being insulting, I felt I was doing my job. But there was nothing personal to our disagreements—we had the same goal, and the same respect for language, even if we couldn't always agree about a semicolon.

What was most extraordinary about his accomplishment was the depth, the detail, of his research. I'd never seen anything like it, and when *The Power Broker* was published, the reaction of his peers among popular historians like David Halberstam, Gay Talese, Theodore H. White, and Robert Massie reflected the same awe. Like them, I was amazed, even if the accumulation of all this research sometimes threatened to sink the ship. I never doubted its accuracy, yet there were times when I just couldn't understand how he had unearthed a given detail. One such anecdote was so particular and yet so obscure that I decided to ask him how he had harvested it. In 1926, Robert Moses's parents were spending a week at the Catskills summer camp for slum children maintained by Madison House, the Jewish settlement house Bella Moses supported (and dominated). That June a New York court found against their son in a complicated and widely publicized trial, and the next morning a young Madison House social worker delivered *The New York Times* to them at the bungalow they customarily stayed in. From *The Power Broker*: "When he handed it to them on the morning after the verdict, and they leafed through it—all the trial stories were on the inside pages now—and learned of the twenty-two-thousand-dollar judgment against their son, they groaned, and Bella Moses said, 'Oh, he never earned a dollar in his life and now we'll have to pay this.'" A good story, but, I asked myself—and then Bob—how could he know what had been said between two people, long dead, on the porch of a cabin well over forty years earlier?

"That's simple," he said. "When I was studying the Bella Moses archive at Madison House, I came upon a list of campers and staff who were there at the camp during that period, and started to try to track them down." In the current New York phone directory he found a number of names that matched, called them all, and one of them turned out to be the name of the young social worker who had brought the *Times* to Mr. and Mrs. Moses on that June 1926 morning, and who had overheard—and remembered—Mrs. Moses's comment. What was most extraordinary to me was that when he was recounting all this it was as if this level of research was to be taken for granted—that this is the way every biographer automatically works. He didn't seem to find it all that remarkable, but I remarked it, and have never again asked him to justify his data to me.

The Power Broker was received with hosannas (except by Robert Moses and those in his camp), won the Pulitzer Prize and the Francis Parkman Prize, and has proved to be a seminal book for those concerned with cities, urban planning, politics, and the nature of power. (Barack Obama, for one, has written of how he was influenced by it in his early Chicago days as a community organizer.) And it made Bob Caro into an esteemed figure. Who could have guessed that it was only the prelude to what he would later achieve?

The big question was whom he would write about next. We had more or less settled on New York's famous Mayor Fiorello La Guardia, who as it happens was a hero in my home when I was growing up—he was practically a patron saint of schoolteachers, and my mother revered him. In *The Paris Review*, Bob remembered the sequence of events this way: "I had seen Robert Moses's life as a way to study how power works in the cities, and I wanted to study the same thing on a national level through the life of Lyndon Johnson, since I thought he understood power better than any other American president. I also wanted to do it in more than one volume, because there were things cut out of *The Power Broker* that I thought should not have been cut... I expected a big fight over this, because back then nobody was doing multi-volume biographies except academics. [He had forgotten Sandburg's Lincoln and Douglas Southall Freeman's Lee.] So I went in to see Bob [me] about it. Before I had said anything, he said to me, Bob, I've been thinking about you and what you ought to do. I know you've been planning to do the La Guardia book, but I think what you should really do is a biography of Lyndon Johnson. And he said, I think you

My grandfather, my mother, my grandmother, and my Aunt Dorothy at home in New York, circa 1910

Little Bobby G with (left to right) my grandfather, my mother, and my father

With tiny baby Roger in the backyard of our house in Cambridge, 1953

Muriel, Roger, and me on the beach, 1958

Martin Provensen's vision of Maria as mother when he heard of her
pregnancy (with Lizzie), 1970

Niccolò Tucci with his daughter (Maria), son-in-law (me), and granddaughter (Lizzie), 1976.
Photograph by Tom Victor

Maria and me at ease (for once), circa 1966

Lizzie and Nicky,
a few years ago

Lizzie and me chatting
as we walk down the
slope from our country
house to her wedding
in the fields, 2000

Maria as Juliet, with Lillian Gish as the Nurse, in *Romeo and Juliet* at the American Shakespeare Festival in Stratford, Connecticut, 1965

Maria with Frank Langella and Gloria Foster, rehearsing Lorca's *Yerma* for the Lincoln Center Repertory Theater, 1966

Maria with Kevin Bacon in the movie
Enormous Changes at the Last Minute, 1983 . . .
with James Earl Jones and Harris Yulin
in Athol Fugard's *A Lesson from Aloes*,
Broadway, 1980 . . . with Debra Messing in
Donald Margulies' *Collected Stories*,
Manhattan Theater Club, 1997

LEFT With Phyllis Levy, circa 1959

BELOW With Tony Schulte, Nina Bourne, and Kay Cattarulla, celebrating something or other at Knopf, mid-1980s

ABOVE Photograph by
Jill Krementz of Alfred
Knopf and me, 1970s: all
rights reserved

RIGHT With Martha Kaplan,
post-shopping, circa 1985

ABOVE Photograph by Jill Krementz of Joseph Heller and me in my Knopf office, 1974: all rights reserved

BELOW With Doris Lessing at my house, 1972. Photograph by Helen Marcus

TOP With Robert Caro, 1974. Photograph by Martha Kaplan

ABOVE With Jessica Mitford in my office at Knopf, 1974

LEFT Mordecai Richler. Photograph by Fay Godwin

ABOVE Photograph by Jill Krementz of Toni Morrison and her son Slade with me at the National Book Awards, 1978: all rights reserved

LEFT With Irene Selznick, 1983. © Helen Marcus

BELOW Photograph by Jill Krementz of Lauren Bacall and me at the Palace Theater in New York, 1979: all rights reserved

With Bill Clinton at his house in Chappaqua, 2004. Photograph by Justin Cooper

With Katharine Graham, 1997

Lincoln Kirstein and George Balanchine in Kirstein's house

TOP With Diane Johnson at Courances, 2010. Photo by Richard Overstreet
MIDDLE Maria with Nora Ephron at my eightieth birthday party, 2011. Photo by Richard Overstreet
BOTTOM Maria with Janet Malcolm, 1989. Photo by Gardner Botsford

Nina Bourne

Deborah Rogers

Lizzie and Michael Young and their twin boys, Jacob and Oliver, 2016

should do it in several volumes. It was really quite startling." I too was sort of startled at having come up with this idea, since I had no real interest in, or knowledge of, Johnson. But it made complete sense—Caro's subject was power, and who more dramatically epitomized it?

The Johnson project was supposed to encompass three volumes, but we got derailed. After the astounding achievement of the first volume, and when he was well into his research for the second, he mentioned to me that the story of the stolen 1948 Senate election could easily extend to a section of a hundred thousand words. I encouraged him to tell it all because I wanted to read it all—always the safest sign for an editor. But *Means of Ascent* would extend to well over two hundred thousand words, and it would be eight years before we published it. It was also the occasion for our bitterest editorial disputes. I felt that Bob was romanticizing Coke Stevenson, Johnson's defeated rival, and he didn't agree. We've never talked about which of us was right. But in the long run, that doesn't matter. A larger story is being told than the story of a stolen election, as is the case with each of the four Johnson volumes to date. *Means of Ascent* anatomizes local politics in revelatory detail and depth—as with all of Caro's books, we end up saying "So *this* is how it works." *The Path to Power* tells the story not only of Johnson's childhood and youth but the saga of hardscrabble Texas during the Depression. The same thing applies even more strongly to *Master of the Senate*: Here is how Johnson operated, yes, but also here is how the Senate really works. And *The Passage of Power* not only thrillingly recounts the Kennedy assassination and the desperate feud between Johnson and the Kennedys but also dramatizes how, in America, power passes—the way our democracy works. Yet even as Caro is exploring these largest of issues, he never strays far from his searing, indicting, yet also moving portrait of Johnson himself. Just like his hundreds of thousands of other readers, I'm beyond impatient to read about Johnson and Vietnam and the drama of his abdication from public life, but what can I do? He and I never discuss content until a manuscript, or part of one, is in my hands.

When we first decided to proceed with Johnson, I wrote to Lady Bird Johnson to urge her to cooperate with Bob. I told her that Caro was a superb biographer—witness the reception of his first book— and, above all, an honest one. I didn't know—*he* didn't know—what his final judgment of her husband would be, but I could vouch for his open-mindedness, and that he was setting out with tremendous admiration for Johnson's accomplishments. That was absolutely true, and Mrs. Johnson was welcoming and cooperative—until it became clear that Caro was investigating things, some of them personal, that she and the Johnson people didn't want investigated. Then the iron gate clanged shut, and he became persona non grata. Can you really blame her?

Caro has written, "In all the hours of working on *The Power Broker* Bob never said one nice thing—never a single complimentary word, either about the book as a whole or about a single portion of the book. That was also true of my second book, *The Path to Power*. But then he got soft. When we finished the last page of the last book we worked on, *Means of Ascent*, he held up the manuscript for a moment and said, slowly, as if he didn't want to say it, Not bad. Those are the only two complimentary words he has ever said to me, to this day." As Ripley famously put it, "Believe it or not." But in case he's still in doubt about what I think of his work, let me say it here: Robert A. Caro is a great biographer, and I've been lucky to be at his side these forty-plus years.

Yet another writer Lynn Nesbit sent to me was Brooke Hayward, just starting out to write about her family in *Haywire*, the moving and painful account of her growing up with her father, Leland Hayward, Hollywood's top agent and a top Broadway producer, and her mother, the wonderful actress Margaret Sullavan, her sister, her brother, and herself. It's a tragic story—Sullavan, a presumed suicide; sister Bridget, a suicide; brother Bill, years later, a suicide. Brooke was the survivor, and she survived to tell the tale. But it was a struggle for her to tell it. She knew what she wanted to say, and she certainly had the talent to say it, but she was almost totally blocked. Friends rallied, Lynn rallied, I rallied, but she was paralyzed. When I realized that part of her problem was a technical one—how to tell the whole family story chronologically—I suggested that she write it in sections, most of them more or less centered on a single member of the family; in other words, tell several stories, not one, that would nevertheless add up to a single story. Somehow that released her. *Haywire* was a Book-of-the-Month selection, was received rapturously by the critics, and spent months on the bestseller list. Over the succeeding years we talked sporadically about her writing another book, about the years of her marriage to Dennis Hopper. It never happened—but it still could.

A few years later, yet again from Lynn, came Barbara Goldsmith's *Little Gloria . . . Happy at Last*, a riveting account of the harrowing childhood of Gloria Vanderbilt, the pawn in a legal circus between her glamorous but hardly maternal mother, Big Gloria, whose sister was the mistress of Edward, Prince of Wales, and her aunt, the powerful, determined Gertrude Vanderbilt Whitney, founder of the Whitney Museum. Barbara was an obsessive researcher, a fanatically hard worker, and a highly capable storyteller. *Publishers Weekly* predicted that *Little Gloria* would be a big bestseller, and it was—as well as another Book-of-the-Month Club selection. And, like *Haywire*, it was made into a much-admired two-part television drama.

And then, in 1982, came *Edie*, an oral history by Jean Stein and George Plimpton of the short, frantic life of Edie Sedgwick, Andy Warhol's protégée and star, daughter of an aristocratic New England family, anorexic, drug abuser, and dead of barbiturate poisoning at twenty-eight. This publication was not a pleasant experience for me. George, not only a good guy but an ultra-zealous worker, was impeccable. Jean, daughter of a movie mogul, was all charm until she couldn't get her way on an issue involving George's credits, and then she played movie-mogul hardball. I, reluctantly, reacted in kind, she was forced to pull back, and although *Edie* was yet another Book-of-the-Month and a considerable bestseller, once the book was on its way to the presses she and I never spoke again.

These three books, all centered on conspicuous and tragic American families, all acquired without my sensing a connection among them, ended up constituting in my mind an unintended triptych. Perhaps they reflected a strong voyeuristic strain in my nature. They certainly represented a strong voyeuristic strain in the reading habits of the moment.

The most unexpected offshoot of these books was that I was

approached by Gloria Vanderbilt herself to publish her memoir of her childhood, *Once Upon a Time*. We didn't know each other, and I was startled when she phoned me out of the blue to ask whether I would read her manuscript and consider working with her. I had heard that she had very much resented *Little Gloria* and so at once mentioned my connection to it. She knew of it already, and it didn't bother her at all—my first indication of how serious a person she was: A lesser woman would have balked. Working with her was completely satisfying, not that her book required a lot of work. The most important thing it had right was the tone, something that, if it's wrong, no editor can fix. The title suggested the fairy-tale nature of the story—the travails of a poor little rich girl (America's most famous poor little rich girl) as she struggled with forces around her that might easily have destroyed a person fundamentally weaker than Gloria. The writing had a tinge of the fairy tale, or perhaps of the poetic, yet the book was palpably accurate and honest.

I came to admire and like Gloria. She, too, had (and I believe still has, forty years later) a powerful work ethic and a determination to do the best job she was capable of. Which meant no defensiveness, no acting out—just serious effort toward a serious goal. I had a slight sense of her existing within a protective bubble, but how not? From the start of her life she had had to find a way to survive bad times lived in the public glare; she was a celebrity from earliest childhood, not unlike Shirley Temple (and born in the same year). But she had found her way through intelligence, strength, and—eventually—healthy life choices and a driving dedication to anything she set out to accomplish, whether it was designing jeans or writing a book. She was also a woman of considerable beauty and allure who didn't try to be seductive, even though there may have been a slight element of narcissism to her nature. Her famous smile may have been frozen, but her mind and spirit were not.

To my surprise, I found myself editing a series of celebrity memoirs—not exactly what I had foreseen for myself when I got into publishing. The most visible of them was Lauren Bacall's *By Myself.* I couldn't resist her—partly because, having met her a few times, I felt I understood her and would be able to work with her. After all, she was a bright Jewish girl (Betty Perske) who was born in the Bronx, grew up in Brooklyn, and went to Julia Richman High School in Manhattan; if she hadn't been a few years older than me we might have dated! (Not that she would have looked at me twice, and I would have been too frightened to look at her even once.) It was adorable, rascally Irving Lazar, the quintessential Hollywood agent of his day, who brought us together, and the two of them had a snappish but affectionate relationship that went back to his palling around with the Bogarts in their heyday. Part of my job was listening to their complaints about each other.

Betty didn't need a collaborator, and in any case would never have put up with one. What she needed was a way to work. After a month or two she told me she just couldn't write at home: too many distractions. So I gave her an office at Knopf, and every day she was in town—*every* day—she turned up and got down to work, writing in longhand on long yellow pads, wandering around the office in her stockinged feet, getting coffee for herself, and chatting with the gang. On red-letter days she'd bring in a box of doughnuts for us, first come, first served. And at the end of every day, little elves out at the front desk would type out what she'd written for me to look over. Although she was notorious in the theater and in Hollywood for being difficult, with us she was relaxed and generous: I came to realize that despite her glamour and fame, she was insecure about her place in the world of acting—a star, yes, but not taken seriously the way Bogart was, or for that matter, her second husband, Jason Robards—so that she still needed the kind of validating support she had from her studio in her salad days. Particularly in regard to how she looked. Can I forget that when I went to Atlanta to conduct a public interview with her for the ABA gala event there—she was the star speaker—my main responsibility wasn't the interview but carrying her electric curlers with me on the train to Texas? (That was during a long period when I wouldn't—couldn't—fly.)

The book came easily—she had an enviable fluency as a writer— and although it needed a good deal of standard editing, it never needed rethinking or restructuring. The crucial thing was there on the page: Betty Bacall. We had only one difficult moment. There was a gorgeous picture of her on the front cover, and on the back I showed her with

Bogart. Absolutely not, she exploded; this was *her* book, not his. That really pushed my buttons. "Listen, Bacall," I said, "people want to know about you and him, and you've written hundreds of pages about him. It's my job to sell your book, he's the major selling point, and he's going on the back cover." "Fine," she said. Like most actors she responded positively to a strong directorial hand. By then we had developed a real . . . friendship? Not exactly, because I don't think she had a talent for intimacy; she was too wary. But she was a good, loyal pal, so I suppose what we had was a real palship, and it lasted for decades.

By Myself was a phenomenal success—a number-one bestseller for weeks and weeks, with hardcover sales of more than three hundred thousand, and even more astonishing, it won a National Book Award. Betty was thrilled, but not surprised. I was thrilled by the extent of the success, too, but somewhat surprised. I hadn't counted on a large Jewish readership that didn't turn out for the usual star memoir. When she died recently, the outpouring of sadness and loving nostalgia revealed what her success had meant to tens of thousands of the Jewish women of her day.

I have a particularly fond memory of her hosting (hostessing?) a gathering of a few close friends of Lazar's soon after his death, in 1993. There had been a big extravaganza in L.A. but nothing public in New York. About a dozen of us—I particularly remember Kitty Hart, Betty Comden, and Adolph Green—turned up at Bacall's apartment in the Dakota for a modest tea in Irving's memory. (Betty wasn't one to overspend.) Everyone told his favorite Lazar story. This was mine:

One day he called me at his usual high pitch. "Kid," he said, "I usually don't send you fiction, but I've got a great first novel that I swear is up to Knopf standards. You know I always give you first crack at anything you want, and nobody else has seen this. It's yours for a quarter of a million!" An expensive literary first novel from Irving was not a comforting thought, but to my surprise when I read it that night I liked it a lot—there was a real voice, and a good deal of craft. It was mild, though. When I called him in the morning I said I thought it was a good book and that I'd be glad to publish it, but that it had almost no commercial possibilities. "The most I could pay you is twenty thousand dollars." There wasn't a moment's pause. "It's a deal!" he shouted. That's why his nickname was Swifty. (Actually, I never called him that—I thought it turned him into a joke. And although in a way he *was* a joke, he was also smart, generous, tenacious, and, despite his charmed career, to my mind sad.)

The year before Bacall's book was published we had brought out another memoir by a famous actress: Liv Ullmann's *Changing*. Like Betty, Liv wrote her own book, but in Norwegian; what I first saw was a translation she had commissioned and overseen. Betty was breezy, anecdotal, opinionated; Liv was serious, reflective, probing. She was also one of those rare actresses—Ingrid Bergman was another—whom both men and women loved, sexy and maternal at the same time. She was *admired*, and her admirers found in *Changing* the woman they believed her to be—and who I believed her to be. They also found in it an unbelligerent but strong feminism as they followed her search for her younger self as an actress, wife, lover, and mother. Meditative, direct, and bighearted, the book was widely praised and highly successful.

Since *Changing* was carefully and affectingly written, editorial work was limited to the cosmetic scrubbing that just about every translation needs. It was through the publishing effort that I came to know and appreciate Liv. Our first meeting was symptomatic. She came, unaccompanied, to my overheated office on a freezing cold day, wrapped in a luxurious fox-fur jacket that she quickly shed. We talked about the book, about the publication schedule, and I could see her start to relax. After a while I suggested I walk her around our offices so she could meet various people whom she'd be involved with, and she stood up and started to put her fur back on. When I asked her why, she blurted out, "Because I'm so fat!" Probably because I was used to this kind of nonsense from my actress wife (another beauty), I automatically said, "Number one, it's boiling in here. Number two, you're not fat. And number three, you're not putting on your jacket." Like Bacall, she was instantly responsive to direction—and reassured about her looks.

More important was her total discipline: no unreasonable demands, no star temperament. We were on a rush schedule and at one point I needed to get a quick approval or rejection of the startlingly severe but elegant jacket design we were proposing. Liv was filming *The Serpent's Egg*—in Berlin, I think. She would be on the set all day, she said, but if the art arrived on time (we were sending it by special courier) she would slip away at eleven in the morning my time and call me with her reaction. Her reaction was totally enthusiastic, as I was fairly certain it would be, but what impressed me was that her call came at eleven—exactly. In this, as in everything else connected to the publication of *Changing* and her second book, *Choices*, her behavior was faultless. It was in her nature: Liv Ullmann is not only a beauty, a talent, and a grand woman, she's a pro.

Professionalism. Again and again I've bored young hopefuls with the unexciting news that though you can't legislate talent into yourself, you can legislate efficiency. It certainly helped my early career that I turned manuscripts around overnight or over a weekend—agents were happy, and authors even happier. I didn't do it in order to score points, though; I just couldn't restrain my curiosity. Besides, why put off reading a manuscript or doing an editorial job? You're going to have to do it sooner or later, and it doesn't take more time to do it right away than after putting it off for whatever neurotic reason. As Lizzie recalled at my eightieth birthday party (the only other one I've suffered in my adult life was for my fortieth), she grew up with the mantra "Do it now. Get it done. Check, check, and check again." I felt the full force of the validity of this when, late in life, I drifted into writing. It made me insane when I would deliver a commissioned piece or part of a book and wait days, sometimes weeks, to hear back from my editor—insane with anxiety and insane with fury. I expected others to do unto me as I did unto others.

Working on books by celebrities was only a small, if highly visible, part of what I was doing. I still thought of myself primarily as a fiction editor. A most important novelist who came to Knopf was John Cheever. He was by then well along in his illustrious career—superb collections of stories and his successful Wapshot novels were behind him. The first book we published was *Bullet Park*, a dark, somewhat obscure parable of life in contemporary America. I thought it was his finest novel to date, and was disappointed when it did only moderately well. Then came *The World of Apples*, a collection. And then *Falconer*, which was rapturously received and to my astonishment rose to number one on the bestseller list and restored his reputation as a major American writer. *Falconer* had sensational elements and was powerfully written, but to me it was less interesting than *Bullet Park*.

It occurred to me that now that his reputation was so high, it was time to gather together the best of his short stories, which by general consent contained his finest writing, and make them available in a giant collection. When I suggested this to John he said he couldn't understand why I would want to do such a thing: The stories had all appeared in previous collections, and no one had bought any of *them*. Well, I for one wanted that book—to read, to own, and to publish. I told him he wouldn't have to do anything: I'd read every story he'd ever written and draw up a table of contents that he could refine as he chose. And maybe he could write a short introduction. So it happened. We had agreed that his pre-war stories were really sketches and should be ignored, and my memory is that he dropped one story from my list and added two. Our superb art director Robert Scudellari (he designed the look of the Library of America) created a remarkable dust jacket—strong silver lettering on a bright persimmon background—and in 1978 *The Stories of John Cheever* was born to ovations, accolades, bouquets, plus months on the bestseller list and a Pulitzer Prize. And financial security for John. Decades later, we can see how its publication confirmed Cheever's place as one of the finest American writers of fiction in the twentieth century.

My other significant engagement with Cheever came after his death, when his family approached me and one or two other publishers about his journals. He had typed them, execrably, and collected them in tiny notebooks, between three and four million words in all—now, of necessity, retyped professionally. I was just in the process of moving from Knopf to *The New Yorker*, but there was no question in my mind: This mass of material was patently uneven, but it was magnificent—a unique, overwhelming achievement. Sonny Mehta, my incoming successor at Knopf, readily agreed, and we paid more money than we should have for the privilege of publishing it. But how to remain Knopf, Cheever's publisher, and let it escape us?

The Journals of John Cheever was the hardest editorial project I ever attempted, partly because of the editorial rules I set myself but also because of the material itself, so much of it bleak and harrowing. What made doing it possible was the support of the Cheever family—their decision, from which they never deviated, to allow me absolute editorial control. Given the pain and, yes, cruelty of some of the material, that was an amazingly brave thing to do.

I had resolved that *The New Yorker*, for so long associated with Cheever, would print large sections of the journals. Because Knopf and *The New Yorker* were at that time co-owned by the Newhouses' company, there were no practical problems in bringing this about, and I was able to edit for the magazine and the book simultaneously. I had decided that the entries would run without internal cuts and as written, except for the kind of manicuring copyediting Cheever always needed (and was grateful for: his talent didn't stretch to punctuation and spelling). The magazine eventually ran nine sections of the journals, in three batches of three excerpts each, spaced about six months apart. Not only did our readers need these breaks but *I* needed them—it was horribly difficult work, and it was disturbing to be so immersed in the hell of Cheever's inner life. Yet working on the journals was also elating, due to the extraordinary quality of the writing and my admiration for his wrenching honesty. My guess is that we printed about 150,000 words in the magazine. (The eventual book was perhaps 20,000 words longer.)

The eminent editor and critic Ted Solotaroff had been one of the several publishers the Cheevers had invited to consider taking on the journals, and when he reviewed our finished book in *The Nation*, he acknowledged that after looking through them for a couple of hours, he had found them "monotonous" and dispiriting. "So," he wrote, "I was very surprised and not a little crestfallen to find myself fascinated by the excerpts of the journals that began appearing in *The New Yorker* last year." And he went on to say, "Now we have a full version of the passages that the editor, Robert Gottlieb, has carved out—about five percent of the total wordage—and my admiration for his editing is even higher since he has assembled this coherent text. It presents Cheever's life in what might be called a final draft: concise, lucid, moving, and brimming with implications. Not since *Look Homeward, Angel* has there been an editorial feat like this." No editor of my generation, however modest, could resist quoting this passage: Seventy years after his death, Maxwell Perkins, Thomas Wolfe's great editor, remains the paragon of paragons.

In contrast to the intimacy I felt with Cheever during this long posthumous process, the lack of intimacy I had with him during our working relationship stands out in almost comical comparison. Cheever was a correct and impersonal presence, at least with me. I can't remember sharing a meal with him, although I recall that Maria and I visited him and his wife, Mary, at least once in their house in Ossining. (Maria's father and Cheever had been friendly colleagues at *The New Yorker*, sharing the same resentments toward the fiction editors that Thurber and Perelman felt toward Mr. Shawn.) As an author he never complained about anything or enthused about anything but was unfailingly polite and cooperative, although late in his life, during the period of his most severe physical and mental collapse, he became uncharacteristically virulent about money. Literally the only sign I ever had from him of his basic satisfaction with Knopf and me came through a weird coincidence. I was working at home one weekend with the radio on and suddenly I heard his voice. It was one of those music programs on which famous people are asked to name their favorite recordings, and this week the famous person was John—I remember one of his choices was a Callas aria from *La Traviata*. The program's host, in between the musical selections, was quizzing him on various subjects, and I heard him ask, "Now that the story collection has been so successful and won the Pulitzer, aren't you being pursued by every publisher in New York?" "Yes," John said, "but my publisher, Knopf, and my editor, Bob Gottlieb, have done an excellent job for me, so why would I change?" I suppose it was too personal a remark for him to have made to me directly.

It was with Cheever's final book—a novella called *Oh What a Paradise It Seems*—that I had an uncharacteristic moment of editorial uncertainty. I thought the book was extraordinarily beautiful, but I felt a hesitation about its conclusion: It just didn't seem fully achieved. I recall asking myself who I thought I was, telling John Cheever to rewrite part of his novel. And then I reminded myself that he had chosen to come to Knopf because he wanted me as his editor, and that suggesting changes to writers was what Knopf was paying me to do, so I pulled myself together. He promptly grasped what I was saying to him, and far from resisting or resenting, he immediately strengthened those final pages. A great relief, and a lesson learned.

At almost the same time we took on Cheever, Knopf began publishing Toni Morrison. She had been an editor at Random House, first in the college division, then in the trade department, where she had built up a significant list of African American writers. Her first novel, *The Bluest Eye*, had been issued by Holt to rapturous reviews (quite rightly), and Bob Bernstein said (quite rightly) that it made no sense for a Random House editor who was so fine a writer to be published elsewhere. Since Random House itself was not a good idea, Knopf was the answer—particularly since, although Toni and I didn't know each other well, we liked and respected each other. That was in 1972, and the next year we published her second novel, *Sula*, the first of her books that I edited. Well over forty years later, as I'm writing this, we've recently published her latest, *God Help the Child*.

We were meant for each other. Although our backgrounds were so vastly unalike, we were exactly the same age and, more to the point, had the same reading behind us. And, most important, we read the same way, so that when I make a suggestion she instantly knows why, whether it's about a sentence or involves a major structural issue: For instance, I thought that one of her later books needed a greatly expanded final third; she saw why and solved the problem swiftly, perfectly, and untemperamentally.

How else was I of use to her? I don't keep track of my editorial interventions, but I do remember asking her to drop the original opening paragraph of *Sula*, which involved reader-unfriendly chickens. And I've had a hand in a number of her titles, the most interesting one to me being the change from *Mercy* to *A Mercy*—a difference that makes much sense if you know the book (which I happen to think is one of her strongest). Our only real disagreements have to do with commas, since she hates them and I love them. I put them in, she takes them out, and we trade. My guess is that she doesn't feel the need for them as strongly as I do because she's *hearing* the text, with the voice in her head supplying the punctuation, whereas I'm *reading* it, without benefit of her beguiling voice.

One intervention that Toni recently reminded me of, when I quizzed her for this book, involved *Beloved*. I had forgotten that her original plan was for it to be the first third of a very long novel about the black experience in America, the second and third sections to take place in much later times. When I read the *Beloved* section I just said to her, "Stop here. This is the novel." (And what a novel!)

Even so, looking back I feel that the two most useful things I did for her had nothing to do with text. After *Sula* I said to her something like, "Toni, *Sula* is perfect—it's contained, it's precise, it's utterly controlled, it's like a sonnet. But you don't have to do that again—you're ready to open up and let yourself go." She knew exactly what I meant, because she was already tugging herself in that direction, but my saying it relieved her doubts about embarking on a daring novel like *Song of Solomon*. And after *Song of Solomon* had its large success, I said to her, "You have to give up your editing job. You have to be a full-time *writer*. That's who you are." By now she was more financially secure, but as she reminded me, she was the single mother of two young boys. I said, "Your agent and I will work out the money side of things. You just write." Again, it was the push she needed in order to do what she already knew she needed to do.

I point to these different kinds of writer-editor interactions to show in how many ways the relationship can be productive when each party to it trusts both the judgment and the goodwill of the other: the writer able to hear with an open mind and lack of egotism what the editor is saying, the editor feeling free to say just about anything with the knowledge that the writer has the flexibility and self-confidence to make use of his advice—or not. Toni, whom many people think of as a diva, is exactly the opposite: First, last, and always she's an artist and a worker.

I was far from the only editor at Knopf working with fiction. Judith Jones, for instance, had been John Updike's editor since he first came to us, long before my day. There was little we could do for John except live up to his expectations in matters of design and production—in fact, he essentially designed his own books as well as wrote his own jacket copy. What a publisher he would have made! Yet he was unassertive about ads and publicity and sales. He was especially unassertive about money, severely limiting the amount he wanted to be paid annually. I was disturbed by the fact that he wouldn't accept advances. When I raised this with him—he had never had an agent, and I was embarrassed that we might be inadvertently taking advantage of him—he explained that he didn't want his children growing up as if the family were rich. (After his second marriage, this changed.)

Apart from pleasant encounters with him as his publisher, I hardly got to know him until I was at *The New Yorker*, from which he had been feeling gradually alienated—I remember him saying to me that he more and more felt that Knopf had become his professional home. At the magazine, where I was very much involved in assigning book reviews, I proposed a few subjects to him: A Library of America edition of Sinclair Lewis was one, and a giant anthology of science fiction another. He was wholly engaged by this kind of assignment, and I had a good time working with him on pieces like these. He was one of the very few writers who dared face directly the Draconian judgments of the magazine's famous chief copy editor, Eleanor Gould. I remember once sitting with him going over the Gould proof, as it was called, and his saying as offhandedly as he could manage, "Oh, let's give Eleanor her parentheses." She had caught him.

Updike was one of the writers Alfred felt proprietary toward—they got along well professionally, but Updike did his best to avoid spending time with him. Another Alfred favorite was John Hersey, who had been with the company forever—through *A Bell for Adano*, *Hiroshima*, and all his other impressive works. Judith watched over him, as well as

Elizabeth Bowen, William Maxwell, and Peter Taylor. And she was the editor of Anne Tyler, already a Knopf author when I arrived (and still one, forty-eight years later). Anne is the least hands-on writer I know, living quietly in Baltimore with her family, almost never giving interviews, and uninterested in being feted by her publisher; in fact, I can remember her turning up at Knopf only once in my almost twenty years there. (I got to know her a little when I printed excerpts from two new novels of hers in *The New Yorker* and worked with her myself to smooth the passage from novel to story. She, like John, was responsive and efficient, and, characteristically, displayed absolutely no ego about her writing. Also like John, she was a total charmer.)

Her books had been selling well, in a modest way, as she quietly built up a dedicated readership. The only contribution I made to her success came with her ninth novel, in 1982. Judith gave me the manuscript, and pointed out that Anne was labeling it "Stories" and had strongly (for her) insisted that it wasn't a novel and shouldn't be called one. I felt it *was* a novel, and suggested that we just shouldn't label it at all—let critics and readers make up their own minds. As it happens, this was *Dinner at the Homesick Restaurant*, which turned out to be her breakthrough book and the first of many bestsellers. It's another example of how non-textual decisions can decisively affect the fate of a book—it would never have done so well labeled "Stories."

Judith, surely the most New Englandy person in New York publishing, was a steady and calm presence in the Knopf mix, unassertive except when pushed to the wall, content in her work and her life. She could charm and cajole Arthur Rubinstein, whose two volumes of exuberant memoirs she guided through the press, and—more central to our financial well-being—she could juggle the formidable egos of her cadre of cookbook writers. Julia Child's ego was too secure, and her sense of humor too robust, to require much coddling, but then there were the amiable James Beard, the taxing Marcella Hazan, the prickly Michael Field, the enchanting Claudia Roden, the equally enchanting Madhur Jaffrey, and the exigent guardians of *The Fannie Farmer Cookbook*, which Judith steered through a complete overhaul. In this area, alas, I could be of no use to her, since I can't do more in the kitchen than boil an egg, and am generally considered food-deaf. Judith was well into her mid-eighties when she retired, by which time she had turned herself into a highly appreciated writer. I hope she's been as fond of me as I've always been of her.

And it was Vicky Wilson (Victoria, if you must) who in 1976 brought us Anne Rice's *Interview with the Vampire*. Vicky was twenty-three when Michael Korda called me from S & S, where she was carrying on to the delight of some, and told me to hire her, so I did. But who could resist her? Bright, sassy, eager, fun—and a handful (she's still a handful)—Vicky has always known her own mind and shared her knowledge with the rest of us, which is what makes her such a good publisher. Instantly she was smitten with Nina, and Nina with her, and her devotion to Nina was total and lifelong. (Recently she dedicated her massive biography of Barbara Stanwyck to her mother, Nina, and me.) More important, she *learned* from Nina, and I like to think from me, too. Whether she adopted me as an uncle or I adopted her as a niece I'm not quite sure, but it's worked out remarkably well for us both—when we're not spatting, we're hugging. Over the forty-plus years she's been at Knopf, she's created her own distinguished list, ranging from Laurie Colwin to Lorrie Moore to William Gass, from important books on film to Sven Birkerts and Martina Navratilova and the champion swimmer Lynne Cox.

We were to share an extraordinary adventure. Vicky was editing the superb book about Marlene Dietrich by her daughter, Maria Riva, and I was so impressed with it that I was considering excerpting it in *The New Yorker*. One day—the day Dietrich died—Vic called and said, in her usual forceful way, "Now don't say no! I want you to come with me and Dietrich's family to Paris and Berlin for the funeral and the burial." I was *about* to say no when it struck me that my Lizzie was in Paris, spending part of her third year in college there. I signed on.

I met the Rivas at the airport. Maria R. was very sympathetic, her husband unwell, her three sons a mixed blessing—the oldest was more or less stage-managing the whole thing. In Paris we stayed at the Plaza Athénée, a far cry from the "atmospheric" Left Bank places I was used to. The service was held in the Madeleine, besieged by paparazzi and conducted by a priest who apparently held the title "*Prêtre des Célébrités*." (Only the French.) Lizzie and her boyfriend were with us, having just enjoyed the most comfortable baths they'd had in months; the Plaza Athénée was worth every franc. At the service we were up front with family and dignitaries—the mayor of Paris, for one. The catafalque went slowly past, adorned by Marlene's *Légion d'honneur.*

The body, with us in tow, proceded to the airport on its way to Berlin, Dietrich having specified that she wanted to be buried in the cemetery, in what had been East Berlin, where her mother was buried. There had been a dispute: The Germans wanted the coffin to be draped with the German flag, Maria Riva wanted the American flag—she and her mother were both American citizens. They compromised on the flag of Berlin. I'd never been to Berlin—a child of World War II, and Jewish, I'd never got past my resistance to everything German (except the music) and had stayed away. The Germans we ran into were on the fence about Dietrich: On the one hand, she was probably the most famous and admired woman in their history; on the other, she had vehemently sided with the Allies against them during the war.

Vicky and I got to the cemetery early, to wait for the family there. It was a glorious hot day. There were grandstands everywhere to accommodate the press and the photographers. Householders across from the cemetery were hanging from their windows, flush-faced and shirtless, staring in. Outside the front gates a small crowd was gathered, carrying a pink banner that read, "Gays and Lesbians of Berlin Say Goodbye to Marlene."

There weren't many people at the graveside: a few German officials, an ancient cousin and her ancient escort, no representatives of the American film industry, and a few German movie stars—Hildegard Knef, Horst Buchholz. As we walked toward the open grave, one actor was quietly saying to another about a TV series he was filming, "Have your agent give them a call—I'm sure they'll find something for you." A TV camera loomed over the gravesite as the coffin was lowered, and Maria knelt, trying to ignore the camera as she said goodbye to her mother, about whom she felt a marked ambivalence. (Imagine being Marlene Dietrich's daughter!) It was a remarkable scene, surreal and distressing and moving, and I was glad Vicky had bullied me into coming.

At the same time Vic was publishing *Vampire*, I was publishing another unique first novel: *Kinflicks*, a bold, dazzling, very funny coming-of-age saga by a bold, dazzling, very funny young woman named Lisa Alther—a novel that is unquestionably the only book ever to boast blurbs from both Doris Lessing and Joan Crawford. Oddly, *Kinflicks* made a large dent on the bestseller list whereas *Vampire* didn't. It's made up for it since, selling close to ten million copies by now—exactly the same publishing history as *Catch-22*. And of course Anne's many later books, under Vicky's guidance, have sold millions more.

And let's never forget Normalsville, that cherished diorama, made up of toy train accessories and tracks, which Vic and I and others created on a Ping-Pong table in an unused back office and which suffered a tragic end when an evil receptionist crept in early one morning and invaded it with toy marines, wreaking havoc and leaving behind plastic pools of blood. *Sic transit.*

Another editor who's been at Knopf forever is Ann Close, who joined us from Harper's in 1970 to strengthen the copyediting department but who then, with a determination that belied her Southern-lady charm (she's a Savannah girl), prevailed on me to make her an editor. And a good thing I did. Among her contributions to the list have been the National Book Award–winning novelist Norman Rush (*Mating*) and the Pulitzer Prize winner Lawrence Wright (*The Looming Tower*). To round out her hat trick of award winners, it's Ann who brought to us our latest Nobelist, the Canadian Alice Munro, with whom she's worked since she acquired Alice's first book published in America, *The Beggar Maid*. That was in 1978.

Ash Green, although primarily a nonfiction editor, discovered George V. Higgins, whose *The Friends of Eddie Coyle* made a big splash, and who went on to write half a dozen more tough, pitch-perfect crime novels set in Boston. Ash also worked with Ross Macdonald, whom we helped graduate from being a much-admired detective novelist to a major bestseller. Or rather the critics, including Eudora Welty in a front-page *Times Book Review* tribute, discovered him, and we caught up. The phenomenon of a popular genre writer being promoted to a literary icon wasn't a new one—it had happened to earlier Knopf detective novelists like Chandler and Hammett. John Leonard in the *Times* put it this way: "Ten years ago, while nobody was looking—or, rather, while everyone was looking in the wrong direction—a writer of detective stories turned into a major American novelist." It's still happening, Elmore Leonard a recent example.

Ash worked with dedication on the books of a number of dissident writers, most of whom reached us through the outstanding work Bob Bernstein was doing with Amnesty International. Among them were Andrei Sakharov, Roy Medvedev, and Jacobo Timerman (although it was I who nervously called William Shawn, whom I didn't know, to tell him about Timerman's powerful account of his torture at the hands of the Argentinian junta, *Prisoner Without a Name, Cell Without a Number*; Shawn acquired it overnight). And it was Ash who fought a long, tortuous war with the late, semi-sadistic (to publishers) but enchanting Spanish agent Carmen Balcells to acquire Gabriel García Márquez. For that alone he deserved the Medal of Honor.

At first Ash had been unsettled by my splashy ways, but he got used to them and I got used to his surface formality. We went on to a decades-long respectful and affectionate relationship, and he remained a central figure at Knopf until his much-lamented death a few years ago.

Another editor with a wide reach was Nancy Nicholas, whose French made her an obvious choice to work on translations—as I've said, a job worse than hell. It was she who handled the three or four books by Milan Kundera that we were fortunate enough to publish, and she was our principal liaison with Marie-Claude de Brunhoff, our justly fabled scout in Paris, who knew everyone and everything about French publishing and about everything else too. Marie-Claude was for me the quintessential Frenchwoman, and we remained close until she died. But Nancy, like most good editors, did a lot of different things. It was she who discovered and nurtured the offbeat William Wharton, whose first novel, *Birdy*, was a critical and popular success (and won a National Book Award). It was she who took over from me for many years and provided the care and feeding of Ray Bradbury—but that was sheer pleasure, since Ray was one of nature's good guys. And it was she who dealt with the demanding but profitable Maida Heatter, who cornered a significant part of the cookbook market with her series on desserts, chocolate, cakes, cookies—you name it, if it's sweet, Maida has written about it and Nancy has edited it.

It was the brilliant Carol Janeway, by common consent smarter than anybody, who became Knopf's Queen of Foreign Rights but also, given her total command of German, was able to bring us the magnificent Thomas Bernhard and the bestselling *Perfume* (Patrick Süskind) and Bernhard Schlink's *The Reader* (which she also translated, for our sister firm Pantheon). I had met Carol when she was a young literary agent in London, soon after she came down from Cambridge. We hit it off, and when she married an American and moved to New York, I hired her to do whatever her talents led her to. Our finest editorial moment together came in 1973 when, in despair over the stilted British translation of Lothar-Günther Buchheim's gripping novel of submarine warfare, *The Boat*, we decided we'd more or less rewrite it. (There was certainly no budget for commissioning a new translation.) This is not the kind of job you can do in the office, and it was summer, and very, very hot. On weekends and holidays Carol would come over to our house and we'd go up to the bedroom (our only air-conditioned room), flop down on Maria's and my big bed, and slog our way through the mess—soul-destroying work, but almost pleasureful when you're doing it with the right collaborator. Every few hours Maria would provide food and drink—at times, more drink than food. We got it done, *The Boat* became a hefty bestseller, and when the excellent German film version, *Das Boot*, came out, it bestsold all over again. But Carol's interests ranged far beyond Germany: She also brought us such disparate writers as the historian Simon Schama and Alec Guinness, whose very successful memoir, *Blessings in Disguise*, she snared for us in the mid-eighties. Carol, who only recently died, all too young, suffered very few people gladly, and I like to believe I was one of them. In all our years of friendship and collegiality, she let me down only once: Because she was such a dazzling speaker, I extracted her promise that she would speak at my memorial service, and I ended up speaking at hers.

Authors from S & S who had come with me to Knopf were producing new books, among them Chaim Potok's powerful *My Name Is Asher Lev* and Joe Heller's *Something Happened*, which I felt then and still feel is Joe's finest novel—indeed, one of the finest novels of its time. Stark, self-lacerating, relentless, it used office life, and the life of an ordinary business executive and family man—a man like Joe, in fact, before he turned into Joseph Heller—as a metaphor for what to me was unquestionably his overriding subject: the power of anxiety. In *Catch-22* the danger was external—"they" were trying to kill him. Now the danger was from inside—he was killing himself through anxiety. And the anxiety proved to be realistic: "Something"—the worst thing—*did* happen. No escape to Sweden in a raft this time. And no comedy to soften the harsh realities of Joe's inner landscape.

I wasn't the only reader who found *Something Happened* a tremendous achievement. Kurt Vonnegut greeted it with unconditional praise on the cover of the *Times Book Review*, and it quickly became a number-one bestseller. It was also quickly forgotten—or, more accurately, ignored; no one who read it could quickly forget it. But it didn't give Joe's readers what they wanted: *Catch-23*. Today, though, I often encounter people who want to talk to me about it and the effect it's had on them. And I was very pleased that in his autobiography, Salman Rushdie calls it "great." Its day will come.

Joe and I worked on it with the same focus and compatibility we had enjoyed on *Catch*—the same restructuring, trimming, rechaptering, recasting sentences. As we were finishing up I said to him, "One last thing. Your man's name is Bill Slocum, but it doesn't sound right to me. I don't think he's a Bill." When Joe asked me what name would sound right, I said, "Bob. He's a Bob." This was one of the very few times I ever saw Joe nonplussed. "He *was* Bob," he said. "I changed him to Bill because I thought you might be upset." I told him it didn't upset me at all. "This guy is nothing like me. We just happen to share a name." So Bill was restored to Bob. This is the closest I've ever come to feeling complete identification with a writer. (A curious postscript—or prescript: When I was eleven or twelve, I hated the blandness of my name. Besides, there were two other Bobs in my small class. I longed for a far more glamorous name: Bill. This was during the period when my ideal grown-up occupation was farmer. I could have been Farmer Bill Gottlieb.)

When Joe was about a third of the way through his next book, *Good as Gold*, Candida showed me the manuscript—and, devious as she sometimes revealed herself to be, she showed it to a couple of other publishers, too. (Joe had quietly let me know that she was doing it.) I didn't think it was up to the standard of his first two books, and told him so, and why. I'd definitely publish it, but not for the money he was hoping for. S & S put up the money—Dick Snyder obviously felt it was a great coup getting Joe back. From the moment Tony, Nina, and I left S & S, he was waging a competitive war with Knopf and Random House, but it was a one-way war: We didn't know we were in it.

Some time after *Good as Gold* was published, to considerable success, Joe almost died from an assault by a rare illness called Guillain-Barré syndrome. When I went to see him in the hospital he laughingly told me of a cuckoo struggle he was having with Snyder over, as I remember it, royalties on the Canadian paperback edition; except he didn't really think it was funny. But it made sense to me: Dick's need to *win* was greater than his need to protect his long-term interests. I remember saying to Joe that I had assumed it would take two books before we were back together again, but it was clearly only going to be one. And so it turned out. A final proof of Joe's cool quality of mind and lack of vanity: The moment I told him I didn't think *Good as Gold* was all that great, he told Candida to grab the highest possible advance for it, since if I was right, and I probably was, it wasn't going to earn out.

Of all the S & S authors who followed us to Knopf, the one I was closest to for the longest time was Doris Lessing. *The Golden Notebook* (1962) had had an immense effect but had sold very few hardcover copies—six thousand, as I recall. But they were the *right* six thousand copies: The book's influence mushroomed and Doris became world-famous, as a writer and as a feminist. (She hated being labeled a feminist, and fought it, futilely, for decades.) Quickly we printed, in two volumes, the first four books of her autobiographical Martha Quest series. (She never stopped denying, equally futilely, that they were autobiographical.) We did collections of her stories. We did novel after novel. I went on working with her for more than twenty years, and loved her until she died.

I first met Doris on one of my early London trips, going to her flat near St. Pancras station and being both startled by her striking beauty and awed by her severe intelligence. She made no attempt to be charming, and I wouldn't have been foolish enough to try to charm her. But somehow over the years we grew closer and closer, eventually sharing our lives as well as our professional obligations to each other; worrying about each other's children—her son, Peter, and my son Nicky had difficulties in common; tracking each other's states of mind; and squabbling, the way you do with family. Indeed, she more than once said to me that we were like an older sister and a younger brother who couldn't live with each other and couldn't live without each other.

People who didn't know Doris assumed that she was in person as severe and uncompromising as her work was. And she *was* those things. But she was also warm, funny, and domestic—when she stayed with us in New York and at our country house, as she did many times, the talk was as much about puddings and plants (she and Maria bonded over clematis) as about our reading. As is true of many autodidacts, she was an obsessive and judicious reader, her house stacked with books everywhere. Like ours. The only thing we could never discuss was her profound devotion to Sufism and its most prominent spokesman, Idries Shah. Not only didn't I know anything about Sufism, I didn't *want* to know anything about it.

One of our running jokes—it ran for decades—was that I claimed she never took any of my editorial advice while she claimed she took all of it. Yes, Doris. In fact, I did get through to her on occasion, but the reality was that she just didn't enjoy rethinking or rewriting. She was driven to write—I remember her saying that she didn't feel she'd been alive on a day she hadn't written—but she didn't really take what she'd already written with great seriousness. When she finished *The Summer Before the Dark* I told her how much I liked it, and that I was sure it would be her most commercially successful book. "How odd," she said, "because it's by no means my *best* book." We were both right.

Perhaps Doris's most striking characteristic was her stubbornness, and the more cuckoo her notions, the more stubbornly she defended them. One that particularly maddened me was her insistence, in the 1970s, that since the world was about to be destroyed in a nuclear catastrophe (see the final Martha Quest novel, *The Four-Gated City*), we should all move into caves dug deep in the Swiss Alps. She went on and on about it so perversely and aggressively that, although I'm in no way a violent person, I actually had fantasies of arriving in London, going to her house, and when she answered the door, putting my hands around her throat and squeezing. So when I got to London I went to her house and rang her bell, but when she opened the door I was so glad to see her that all I could do was hug her.

Possibly her nuttiest notion was her insistance on publishing two novels under a pseudonym. She had her loyal agent, Jonathan Clowes, submit the first "Jane Somers" to both me and Tom Maschler at Cape, who was not only her publisher from the beginning but a close friend. Tom got an unenthusiastic report from one of his sub-editors and rejected the book. When Jonathan sent it over to me (I was in London at the time) I knew at once it was by Doris—but as I told her, it wasn't very hard to see through the pseudonym since only the day before, on a walk around Queen Mary's Rose Garden, she had been expounding the very ideas and attitudes that permeated the manuscript. This was not what she wanted to hear: She preferred to believe that I was brilliant and Tom was an idiot. What was nutty was her reason for concocting this farce. She was determined to prove that a novel by a complete unknown would receive less public attention than a novel by a world-famous writer. Who would have thought it! (I readily published it under her pseudonym, with the predictable results.)

When I attacked her for the umpteenth time about her stubbornness in defending her cranky notions, she challenged me to name other people who thought she was stubborn. "No problem," I said. "Let's just ask Tom. And Peter. And Jenny." (Peter was her son, Jenny was the formidable writer-to-be Jenny Diski, her more or less adopted daughter.) "No need to ask *them*," she said. "They say exactly the same thing you do." How not to love her?

When I left Knopf for *The New Yorker* Doris moved on to another American publisher but went on showing me her new work first. As usual, she would listen intently to what I had to say and then do nothing about it. "So explain something to me, Doris," I said. "Since you never change anything I want you to change, why do you want my opinion? I'm not at all offended, just curious." "But it's simple," she said. "I'm just always hoping for your approval." I was completely dumbstruck. This was Doris Lessing? Well, yes, because Doris Lessing was many things, and almost all of them were original and unpredictable. The world got to see that firsthand when, late in the day, she was awarded the Nobel Prize. The clips on television of her sitting down on her front steps grumpily expressing her irritation at having her life interrupted this way were an amazement to people—except to those who knew her best.

Doris wanted me to come to Stockholm with her, and I made all the complicated arrangements, planning to fly from Paris, where I was at the time. But at the last minute she was in too much back pain to make the trip. I canceled my arrangements despite her urging me to go to the ceremonies with the rest of her nearest and dearest, and went to London instead, more eager to see Doris than Stockholm. The last time I was with her—she was in her nineties—her mind was wandering. It was painful to witness. My only consolation when she died, not long after, was that Peter, whom she had spent her life looking after, had died months earlier without her being aware of it.

Two other writers with whom I worked won the Nobel—Toni, of course, and V. S. Naipaul. When I say "worked," I don't mean editorially, since Vidia didn't welcome editorial suggestion, and fortunately didn't need it. *In a Free State*, *A Bend in the River*, and *Guerrillas* were searing novels, and his nonfiction writing, beginning with *The Loss of El Dorado*, was equally strong. We maintained a polite professional relationship—occasional dinners in London or New York which I found strained: I sensed a streak of narcissism in him, and too much (barely) repressed anger. He was also a snob. But what a superb writer!

Another first-rate writer whom I came to dislike was Roald Dahl. Alfred had spotted his matchlessly macabre stories in *The New Yorker* and invited him to join Knopf, but by the time I arrived on the scene, most of his wildly successful work was being done for the juvenile division, which had published *Charlie and the Chocolate Factory* and *James and the Giant Peach.* His behavior to the staff there was so demanding and rude that no one wanted to work with him, and in any case there was no one there who was elevated enough for him to deign to deal with. Roald was a tremendous charmer, and Maria and I had come to enjoy spending time with him—and even more, his beautiful and tragic wife Patricia Neal. But his behavior at Knopf grew more and more erratic and churlish. Secretaries were treated like servants, tantrums were thrown both in person and in letters, and when Bob Bernstein, as head of Random House, didn't accede to his immoderate and provocative financial demands, we sensed anti-Semitic undertones in his angry response.

I was somehow exempted from his disagreeable behavior, and we had worked congenially on three or four books together, but when he sent me a letter filled with complaint and threatening to leave Knopf unless we kowtowed, I decided that enough was enough and sent him a blistering reply saying that the question wasn't whether he would leave us but whether we would continue to put up with him. And that was that. It was a very foolish act from a profit-and-loss point of view, but a very gratifying one, particularly since it made me a hero with all my colleagues who had been his victims. Along the way I had steered him to Tom Maschler at Jonathan Cape, a more than adequate thank-you to Tom for steering John Lennon and Salman Rushdie to me—I suspect he ended up as Cape's most profitable author. From the very start of his tremendous career Tom had a golden touch—for both recognizing talent and promoting it. (I could never decide whether I was flattered or irritated when in England I was occasionally identified as the American Tom Maschler.)

Tom had grown up as a refugee boy in England, and was very much a self-made man—a brilliant publisher and a natural entrepreneur; a swashbuckler. We spent a lot of rewarding time together over the years, both personally and professionally, and eventually I was able to do him the service of convincing Si Newhouse to buy Cape, in the process making Tom a rich man.

Another famous English writer I worked with, Anthony Burgess, was never disagreeable—in fact, he was consistently charming—but he was somewhere on the idiosyncratic/outlandish spectrum. He came to Knopf through his then agent, my friend Deborah Rogers, who told me that when his first wife died (of alcoholism) he felt that as a gentleman he owed it to Deborah to propose to her. She was no more interested in this marriage than he was and they got along very well in their professional relationship until his second wife, Liana, an Italian virago who had been his Italian translator, hooked him. She hated everyone he had been involved with before she came along, including his agent (Deb) and American publisher (me).

Even so, the Burgesses, who were living in Malta for tax reasons, invited themselves to stay with us in New York—along with Liana's six-year-old son, Andrea (who turned out to be Burgess's son too). It was in the middle of a heat wave, Maria was pregnant, and we also had staying with us an Italian friend of Maria's, a famous model, Benedetta Barzini—daughter of Luigi Barzini, author of *The Italians*—and her film-director husband, a Maoist on a Zen-macrobiotic diet who spoke no English. Oh yes—Benedetta was even more pregnant (with twins) than Maria, was bulimic, and all she wanted to talk about was Italy's version of the La Leche League, devoted to breast-feeding. Liana and Benedetta loathed each other on sight, and were constantly whispering imprecations about each other in Italian to whichever of us they could corner. Burgess was smoking heavy cigars nonstop, making both pregnant women queasy, and usually playing the piano very loudly. (It was from him I learned that wonderful song "A Nightingale Sang in Berkeley Square.")

One day after almost three weeks, Liana took Maria aside and whispered to her dolefully that we might have to throw out the mattress she and Burgess had been sleeping on—"Everybody in Malta has them!" "Has what?" "Bed lice!" Our dog (Sweeney) was constantly humping little Andrea while Burgess muttered, "Ho ho! Dogerasty, dogerasty!" And the heat had become unbearable—we were un-air-conditioned. *Basta*, as they say in Italy. We played the classic farce card, one day just decamping, leaving a note behind and going to stay with Maria's friend the actor Brian Bedford in the country. For all I know, the Benedettas and the Burgesses didn't notice we had left, but when we got home they had all vanished. Burgess later wrote that he and Liana and Andrea had stayed with us "a day or two."

There had never been real editorial interaction between Burgess and me—it wasn't needed—and after half a dozen or so books, Liana pried him away from Knopf. This is what he (or she) wrote about me in his amusing memoir *You've Had Your Time*: "Gottlieb was the cleverest kind of New York Jew. He had sailed through Harvard and Cambridge, never sufficiently stretched by his tutors, had actually read the entire New York edition of Henry James that rested on his drawing-room shelves, and was an acute spotter of literary worth that was also profitable." It took Anthony Burgess to get me into Harvard!

One of the more unpleasant moments I've had with a writer (from my point of view) was with Salman Rushdie. Prompted by Maschler, I had read the manuscript of *Midnight's Children* in London, been as impressed with it as just about everybody else has been ever since, and acquired it for us. I remember describing it at our monthly editorial meeting and remarking that I was aware that books about India were commercially hopeless but that this book was so extraordinary that we couldn't be Knopf and not publish it. Salman came to New York and was nice, agreeable, friendly. (I remember taking him to see Balanchine's *Jewels* at New York City Ballet, and his pleasure in it.)

Two years after publishing *Midnight's Children*, which won Britain's Booker Prize, we published *Shame*, another superb novel. But something had changed: Salman. From the moment he won the Booker he seemed more demanding, less cordial. His old associates were dismayed. I left Knopf, he left Knopf. We had pleasant dealings with each other when I published an essay of his on *The Wizard of Oz* in *The New Yorker*, but then no contact until, in 1993, we both were present at the premiere of the opera *Baa Baa Black Sheep*, by Michael Berkeley, at the Cheltenham Music Festival. I was there because Michael was the husband of my beloved Deborah Rogers, and naturally a friend of mine as well.

Salman had behaved atrociously to Deborah (among many others), but she had rallied to him when he first came under the threat of the fatwa, and they had resumed some kind of relaxed relationship—again and again she and Michael provided refuge for him in their secluded house just across the Welsh border. When he and I ran into each other at Cheltenham, he almost immediately began to complain of the police and the restrictions they continuously placed on his movements—for years they had been protecting him, at Britain's expense. Embarrassed, I tried to change the subject by commiserating with him over the fact that if he had only known in advance what was going to happen, he could have dropped or changed a few lines in *The Satanic Verses*, saving the lives of the people who were assassinated because of their professional involvement with it. In a fury he turned on me, sputtering, "Why would I have done that? It's not my fault that they were killed!"

In his strange but compelling autobiography, *Joseph Anton*—narrated in the third person—he relates this incident almost accurately, except for setting it in the trendy Groucho Club in London, at a birthday party for two of his close friends (and mine), the prominent publishers Liz Calder and Carmen Callil. Why would his memory fail him in this regard? Not that it matters, except that it calls into question the accuracy of other things, of more consequence, that he reports. I'm glad, though, that he goes out of his way to salute the work we did together, and the pleasure we had doing it, on the *Wizard of Oz* piece; on that score, our memories coincide.

One of Salman's steadfast friends, Antonia Fraser, has been a good friend of mine as well, and for forty years. I had thought her *Mary Queen of Scots* a terrific book, although it leaned toward hagiography, whereas I've always felt that Mary was a foolish troublemaker. Even so, I doggedly tracked Antonia down, announced that I was going to publish her, and we went on to do six major books together—from *Cromwell* to *The Six Wives of Henry VIII*, the idea for which popped into my head when one day Antonia came to see me at *The New Yorker*, bemoaning the fact that she didn't know what to write about next.

She went on to other projects and publishers, but our friendship was based on more than our shared professional life and has never faltered. A great deal of it has had to do with our almost unnatural passion for reading just about everything—writers as diverse as John Cheever and Georgette Heyer, Queen of the Regency Romance. And there was a growing affection over the decades. When Antonia married Harold Pinter, I was concerned for our friendship, given his almost rabid allergy to America. But his behavior to me and Maria was always impeccable (politics were never discussed), and the last time I was with him and Antonia—a quiet dinner in a quiet London restaurant—the barriers came down with the help of a good deal of wine, and there was something approaching intimacy. His health was dreadful and soon afterward he died, leaving me sad not only for Antonia but for the loss of a new friendship, and grateful for having found it just in time.

There is no more industrious and rigorous worker than Antonia— her (our) great luck is that her brains are the equal of her beauty. Oddly, I became a kind of family publisher, working late in her life with Elizabeth Longford, Antonia's superb biographer mother (her *Wellington*, alas not published by us, is a classic), but I had the pleasure of seeing her through several books. And eventually—and still—working with Antonia's daughter Flora Fraser, yet another paragon of intelligence, industry, and charm. We've got five books under our metaphorical belt, ranging in subject from questionable characters like Emma, Lady Hamilton, and Pauline Bonaparte, to the irreproachable George and Martha Washington. Flora likes to recount that after her *Beloved Emma* was launched, we were discussing what she might tackle next and I came up with the infamous trial of Queen Caroline. "Perfect!" Flora said, and got to work. Years later, when we had become good friends, she confessed that she hadn't had a clue about Queen Caroline (wife of George IV, previously the Prince Regent) or what she was being tried for (adultery). Soon, given her passion for research, she knew everything. Antonia and I liked to joke, after Flora married a Soros, that if either of us was ever down on our luck, we could find shelter in Flora's magnificent home.

As I went on, I grew more and more interested in biographies— reading them, editing them, eventually writing them. What can be more fascinating than peoples' lives? That certainly applied to Antonia's and Flora's subjects, and to Robert Massie's Peter the Great, that towering and engrossing figure. Massie didn't have problems with his prose; what in my opinion he needed was someone to help him clear enough of the forest to let the important trees show through more distinctly. Historians, biographers, even editors have their hobbyhorses, and Bob Massie's was naval warfare. (He went on to write two books on how it was waged during World War I.) Peter's life was a natural fit in this regard: Not only had he worked in a Dutch shipyard when he was in his twenties, but he was tireless in his determination to make Russia a naval power. But a biographer with a special interest can inadvertently skew a book in its direction. I remember sitting for days in a jury room and, while waiting to be impaneled, applying my pencil to galleys of *Peter the Great*, getting it back to land. *Peter* was a tremendous success and won a Pulitzer, which it undoubtedly would have done with all the navies left intact. But then most cutting is done because an editor's reading antennae tell him it will edge a book closer to its Platonic self, not to make it more commercially successful. It's the book that comes first (or should), not strategy or ego.

Another historian who moved to Knopf was the renowned Barbara Tuchman, who had already won *two* Pulitzers—for *The Guns of August* and her book on the World War II general Joseph Stilwell. It was a feather in our cap to add her to our list, and she felt it was, too— noblesse obliged. What a curious person she was: in some ways modest and generous, in others insecure and demanding. Barbara's uncle was Roosevelt's Secretary of the Treasury Henry Morgenthau and her father was the financier Maurice Wertheim: In other words, she had an upperest-crust German-Jewish background. There was a family com- pound in Cos Cob, Connecticut—a scattering of houses through exten- sive woods, but nothing elaborate or showy. It was the Jewish equivalent of old-time New England money. Barbara's husband, Lester, was an affable doctor, ready to pour you a drink, and Barbara was gracious without being graceful, nice with our kids (she had three daughters of her own), simple in her manner, and yet she was . . . grand.

The first book we worked on together was *A Distant Mirror*, a strik- ingly original concept and performance, about the disasters of the fourteenth century—the Black Plague, the Hundred Years' War, the papal schism—as reflected in the life of a great French aristocrat and reflecting the disasters of our own time. When she had finished several chapters she would send them to me and I would tactfully (I hoped) do some modest cosmetic editing, with perhaps an occasional suggestion for trimming or expanding. Then I'd go to her apartment—something I rarely did for a writer—and painfully, tensely, we'd go over all my notes. She did not like being faulted, yet she was too honest not to be convinced by at least some of them. I was really startled (and amused) when, on her acknowledgments page, she thanked me for my "enthusiasm and belief in the book as well as judicious improvements." *A Distant Mirror* was a huge success—the right book at the right moment, a moment (1978) when Americans were increasingly doubting their way and may have been relieved to read about a time when things were so much worse. And Barbara's gift for narrative brought it all vividly to life.

It was this gift that guaranteed her books such a wide readership. Her examples of human foolishness in *The March of Folly*—the self-destructiveness of the Trojan Horse episode; the refusal of the Renaissance popes to cure the excesses of the Catholic Church, thus leading to the Reformation; the blindness and blunderings of George III and his ministers leading to the American Revolution; and America's disastrous adventure in Vietnam—were provocative, and her dismissive tone toward those who disagreed with her did not go down well. But even her harshest critics from the academic world acknowledged that she told her stories effectively. And her final book, *The First Salute*, again about the American Revolution, received the same grudging admiration.

Unfortunately, we had a severe disagreement and a real rupture in our relationship when she learned that, as Knopf had always done with its books on American history, we had shown that final text to authorities in the period, who in this case suggested that much of her research was outdated. I was hardly aware that we had gone through this exercise, since it was an automatic process for us, but she certainly should have been consulted beforehand, and appropriately it was I who had to explain and attempt to mollify. I can't say I succeeded. Barbara, who had waged a career-long struggle defending herself against accusations that she had no real academic credentials, was humiliated, even though none of this became public, and she lashed out. I was particularly saddened because she was not well and, indeed, died a year after *The First Salute* was published.

Even at the height of our quarrel I remained fond of her porcupinish self, and admiring of her achievement. But her sense of entitlement was sometimes hard to deal with. She was, for instance, the only writer I've ever worked with who berated me for not trying harder to persuade the Nobel Prize people to award her the literature prize—not that I would have known how to go about this, even if I'd wanted to.

Why were famous writers like Tuchman and Fraser and Massie and Cheever ready to come to Knopf? In some cases, perhaps, for me as editor, but I had come to realize that I was not the only one for whom the Knopf name had always held great resonance. Once the house began to show renewed energy, there was no difficulty attracting writers to the home of the Borzoi. The quality of our design and production was a further attraction. Perversely, at first I found this phenomenon unsettling—even a little irritating. Nina and Tony and I had spent so much energy trying to convince the publishing world that Simon and Schuster was a place of distinction—"Please pay attention to *A Legacy*! Please try *Catch-22*!"—that we weren't quite sure how to behave in a situation where everything we published was presumed to carry distinction because we were . . . Knopf. It was particularly unsettling when books of ours that definitely lacked distinction nevertheless received the benefit of what was something of a free pass. We got used to it, however, the way one always gets used to being spoiled.

By the mid-seventies the house was humming. We were seen as having preserved the reputation Alfred and Blanche had earned, while branching out in new directions. The list was almost bizarrely various: from Bruno Bettelheim to *Miss Piggy's Guide to Life*; from my personal list of dance books to the Audubon nature guides (tens of millions sold); from Jill Krementz's charming and highly successful *A Very Young . . .* series, beginning with *A Very Young Dancer* (one hundred thousand copies sold!), to Bruce McCall's *Zany Afternoons*; from Barry Commoner's *The Closing Circle* to B. F. Skinner's *Beyond Freedom and Dignity*; from Bob Dylan to Diana Vreeland.

Although I had a good time guiding Miss Piggy to the bestseller list, she and I never became close. As for Diana Vreeland, I didn't know what to expect. I hadn't met her before I took on her memoir, *D.V.*, and I wasn't a fashion person, as anyone who's ever noticed how I dress will testify. (I remember Ash Green remarking that I could put on a new suit for the first time and in half an hour look as if I'd slept in it.)

One tends to forget that people who are "iconic" aren't iconic to themselves unless they're fools, and Diana was certainly not a fool. She was a riot—a riot of excess, generosity, outrageousness, and formidable powers of invention. Her famous maquillage, her famous apartment with its mirrors and red festoons and blackamoors, her raspy seductive voice might have been scary if they weren't so amusing. She made no secret of the fact that she preferred fantasy to mere data—why tell the truth when the truth is so often dreary? Either improve on it or ignore it. But beneath the fantasy was a core of iron will, under the maquillage was dignity and a profound privacy. Above all—it was the hallmark of her entire life—D.V. was a worker. And like all true workers, she loved work not just for the results but for itself. She knew she was alive when she was at work.

It takes one to know one. And we had a third driven worker on board: George Plimpton again, this time throwing himself into his co-author role not only with respect for the process but with respect (and affection) for his collaborator. He went back and back again to the tapes of his debriefing sessions with Diana, and made more and more new tapes, urged on by my eagerness for more and more stories. Were they true? Had she, in Paris in the twenties, really gone to a Brigitte Helm movie set in darkest Africa only to find herself sitting in the balcony next to Josephine Baker and Josephine's pet of the moment? "Darling," whispered Josephine, "I've brought my cheetah to see the cheetahs!" Do you care if it really happened? I don't.

Bruno Bettelheim, unsurprisingly, had very little in common with Diana Vreeland, although he too had been accused of bending the truth on occasion and he too was a passionate worker. We did half a dozen books together, the most famous of which was his original and provocative take on fairy tales, *The Uses of Enchantment*. Bruno's reputation from his years running Chicago's Orthogenic School was that of an authoritarian, almost brutal leader, but as a writer he was astonishingly modest and unassuming. He knew his English was not what he would have liked it to be and he always employed a freelance editor to brush it up before submitting it to his official editors. Even so, his prose required a great deal of untangling and he was fulsomely grateful for the work we did for him. *The Uses of Enchantment* seemed to me an extraordinary work, but parts of it were hard going, and there were passages that I found over the top and unconvincing. Since I was the beneficiary of a Freudian analysis, I was very sympathetic to Bruno's Freudian take on fairy tales, but at times I was baffled, and at other times I simply couldn't accept his convoluted reasoning.

I typed out a series of remarks and questions and anxiously sent them off to him in Chicago. When he sent in the rewritten text I was taken aback and dismayed to see that in several cases he had simply inserted into it, verbatim, sentences I had written to him. But what did I know? I was just doing what editors do: probing. I certainly had no belief in the validity of my "insights"; I was only trying to steer him toward clarification or rethinking. When I called him almost in a panic to beg him to say what *he* thought rather than what I (vaguely) thought, he was adamant. I felt that he did this out of courtesy—and his respect for those who spent their lives dealing with the written word. Certainly he had an old-world deference toward "literary" people and a touching hope that his writing was up to their standards.

Only very rarely did Maria ask to meet one of my authors, but Bruno was an exception. She had been grateful to find approval in one of his books for continuing to breast-feed Lizzie longer than was fashionable at that moment (only nine months, actually), and she wanted to ask him whether she should be worried that Lizzie woke up so often during the course of the night. (He didn't think she should be worried—but then, he wasn't spending sleepless night after sleepless night.) Bruno accepted my invitation to come to our house for lunch, and when he turned up he was a model of Viennese politeness. Lizzie was happily playing underfoot while we ate, and suddenly he said, "I've been watching your lovely daughter, and it occurs to me that..."

And he broke off. "Yes?" "No, I shouldn't say anything—I don't want to take the chance of offending you." Needless to say, we were desperate to hear whatever he might have to say, and finally prevailed on him to go on. "Well, if you absolutely insist, and forgive me if this is rude, it did occur to me that your daughter is already considerably more secure than either of you." Can there be parents in this world who wouldn't have been thrilled at this verdict? "SECURE—BRUNO BETTELHEIM." Her first review.

Bob Dylan also came to our house once, but under very different circumstances. I had agreed with his lawyer to publish a collection of his lyrics—to be called, oddly enough, *Lyrics*—that was to include his entire output of songs from 1961 to 1982. Almost from the start of his career I had been impressed by him, and when in 1965 I heard "Like a Rolling Stone" over the radio the day it was released as a single, I was bowled over in a way I hadn't been since the first time I heard Elvis's "Heartbreak Hotel" almost ten years earlier—pop music had always been one of the great passions of my life. Most of my dealings with Dylan were either on the phone or through his woman-Friday, Naomi Saltzman, a nice Jewish mother hen who made his everyday activities possible and was great to work with because she was utterly devoted to his interests yet also practical and realistic. One night she had me and *my* woman-Friday, Martha Kaplan, to her apartment for dinner with just her husband and Bob. It was a revelation. This genius rebel and tremendous star was almost childlike—you felt he barely knew how to tie his shoes, let alone write a check. Most touching was when he tried to help with the dishes. How did this naïve behavior square with the snarling, rasping fury of "Like a Rolling Stone"? There was more than one Bob Dylan.

Once the text of *Lyrics* was organized and tweaked to his satisfaction, there was a major bridge to cross: the book's design. It was to include a number of his drawings, and he was very focused on how they, and it, would look, but he couldn't or wouldn't tell me what he had in mind. I asked our hippest art director to come up with something, and sent his elegant design down to Naomi for Bob's approval. His approval didn't come, so I suggested we get together to talk about it, and since I didn't want to expose him to the curiosity of the entire office, we decided he would come over to my house at lunchtime. Which he did, in his usual scruffy guise, actually not so different from my own usual scruffy guise. He had asked for a tuna sandwich, and one was waiting for him. For twenty minutes or so we danced around the subject of his visit, but he was tongue-tied—he couldn't explain what he didn't like about our first stab at a design and he couldn't articulate what direction he thought we should take next. Finally, in desperation, I told him I just had to have a clue, and after more backing and filling he managed to stammer out that maybe we could come up with something a little more . . . "Midwestern"?

With that clue, if that's what it was, I turned to our chief book designer, Betty Anderson, a fragile aging lady from South Carolina who wore white gloves to the office and had lunch every day at the very ladylike Women's Exchange. Betty had heard of Bob Dylan but had never heard any of his music, so I loaned her my complete collection of Dylan LPs and she bravely took herself off to see *Dont Look Back*, the D. A. Pennebaker documentary, which was being revived at some theater near her. She loved the music, she loved the movie, she loved Dylan, and she quickly came up with simple, handsome designs that I messengered downtown to Naomi. Two hours later my private phone rang in my office. A voice I barely recognized said, "Bob? Bob Dylan here. I got the designs. I love them. Don't change a thing. Thank the lady." He was transformed—here was the Bob Dylan who bestrode the world; confident, excited, in charge. I didn't tell him that Betty was Southern, not Midwestern.

As for that woman-Friday, Martha Kaplan, she was the greatest gift I ever received from my old sidekick Phyllis Levy, who in the early seventies was the fiction editor at the *Ladies' Home Journal*. Knowing that I was looking for someone to back up Toinette, she proposed Martha, who was doing preposterous things at the magazine, like being the poetry editor. I liked her on sight, and came to love her. She was a sturdy young woman without the slightest pretention, but her integrity, her decency, were so patent that I would have been insane not to claim her for us, and for me. It took time to realize that beneath her modesty there were at work a canny intelligence and a severely judgmental nature. She was generous in her opinions, but once you had trespassed on her sense of what was and wasn't acceptable behavior, it was over.

Within a few years I was sharing everything with her—the problems, the doubts, the satisfactions—always relying on her common sense and sound judgment. And then we discovered that we had interests—obsessions—in common. Somehow or other we began taking trips together: trips to the Midwest, to New England, to the South, searching out flea markets and junk stores, eating in diners, staying in motels. (Maria was thrilled: She didn't have to go! And, better still, didn't have to feel guilty about not going.) I was in the grip of the most persistent of all my collecting manias: the plastic handbags of the 1950s, which I had stumbled on by accident in a junk store and starting buying without really knowing what they were, charmed by the extravagance of their design and the outrageousness of their materials. Theirs was the era of Cadillac tailfins and Miami Beach's Fontainebleau Hotel. For at least half a dozen years I chased after these exotic objects with the determination of Captain Ahab on the track of his whale, though with less destructive results. After I left Knopf, Vicky Wilson published my book about them.

It wasn't only handbags. I was also collecting Scottie memorabilia (much as I disliked Scotties) and god knows what else—oh yes, macramé owls and sets of patio glasses. (Martha had her own priorities, the most important of which was her deer memorabilia collection, of which I was a proud co-curator.) We would fly to Chicago, say, rent a car, and set out through Indiana, Ohio, West Virginia—usually two weeks of exhausting activity, my only real vacations, and far more to my taste than traipsing through Louvres and Uffizis. Once a day I'd have to be on the phone with the office, making a score of decisions, sometimes standing out in the hot sun talking from a garage-side phone booth for an hour. Martha and I were perfect companions, with plenty to talk about but no need to keep talking. We could drive for hours in contented silence. And we knew each other's needs. I knew when she would implode if she didn't get hold of some orange juice very soon. She knew when, after a sequence of four or five less than delightful motels, I would need a night in a real hotel with a real dining room.

Some years we would meet up with our food-critic authors, Jane and Michael Stern, as when one summer we all tooled into Nebraska City, Nebraska, to check out a fried-chicken restaurant they were planning to write about, and where you sat at long trestle tables with local farmers, with great bowls of tapioca pudding waiting for you to dig into before you went for the chicken. And what about the bowls of chocolate pudding nestled among the greens of the gigantic salad bar in Des Moines' leading steak house?

The major side benefit of these excursions was getting to know parts of America I had never even thought about and which I came to respect and admire. I've never forgotten the time Martha and I were driving along an obscure road in southern Pennsylvania and noticed a group of well-dressed, mannerly, middle-aged men and women picketing a strip mall. Why? We stopped and got out to talk to them. Their placards announced their upset with a small video-rental store that dealt in sex videos. But far from being the rabid born-again bigots I assumed they must be, they were obviously decent Middle Americans confused and mortified by what was suddenly taking place in their world. Yes, sexual liberation was bound to come, and it came none too soon. And yet it had come too fast for people like these—people who, I assume, constituted Nixon's silent majority and who hadn't yet absorbed the changes our culture was undergoing. This tiny moment helped steer me toward a growing awareness of the ugliness of demonizing people you don't agree with.

Maria couldn't have gone off with me into the wilds of Indiana or Nebraska even if she'd wanted to. From the moment Lizzie was born, early in 1971, she couldn't bear to be separated from her; not since Madame de Sévigné has there been a more devoted mother. She could barely leave the room Lizzie was in, let alone the house. It had been an easy birth—I was in the hospital room with her, checking over Cynthia Ozick galleys while helping count Maria's contractions à la Lamaze— and it was over almost before it had begun. Like all fathers (and others, too, I imagine), I found seeing a baby being born an astonishment. One moment there were five people in the room—us, the doctor, and two nurses—and the next moment there were six.

From the minute she was born, Lizzie was cheerful, genial, curious about the world and amused by it. (Her only flaw, as already noted: She preferred being awake at night to sleeping.) For Maria, nursing and obsessing away, it meant a halt in her career, which at that moment she hardly registered. She managed to do a limited run of Molière's *L'École des femmes* on Broadway with Brian Bedford by dashing down the steps of our Forty-eighth Street brownstone, rushing to the theater, rushing out of the theater at the end of the (short) play, and dashing back up the brownstone steps just in time to nurse Lizzie: She never missed a feeding.

Maria's early career had involved a long series of poetic or persecuted ingénues—Cassandra in *The Trojan Women* at the Circle in the Square; at the Shakespeare festival in Stratford, Connecticut, everything from Juliet and Ophelia to Antigone, both Hermione and Perdita in *The Winter's Tale*, Irina in *The Three Sisters*, Elizabeth in *The Crucible*, and (a relief from injured innocence) Regan in *King Lear*, frightening even me with her warped malice. She had been the young girl, Alexandra, in Mike Nichols's famous revival of *The Little Foxes* (their close friendship would last until his death), "The Girl" in the controversial German play *The Deputy*, and had been nominated for a Tony for the role of Maureen Stapleton's daughter in a revival of *The Rose Tattoo* (decades later she would play the mother). For six months she suffered as the battered heroine opposite Yaphet Kotto in *The Great White Hope*. She had seemed to glide from one important production to another.

But when Lizzie was two and she was ready to go back to work in the theater full-time, it proved to be difficult. She had changed—she was no longer a poetic ingénue. And the theater was changing. The heyday of the classics on and off Broadway was over. Luckily, the summers at Stratford were replaced by many contented summers at the Williamstown Theatre Festival, in western Massachusetts, where she could install herself with our children and perform Chekhov, Gorky, and Tennessee Williams. She particularly loved acting Williams (her first role on Broadway was in the original American production of *The Milk Train Doesn't Stop Here Anymore*), and he loved her: "I am not a believer in auras that surround people like colorful halos," he wrote about her to his great friend Maria St. Just, "and still I always seem to think of Maria as bathed in a wonderful, late-afternoon amber—a color that comes from her incredible warmth, humor, and intelligence . . . I don't know what keeps Maria acting, unless it's her undying, selfless love for it. That's rare—a performer who acts simply for the love of and propagation of theatre."

She had become a powerful dramatic artist—shattering, for instance, in *The Heiress*. (Ruth Goetz, who with her husband was the co-author of the play, told Irene Selznick that she was the most moving Catherine she had ever seen.) Later, she would find her finest role as the emotionally disintegrating wife in Athol Fugard's *A Lesson from Aloes*, with James Earl Jones and Harris Yulin. And—a formidable reader and naturally gifted writer—she would translate (and appear in) a group of plays by the great Neapolitan playwright Eduardo De Filippo. Recently she was on Broadway in a long-running revival of Schiller's *Mary Stuart*, whose spectacular star, Janet McTeer, has become the closest friend she's ever had in the theater—even more spectacular as a person than as an actress.

Somehow she managed to juggle her demanding work schedule with the demands she always made on herself as a mother. Many actresses stay out late, sleep in late, take care of themselves. We had help at home—a housekeeper, au pair girls—but Maria wanted to do everything for her children herself, which meant tearing around Manhattan in our station wagon delivering them to schools, playdates, birthday parties, before picking them up and rushing home to cook our dinner in time for her to get to the theater the traditional thirty minutes before curtain time. But she couldn't bear to leave the children to be put to bed by me or her mother or Nina, whoever was on duty that night, and as it grew later and later, Lizzie and I would ritually chant, "It's time to . . . WATCH . . . THAT . . . CLOCK." And as she ran out the door the phone would be ringing: her stage manager, wanting to know where she was. "On her way a quarter of an hour ago. She'll be there any moment."

I knew it wasn't true and he knew it wasn't true, but we also both knew that she'd be there in time. Fortunately she isn't the kind of actor who needs to "prepare" backstage: As I've said about her for fifty years, for Maria if a thing is worth doing, it's worth doing fast. She's had a full and fulfilling work life, yet not what it might have been if she had been as interested in forging a career as she was in acting itself.

Since during my years at Knopf I was working nonstop at home as well as at the office, and also for many years helping run New York City Ballet, neither Maria nor I had time for non-essentials. Luckily they didn't call to us. Our idea of socializing was being with close friends at home. I hated dinners out. Restaurants didn't appeal to me. I didn't go to movies or parties, play sports or watch sports. I literally didn't know how to turn on the TV. But none of this was in the spirit of sacrifice, any more than Maria's devotion to our family was. Work and family life were what we loved, and everything else was more or less a distraction. When on weekends we were at the beach, in Nina's little house on the dunes, I slept and slept, edited and edited. Nina practiced on her recorder and taught Lizzie how to make beds. The dog of the moment barked and barked. And Maria put delectable food on the table when she wasn't flying in a tiny plane into the tiny East Hampton airport from Stratford, Connecticut, having just died as Ophelia or Antigone.

When we started living together I had said, in my tactful way, "Muriel was a terrific cook. I'm used to good food. You have to learn how." My word (naturally) was law, and once I brought home a copy of Julia's *Mastering the Art of French Cooking* for her, Maria plunged into learning. But not Julia's way. Cookbooks inspired her, but basically she improvised her way into becoming the excellent cook she is (when she chooses to be). Tell her that eleven people are coming for dinner next Thursday and she shuts down. Call her at seven to say that you're bringing half a dozen people home for dinner at eight, and there's a royal feast.

In 1978, our son, Nicky, was born. I was already a father twice over—first Roger, then Lizzie—and had no urgent desire for a third child, but it was obvious to me that Maria would never feel complete without a second one. And Lizzie was desperate for a baby sister or brother—to such a degree that I actually asked Bruno Bettelheim for advice. He was sympathetic but firm: "The question, my dear Bob, is not whether your daughter wants you to have another baby but whether *you and your wife* want to have another baby."

Everything about Nicky was difficult from the start: a difficult pregnancy, a difficult birth, a difficult infancy. He didn't want to eat, he didn't sleep, he was an unhappy little person. Even Lizzie, who at seven was in an ecstasy of sisterhood, could see that things weren't really right. After some months Maria noticed that he was having odd tics, almost mini-convulsions, that no one else noticed. I was in London, having dinner at Edna O'Brien's, just the two of us, when Maria called me there to tell me, with extraordinary calm, that she had taken Nick to New York's leading neurologist for babies and had just been given the diagnosis: a rare disease that attacked the brain, a disease that no one understood and that might or might not be relieved by cortisone. The disease would go away, but the potential after-effects ranged from "minor learning disabilities to total vegetable retardation." And, oh yes, there might be attacks of epilepsy. Deborah, with whom I was staying, got me on a plane the next day, and I remember thinking as I crossed the ocean, "Our lives will never be the same."

It was true and it wasn't true. All our time and emotional energy were of necessity focused on the baby, but life went on. It became apparent that he was on the less dire end of the spectrum, but in essence he had shut down: almost no reaction to the world around him. And there were two grand mal seizures, while Maria was alone with him and Lizzie at the beach. (Dilantin put an end to them.) Our loved ones all rallied, but what was there to say or do? One friend said to me, "And how terrible that this should happen to you and Maria of all people!" "No, that's not right," I heard myself saying. "If this had to happen to anyone, at least we have the means to deal with it—access to the best doctors, money for the best treatment, and enough emotional stability not to go under." This was the first intimation I had that, at forty-seven, I might actually have become an adult.

Maria, suffering so deeply, stayed controlled and resolute. As for Lizzie, when Nicky was about nine months old (she was eight by then)

I said to her one day, "You know, darling, I know how hard this has been for you. First of all, you really don't have the baby you wanted so much—he's just not there. And on top of that, until Nicky was born you had Mommy's total attention, and now she's almost completely focused on Nicky and you're left with me." After a moment she said quietly, "Yes, I do miss Mommy some of the time, but I love Nicky and I know he needs her, so it's all right." That's when I knew that I didn't have to worry about the kind of person she would turn out to be.

As the years passed (and pass), Nick has surpassed all expectations. He was three before he learned to talk, and then it was slowly, word by word, as if he were learning a foreign language; today he's among the most verbal people I know. He couldn't really communicate with others—he couldn't answer questions, for instance; you had to give him choices—but he wanted to be in touch with people. So he drew on his extraordinary aptitude for arithmetic, and when a stranger said hello to him, he would answer, "What day were you born?" and when the person gave him the date, he would instantly say, "That was a Thursday," or whatever the correct answer was. (One woman whom he approached in Central Park said sharply to him, "You shouldn't talk to strangers." "Are you a stranger?" he asked.) He couldn't tell you what he'd had for lunch, but if you asked him (as he loved you to do) what seventy-six times eighty-three was, say, he would whip back, "Six thousand three hundred and eight." A lot of his time alone with me was spent calculating square roots. It was a little nerve-wracking, but fortunately he grew out of this kind of savant behavior as he very slowly edged toward normality.

It was almost impossible finding schools for him. As he matured, it became evident that he was much too smart for schools for intellectually challenged kids and much too well adjusted and happy for schools for emotionally damaged ones. He wanted to be "normal," yet once he was a teenager he couldn't keep up socially or emotionally with his peers. The one high school that would accept him was the Scuola d'Italia. (He was bilingual, his talent for languages as remarkable as his talent for math.) What saved him, and us, was his sense of humor, his charm, and the buoyancy of his nature. And also his abilities and sense of responsibility. The jobs he does, he does extremely well, though problems can arise when he fails to make a certain connection and does or says something inappropriate. In other words, he has a relatively light version of Asperger's syndrome—something no one in America had heard of when he was little and which came as a revelation to us when it emerged as a phenomenon. Today, schools and neuropsychologists would instantly identify his symptoms and move to counteract them. Back then, all we heard from educators and psychologists was "We've never seen anyone like him." He's a big guy, overweight, good-looking, who's never smoked, drunk, drugged, or acted out sexually. (He remains steadfastly loyal to his first hero, Mr. Rogers, and with his combination of charm and persistence he's established an ongoing phone relationship with Fred Rogers's remarkable widow.)

Of course, when at first he was so ill, and later so apparently backward, we were in the grip of pain and anxiety. Maria had no problem in expressing her feelings—to me, to her friends—but I specialize in holding my feelings in: The more distressed I am, the less I show it. This, however, was not a time to shut myself down. Once, I allowed myself to cry in front of Maria—I felt it was important to let her know how deeply upset I was. And then one day in the office, at lunchtime, I shut my office door—something I never did—and called someone who was as close to a soul mate as I had at that time: my extraordinary friend Irene Mayer Selznick. For an hour I cried on the phone while Irene listened. And then we hung up, I opened my door, and I was okay.

Irene. She came to me via Walter and Jean Kerr, who worshipped her. The daughter of Louis B. Mayer (MGM), the ex-wife of David O. Selznick (*Gone with the Wind*), she was quintessential Hollywood royalty, who, when she divorced David, moved to New York and produced *A Streetcar Named Desire*, becoming Broadway royalty. But I knew almost nothing about her when she first arrived in my office—quiet, contained, yet very highly charged. She had decided, she told me, to write a memoir, although she dreaded being indiscreet and resisted invading her own privacy—the title of the book was to be *A Private View*. It was family matters that impelled her to break the silence: her determination to set the record straight. But could she write? She had brought me about thirty pages that she had dictated to her assistant, and would await my verdict. She was not demanding, not grand in any way, but she was the only person in all my years whom I escorted downstairs and into a cab. This must have been in 1975, when she was sixty-eight years old.

We made an appointment for me to come and discuss her pages the next afternoon at her sprawling apartment at the Pierre hotel (windows facing all four directions), where she had lived for decades. I arrived for a drink at about six. We were still talking—and talking and talking—at midnight, not even taking time out for a meal. The business of the book was quickly settled: What she was doing was dazzling, the tone unique and riveting, her words revealing a remarkable honesty and degree of unsparing self-knowledge. At once I said I would publish it. But what kept us talking for six hours—and then for fifteen years, until the day of her death—was an affinity so pronounced that it almost made me a believer in the "separated at birth" syndrome. The fact that her birth had taken place twenty-four years before mine was irrelevant. It wasn't only that our ideas and reactions were totally similar but that her gimlet-eyed rigor about life totally resonated with me.

Irene, in her uncompromising way, went into battle mode. She had agreed to write a book, and now she was going to do it, focusing on it with an intensity and single-mindedness that were new in my experience. "I'm going to give a big party for everyone I know. It's going to be a farewell appearance. Then I hunker down and do nothing but the book." And that is what she did. For seven years she worked with her clever and sympathetic assistant Anne Grossman, known as Cookie, who would come in almost every day and scribble down Irene's memories and thoughts, prodding her, encouraging her, and dealing with her turbulent emotional ups and downs. (With Irene, everything was drama—no wonder she was so successful on Broadway.) These scribbles, some no longer than a sentence, would then be filed in folders labeled by subject: Mother, Brando, sister Edie (her bête noire), *Gone with the Wind*. Slowly through the years the folders fattened, and eventually the two women started to stitch their contents into a coherent narrative.

So the book was writen by accretion, but the results were startlingly penetrating and oddly fluent. Then the process faltered, or Irene's confidence did, and I decided I had to intervene. By this time we had each other's complete confidence, something neither of us guarded creatures easily bestowed. I decided to move into her apartment for three days and do myself what stitching remained to be done. We never stopped except to sleep—no going out, no formal meals. I went through the famous folders, startled to find that there might be three versions of the same story told in the exact same language but dated years apart. By the end of the third day we had the book, which went on to acclaim and even a modest commercial success, despite Irene's almost phobic reluctance to appear in public and promote. She was a reformed stutterer, for whom public speaking was torture, and she had always shunned the limelight, although everyone who knew her well—beginning with her father and her ex-husband—depended on her for counsel. She was the power behind a number of thrones.

During these years, and the half dozen that followed, we were in constant touch. At least once a week, usually at midnight, we would be on the phone for an hour or two. Often I would go up to the Pierre for a talkathon—about my family, her family, Hollywood, the past, the present, the future. Her severity of judgment combined with her immense reservoir of sentiment was perpetually seductive to me, and my judgmental nature met hers with glee and mutual respect. We disagreed only about her sons, Jeffrey and Daniel, who were constantly in and out of favor with her. I strongly disapproved of the way she used money to control or influence them, which is the way her father had tried to control Irene and Edie. Once she had said to him (and she loved him deeply), "Dad, I can't afford your money," but she couldn't apply that understanding to her dealings with "the boys," the term she went on using about them when they were in their late forties. I couldn't cure her of that either. Yet she understood the damage Louis B. had done to her life, refusing to let her go to college (where you encountered boys and lost your virginity) and murdering her powerful desire to become a doctor. Among the mementos of her early life that she entrusted to me were her Girl Scout badge and her letter of acceptance from Wellesley, to which she had secretly applied and which she was then forbidden to attend.

She was deeply interested in my family and life. She liked Maria (and Maria her, although like most people she was a little nervous of her), she found Lizzie charming, but Nicky was the child of her heart. She had no grandchildren of her own, and she was invested in this baby. Nick was born in the Southampton hospital, and when he was a week or two old Irene decided to come and inspect him. She hired a car and driver and one weekday she and I were driven to the beach for the inspection. When it was concluded to her satisfaction, she delivered judgment: "He reminds me of my father." I remember thinking that if your week-old infant had qualities in common with Louis B. Mayer, you were in for a bumpy ride. But when through the worst of his illness he demonstrated overwhelming willpower and determination—forcing himself to walk even though he had no connection with the people he was walking toward—we recalled Irene's pronouncement.

Irene was with us every Christmas for many years, and most Thanksgivings. The discussions over presents were obsessive, and she had a formidable appetite. (She was also amazingly strong—she had been an athlete as a girl and her shoulder massages were deadly.) She was also obsessive about her will, another family tradition. She would worry over it, revise it, drive her lawyers crazy over it. Again and again she tried to get me to discuss it with her, but I just wouldn't do it. "I don't want to think about what happens if you die." "Not 'if'—'when.'" After half a dozen years I reluctantly decided that this was something I could do for her if I gave up being over-fastidious, and agreed to take part in her calculations—but only on condition that the only things she could leave to me were the hideous leatherette Barcalounger in her library that I had spent so many hours stretched out on, and the green crocheted afghan that I would fling over myself.

Another thing I was able to do for Irene, after much protest, was join the board of the Louis B. Mayer Foundation. At that time her older son, Jeffrey, was president, but needless to say Irene was the power behind that throne too. I finally said I would do it if the focus of its (modest) philanthropies would include film restoration on the same level as medical research, which had been Mr. Mayer's main interest—what did I know about medical research? The board shrank, and when Jeff suddenly died, our administrator told the two of us who were left—myself and dynamic Carol Farkas, who was the medical expert—that one of us had to take over. Here is how the power struggle played out: "You!" Carol said. And almost twenty years later I'm still running the foundation, in total accord with Carol (and now her daughter, Judi) and my great friend Elliot Cattarulla, whom I brought in to stabilize it and me. And we've done good things, in both the film and medical worlds. I think Irene would be pleased.

Irene also presented me with Katharine Hepburn. The two of them, both born in 1907, had become close friends in their early thirties, palling around in slacks (still considered daring) and trespassing in the swimming pools of people they didn't know, just to be audacious. Louis B. approved of Hepburn—he had been impressed by the business-like way she had come to him to offer MGM the film rights to *The Philadelphia Story* (which she controlled); their paths had never crossed before.

Irene was one of the very few people in on the ultra-secret Hepburn-Tracy relationship. One of the things she liked most about Kate was her insistence on her privacy, and she was drawn to Kate's nonconformist approach to Hollywood and its trappings. In fact, Hepburn didn't like being in California, didn't enjoy the ups and downs of her movie career (top star one day, box-office poison the next), and thought of herself as a New Yorker, grounding her life in the Manhattan townhouse she had bought in the early thirties and her family home in Connecticut. As it happened, her New York house was located in the same Turtle Bay Gardens where our house was, so we were neighbors.

In her intense but controlled way, Irene went on the warpath, essentially forcing Hepburn to meet with me and agree to write a book. She warned me that Kate was avid for control, competitive, demanding, but also a serious worker who would meet her commitments. And she not so much predicted as took for granted that Kate would try to take me over—from her. This seemed utterly preposterous. What would

Katharine Hepburn want with me? It would be some time before I began to understand her need not only for attention but for adoring acolytes.

The book was *The Making of the African Queen* (subtitle: *How I Went to Africa with Bogart, Bacall, and Huston and Almost Lost My Mind*). The work went easily—I would walk through our common garden and in through her back door to go over new pages with her, usually in her bedroom: She liked to receive in bed. Just as the manuscript was more or less complete, the news broke in the *Times* that I was leaving Knopf for *The New Yorker.* That morning, in a fury, she barreled into my office, uninvited and unannounced, to denounce my treachery. I had tricked her into signing a contract when I knew I wouldn't be there to oversee her book and its publication. I was able to calm her down by telling her the exact truth (not that she wanted to hear it): My arrangement to leave Knopf was less than a week old, and nobody knew about it except my family, Martha Kaplan (who was as eager to make the move as I was), and two close friends. And in any case, I would go on working on the book and overseeing its publication, since Knopf and *The New Yorker* were co-owned and I wouldn't be relinquishing my links with the former, I'd just be located in a different office.

She calmed down and life resumed. But as time passed, I sensed that her need to stay in the public eye was growing more and more frantic. She was lending herself to movie and television projects that were unmistakably inferior—and she certainly didn't need the money. Instead of protecting her privacy, she was flaunting her presence: She'd lean out of cab windows and wave at people, or stand outside her door on Forty-ninth Street longer than she needed to, enjoying being recognized. All this maddened Irene, whose privacy was becoming more, not less, important to her. The breaking point came when Kate participated in a TV special about Tracy, and invited Irene and me to attend a screening of it in a Broadway theater. When she began describing how she had knelt by his bed while he was dying, and then packed up her things to leave before Mrs. Tracy arrived (she changed her mind), I thought Irene was going to implode in rage and mortification. The final straw: Hepburn led onto the stage Tracy's ultra-reserved daughter, whom she really didn't know, as if to sanctify the famous romance. "This is vile," Irene muttered as we made our escape.

From then on she did everything she could to ward Kate off—but Kate wasn't someone capable of letting go. There were countless invitations; she even "dropped in" at the Pierre, but Irene wouldn't let her upstairs. One morning Irene called me at the office—something she almost never did, having been trained by her father "not to bother busy men at work"—and she was seething. "You won't believe what *she* has done now! She has *dared* to invite me to have dinner with Michael Jackson! Is she insane?" To her, Michael Jackson was just another symptom of Kate's vulgar and pathetic desperation to stay up to date and in the limelight. "What did you tell her?" I asked. "I said I was too fragile to climb her stairs." Confrontation was not Irene's style. Saddest was her increasing feeling that she had been deceived all those years ago, that Kate had never been the fine person she had taken her to be; that she had been used. I didn't believe it until, not long before she died, Irene gave me all her letters from Kate, scores and scores of them, mostly addressed to "Sister Irene" and signed "Sister Kate." They were casual, breezy, informative, and, I sensed, dutiful—often Kate would move into Irene's Beverly Hills house while she was making a movie, and was conscientiously reporting back to her hostess in this series of bland bread-and-butter letters. "I don't want the wrong people to get hold of the letters," Irene said, "particularly *her*!" This was one of the reasons she made me her literary executor.

The final drama between these two fierce women had to do with a Bessarabian rug—a long, woven runner that ran down a long hallway in Irene's apartment. Kate wanted it. And many years before, she had made Irene promise to leave it to her in her will. Now Irene balked. "She's not getting the Bessarabian rug!" she announced. "She's not getting anything!" I thought it was comical, but Danny Selznick knew better, calling me to say, "Bob, you have to convince Mother not to do this. It will be a *shonda*! And Jeff and I will be left to deal with it." Once he had explained to me that a "shonda" was a scandal in the family, I took his point and slowly did convince Irene that even though Kate was now beyond the pale, she should honor what had been a long-standing closeness. "All right," she finally agreed, "but she's not getting the rug," and she left Kate an innocuous gilt hand mirror from her dressing table. Honor was saved.

The first time we ever met, me in awe, I had said to Kate, "The other night I saw one of your movies in which your face was more beautiful than anyone's I've ever seen other than Garbo's." "*Alice Adams*," she said, and she was right. But the exchange we had that I remember most vividly was on the phone one morning when a blizzard had piled up snow so high that New York was shut down. Kate's secretary and cook came in every morning, but she was alone in the house at night, and on this morning they were not going to make it in. She was old, and I decided to call her, to see if she needed anything. The phone rang and rang, and I was beginning to worry when she finally answered. "Sorry it took me so long," she said, catching her breath. "I was up on the roof shoveling the snow off. Very important to do. If you don't know how, I can come over and do it for you." What a dame! Or, at least, what a performance. I was fortunate to have been long gone from Knopf when it published her fuller memoir, *Me*, a thorough mess of a book. Yet at least the title was accurate: From first to last she was about Me.

You'd have to look very far to find an elderly woman more unlike Hepburn than the remarkable photojournalist Eve Arnold. She came into our lives in the late 1960s and never departed until severe old age ungenerously robbed her of her amazing vigor and vitality. The first book we did together was *The Unretouched Woman*, which included some of her most famous photo-essays—of her friend Marilyn Monroe, of Harlem fashion shows (in the 1950s), of aristocrats in England and Malcolm X and migrant workers on Long Island. She had more or less picked up photography on her own with a boost from Alexey Brodovitch, then was championed by Henri Cartier-Bresson into becoming one of the first two women photographers to join Magnum.

Eve was tiny, tough, feminine, loving, and wonderful to work with. We saw eye to eye and were hand in hand and cheek by jowl through the half dozen or so books we did together over the years, including *In China*, her astonishing pictorial overview of that country, made possible in that difficult time by the intercession of her old friend Zhou Enlai.

(Another old friend, John Huston, deployed her on the sets of many of his films, including *The Misfits*—trusted not only by him but by Monroe, Gable, and Arthur Miller. But then everybody trusted Eve, from Joan Crawford to Mongolian herdsmen to women in purdah.) She was another author who was loved by our whole family—and often with us for festivities and adventures in town and country, New York and London. Best of all, she was a kind of extra grandmother for Lizzie and Nicky.

A unique nonfiction bestseller, and pure joy to publish, was Robert Townsend's *Up the Organization: How to Stop the Corporation from Stifling People and Strangling Profits*, which we thought had a good chance but had no notion of just how good a chance it was. Townsend, who had been head of Avis—he masterminded their triumphant "We try harder" campaign—was a maverick, and proud to be one. When we all met he decided that we were the right team for his quirky, funny, and provocative ideas on how businesses should be run and, more to the point, how they shouldn't be run.

As I remember it, he wanted no advance or a very modest one; he just required us to match the best boilerplate terms we gave our top writers. He had no agent, and announced that he would sign our contract without reading it or giving it to his lawyers, since if they got involved we'd have finished books long before it was signed. (He practiced what he preached. And so did we. We had sold more than twenty million copies of the Audubon nature guides before we had a signed contract for them with their packager.) Since this was the way I myself operated, a successful marriage was in the cards. Townsend was totally open to editorial tinkering, which was all that was required, and was ready to promote his book heartily. The only problem was the title, which all of us at Knopf hated, starting with me. Again, he was amenable to changing it, but after months of frustrating failure, we couldn't come up with anything anyone liked. *Up the Organization* stayed *Up the Organization*.

A pre-publication excerpt ran in *Harper's* magazine and something happened that I'd never witnessed before and haven't since. (This was back in 1970.) Finished books were not yet in the stores the day the issue of *Harper's* hit the stands, and people started finding their way up to the Knopf offices, demanding to buy the book at our front desk. Talk about straws in the wind! We were number one on the bestseller list for a couple of months and quickly sold three hundred thousand copies. Later, Townsend wrote a successful update, but never something really new. I was disappointed. His ideas on being a parent were as radical as his ideas on business—he had five children, and he was clear-eyed about them. The book I hoped for was to be called *Please Don't Call Me Till You're Forty*, his mantra, but alas it never happened.

So Townsend was a one-off, and not the only one we had fun with in these years. A friend showed me clips of a hilarious illustrated "novel" that was running week by week in the counterculture newspaper *Pacific Sun*. It was called *The Serial*, because it was a serial. Subtitled *A Year in the Life of Marin County*, it went for the jugular about that heartland of New Ageism, birthplace or at least home territory of such phenomena as jogging, organic food, wife-swapping, est, and the Sierra Club. We laid it out in fifty-two outsize spreads and spiral-bound it—it was the closest I ever came to a graphic novel—and it took off, with the help of such diverse enthusiasts as George Will and Lincoln Kirstein. Alas, Cyra McFadden never wrote another serial, but she did write a first-rate memoir, *Rain or Shine*, about growing up on the rodeo circuit.

And then there was a bit of French New Ageism, Frédérick Leboyer's *Birth Without Violence*, with photos, translated by Carol Janeway and me, which persuasively advocated plunging newborns into warm water to help in the transition from the womb to the outside world. (When Nancy Nicholas was in Paris, she went to see Leboyer to bring back more photos. He grew concerned about her nasty cold and offered to give her a warm bath, since "re-creating the birth experience" was a surefire help in healing.) Like *The Serial*, *Birth Without Violence* quickly sold more than a hundred thousand copies.

As for *Miss Piggy's Guide to Life*, it was very funny, and a smash hit. *The New York Times* commented, "A curious fact about *Miss Piggy's Guide to Life* is that it is published by Alfred A. Knopf, a firm for whom literary authors have consistently brought home the bacon." I'm quoted as responding, "Knopf is not always what people think it is."

Another book we published that caused some eyebrow-lifting was *The Hite Report on Male Sexuality*. Shere Hite's report on female sexuality had been a great success and a cause célèbre, and the follow-up came to us through an editor who then got out of town, leaving me to inherit it. To my surprise, I liked Shere—her gumption, intelligence, and dedication. And her striking red hair. (She had posed nude for *Playboy* while studying for her PhD at Columbia.) There was a lot of resistance by scientists to her methodology, but she was far from an amateur sociologist and was scrupulous in her research. To come up with the data for her book, she had distributed many thousands of exhaustive questionnaires, and had then distilled what she learned from the more than seven thousand men who responded. For me, the interest lay in those responses. Reading them raw and undigested—I must have read several hundred of them—was a revelation, not because of the sexual material, which was what you would expect, but because of the emotional life so many of these men were reporting. They had never been able to communicate with their parents, with their siblings, with their wives or friends. They were locked inside themselves, and in pain. (And I thought *I* was emotionally unforthcoming!) This was some of the most distressing reading I've ever done, but it confirmed my view that this Hite Report was worth publishing.

Although we were inclusive enough to embrace Shere Hite, Frédérick Leboyer, *The Serial*, and Miss Piggy, there were perfectly okay books I didn't feel needed to be published by us. NFK, I called them: Not For Knopf. It was a snobbish way of expressing my view that although we could and should publish all kinds of books, including the unexpected, we shouldn't publish books that weren't the best of their kind: the *best* cookbooks, the *best* nature guides, the *best* genre novels. No one needed Knopf to launch second-level work, and our doing so would only lose us the edge that being Knopf gave us. *Interview with the Vampire* was a perfect example of original and distinctive commercial fiction. Another was Tom Tryon's first novel, *The Other*—an outstandingly written and utterly gripping psychological horror story that was greeted with cheers by critics and the public.

Tom's history was hardly that of your average bestselling novelist. He was a Yale graduate and a graduate of Hollywood, his limited acting career there capped by his playing the name role in Otto Preminger's *The Cardinal*. In his early forties he decided to switch to writing, and quickly he produced *The Other* and a series of other chilling, and successful, novels.

We had a sunny relationship from first to last. No one ever worked harder, no one was easier to work with—Tom was determined to be as good a writer as he possibly could be, and he soaked up editorial suggestion. Yes, he was (and looked like) a star—he was certainly the handsomest writer I ever worked with—but he had a firm grip on his potentially self-destructive qualities and they never interfered with his work. An example of his professionalism and modesty: When I proposed that, because Paul Bacon's jacket art for *The Other* was so smashing, we should let it stand alone—without the author's name—Tom, with his college background in art and design, instantly saw the point, and enthusiastically approved. I can't think of another writer, let alone a movie star, who would have agreed to such a thing.

Another area in which I felt we published the best was the spy novel. In the 1970s and '80s I had the fascination of working with England's two most successful spy writers, John le Carré and Len Deighton, part of the pleasure lying in their almost ridiculous dissimilarities.

Len was straightforward, direct, a superb researcher on World War II military subjects (the first book of his I worked on was the widely admired nonfiction *Fighter*), a highly popular cookbook writer in Britain, and a skilled graphic artist. And he was a highly prolific writer of novels, starting with *The Ipcress File*, the film of which cemented Michael Caine's rise to stardom. With Len, between the desire and the act fell no shadow. He wrote fast, he didn't worry, he dealt with problems briskly, and he showed very little temperament, unless someone screwed up.

We spent almost no time together—the work was done by phone or mail, mostly the latter, and mostly cosmetic. The most excited I ever saw him was when we supplied a first-rate copy editor for *Fighter*, after the British edition had already been published. (We always re-copy-edited British editions, which I have to say were at that time unbeliev-ably slapdash.) She found hundreds of errors, both substantive and grammatical, and after his initial shock, he declared her a national treasure and for future nonfiction books took to traveling with his manuscript to where she lived—Iceland, I think, or maybe Ireland—and hiring her to work with him for weeks at a time. In other words, he was both sloppy and a perfectionist, and without vanity where his work was concerned; he certainly didn't obsess over the reception of his books, either by critics or the public. I felt that for him writing was a job he knew he could perform effortlessly, efficiently, and profitably; not that he was indifferent or lazy about it, far from it, but that it repre-sented a sizable but not central place in his inner life. What do I know, though? I liked him, I respected him, but I certainly didn't know him.

As for le Carré, where to begin? At the beginning—how we met. In the sixties, on one of my London trips for S & S, I called on the com-mercial publisher Hodder & Stoughton, I'm not sure why. They set up a meeting with several extra-rights people, among them Jane Eustace, a very pretty, very nice (and very capable) young woman who helped me acquire the rights to R. F. Delderfield's *A Horseman Riding By*, a "saga novel" I had spotted in the window of Hatchard's bookshop.

Jane and I would get together whenever I was in London—she'd go with me to a dinner or to the theater if I needed a date; she'd help me shop for Maria; we gossiped. It was a totally pleasant and placid palship. Time went by, and suddenly Jane disappeared—not a sound out of her, not even a Christmas card. And no one seemed to know where she was. Then in 1970 Maria and I were in London and scheduled to have dinner at the home of a publisher friend. Out of the blue, Jane called me at Deborah's house, where we were staying, to say that she'd be at our dinner party that night. And "Oh," she said, "I should tell you that I'll be with the man I've been living with in Switzerland. David Cornwell, who's John le Carré." I was so pleased to be back in touch with her that I barely registered that news. But when we arrived at our host's, and Jane introduced me to the Master, I instantly realized that this was an audition: I've never in my life been observed so intently. As I said to Maria as we walked home, "This guy's mind is a lot more complicated than mine—than anyone's—so whatever this is about I'm not going to try to out-think him." I adhered to my own good advice through the many years of our relationship.

Jane called the next morning (I had passed inspection) to say that David wanted to change American publishers and would like me to read his new manuscript, which was in a totally new vein—not a thriller or spy story—and which nobody else had seen. I would, however, have to come to their flat and read it there, lest . . . lest what? I was *in* a spy story, but didn't know why. But I was excited by the opportunity, went to their place, and was left alone there to read. This was *The Naïve and Sentimental Lover*, the most unsymptomatic, because the most personal, of all his books, a painfully raw re-imagining of David's long, tormented first marriage. It was certainly not going to become a runaway bestseller like *The Spy Who Came in from the Cold*, *A Small Town in Germany*, and *The Looking Glass War*, but it was interesting, even compelling, and I certainly wanted to publish it.

So began one of the most stimulating author-editor relationships of my work life. On the personal level it was highly agreeable since David was so charming, so funny—a fabulous mimic with a devilish take on people—and so intelligent. He loved food and wine, and he loved striding across the fields in Cornwall where he and Jane mostly lived, avoiding the oppressive (to him) London literary world. I didn't care about food and wine, avoided the outdoors when possible, and had a good time in my London world. But at least we had reading as a mutual passion. I think it's accurate to say we really liked each other, even apart from our professional relationship, although I never stopped feeling I was being appraised, that he was figuring things out that didn't need figuring. It was just his nature to be wary, to be one step ahead of the game, even when there was no game. (A footnote about food and wine: At some point, David had his agent insert into our latest contract that I would take him out to at least one first-rate restaurant when he was in New York; he was tired of our sandwich lunches in my office and the tacky ethnic places I preferred for dinner. I was less amused by this than he was. Years later I discovered that Maxwell Perkins had had exactly the same eating habits I did. At least in that regard I had lived up to his example.)

The Naïve and Sentimental Lover confused the le Carré readership, but it did reasonably well, and then came the superb "Smiley trilogy," beginning with *Tinker, Tailor, Soldier, Spy*, which shot him back up to the top, where he belonged. It had an extremely intricate plot, and we did a lot of work on it—totally gratifying, since David was one of those rare writers who loved going back to his book, rethinking, rewriting; all he needed was a suggestion that made sense to him and he was off and running. I remember saying to him that the character Connie Sachs, the superannuated spymaster who remembered everything, was so extraordinary that I wanted more of her. He couldn't wait to get back to her, and in a week or so I had twenty or thirty terrific new pages—a few too many. No problem. A little trimming and Connie emerged in her full glory.

I loved David's relish for this kind of work. Other writers, as I've said in relation to Doris Lessing, simply can't revisit a finished manuscript—when it's done, it's done. I once asked Len Deighton to rethink a book and he was perfectly willing to try, but what he more or less did was retype it. I remember pointing out to him on another occasion that a minor character who was shot and killed on let's say page 49, emerged in good health at a cocktail party a hundred pages later. "Brilliant!" he exclaimed. "Thanks! I'll redo this!" And he did. Now on page 49 this character was "shot and almost killed."

Jane now oversaw all David's publishing affairs, which were highly complex since every book had to be launched in so many languages. "Launch" is the right word: These occasions, approximately one every three years, were like full-scale invasions. And because the editorial input came from me, his American publisher became the launchpad ... to David's regret, because he was an Englishman and a patriot, however much he deplored certain of England's attitudes and methods.

His life was now settled. He and Jane had homes they loved and a son they loved even more. (He had three sons from his first marriage.) Book after book was received rapturously—the second and third

Smiley, *The Little Drummer Girl, A Perfect Spy* (to me his most interesting and moving book, with its portrait of his con-man father). I found the title somewhere in the text, but to my mind David himself, rather than his hero, Magnus Pym, was the perfect spy.

Some writers stay with one publisher throughout their career: Knopf published all of Updike except his first book of poems, all of Anne Tyler, all of John Hersey, just about all of Anne Rice, just about all of Alice Munro. Other distinguished writers accompanied their editors to Knopf when we hired them. The most talented of these was David Segal, whose passion for literature combined with his impeccable taste had made him a significant figure in publishing, to such a degree that when Harper's was trying to figure out what it was doing—it took decades (and Jane Friedman) to succeed—it offered David the job of editor-in-chief. This was a lunatic idea, since he was neither an administrator nor boss material; his consuming interest was the books and writers he himself worked on. As it always does, the Peter Principle did its deadly work, and he was fired.

I knew David Segal slightly because I edited and was fond of his wife, Lore Segal, and I immediately offered him a job. When he came to us he brought with him an extraordinary list of writers—Cynthia Ozick, John Gardner, William Gass, Gail Godwin, among others—though they weren't the primary reason I wanted him to join us. I simply felt that a man of his quality shouldn't be out of a job, and that just as Knopf should be there to publish certain books others might shy away from, we should be there to give harbor to certain exceptionally talented men and women. (The same thing happened, years later, when Gordon Lish lost his job at *Esquire.*) David, not a particularly comfortable man, fit in well at Knopf, no doubt in part because I trusted his judgment and more or less gave him carte blanche, but also because, as it still is today, Knopf was a congenial place to work.

It was a terrible blow when he died suddenly, only a year or so after he came to us. Although his taste in fiction was more adventurous than mine—another reason I had wanted him at Knopf—I took on a number of his writers at his death, most gratifyingly Ozick and Gardner. With

Gardner I enjoyed a smooth, interesting, productive, and impersonal relationship—he must have done a dozen books with us, beginning with *Grendel* and on through *The Sunlight Dialogues*, *Nickel Mountain*, and *October Light*, as well as other fiction, poetry, stories, his biography of Chaucer, and his controversial *Art of Fiction*. He was receptive to editorial suggestions, but they can't have been of much consequence since I don't remember any of them. To his astonishment (and mine) he became a bestselling author, but that didn't change him or his way of life, so different from mine that it isn't surprising we never became close other than professionally. John seemed to me to have a large, unselfish nature, with a streak of self-destructiveness to it. He was highly likable, but I liked him better than I knew him.

Cynthia, on the other hand, was lovable—her mind fierce, her manner girlish. And her writing was powerful, at times transcendent. It wasn't easy to recognize the writer in the woman, but I cared for both. In the years we worked together, she was living a somewhat hermetic life, devoted to her husband and daughter and, although she lived in nearby Westchester, more or less out of the literary swing. We would see each other perhaps once a year, but our meetings were intense and personal; I think I was helpful to her in dealing with her doubts and hesitations and pushing her to have more confidence in herself, although I sensed that beneath her qualms and protestations, she knew exactly how good a writer she was. Certainly the critical establishment knew.

When I was at *The New Yorker* she wrote several long, brilliant pieces for me—acute criticism and telling memoir—as well as exemplary fiction. I think it's a tribute to us both that my incomprehension of, and lack of interest in, Judaism never gave us a moment's difficulty, at least as far as I'm aware. We certainly never had a difficult moment, though I was slightly taken aback when one day she asked me for a lock of my hair—a first and last such request in my experience. I was too embarrassed to comply. (She now denies this incident!)

I also worked for a while with Gail Godwin, but that didn't pan out. She didn't want to be considered a "literary" writer, and that's the way I foolishly saw her. She moved to a different publisher, who paid her a good deal of money and succeeded in helping her next novel, *The Odd Woman*, become a big seller—a fortunate outcome, if not for me.

There are many reasons writers switch publishers. Money certainly is one of them: When a writer or his agent wants more than the publisher thinks is prudent to pay, or another publisher has flashed bigger bucks. When a writer and his editor don't really understand (or like) each other. When a writer doesn't feel that his publisher really believes in him. When a writer feels that a change of publisher might change his luck. When a writer is having a mid-career crisis and just needs to make changes in his life, which often involves changing spouses as well as publishers. Sometimes it works out well—the change revitalizes the career. Inevitably, when a writer jumps ship, particularly when a friendship has grown up, the abandoned editor feels aggrieved. It's hard to convince a colleague (or oneself) that it's not personal—that a writer's chief concern is, and should be, protecting himself and his books as he thinks fit. If the editor and publisher don't provide that sense of security, they're not doing their job, which is first, last, and always a service job: What we're there for is to serve the writer and the book. That doesn't mean I haven't been stung when an author I valued moved on.

Don DeLillo was one. I had read and admired his first three novels, then published four more, then was cold-shouldered. I liked him but wasn't at ease with him—and sensed that he felt that way about me, too. I disliked his agent, and no doubt she reciprocated. For a few weeks I felt badly used when he decamped, then remembered how many writers had come to me under similar circumstances.

I worked with Denis Johnson on his first three novels—his agent had sent me the manuscript of *Angels* and I bought it the next day. Denis was not only an extraordinary writer but an appealing and decent guy; he wandered off at some point after I left Knopf for *The New Yorker*, which I could hardly resent.

I worked with the very appealing Robert Stone on two exceptionally powerful novels—*A Flag for Sunrise* and *Children of Light*. I thought he was one of our best novelists, and the first book, in particular, was a critical triumph, but we didn't really succeed with it commercially. Was that why he floated away?

I can't say I edited William Gaddis's *J R*, although I remember trying. He was unrelentingly disgruntled, perhaps "touchy" is the better word—but writers *are* touchy. The problem was that although reviewers were mostly in awe, the book didn't sell. (The National Book Award came along too late to help, and in those days wasn't really a spur to book buyers.) I had paid Candida a higher advance than was realistic, there was no way it could earn out, and Gaddis blamed Knopf for lack of publishing commitment and then for not making him financially whole. Although I admired his writing and his intelligence, and was impressed by the large reputation of his earlier novel, *The Recognitions*, both it and *J R* seemed to me more constructs than novels and, feeling that way, I shouldn't have taken him on. On the other hand, I very much liked Evan Connell's *Mr. Bridge*, and Evan, too—a laconic man who seemed to me both intensely moral and naturally elegant. His career was an odd one, my attention wandered, and we drifted apart.

As for Gordon Lish, as I've said, when he lost his prestigious job as fiction editor of *Esquire* I felt that someone of his unique talent should join us—besides, far more than was true with David Segal, Gordon's taste and mine were vastly different and I hoped would prove complementary. An even greater disparity was our approach to editing. He had a profound need to put his imprint on fiction—to steer his writers toward his own aesthetic. It wasn't a matter of ego, although he certainly enjoyed the guru status he had attained; it was zeal.

Over the decades, Gordon proved to be of considerable value to the world of American fiction—as editor, teacher, exemplar; perhaps not as writer. He also, along the way, did damage to some of his writers by distorting their natural bent. As I've tried to drill into countless aspiring editors, the most damaging thing an editor can do to a writer is to try to change a book into something other than what it is, rather than try to make it a better version of what it is already. Yet Gordon was always touchingly eager in his support of his writers, and in his general desire to please.

Gordon was, in fact, a charmer—and it was genuine charm, the charm, say, of a Candide. He also seemed a little nuts, but that was part of his charm. He stayed on at Knopf for many years after I left— testament to the loyalty of the firm and the generosity of Sonny Mehta. But also to Gordon's persuasiveness and to the writers (Amy Hempel, for one) he brought to us.

When after the many years of their highly publicized (too highly publicized) collaboration he and Raymond Carver fell out, I tried to be useful to Ray, for one thing helping put together the collection called *Cathedral*. I found him tremendously sympathetic—I suppose I saw a man whom life had sorely beset, though what did I know about alcoholism, drugs, or for that matter, working-class life in the far west? He seemed to me someone who had come through and found inner equilibrium; that his opacity wasn't excluding but central to him. I understood that all I could do for him was provide him with a responsible and hospitable publishing environment.

And then there was Harold Brodkey—brilliant, maddening, tricky, self-destructive, troublemaking, irresistible; he and Gordon had tormented each other for years. He was a sacred icon at Mr. Shawn's *New Yorker*, perhaps Shawn's favorite writer of fiction after Salinger, and Harold dazzled in the same way Salinger had—and with the same narcissistic obsession with childhood and adolescence. (The *New Yorker* fiction department was far from pleased by this favoritism of Shawn's.) Harold had embarked on what was meant to be, and was heralded (by himself loudest of all) as, a major work to be called *A Party of Animals*.

Lynn Nesbit was his agent, and she had sold the book to Joe Fox at Random House, but as time passed and the book grew longer and longer but not closer and closer, at Harold's insistence the contract was switched to Farrar, Straus and Giroux for more money. It fared no better there, and when I arrogantly decided that I was the one who could wrest a novel from the material, it passed to me—in exchange for yet more money. Harold had by this time married the writer Ellen Schwamm, whose two novels I had edited—the latter, *How He Saved Her*, being an account of how he took over her hitherto conventional life. (Harold, with his diabolical psychic potency and ambiguous sexuality, would not have been every woman's cup of tea.)

A Party of Animals was, with Truman Capote's *Answered Prayers*, one of the two most famous unpublished novels of its time, though by no means was it an unwritten novel. Nothing could stop Harold from turning out hundreds of pages about his childhood and family in Saint Louis, even though the book had started out as an account of a certain style of life in New York. We had long, amiable talks about it, which after several years I realized were going nowhere. Eventually I concluded that he was never going to pull this material together. Much as he wanted to be Proust, he lacked Proust's discipline, to say nothing of his talent. I asked him to give me the thousand or so pages that now existed and told him I was going to try to organize or shape them into a coherent narrative. I also told him I was fully aware he would reject my version. But at least there would *be* a version.

I spent months hard at it, and produced what seemed to me a coherent and compelling text. The talent was his, the readability mine. As I had known would happen, he didn't want this version published; he was full of compliments over the job I'd done, but it wasn't his book. And he was right—it was too conventional, too orderly for him. I was content with his decision: I had done what I could do, and felt relieved of responsibility. Unfortunately, there never would be a satisfactory finished book, although later on chunks and snippets of it appeared here and there. Harold's talent was large, but his ego was colossal, and it did him in—not because he rejected my diligent efforts, but because his inflated view of his genius kept him from exercising that talent fruitfully.

More rewarding to me was Alfred Kazin, whose masterpieces *A Walker in the City* and *On Native Grounds* I had grown up on. He was one of a group of writers and intellectuals Maria had been exposed to as a child—Mary McCarthy, Saul Bellow, Saul Steinberg, Albert Camus, Hannah Arendt—so I had some advance warning of his grumpiness, pugnacity, and appeal. He seemed to me always in contention, but with whom? And for what? The literary and political wars of the thirties and forties were before my time, but they weren't before his, and he was still fighting them. There was no contention between us as writer and editor—perhaps he sensed my admiration for what he had accomplished. I hope I was helpful to him on the two books we did together, *New York Jew* (after all, I was one too) and *An American Procession*, his Olympian reconsideration of our nineteenth-century literature.

The most complicated, interesting, and challenging man I was working with toward the end of my years at Knopf was Elia Kazan. He had been the great theater figure of my youth—director of Tennessee Williams, Arthur Miller, et al.; founder of the Actors Studio and Method acting. And then he became the man who Named Names to HUAC. When Irving Lazar suggested I become his editor after the gigantic success of his novel *The Arrangement*, 1967's bestselling work of fiction, I cautiously agreed. I had admired the naked force of that book, but it was so obviously autobiographical that I wasn't sure he could write any other kind of novel. Also, Irene, who had tangled with him when he directed her production of *A Streetcar Named Desire*, warned me about his duplicity—and his fatal charm.

Although I could recognize the qualities Irene had alerted me to, I found him almost painfully serious and raw. When he decided to write his autobiography I paid Irving far more money for it than it could possibly justify, but I never regretted it: *A Life* is one of the most remarkable memoirs I've ever read, and certainly the most gripping and revealing book I know about the theater and Hollywood. Even more extraordinary are the passion and integrity with which Kazan tries to understand and expiate the dark passages of his life and to chart the harrowing struggle he waged in order to become his true self.

I was leaving for *The New Yorker* as we were getting the manuscript in shape—the editing was intense but cloudless—and from then on Kazan was in the hands of my most valuable and valued secret weapon, Kathy Hourigan, who steered him though later books and even now is working to further his legacy, having recently published a collection of his remarkable letters. For once (and it was only once), Irene had been wrong: The impossible, irascible, untrustworthy Kazan had been the perfect author.

Today the world thinks of him almost entirely as a movie director. His novels aren't read, and no one cares about theater history; film replaced the stage as the essential form of entertainment (just as, in turn, television has replaced film). But I grew up oddly unaffected by the movies: My parents weren't really interested, and apart from the required kid movies—some Disneys (*Fantasia*, because it was cultural) and *The Wizard of Oz* and *National Velvet* and *Lassie Come Home* and Abbott and Costello (I still remember the martyrdom my parents underwent when I dragged them to *Buck Privates*), it wasn't until I was in college that I started taking an interest. And then it was mostly upper-brow: Carl Dreyer's masterpiece *The Passion of Joan of Arc* at MoMA; *Ivan the Terrible* and *Battleship Potemkin* and *Alexander Nevsky*, or Harry Baur double-bills of *Crime and Punishment* and *Les Misérables* at the Thalia; or what we generically termed "foreign film"—post-war Italian neo-realism, Michèle Morgan and Jean Gabin suffering in French, *Les Enfants du paradis*.

Only later did I fall for Hollywood, and particularly the Hollywood of the thirties and forties, first and foremost Astaire and Rogers, with Arlene Croce's groundbreaking book about them pointing the way. (Well, if you were passionate about dance, you were passionate about Fred and Ginger. George Balanchine, for instance, thought that Astaire was the world's greatest male dancer, and was in love—from afar—with Ginger.) When I arrived at Knopf, it had just published Kevin Brownlow's seminal book *The Parade's Gone By . . .* , and soon I was working with Walter Kerr on *The Silent Clowns*, still the finest book on Chaplin, Keaton, Lloyd, and the Mack Sennett gang. Walter was widely known as a theater critic—I had done several books with him at S & S—but for me *The Silent Clowns* is his most significant work.

And then came a vast project, certainly the most opulent and perhaps the most informative book ever published about the making of movies: Ron Haver's *David O. Selznick's Hollywood*. Ron was the head of the film department at the Los Angeles County Museum of Art, and not only an obsessed researcher and a fluent writer but also a selfless and generous friend. His book was insanely elaborate, with fold-outs, punch-outs, metallic printing—a production as colossal as *Gone with the Wind*, which it celebrated in ultra-lavish Technicolor. (Luckily for me, I was the only person aware of the costs this extravaganza was incurring.)

We bonded transcontinentally throughout the endless time it took to pull this one together, a period that witnessed the flourishing of non-network TV, leaving new stations with not much to broadcast but old, old movies too obscure to have been shown on the *Late Movie* show and now exhumed for buffs yearning to see forgotten Helen Twelvetrees weepers (she was known as "tear-stained Helen Twelvetrees") and Zasu Pitts laugh riots. It was also the moment when taping from TV became possible, and since so many stations broadcast locally in L.A., I ruthlessly took advantage of Ron's good nature: Every Sunday morning by phone we'd go over the coming week's schedules and he'd start taping . . . and taping . . . and taping. Eventually, I accumulated some two thousand titles, many of them movies I'm sure no one had looked at in thirty years. (Where could they have seen them? Hollywood had no interest in its old product—no interest and no respect. Until recently, certain of the studios were criminally negligent about what is our legacy as well as theirs.) It was Ron who, rummaging in the Warner vaults, would discover the missing footage of the Judy Garland *A Star Is Born* and write a book about it (which Martha edited). He and I stayed phone friends for years until he grew desperately ill, then died. He had been in such strong physical shape that it was months before his doctors realized that what he was dying of was AIDS.

The most unlikely film project I was involved with was the amazing collection of essays by the silent-film icon Louise Brooks. It was called *Lulu in Hollywood*, after her central role in Pabst's *Pandora's Box*, and it did not disappoint the many admirers who had rediscovered her in Kenneth Tynan's famous article about her in *The New Yorker*, "The Girl in the Black Helmet." (William Shawn was another worshipper.) She lived, reclusively, in Rochester, New York, and had no interest in coming to the big city. I, like an idiot, made no pilgrimage to Rochester, so our discussions about the book were limited to a modest correspondence and some phone calls, all of which were low-key, sensible, and totally absent the eccentricities for which she was famous. When the book was successfully launched she sent me a token of gratitude, even though I was the one who had cause to be grateful. Don't try to guess:

It was a Modern Library edition of *Thus Spake Zarathustra*, inscribed to her by Robert Benchley.

My increasingly heated interest in popular culture spread from movies (and dance) to the great lyricists of what we now call the Great American Songbook. In 1983 we published the first of the definitive "Complete Lyrics of . . ." volumes, *The Complete Lyrics of Cole Porter*, edited by Robert Kimball, then and now the number-one Porter expert. Bob was compulsively meticulous as well as comprehensively knowledgeable, a kind of Bob Caro of the field—and, also like Bob Caro, he took a long time polishing his work. Kimball went on to Lorenz Hart, Ira Gershwin, Irving Berlin, Frank Loesser, and Johnny Mercer, sometimes with collaborators, usually not. These were elaborate publications, expensive to produce, priced high, and with a limited readership— definitely not winners by profit-and-loss standards—but here again I was lucky not to have anyone looking over my shoulder. I simply felt these were essential books and that we had to publish them.

The icing on the cake was Kimball himself, a total pleasure to work with and to know, except for his incurable dilatoriness. But I had my revenge. Once Martha and I were driving through New Haven and spotted Bob in the street. We slowed down, drew up beside him, and I shouted at him through the car window, "Where's my manuscript?" Boys must have their fun.

By the time I got to Knopf I had ceased enjoying the supposedly unavoidable business lunches that editors like to pretend are essential to their wheelings and dealings. And they are—when you're first meeting people, establishing yourself, creating the relationships that will underlie or cement your future career. Also, they're heady: Eat, drink, and be merry at the company's expense. But enough was enough. I soon realized that there was just too much to do at Knopf, and I couldn't spare a couple of hours every day to overeat and overdrink. (Back then drink meant martinis or Bloody Marys, not a glass of white wine. I'd come back to the office dazed and not very useful.) So I just cut out The Lunch. A sandwich in the office, an outing to a local fast-food joint, a walk in the park with a writer, was the new regime.

This would hardly be worth noting except that it led to one of my very happiest professional and personal relationships. *The New York Times Book Review*, in all its high seriousness, decided that it needed to give the world a feature story about the lunch habits of prominent editors, and assigned it to the young freelance journalist Nora Ephron. She came to the office (for the obligatory sandwich), and within minutes I could tell that she was as embarrassed as I was to be having a discussion about this dopey non-subject. Within an hour we both knew that we were going to be friends.

Soon I was her publisher. Soon we were palling around. Soon she and Maria had become close. Nora was married to Carl Bernstein and was living in Washington, but summers were spent in the Hamptons, where Nora created perfect homes and produced perfect meals. She was pregnant with her first son, Jacob, while Maria was pregnant with Nicky—a lovely coincidence for them both. And who can forget the combined first birthday party for the two toddlers at Bridgehampton's Candy Kitchen? But Nora's marriage was unraveling, and while she was in New York giving birth to her second son, Max, just fifteen months after having Jacob, she confirmed for herself the ugly news that Carl was still conducting an affair with Margaret Jay, wife of the British ambassador.

That was it for Nora. Maria had once said to her that she could always come to us if she needed a place to stay in New York, and now she called from her hospital room, told Maria what had happened, said she wasn't going back to Carl (and Washington), and asked if she—and Jacob and Max and her au pair girl and Max's nurse—could move in with us while she sorted out her life. ("Us" at that time was Maria and me, Lizzie, little Nicky, and *our* au pair girl: Susan Finkelstein, then pre-med, later a successful child psychiatrist, today a close family friend and support to us and to grown-up Lizzie and Nicky, and adored "aunt" to Lizzie's twin boys; their Nina, in a way.)

It was a crowded house, but despite Nora's unhappiness, a determinedly cheerful one through Thanksgiving, Christmas, and well into the new year. Carl kept calling and coming around, both to see his new baby and hoping to win Nora back, but she was having none of it. (It didn't help when Carl wooed her by saying that if she would only agree to go into marriage therapy with him, he would "put Margaret on hold.") Nora's heart was broken and her pride shattered, but she knew her mind and she was determined not to expose her distress to the world. It was wonderful to be able to give her the shelter and privacy she needed, and there are far worse things than a crowded house. All of which goes to explain why her immensely successful novel *Heartburn* (complete with recipes), which transformed this painful event into comedy, was dedicated to Maria and me. But the true reward was that living together under such stressful circumstances transformed a pleasing friendship into a lifelong intimacy.

Throughout the seventies and eighties I was in London just about every year, staying with Deborah, seeing publishers (Tom Maschler, first on the list) and agents and spending time with authors who had become friends—Doris first of all; David and Jane Cornwell; Antonia Fraser; Margaret Drabble, whom I liked tremendously and worked with on half a dozen novels (not that much work was required). There was also the problematic Richard Adams, some time after his *Watership Down* glory days. I gathered that Richard was disliked in the London literary/publishing world for his very politically incorrect views, and his sometimes supercilious manner. But we got along well, partly because he found the editorial process interesting but also because he, too, was an obsessive reader. One day he paid me the ultimate compliment at his command: "You know, my dear Bob, sometimes I think that—apart from myself, and given that you're an American—you're the best-read man I know." You can see why he rubbed people the wrong way, but I found it a generous thing to say, and touching as an example of how he just didn't understand how he affected others.

Perhaps the most surprising fruit of my London trips—to me, then and now, a real coup—was the beginning of my partnership and friendship with the historical novelist Dorothy Dunnett. I had read— devoured, really—the six long volumes of her Lymond Chronicles, starting with *The Game of Kings.* Her dazzling combination of deep research, a kind of Dorothy Sayers–like witty approach to romance, and utterly thrilling set-piece scenes à la Dumas, was unique, and her plotting masterly: The suspense never let up. I was sixty pages from the end of the final volume, *Checkmate*, when at four in the morning I had to go to sleep. The next morning I did something I've never done before or since: I stayed home from work to finish a book.

I was paying a courtesy call on Graham Watson, the head of London's powerful literary agency Curtis Brown, which represented both Antonia and Vidia Naipaul, and he was tempting me with one literary name after another, all of whom I was politely sidestepping, when I noticed that on a low shelf in his office all the Dunnetts were lined up. To his astonishment, since he had me pegged as "literary," I told him I desperately wanted to publish her, not only because I loved her books, but also because although she was a bestseller in Britain, she hadn't broken through in America and I was sure it was because she was being presented as a typical bodice-ripper rather than as the uniquely imaginative and compelling writer she was.

Dorothy was free! He rang her in Edinburgh, where she lived with her distinguished husband, Alastair, editor of *The Scotsman* (and later head of Scotland's offshore oil industry), and she rushed down to London to meet me. Yet again it was love at first sight. Dorothy was a dynamo, who had effortlessly made the transition from successful portrait painter to successful novelist, while enjoying a fulfilling marriage and raising two splendid sons. Her secret, she confided, was that she had never cooked a meal in her life.

We began with *King Hereafter*, her original and provocative novel about the historical Macbeths, and went on to a series of amusing detective stories. But I was hoping that she'd start on a big new series, and when I told her so on one of her trips to New York she said she'd love to, but what should be their overarching metaphor, the way chess was for the Lymond Chronicles? "The signs of the zodiac," I blurted out, not having given the question a moment's thought, and eight volumes of the "House of Niccolò"—set in the fifteenth century, a hundred years before Lymond, and ranging across the known world—were the result, ending with *Gemini*, published only a year before Dorothy's death. (There was no question of her dying before she had completed her life work.) Not only was there a tremendous boom in her popularity when Vintage republished the fourteen long novels, and a serious reconsideration of her merits, but her fanatical worldwide readership goes on carrying the torch with such events as IDDD (International Dorothy Dunnett Day, in case you didn't know), celebrated annually with orchestrated readings and celebrations. You can see why I'm proud.

Despite all the pleasures and satisfactions of my publishing life in London, for me the important thing in England was the time I spent with Deborah Rogers. For whatever reason, through thick and a good deal of thin, we always had the greatest fun together, as well as the greatest belief in each other, in a deep relationship that seemed to exist without psychic or sexual elements—a siblinghood free of the unfinished business of childhood, to borrow Freud's luminous phrase. And free of the jealousies that close relationships can harbor; I am (or was) a possessive person, but I got along perfectly with her longtime boyfriend Andrew, and was delighted when she met and married the composer and broadcaster Michael Berkeley (now Lord Berkeley, making Deb late in life Lady Berkeley—a family joke, because for decades, when she was in her over-gracious mode, I called her Lady B, short for Lady Bountiful).

When in 1968 she first set up her own agency, Deborah Rogers, Ltd., it was in two rooms over a fish-and-chips shop in far-from-classy Goodge Street. A year later she expanded by taking on board my old S & S colleague Pat White—beautiful, capable, unswervingly loyal—who had decided to move to England and whom I introduced to Deb. (Apart from everything else, Pat added to the colorful ambience of the typical Rogers office by installing her three dogs at her desk every day.) Pat's loyalty extended to me, and I was staying with her almost fifty years later when I came to Britain for Deb's funeral in Wales, and months later for the extraordinary memorial service held for her in the church of St. Martin-in-the-Fields, 750 people in tears.

Deb and I were always rushing off on last-minute expeditions. "Let's cancel our meetings tomorrow and go to Brighton." "Let's take tomorrow off and try Herne Bay" (a seaside resort town famous for its rock candy). "Let's take a week off and go to Ireland," where neither of us had ever been. The only way to go was by air, and we shared a pathological terror of flying—for fifteen years I went back and forth to England by ocean liner. As it turned out, each of us was so anxious for the other one on the flight to Dublin that we didn't have time to be scared for ourselves. During two other summers we spent a week on the canals, in those little barges that you maneuvered through the narrow bridges and easy-to-handle locks. The first time, Andrew was Captain, Deb's super-capable sister, Sue, was Mate, Deb was Cook, and I was Passenger. The second time, Maria and toddler Lizzie came along, with Karen Provensen as our au pair girl. Best of all, perhaps, were the many long weekends at Stanage, the pile—crenellated walls, gardens laid out by Repton—where Deb and Sister Sue had grown up, on an estate of twenty-five thousand acres in Wales. Their mother, Stella, had been a successful ingénue in the West End (she was the goddaughter of the great Mrs. Patrick Campbell, Shaw's original Eliza Doolittle), until she was swept up by Guy Rogers, a successful businessman who worshipped her and their two girls when he wasn't growling at them.

I suppose that what Deb and I had most in common was a fanatical interest in other people (rarely ourselves)—friends, friends of friends, colleagues, people encountered casually, total strangers glimpsed in restaurants, buses, anywhere. I knew everything about the agency, she knew everything about Knopf. She and Maria grew closer and closer through the years. (Once, when she was in personal crisis, she called Maria and asked her to fly over to help her through—it was Maria she wanted, not me.) Although on the surface they were totally unalike, these two women were extraordinarily alike under the skin: the same pride and intelligence hiding beneath girlishness or faux-naïveté; the same fortitude; the same demented mothering. The same superb—and spontaneous—cooking. The same ability to get more done than any three other people while leaving chaos in their wake. Many times I asked myself, and them, too, what I had done to deserve two such impossible females in my life.

Deb, as I've written, was at our wedding. Years later, we were there at Kennedy Airport when she and Michael stepped off the plane from Arizona with tiny newborn and newly adopted Jessica. We lived in each other's houses and shared the same timeworn jokes. (One example: At a dinner party that the extraordinary Tony Godwin, chief editor of Penguin, gave for Maria and me—he had recently shed his very nice wife—all the work had been done by Deb and Maria, and when we'd eaten and the two of them stood up to clear the table, Brigid Brophy, a well-known lesbian novelist who was one of the other guests, spoke up sharply: "Don't *you* get up, Maria. *Your* job is to sit there and be beautiful." We never let Deb forget it.)

These are the family memories and jokes that bind people together for life. When she came over to Paris to spend my forty-fifth wedding anniversary weekend with me (in the absence of Maria), Deb was as happy and energetic as I'd ever known her—we had a joyous reunion, but then all our reunions were joyous. She called from London on Monday morning. She called again on Wednesday morning, full of beans. Late that afternoon Michael called to tell me she was dead—she had died of a heart attack while parking her car outside their front door.

It's the death I'll never get over. As I said when I spoke at her memorial service in London, in October 2014, she was the sister I never had, and the friend of my heart for fifty years. Why did we love each other on sight and forever? No one is wiser than Montaigne, and this is what he had to say about his instant and profound bond with the man he would be closest to, beginning when they first met, late in his life: "If pushed to say why I loved him, I feel it can only be expressed by answering, 'Because it was him, because it was me.'"

And yet although we were in the same business, Deb and I had hardly ever done business together—I could no more have asked her to move an important author my way than she could have tried to "sell" me on someone. There were a very few writers scattered over the years: Burgess, J. G. Farrell (the remarkable *Troubles* and *The Siege of Krishnapur*), and, out of left field, Penelope Leach. I had noticed in a London bookstore a Penguin book called *Babyhood*, anatomizing the behavior and development of children from birth to two. Deb was Leach's agent and assigned me the American rights. This was not the kind of book I usually brought home from England, but I was convinced of its validity and utility. Back home I asked for a photo of a wholesome baby for the cover, and to my amazement our art director set up an elaborate and expensive photo shoot, the results of which were fakey and unconvincing. "Horrible!" I blurted out. "Go around the office and ask every parent we've got for a baby picture and choose the best of them. Here!" I said, grabbing a picture of tiny baby Lizzie from my desk; "Start with this." The search went no further, which is why Lizzie (uncredited) found herself on the cover of *Babyhood*, and indeed is still on the cover hundreds of thousands of copies later, since the book has never been out of print. We then introduced Penelope to the British packaging firm of Dorling Kindersley, which took her on to write the text of what would turn out to be a child-care bible: *Your Baby and Child*. With more than two and a half million copies sold, it's become the most successful rival and/or supplement to the immortal Dr. Spock. Kathy Hourigan has nurtured Penelope at Knopf for forty years now; I can only remember meeting her once. But I had done my part.

I never had a long-range plan for Knopf, and Bob Bernstein as president of Random House never tried to steer me in any given direction. Since we were always healthily profitable, my view (and his) was that it wasn't anybody's business how we got there, so there was no questioning whom I hired or what I published. Our process was simple and quick: When an editor wanted to acquire a book, he or she just told me and I said yes or no, and decided how much money we could pay. The calculations went on in my head, so no time was wasted in concocting abstract profit-and-loss statements that were pure guesswork. (At least my off-the-cuff decisions were backed up by experience.) And I read more or less everything—not only manuscripts up for consideration but commissioned manuscripts when they were delivered. Otherwise how could I have decided on print runs and promotional plans?

During the almost twenty years I was at Knopf, the book business was changing in many ways, but my head was buried in the specifics of editing and publishing, and so I just tried to adapt to the more visible changes rather than anticipate them. For instance, I had grown up at a time when our main selling tool was advertising. But as the cost of ads rose far more steeply than the income from book sales warranted spending on them, ads became less and less practical, although they remained important to writers, who not only enjoyed seeing them but took them as a gauge of their publishers' belief in them. It was now promotion that dominated—the promotion of merchandise with book-sellers by way of discounts and co-op campaigns, all handled by the sales department, and author promotion. What had really begun with Alexander King on the Jack Paar show had become the most effective way of selling books, or at least certain kinds of books. We couldn't sell a French novelist by sending him on a nationwide tour, but we could send a Bacall or a Julia. And it began to be productive to send less celebrated authors to carefully chosen venues—literary bookstores, local radio and television stations that focused on cultural matters. There were writers who didn't like doing such things, but most enjoyed them, even the stressful book-signing events at which almost nobody might turn up.

Our good fortune was that as author promotion was becoming an essential publishing tool, out of our organization sprang the perfect person to handle it—the young, confident, and irrepressible Jane Friedman, who had arrived at Knopf (as a secretary in the publicity department) a few months after I did. Baby Jane, as we liked to call her, was a dynamo—and a take-over one. No one ever said Jane was a fragile flower, but fragile flowers can't do promotion, and she was not only amazingly effective but loving, loyal, sentimental, and giving. Like everyone else, she sat at Nina's feet, and when we talk about Nina today, tears still come to her eyes (and mine). Authors were crazy about Jane because she worked so hard for them *and* was so positive and cheerful. (Some of the relationships she formed back then, like her near-partnership with Michael Crichton, lasted for life.) Jane was boisterous—to some people perhaps over-boisterous—but I enjoyed her and was glad to harness her energy, or to put it more accurately, not get in its way. She also had a strong entrepreneurial streak, something I totally lack; it was she who masterminded Random House's audiobooks division and administered it into profitability. When Sonny Mehta took over from me, in 1987, Jane became his right hand, and sometimes his left hand too, until it became obvious that she needed her own thing to run. Random House ignored her credentials, so off she went to revivify HarperCollins, and eventually to start up her own company. Through all of which she's remained exactly who she was at the start: irrepressible, a loving friend, and unqualifiedly sure of herself.

As promotion grew in importance as a sales tool, so too did the rise of the bookstore chains, in particular Dalton and Walden. Suddenly their stores were everywhere across America, bringing books to small towns and suburban malls. In my youth, if you lived in a small town you could join a book club or go to the public library (if there was one), or you could try to find something to buy in the local drugstore's paperback rack—a choice more or less limited to Mickey Spillane, Erskine Caldwell, and Erle Stanley Gardner, with a sprinkling of Agatha Christie for class. And years later when Dalton and Walden imploded, there was Barnes & Noble. (The days of Amazon as the latest channel between publishers and readers were well in the future.)

How the chains affected us most was that more power was in the hands of fewer buyers, and they began pressuring publishers for higher discounts as well as influencing the size of our first printings by the size of their initial orders. Small bookstores could still acquire merchandise from jobbers, but the balance of power had changed, especially when department stores began closing down their book departments, which had once been major players. Macy's, for instance, had for decades sold tons of books; it was big news when in 1936 they discounted *Gone with the Wind* (the first novel to be sold at three dollars) to ninety-nine cents for a special promotion.

When a book was by an established genre writer, the chains knew exactly what to order, since they had data from the author's previous books. But when it came to a writer like Updike—the commercial possibilities of whose books differed widely, since he wrote such different books—the chains were out of their depth. If his previous book had sold forty thousand copies, they would order in relation to that number, whereas we knew that the new book might sell barely half that—or double that. So I had to struggle with the sales department over our first printings, since the salespeople, naturally, were always glad to push the numbers up. (They weren't responsible for returns, an increasing problem as the eighties rolled by and the chains were over-ordering so as not to be caught short of stock in case a book took off.) This was not amusing.

In fact, for me—and it took some time for me to acknowledge this to myself—the amusement was draining out of things. I was doing more and more, and our profits were consistent, but the personal cost was mounting. And I was finding less satisfaction in individual successes than I once had. When a book hit the bestseller list, when an important author joined us, when a major award was won, it had always been a moment for celebration. Now it was just a relief—okay, this worked, so on to the next. It wasn't being jaded, it was exhaustion.

What changed everything for me was the sale of Random House, in 1980, to S. I. Newhouse. RCA, which had previously owned us, was clueless about publishing, and uninterested. The two board meetings with RCA executives that Bob Bernstein induced me to attend were so paralyzing, and the directors so thick-headed, that I just refused to attend another one. One of Bob's greatest contributions to the well-being of all of us at Random was to provide a solid barrier between us and the potentially disruptive ownership. What more important function can the head of a subsidiary company perform?

When Bob summoned me downstairs to our boardroom to meet the new owner, I knew nothing about Si except that he owned Condé Nast. I was dressed in my usual high style—unpressed khakis, white sneakers, and a particularly sloppy cardigan. And there was the new owner, dressed more or less the same way! From the moment we met, we got on well, and as time went by, Si came to me again and again to discuss the company. And then as someone to spend time with away from work, particularly when he discovered my passion for old Hollywood movies: Every week or two he would ask a dozen or so friends over to his East Side brownstone and project movies for us. More to the point, he was a passionate reader—books were everywhere in his house and he was always talking about what he was reading. His daughter, Pamela, once said to me that she thought her father had bought Random House to justify all the reading he was doing anyway. And his wife, Victoria, who herself had been in publishing, was and is an equally ardent reader—and has remained a great friend.

A real problem was that Si and Bob didn't get along. Or maybe it was that they just didn't know how to talk to each other. Si, unless you really interested him, was all business. Bob loved to expatiate on his passionate extracurricular—and important—work for international human rights. And, like his mentor Bennett Cerf, he loved telling jokes. It made Si wild. Three times in five years he asked me to re- place Bob as president of Random House, and I said no three times, each time more emphatically and ungraciously. First of all, I would never have done that to Bob, who had been extraordinarily good to me through the years. (He once said to Maria, "If only Bob would say behind my back all those things he says about me to my face.") But also, as I kept telling Si, this would be yet another extreme example of the Peter Principle at work. Why take me—whose talents lay in editing, publishing, and presiding over a small harmonious group of people— and give me a job isolated from the real workers and the real work, making decisions about such matters as how much more warehouse space we needed in Maryland? Besides, although I didn't say this, what was in it for me? I made enough money, I had enough responsibility, my reputation in the business was secure, and I had heard enough from Bob over the years to know just how knotty and daunting were the problems he faced—and I would have to face. Finally Si got the message, and luck- ily he wasn't the kind of man whose amour propre would be offended at being turned down this way.

At some point he started quizzing me about *The New Yorker,* for which he had a lifelong veneration and which he had recently acquired. What did I know about Mr. Shawn's succession plan? Nothing. What did I think about the magazine's current state? Less exciting than it used to be. What did I know about this young guy, Bill McKibben, whom Shawn had mentioned to him as a possible heir? Only that he was very young and very earnest, and not very popular with his colleagues—considered by them an even less plausible candidate than Jonathan Schell, at the idea of whom the staff had previously rebelled. (I had published Jonathan's *The Fate of the Earth*, and liked him a lot.) Did I have any ideas about other potential candidates? No, because although I had several friends at the magazine, I was in no way knowledgeable about it. What I did know something about was the way various editors at the magazine had been tantalized by Shawn with vague promises about the future, only to have those promises melt away. The best-known victim was the talented and much admired Bill Whitworth, who got so fed up that he quit and became editor of *The Atlantic*, where he did a splendid job.

This was not a promising history for a man like Si Newhouse, who made snap decisions and carried them out speedily. Indecision, delay, hesitation were simply not in his nature, and he had no tolerance for them. Meanwhile, Shawn was approaching eighty, and although he had sent up trial balloons like Schell and McKibben, he was clearly not going to act. But even Si, who had a reputation for firing people, understood that he should not, and could not, fire the most revered editor in America. He was a frustrated owner.

And then I realized that he was narrowing in on me. This was at a time when I was beginning to be restless about the relentless demands of my publishing life, and given my lifelong addiction to the magazine, I was attracted by the idea. Finally he asked me whether I would consider taking the job, and I said I would—when the time came. And if it wasn't too late. I was in my upper fifties, and the magazine didn't need another aged editor.

We put it on nervous hold, but as time went by I grew more and more stressed by the situation. I was certainly okay where I was at Knopf, and I was pretty sure I'd be okay at *The New Yorker*, but I wasn't okay not knowing what my life was going to be. One day I said to Si that the situation was really upsetting me, and that I wanted to shelve the idea entirely: When eventually Shawn retired, or was incapacitated, Si could decide whether he still wanted me and I could decide whether I still wanted the job; if he had changed his mind at that point, no hard feelings. The moment we agreed on that, I felt tremendously relieved and just forgot about it.

It must have been about six months later that Si called me one day in the office during lunchtime, sounding atypically excited, and asked whether he could come right over to see me. As soon as he arrived he blurted out that he had just left a lunch with Shawn, and Shawn had resigned! Was I prepared to take over? It had to happen quickly, before Shawn changed his mind. Si reported that Shawn had said to him, "Mr. Newhouse, would you welcome my leaving sooner rather than later?" and when Si said yes, went on to say, "Then I will." "Good," said Si, and left the restaurant to call me. As far as he was concerned, it was over: Shawn had resigned. Later, when I came to understand Shawn better, I realized that for him, this exchange was only the first move in what would have been a drawn-out affair of qualifications and procrastinations, which is how he had dealt with the issue of succession for so many years. Having spoken to both men about what had happened—surely the only person who did—I'm certain that Shawn didn't understand that in Si's eyes he had resigned, so that later he could honestly assert that he had been fired, and that Si was equally certain that Shawn *had* resigned, so that he was free to move on without guilt. The ultra-forceful Newhouse and the passive-aggressive Shawn were constitutionally incapable of understanding each other.

I said to Si that I would take the job, but that we should be in agreement about a few things before we formalized the arrangement. I told him that I revered what *The New Yorker* was and didn't want to see it change into something different; that I thought it needed new energy, but that I was a conserver by nature, not a revolutionary, and that if he wanted a different magazine from the one he had, I wasn't the person for the job; that I felt I could make it a better version of what it was, not turn it into something it wasn't. That was fine with him. Then I asked him to promise me that if he changed his mind at any time, he would give me advance warning and tell me directly, not fire me abruptly and publicly, as he had done to several of his well-known editors. He gave me his word, and started to tell me what he planned to do for me contractually. As I'd done almost twenty years earlier with Bennett Cerf, I told him that I'd just had a substantial raise at Knopf and didn't want more money now: Again, I didn't want so important a life decision to be affected by financial considerations. It's fair to say that he was taken aback. But we went ahead.

A couple of months after I was installed at *The New Yorker*, at one of our regular lunches, he announced that whether I liked it or not, in light of all the disagreeable publicity my accession had involved he was raising my salary—I think it was by twenty-five thousand dollars. I was about to refuse indignantly, but then decided that this would be too ungracious, even for me, so just said, "Well, thank you." The thing I really did appreciate was when at a later lunch, and with some embarrassment, he handed me a package, saying, "I saw this and thought you might like it." He was right. It was a beautiful vintage photograph, suitably framed, of Fred and Adele Astaire.

WORKING

The New Yorker

THE NEWS that I was going to replace William Shawn at *The New Yorker* was front-page news—in fact, it appeared on the front page of *The New York Times*, along with my picture. Even so, as was the case when I went to Knopf, I wasn't the story—the story was about the fate of the magazine that to hundreds of thousands, perhaps millions, of people was an essential part of their lives. I was one of them, and had been since I first started scanning the cartoons when I was about twelve, the way so many readers have been drawn into the magazine. First the cartoons (what could be more sophisticated for a precocious kid than "getting" Addams, Arno, Hokinson, and Thurber); then the humor pieces; then on to the fiction. By 1946, when Harold Ross, the founder, devoted an entire issue to John Hersey's *Hiroshima*, I was religiously reading every word he chose to run.

William Shawn, Ross's successor, was as highly regarded as Ross had been. He was a sacrosanct figure, despite Tom Wolfe's notorious 1965 attack on him, "Tiny Mummies!," in *New York*. He had carried the magazine to amazing success, both literary and financial. But by 1987, when I took over, the magazine had become less vital. All too often I found myself turning its pages rather than reading them.

I had understood that my appointment would be greeted with a blast of speculation and/or resentment, although I hoped there would also be a degree of goodwill—I wasn't, at least in my estimation, a barbarian at the gates. But the circumstances of Shawn's departure were so shrouded in confusion and obscurity, aggravated by deliberate obfuscation, that what in an ideal world would have been an orderly and polite transfer of authority became a scandal. To begin with, when Si Newhouse bought the magazine he had assured the staff that he would consult with them when the time came to replace Shawn. This he failed to do—partly, I suspect, because he didn't *know* the people there, but also because he didn't want to. He wasn't used to being second-guessed, let alone first-guessed. It was *his* magazine, and he would do what he wanted to with it. But he took the responsibility seriously. He venerated *The New Yorker*, which is why he overpaid for it, and whenever we had talked about it over the previous several years it was evident to me that if Shawn had proposed a plausible candidate to replace himself and a reasonable timetable for his departure, Si would have been relieved. Given Shawn's nature, however, that was an impossibility, and Si, extremely impatient by temperament, erupted when Shawn, without knowing he was doing it, gave him the opening.

The staff and the writers at *The New Yorker* were shocked, dismayed, and scared when the news broke, and who could blame them? They were also angry, since Shawn let it be known that he had been abruptly fired. Lillian Ross, Shawn's mistress of many years, stoked the fires; it was she who came up with the idea that everyone should sign a letter to me, asking me to withdraw from the job. (When, years earlier, Si had bought the magazine, she had wanted everyone to line the halls and stairways and cry "Shame, shame" when he put in his first appearance. Wiser—or saner—heads prevailed.)

No sooner had The Letter been hand-delivered to my door than the phone rang, and someone told me that this was the *wrong* letter, that I should ignore it and wait for the *right* letter, which was on its way. This did not speak well for the efficiency of the gang on Forty-third Street, but they were overwrought. The right letter proved to be polite, pleasant, and pointless—can anyone other than Lillian have been naïve enough to think that either Si or I would pay any attention to it? But I appreciated that this was an acceptable way for Shawn's colleagues and friends to publicly rally to him, and—as requested in the letter itself—I didn't take it personally. I also decided not to focus on the long list of names attached to the letter, particularly once I had glanced down it and noticed that Janet Malcolm, one of my closest friends, was on it—someone who certainly didn't bear me ill will. I deliberately didn't go through the list name by name, so as not to be aware later on of who had signed it and who hadn't.

I called Mr. Shawn the morning the announcement was made, to pay my respects and ask him how he wanted us to proceed. We agreed to meet for lunch the following day, at the Algonquin (of course), and the first thing I did was hand him a short note to the staff saying that I *did* appreciate that the letter was not meant personally and that I was going to take up the job as announced, eager to work with everyone. Or something like that—I jotted it down fast, didn't dwell on it, and didn't keep a copy. Shawn, when he read it, graciously said that although he regretted my decision, he thought I had expressed it as well as it could be expressed, and said he would post it in the halls when he got back to the office.

The lunch was not made easier by the hovering presence of a photographer who not only burst into the dining room and took a hideous shot of the two of us that later appeared in *New York* but pursued us out onto the street at the end of the meal—I managed to distract him as I rushed Mr. Shawn into the *New Yorker* building before he could be exposed to more of the publicity he hated. Our conversation had been as cordial as it could have been under the circumstances. I asked him what kind of timetable he would like us to proceed with, how (or if) we should overlap, etc. We agreed that I should spend a week in the office while he was still in charge, to give me a chance to begin learning the ropes from him directly, and he named a date. (I was startled to read somewhere recently that I had given him three weeks to clear out his office and go.)

The fact of The Letter made the whole thing into a force-ten media event: As I remember it, the *Times* ran big stories three days in a row. I hadn't anticipated this level of interest—of hysteria—and I got my first taste of it the night the first *Times* story ran. I was at a New

York City Ballet performance at the State Theater, and as usual there were twenty or thirty people I knew in the audience. At the intermissions, old acquaintances suddenly seemed shy and avoided me, near-strangers rushed up to congratulate me, dozens of people I didn't know stared at me. This was not delusion or self-consciousness, it was blatant, and it confirmed my long-standing belief that being a public figure is hell. I was to discover that it's not easy for the editor of *The New Yorker* to maintain a low profile (although I don't believe that anonymity was my successor Tina Brown's highest priority). When I wouldn't talk to journalists, I was biting the hand that was now feeding me. When I did, things I said casually were taken out of context and turned into stories. Which perhaps I should have expected, but I wasn't used to being news.

My first order of business, in any case, was to help Knopf settle into its future. When the decision was made that I was to leave, Si and Bob Bernstein wanted to know who I thought should replace me. I told them it had to be Sonny Mehta, from Picador in the U.K., who not only had the crucial passion for books of quality, and the knowledge of how to publish them, but who had something I lacked—a significant presence in the world of international publishing: a presence at the Frankfurt Book Fair, for instance, which I had succeeded in never attending, much happier having Carol Janeway and Tony Schulte over there engaging with the foreign big shots while I stayed home, putting the cat out at the end of the workday and locking the back door. When Si and Bob asked who my second choice was, I said there was no second choice, so they'd better secure Sonny. If I'd given them a list, we'd still be discussing it now, but as it happened, there was no list: In my mind, Sonny *was* the only plausible candidate, not that he was aware that he was a candidate until he was offered the job. Very few people at Knopf knew him other than Carol, who had been at Cambridge with him, so I had the satisfying task of reciting his virtues to his new colleagues. Fortunately for all, he came, he saw, and he took over, and by now has been at Knopf far longer than my mere nineteen years.

As for my own new colleagues, I knew very little about them. But I had heard many good things about Chip (Charles) McGrath, who had been one of those Shawn had tantalized with the idea of being a possible successor. The day after the announcement was made I called him and asked him to have dinner with me that night. Reluctantly he agreed—like everyone else at the magazine he was in a state of shock—and when we met he was naturally somewhat ambivalent, but then so was I. Within minutes, though, I invited him to become deputy editor. And so, eventually, it happened—to my good fortune, and I think he would agree, to his. Certainly our relationship, which started off under these rocky circumstances, grew into a happy one, and is still that today, almost thirty years later. Maybe it worked so well because although we're so unalike—Chip so circumspect, me so exuberant—we're equally fanatical about work. And our judgments almost always coincided. Throughout my entire stretch at the magazine, for instance, he and I together edited the "Talk of the Town" section in harmony and with growing respect for each other's editorial skills.

There was an important job Chip agreed to perform in the weeks before I was to arrive on the scene. One of the myths about *The New Yorker* was that there was a large bank of first-rate material waiting—some of it for years—to make its way into the magazine. Since, beginning on my first day, I would be scheduling upcoming issues, I needed to know what was immediately available, and I asked Chip to plow through this famous bank and pass along to me everything he felt was viable. To our surprise and distress, the cupboard turned out to be nearly bare, at least of pieces one would feel good about printing. The myth was a myth, and we should have anticipated that: An editor as gifted and enthusiastic as William Shawn would not have kept a hoard of gems locked away. As I was to discover, if you're the editor of a magazine and something exciting turns up, your impulse is to get it out there to your readers as fast as you can.

It was a scramble to fill the first issues I was now responsible for, but there was no panic, and I was enjoying getting to know people and beginning to understand the superb machinery that kept the magazine running smoothly. My job was to feed the machine, and my luck was that the way I had run things at Knopf was very much the way Mr. Shawn had run his magazine: Everything came to him for decision, and then his decisions were implemented. The job as he performed it, I came to realize, was like the job of a heart—everything flowing to and from it, to keep the system going. Since that had been my way at Knopf, *The New Yorker* got what amounted to a heart transplant. But not every boss likes to work that way. It was much more natural for Sonny to delegate, to consider, to step back. As a result, he had a rougher time than I did—Knopf was used to my way of doing things, and so the transplant there was less simple: a brain, perhaps, substituting for a heart. (Not that Sonny wasn't and isn't a feeling person.) When we compared notes a year after the changeover, he told me he had spent endless time trying to figure out what my systems were, before finally realizing that *I* was the systems.

The week I spent in the office with Mr. Shawn was manifestly terrible for him. He did his best to explain and demonstrate, but he couldn't bring himself to ease my way with his people—which was everyone. I took myself around the office, introducing myself, asking questions, no doubt over-talkative and over-friendly. Shawn was famously shy and secretive. I blurted out what was on my mind; he was enigmatic, cryptic, Delphic. I could see that people were perplexed by what, and how much, I was saying to them. Much later Chip told me that in these first months, because he was spending so much time with me he became something of an interpreter. "Bob passed me in the hall this morning and asked how I was coming along with my piece. What do you think he meant?" It took even him some time to grasp that I meant just what I said. For some people this was a relief; for others, it was jarring.

Shawn was so soft-spoken that you weren't always certain what he was saying, nor was he easy of access. To enter his office you had to pass through *two* closed doors, and then only after making an appointment. Almost my first action after he was gone was to have one door removed and the other always left open. (Joe Heller could have written the first line of *Something Happened* with me in mind: "I get the willies when I see closed doors.") I was comfortable having people rush in and out, and I needed to wander the halls a couple of times a day, either on official business or just to chat—a burden, sometimes, on hard-pressed workers. But I couldn't help being gregarious any more than Shawn could help being... being what? Reserved? Cautious? Secretive? His colleagues at the magazine, all of whom knew him far better than I did, have failed to diagnose or analyze him. It's been suggested that he changed significantly—grew more embattled, even embittered—after the failed attempt of a number of staff members to unionize the magazine in 1976 and the staff's rejection of Jonathan Schell as his possible successor. Certainly, something happened to him, or within him, that led Roger Angell, who knew him longer and better than anyone, to refer to him in his late tenure as "a Lear in his old age, wishing obsessively to hold the magazine in his hands forever." It was a tragic end to one of the great careers in American journalism, and I did not enjoy observing it at close hand.

Only slowly did I come to realize what his way of dealing with people had done to some of those who were in thrall—in fact, who accepted his exacting paternalism as something almost sacred. But I had witnessed something of the same phenomenon at New York City Ballet, where Balanchine was the beginning and end of everything—many of the dancers had been with him since they were eight or nine, and he had been the determining factor in their lives. In addition, he was a true genius, and the entire dance world knew it. How argue with George Balanchine? How displease him? After his death, certain dancers began to express resentment at the total sway he had held over them, and during the years to come, the same thing happened to certain *New Yorker* writers—they began to resent having been infantilized, even while maintaining their admiration for, and gratitude to, the man who had so bountifully presided over their careers.

Martha Kaplan joined me the day after I arrived, and as the new executive editor, she quietly began taking various practical matters into her hands—matters dealing with payments, offices, contracts; and more personal issues that arose from people who didn't feel comfortable coming to me. Since we had worked together for so long, and I had such complete confidence in her judgment, she could speak for me, and since she was obviously neither a power seeker nor a game player, she gave off no threatening vibrations: She respected everyone, was direct and candid, and just got things done. On the Thursday of our week together, Mr. Shawn said to me, "I'd like to meet your Miss Kaplan. I've been hearing good things about her." I ushered Martha in, the three of us talked for half an hour, and after she left he said to me, "I've spent my life looking for someone like that to help me." I managed not to say, "You don't look for someone like that. You meet someone you like, make a connection, develop an affection and a trust, and create a strong working and personal relationship." It just happens—or it doesn't.

It was a sad thing that William Shawn's final weeks at *The New Yorker* were so distressing for him, and that his distress was so publicly aired, although perhaps it was somewhat assuaged by the public sympathy that came his way—I hoped it was. He hadn't been able to embrace me, but he had remained courteous and, intermittently, helpful. I didn't think of myself as a usurper—I'd been offered a job and had taken it—but he must of necessity have seen me in that light. It emerged later that he had rented an office down the street, certain that I wouldn't be able to put the magazine out and that Si Newhouse would have to call on him to step in and save the day. But even if I had fumbled, the system, which, thanks to Shawn, had a sturdy life of its own, and the dedicated staff would have covered my tracks. I didn't fumble, though—at least not in my own eyes; as usual, manic energy and blind self-confidence carried me through.

Shawn's anchor at the magazine, and in his life, had been the writer Lillian Ross, who, I soon came to realize, was disliked, mistrusted, and resented; she was The Favorite, like a *maîtresse en titre* at the French court, while *la Reine*—the kind and likable Cecille Shawn—presided over hearth and home. That Lillian and Shawn shared an apartment a few blocks away from where he and Cecille and their children lived was a not-so-secret secret, until in her memoir, *Here but Not Here: A Love Story*, Lillian embarrassed everybody but herself by officially informing the world about it . . . and much more.

Oddly enough, I had a relationship with Lillian that went back to my Simon and Schuster days, when I shepherded several of her books to publication, most notably her coruscating series of interconnected stories about psychoanalysis called *Vertical and Horizontal.* This event coincided with my own analysis, and I was faced with the difficulty of confiding to my analyst that I was the editor of this barbed and controversial account of the kind of thing he and I were doing together. (He had to be told—there are no secrets in psychoanalysis.) I have to confess that I was amused, and maybe even gratified, when I sensed that, for once, I had his full attention.

During the height of the civil rights movement, when I was intensely involved with SNCC (the Student Nonviolent Coordinating Committee), I invited Lillian to attend a meeting, hoping she'd write a "Talk of the Town" piece about it. Not only did she come, she brought Mr. Shawn with her, my first sighting of him, and my first indication that they had an extra-curricular relationship. When her account appeared, I was taken aback—disillusioned, really—to realize that though its heart was in the right place, it was far from accurate in detail. So much for *The New Yorker*'s sacred principles and its fabled fact-checking department.

A number of years after this, she called me out of the blue to say that her dog had had a litter of puppies, and would I like one (at a bargain price)? That was when I began to think she might be cuckoo. I had long been put off by her golly-gee, naïve-girl-reporter manner—presumably the tactic that had led so many of her interviewees to open up to her, to their eventual discomfiture. Yet what a terrific reporter she had been!

Lillian vacated but did not surrender her office when Mr. Shawn left, and some months later she telephoned and asked to see me. When she came in she asked me to shut my door, a bad sign. Then, in a scene out of a thirties weeper, she pleaded for her man. Surely, she said, it would be a blessing for our authors, and a big help to me, if I offered "Bill" an office down the hall from me; he would proffer editorial aid and personal comfort to all who sought him out. I wondered aloud whether Mr. Shawn was aware of this proposal. "*Bill*," she said; "he hates all this 'Mr. Shawn' formality." Since, however, he had never invited me (or almost anyone else at the magazine) to use his first name, I continued in the formal vein. No, she went on, she had thought it up all on her own. How to respond to this preposterous suggestion? With the truth—or part of it. "Lillian," I said, "however constructive such an arrangement might prove to be, there isn't the slightest chance that Si Newhouse would ever countenance it." Our moment of drama was over.

To end the Lillian saga: Some time later someone passed along to me a movie script she had written about a great and noble magazine editor ousted by a coarse mogul and replaced by a clever but brash young book-publishing executive (not an editor, however; a public relations/marketing man.) The heroine—an intrepid young girl reporter—came to the rescue when this poor specimen failed at the job, by convincing the mogul to bring back the great man. And *then*—this was the beauty part—she married the young publishing guy, who had gone back to where he belonged: marketing. This amazing fantasy made the rounds of the upper echelons of the magazine, to the delight of all, but got no further: Can Lillian really have believed that anyone would produce such a movie? I suppose I should have been flattered that her stand-in's favor had fallen on brash me.

It's been suggested that it was because of my upset at The Letter that I didn't pursue changes at the magazine as swiftly and radically as I might have wanted to. I don't understand why anyone would want to go on regurgitating this kind of speculation almost thirty years after the event—I mean, who cares? But apparently people do speculate, so let me clarify. As I've said, I was in no way upset by The Letter, nor had I ever had radical ideas about changing *The New Yorker*. What I wanted to do was slowly revitalize it. I had forgotten The Letter within a week of my arrival.

Besides, my first priority was not to make changes but to understand how things worked. I had to learn both the process and the cast of characters. First of all I had to come to understand and appreciate the outstanding abilities of the two senior nonfiction editors, Pat Crow and John Bennet, the first from Arkansas, the second from Texas. Each of them had complete command of style and, even more important, structure. Their writers trusted them, the staff trusted them, and quickly I trusted them. Pat—outspoken about everything, and never a

Shawn idolater—quit when he started questioning the direction the magazine was taking under Tina Brown (and, to the dismay of everyone who loved him, which was everyone, died several years ago). John, more private but no less articulate (or eccentric), continues on with his dedicated service to writers and the magazine, where he's been at work since 1975.

It was obvious who and what the checkers were, and the copy editors, and the art department, and the heroic production guys, but who, for instance, were those seemingly functionless people who populated a number of small offices up and down the halls? When I went over the list of their names, there were writers I had never heard of—mostly men in their seventies, even eighties, who were given annual contracts but didn't write and used the office as a kind of club. I'm not speaking of superb talents like Joseph Mitchell, a hero to all, though tragically blocked; I'm speaking of un-talents, who were in essence pensioners. There were also editors no longer (if ever) competent, to whom occasionally I would assign pieces, to my eventual regret. No adequate financial arrangements had been put in place for these superannuated employees, and this was Mr. Shawn's generous way of taking care of them. Since I had never been able to fire people, and the situation was no fault of theirs, I kept them on until some disappeared through attrition and others just slipped away when after more than fifty years the magazine moved—from Forty-third Street to Forty-second Street— and there were fewer offices available. (On the day of the move, after everything and everyone was gone, Martha and I walked through the empty five floors the magazine had occupied, appalled by the newly exposed wretched physical condition of the place, yet sentimental about it. I had until the last minute deliberately kept the large, handsome photograph of Harold Ross—a Karsh?—hanging in its highly visible place in the main hallway, and now I carried it myself to the new building and placed it in an equally prominent position there. We had already salvaged the famous "Thurber wall," covered with his drawings, and installed it on the next block.)

Ross had created a unique institution, a byword for sophistication, honesty, and liberalism. Shawn had presided over its transformation into a crucial American cultural phenomenon—and an immensely profitable one. But by the mid-eighties, that profit had dwindled away. When I arrived, as I remember it, the magazine was losing about twelve million dollars a year. When I departed, five-plus years later, Steve Florio, the obstreperous but somehow likable publisher, and I were within two million dollars of breaking even, and on target to get there within a year. (Five years after that, I was told, the losses had soared to twenty million dollars.) But turning the ship around for the long haul depended on reversing the perception that *The New Yorker* had lost its edge. The only way I could think of to bring that about was to attract new readers and advertisers by offering them new writers and sharper art: Even the famous cartoons had become too predictable.

Not that attracting writers was a problem. Almost every freelance writer was glad to appear in the magazine, both for the prestige and for the high rates we paid, though money was never spoken of. Mr. Shawn's method was simple: He accepted a piece, and the writer was paid whatever Shawn felt was appropriate. No discussions, no negotiations— and no complaints. This was certainly a tradition I could take to, after so many exhausting years of negotiating book contracts. Soon after I began, Lynn Nesbit offered me David Rieff's book on Miami for excerpting, and I decided I wanted to run a big hunk of it. "Wonderful," Lynn said. "What will you pay?" "When we've made our final cut and know how long it is, I'll send you a check." After a long moment she said, "You really mean it, don't you?" "Yep." It was the shortest negotiation we ever had. But when our check arrived, she and David were very happy.

One of the magazine's finest traditions had been its overseas reportage, which flowered during World War II and climaxed with *Hiroshima*. But by 1987, when I arrived, the tradition was dying. Jane Kramer was writing strong pieces from Europe, and Amos Elon from Israel, but most of the world was under-reported or unreported. I knew very little about journalism and very few journalists, so had to depend on good fortune to help me find new writers to match the old. The greatest stroke of fortune brought us Alma Guillermoprieto, whose daring and provocative reporting of the struggles in El Salvador and other Latin American countries had won her an enviable reputation.

But she wasn't a comfortable fit with *The Washington Post* and *Newsweek*, and when her agent, Liz Darhansoff (Tony Schulte's wife), proposed her to me, I grabbed her. Two quick, tough pieces about Nicaragua, and then she was in town and came to the office.

Yet again it was love at first sight—but who wouldn't love this strikingly handsome, fiercely determined, fearless, and funny person? When I invited her to become a staff writer, she hesitated—apparently she'd been thinking of going to Moscow for a few years to learn Russian. I was not amused. As she remembers it today, I said to her, "I'm going to tell you something, and I want you to listen carefully and repeat every word after me: Just because you're doing something well doesn't mean it's not worth doing! Let that be your mantra." Since Alma is a reliable reporter, I have to believe I actually said that, or something close to it.

So she stayed. I sent her everywhere, because I knew she'd come back from Bolivia or Brazil or her native Mexico with original and revelatory stories. (Readers of *The New Yorker* and *The New York Review of Books* are still benefitting from her driving curiosity and powerful prose.) I became her book editor, too, and she became a close family friend—staying with us again and again in New York or in the country. It's been more than twenty-five years now. Not only is she a MacArthur Fellow, but we see eye to eye on kitsch. Her only flaw is that she has bad feet—a legacy from her early years as a modern dancer—which hampered her when we tooled around Portugal and Spain together in 1998.

Alma was a pal of the amiable Ray Bonner—they had both been in serious danger when, embedded with the FMLN, they reported the Mozote massacre in Salvador, to the fury of the Reagan apologists for the ruling oligarchs there. Easygoing Ray was delighted to be dispatched anywhere, so I dispatched him first to Indonesia, where he spent six months gathering material for an authoritative report on that fourth-most-populous country in the world which no one seemed to know anything about. (We heard later that his two-part article became required reading at the State Department.) And then he did the same for Peru and Kuwait and Kenya and other far-flung locations, and with the same strong results and the same somewhat goofy what-the-hell approach to work and the magazine that made him so endearing. Equally hardworking and responsible, though perhaps more sober than goofy, was Milton Viorst, who parsed such knotty parts of the world as the Middle East for us and whose lucidity and good judgment made his subjects understandable to non-experts like me—and most of the rest of us.

It was also highly satisfying to be able to deploy young Mark Danner, who, when he sent me clips of his work, I pounced on. The reporting for his three-part piece on Haiti was remarkable, and I would gladly have sent him elsewhere, but he got trapped (for years) in trying to turn those pieces into a book. (Eventually he wrote a magisterial piece on the Salvador massacres for Tina.) But his being grounded in America made him available for a crucial job—writing "Comment," particularly important when Jonathan Schell departed. Mark was to a large extent our voice on the Gulf War, on Iraq, on Iran-contra. Everything about him was first-rate—his research, his intensity, his moral compass—except his work patterns. No one was ever later with copy; no one ever went on gnawing at it later in the day than he did. He drove the staff to madness, but he was worth it. I liked everything about him (including his mother, with whom I bonded instantly when he brought her into the office—to his intense embarrassment). Eventually he found the perfect home for himself at *The New York Review of Books*, where he had in fact started out as one of Robert Silvers's seemingly endless supply of talented young assistants.

I wanted a new shrewd take on the British—the inestimable Mollie Panter-Downes had retired in 1984—and talked Julian Barnes, whose novel *Flaubert's Parrot* I had bought for Knopf (which still publishes him), into contributing a series of penetrating and amusing reports, and, closer to home, prevailed on Joan Didion to write for us from California, her natural turf but to me almost as foreign as El Salvador or Indonesia. The last new reporter I welcomed to the magazine was David Remnick, whose writing from Russia in *The Washington Post* I greatly admired. We didn't coincide at the magazine for long, but he turned out to be the most fortunate hire of them all.

Meanwhile, many of the writers whom Shawn had brought in from the mid-sixties on were writing superbly. The one I knew best was, indeed, Jonathan Schell, Wally Shawn's roommate at Harvard, who in the eyes of many was like a third son to Shawn, and perhaps his favorite writer. Jonathan came to prominence with his powerful article "The Village of Ben Suc," which appeared in the magazine in 1967 and then as a book published by Knopf half a year before I arrived there. He became the leading editorial spokesman for *The New Yorker*'s (that is, Shawn's) political viewpoint, dominating the "Comment" section at the front of the magazine, and he was passionate and fearless—admired by many, including me, but considered self-important and humorless by some others. He wasn't, however, interested in popularity but in getting his message across.

In 1982 Jonathan wrote his alarming *The Fate of the Earth*, about the overwhelming dangers of nuclear war, which appeared almost simultaneously in the magazine and as a Knopf book. Shawn made it a condition of our proceeding that no one on the outside was to know even what the subject of the book was until the day it began running in *The New Yorker*: Not only could no advance galleys be sent out, but I wasn't allowed to tell our sales force anything but the name of the book and the author. At our sales conference I just announced that a book of major importance was on the way, and that the salesmen—and their bookstore customers—should just take my word for it that it would cause a sensation and would sell. Somehow it worked.

Shawn himself wrote the jacket copy, and I had the unenviable job of requesting certain changes—in other words, of editing the most admired editor in the world. I had no changes of substance to suggest, but his text had to be gentled into "selling" copy. In a long telephone conversation—the first extended conversation I ever had with Mr. Shawn—we went over it all, phrase by phrase, with ease and not the slightest resistance on his part. It was a lesson to me, and one I had internalized by the time I myself started writing and was dealing with younger editors who were clearly nervous of *me*, though how anyone could be nervous of me was beyond my understanding.

Jonathan was one of only three people other than Lillian Ross who left the magazine when I took over—a departure I very much regretted. (The others were Bill McKibben, who a few years later came back, and a minor fiction editor.) I regretted Jonathan's absence both personally and professionally, but most of all I regretted it for him. *The New Yorker* had been his home, and I believe that he never recovered from being ripped from it. My only severe criticism of Shawn is that he accepted this sacrifice from someone who loved him and whose loyalty to him was beyond doubt—accepted it, and clearly had expected it. I came to believe that Shawn would have been glad to see a mass departure from the magazine when he was, as he saw it, deposed.

The most satisfying (to me) group of writers I inherited was the extraordinary cadre of critics who were overall the most admired American writers in their fields. In dance there was Arlene Croce, in my view the finest mind ever to have engaged her subject and, coincidentally, a friend and author from my Knopf life. In jazz there was Whitney Balliett; in fashion, Kennedy Fraser; in photography, Janet Malcolm; in books, John Updike (among a number of others)—also the mainstay of the fiction department. And in baseball, there was (and still is) the incomparable Roger Angell. Most famous and/or notorious—and influential—was Pauline Kael. To this formidable list I slowly added Ingrid Sischy (to replace Malcolm on photography; Janet wanted out); Adam Gopnik on art (he had come to the magazine with me from Knopf); Claudia Roth Pierpont, with her highly original literary mind (and later a close friend); and Louis Menand. I never did succeed in finding equivalent talents to cover theater, television (Michael Arlen, alas, had retired from the field), or music—classical or pop—although I tried.

I also inherited a strong group of short-story writers, a number of whom I already knew and admired. Updike was the most prolific (and probably the most talented) of them; if he had a rival it was William Trevor. Alice Munro, a newcomer, was already a commanding voice—she, like Updike, was published by Knopf, though I was never their editor. There were Raymond Carver and Ann Beattie and Mavis Gallant and Deborah Eisenberg and the influential Donald Barthelme, and many more. But the fiction department was inhibited in its choices by a number of Mr. Shawn's strictures about language and subject matter. (Sex was a problem. In fact, mentions of all bodily functions except crying were likely to be vetoed.)

Since I was an editor and publisher of novels, I came with no ground rules about fiction, and so, automatically, the range of subject matter and style was able to expand. If we thought it was good, we published it. The "we" was the fiction department, who fed me material, plus myself, who was far more devoted to fiction than Shawn had been—like Ross before him, and David Remnick today, he had emerged from journalism. Here's how it worked: The numerous fiction editors included among others Chip, Daniel Menaker (himself an excellent short-story writer), Veronica Geng, and at the helm, the venerable, strong-minded (and sometimes grumpy but always generous) Roger Angell. One of them would like a story, present his arguments for it, pass it along to his colleagues, who would append their opinions, and whether or not there was a consensus—and very often there wasn't—it would come to me for judgment. I was always curious about these opinions, and respected the intensity and integrity behind them, but my own ideas about fiction were as strong as these, so there was no negotiation, just a quick yes or no. Well, somebody had to decide.

Dan Menaker, in his memoir, *My Mistake*, remembers my time as "perhaps the best professional years of my life, thanks to Gottlieb's eclectic taste in fiction and his willingness to take chances with new writers," and more, too embarrassing to quote. He cites, among many others, Jennifer Egan, Michael Cunningham, Allegra Goodman, Amy Bloom, Abraham Verghese, Richard Ford, and George Saunders. Among those I myself added to the mix were Anne Tyler and Margaret Atwood. And Haruki Murakami. Because I felt absolutely sure of myself in regard to fiction, this proved to be one of the easiest parts of my job, though I also enjoyed vetting the poetry which Alice Quinn, my old colleague and close friend from Knopf and later the magazine's poetry editor, passed by me. She was kind enough to act as if my comments were to the point.

The two funniest writers nurtured by Shawn were the much-loved and admired Ian (Sandy) Frazier, whose "casuals" were (and still are) hilarious and who developed into a substantial nonfiction writer, and the quirky, flirtatious fiction editor Veronica Geng. Veronica was both thorny and charming, her humor complicated and sometimes too oblique, but I liked her a great deal, and she got used to me after I survived a trial period during which she did her best to provoke me. I was very moved when she asked me to come to see her in the hospital, where, in her mid-fifties, she was dying of a brain tumor, and I was terribly saddened to see her in this dreadful state.

It was at the curious (because totally unorganized) gathering of her friends to celebrate her rather disorganized life—held in a little old-fashioned Italian funeral parlor on the Lower East Side—that I had a highly satisfactory encounter with one of Shawn's pets with whom I definitely didn't get along: his (then) daughter-in-law Jamaica Kincaid. When I took over, Jamaica had been working for a long time on an extended semi-autobiographical piece on colonialism in the Caribbean, where she had been born. When she turned it in, it was obvious to me that we couldn't possibly run this protracted, unmediated roar of rage. I went to her office and broke this unpleasant news, adding that since it had been commissioned, we would pay her the full amount she would have received if we had run it—this was standard *New Yorker* policy; Shawn didn't believe in kill fees. (I agreed with him. Something like this was our mistake as well as the writer's.)

Jamaica's anger at me was more or less on a par with her anger at colonialism, and I gathered that she bad-mouthed me long and loud. Suddenly in the dim funeral parlor I saw her bearing down on me—a ship in full sail. "Bob!" she said portentously; "Bob!" "Jamaica!" I said. "Bob, I owe you an apology." "You do?" "I misjudged you," she said. "I've come to realize that you're really a good person." "Well, that's very nice of you, Jamaica, but I didn't know we had a problem. Hope all's well with you," and I moved away. Undoubtedly, she had anticipated explanations and reconciliations in this highly public circumstance, but I saw no reason to gratify her. What had changed her mind about my deficiencies of character? I can only guess. Some time after

Mr. Shawn died, I was able to help his widow, Cecille, straighten out a problem she was having with some of Si's myrmidons, and since Jamaica was at that time married to one of Cecille's sons, this simple act of respect may have made a positive impression on her.

Another writer I was exasperated by was Pauline Kael, who for years had warred with Shawn over his efforts to rein her in. (Sometimes he won, sometimes she did.) Like almost everyone else, I admired her acuity and style, if not always her judgment, and I certainly recognized how important she was to our readers and to the world of movies. We hardly knew each other, but after I'd been on the job for a year or so, someone passed along to me a copy of an obscure journal in which she had gone out of her way to criticize the magazine and me. This was hardly a federal offense, but I felt it was uncivil and disloyal, considering that the magazine paid her way. I just sent the article down to her office with a note attached, saying, "Thanks for your support, Pauline." No answer, and since there was no reason for us to meet, we never did.

But I have a favorite memory of her, from an occasion years earlier. Maria, Lizzie, and I were spending the weekend at the house in Sheffield, Massachusetts, that Janet Malcolm and her husband, Gardner Botsford, had built, and Pauline, who lived nearby, came to dinner, arriving by taxi (she didn't drive) in her little white sneakers. By the time she left, she had managed to insult every one of us except ten-year-old Lizzie. Gardner had been her long-suffering editor for years, so the bile she directed at him made some kind of sense for someone who resented authority as much as Pauline did (she liked to refer to him as the Ripper). But she'd never met Maria or me. For instance, she said to Maria, "I was in your family's apartment once. Your father was carrying on, and I remember that your mother was a particularly ugly woman." This was not only gratuitous, it was nuts, since Laura Tucci was a famous beauty. Pauline's aggression was so gratuitous that all of us, including Janet's daughter, Anne, then about sixteen, and even Lizzie, went around for the rest of the weekend remembering more and more disagreeable things she had said. I don't even think it was deliberate—it was just who and what she was.

It was not surprising that we were at Janet's house. Sometime in the mid-seventies Maria, out in the common garden behind our house in Turtle Bay, spotted a young girl she had never seen before and thought, "Hah! A possible babysitter." The girl was Anne Malcolm, and she had just moved with her mother into a house almost directly opposite ours—Janet had recently married Gardner, and they had re-taken possession of the house where he had raised his first family. Anne came over to our place, she and Lizzie were instantly making play-dough ornaments together, the six-year difference in their ages vanished in an instant and forever, and soon we were bound to Janet and Anne in a familial intimacy that has never dimmed—Christmas dinner in our house for almost forty years; Anne and her husband, Richard, and their daughter, Sophy, with us in the country every Thanksgiving; to-gether in ups and downs. It was Janet who went with Maria to the child neurologist to hear the diagnosis of Nicky's dire condition, and Gardner who wept when he heard the verdict. Brilliant, quirky, adorable Anne spent a great part of her adolescence in our house—her own brilliant father, Donald Malcolm, yet another *New Yorker* writer, had died, and I was happy to be some kind of father or uncle or mentor or playmate for her, although I didn't do play-dough. (I did books, however, and that's where our minds met—particularly over Dorothy Dunnett.) And we all ganged up on Janet when she insisted that her cat, Despard (named by Anne for a Gilbert and Sullivan villain), would on request raise one paw as if to shake hands. Despard would be placed on the dining room table and Janet would murmur, "*Do* it, Despard," and the rest of us would chime in, "*Do* it, Despard. *Do* it, Despard." And yes, Janet, Despard *did* do it—when he chose to, and in no particular response to our blandishments. You can't turn a cat into a dog.

Among the other things Janet and I shared: any awards that came our way, beginning with something we referred to as the Golden Turd, a bronze sculpture she was given for her book *Psychoanalysis: The Impossible Profession*. (She, like me, had experienced—and benefited from—a full Freudian analysis.) It went back and forth between us at Christmas and birthdays, and was even slipped into each other's houses through our back doors, until one Christmas she lost it in a taxi going home after dinner. But we Freudians know why people "lose" things.

Because Janet's writing is so formidable, people assume that *she's* that way too, and she can be. But for us she's nearest and dearest. Our bedroom window looked out across the garden and down into her kitchen, and we'd be endlessly on the phone while she cooked. When Anne hosted teenage overnight parties, Janet would come over and sleep on our living-room sofa. Sometimes we squabbled—so what? And we managed to get through and past the awkwardness that naturally arose when I took over from Shawn—Gardner was a child of *The New Yorker* (his stepfather being the owner, Raoul Fleischmann), and I was a professional outsider even if I was a domestic insider.

One lunchtime—it was a beautiful Sunday in June in the early eighties, well before I left Knopf for *The New Yorker*—I got home from a thrilling trip to a flea market downtown and found the house empty and the back door to the garden open. That meant the family was over at Janet's, and when I walked a few steps down the center path, there they were eating lunch in the Botsford garden: Maria, Lizzie, Nicky, and Maria's father, Nika Tucci. And the Botsford-Malcolm clan. And a man and woman I didn't know. Introductions, but I didn't catch the names. I had some food and left—the man gave off what I felt to be so powerful an aura of narcissism, of overwhelming self-satisfaction, that I literally couldn't bear to be in his presence. That evening when I called Janet to apologize for leaving so abruptly, I asked who this man was. "Jeffrey Masson," she said; "the person I mentioned to you whom I'm writing about." "How can you spend time with someone like that?" Janet just laughed. Meanwhile, Maria had told me that when Nika was introduced to Masson, he said, "I believe I've met one of your ex-girlfriends," to which Masson replied, "I've had so many, I can't really remember them all." To which Nika responded, "I feel sorry for you."

So Janet wrote *In the Freud Archives*, which was published first in *The New Yorker* and then by me at Knopf. And there followed the famous lawsuit brought against her by Jeffrey Masson—one technical aspect of which went to the Supreme Court. My second and last encounter with Masson took place when he and I were both being deposed in the

Knopf offices. He was cordial, I was cordial, and I had the exact same feeling I had had about him before. Fortunately, justice was done and Janet was exonerated. But I had learned a lesson about the overwhelming need of narcissists to be in the right, and to punish those by whom they feel slighted. The key issue in the Masson-Malcolm controversy had to do with several things Janet had quoted him as saying but for which she couldn't find the notebook that contained her handwritten notes. Some years later, the missing notebook was found, when Janet's two-year-old granddaughter, Sophy, crawling around a room and pulling books from low shelves as tots will do, pulled it out! There were the handwritten notes, just as Janet had testified to them. Justice had already been done, but if there were any lingering doubts, this singular turn of events put a stop to them.

The New Yorker checking department came under tremendous pressure during the trial. It had already been traumatized by the uproar involving the legal actions among Renata Adler, General Westmoreland, CBS, and *Time* over pieces written by Renata for the magazine (also later published as a book by Knopf). She had never been a favorite of the checkers—they felt, rightly or wrongly, that they had been sandbagged by her in the Westmoreland crisis.

I knew Renata well, having edited (if that's the word) her second novel, *Pitch Dark*, almost losing my mind, or at least my cool. She was talented, she was amusing, she was cooperative, but she couldn't make up her mind—things were changed, re-changed, de-changed. No comma, let alone word or phrase, escaped her frantic need to second- (third? fourth?) guess herself. My fondness for her carried me through this ordeal by irresolution.

It did not survive the ordeal of the Robert Bork Supreme Court nomination, in 1987, about half a year after I arrived at *The New Yorker*. It was Renata who wrote the magazine's savage (and, in my view, justified) denunciation of Bork as a potential justice, and I gave her the entire "Talk of the Town"/"Comment" section to state her case. At that time, every issue closed on Monday afternoon, but on this occasion we didn't finish until after two a.m. In my office had gathered the usual team: the writer (Renata), the editor of the piece (myself), the checker, and the official "closer," whose job it was to make sure that everyone's fixes were incorporated in the final proof. On this occasion the closer was Eleanor Gould, the genius copy editor who did proofs on every piece of nonfiction the magazine ran—Shawn's favorite of favorites, and quickly mine, too. But the problems here were not copyediting ones, they were questions of fact, or the verification of facts.

Our chief checker, Martin Baron, the intensity of whose devotion to our enterprise was on a par with Miss Gould's, and who felt burned by the Westmoreland experience, took us slowly through his proof, point by point and contention by contention. Renata was comfortable in embattled positions, and as the discussion grew more and more heated, her stance grew more and more combative. After four or five hours of negotiation, everything came down to one particular assertion for which Martin could find no verification. Naturally, Renata defended it.

The more I considered it, the more I felt justified on insisting that without supporting evidence it had to be removed—and the more strongly she insisted that it stay. Since time immemorial (1925, when the magazine started publication), it was a given that no word could be changed without the writer's agreement, a tradition I wholeheartedly supported. But I was under no obligation to run a piece I felt was both factually fragile and legally dangerous. As we approached two in the morning, I said to Renata that if she didn't abide by my decision, I would have to abort the piece, however much I admired it, and somehow fill the "Talk" section with other material we had on hand. She yielded but stormed from the room. And she didn't forgive me, as became evident when, in 1999, she published her memoir, *Gone: The Last Days of "The New Yorker,"* so far from reliable that it was a sitting duck for a piece I wrote about it (and Lillian's memoir too) for *The New York Observer.* Only very recently, when, to our mutual surprise, we found ourselves sitting next to each other on a plane and having a happy conversation, was the breach healed.

That Monday night, I was later told, was the latest closing in the history of the magazine, but no one present was fazed by that. I begged the septuagenarian Miss Gould not to come in the next day, but she looked at me as if I were crazy. "Since Freddie died," she said—her husband, Frederick Packard, had been another mainstay at the magazine—"it's been the easiest time of my life. I can stay up till all hours, I can work weekends, I don't have to cook. Of course I'll be in tomorrow." That was Eleanor.

Eleanor Gould, who worked at the magazine for just under fifty-five years, was given (by Ross, I think) the title "the Grammarian." (I would have called her the Indefatigable.) All day, every day—did she ever call in sick?—she sat in her office skimming her pencil over our long proofs and leaving them covered, often every inch of them, by her snail marks that made strong men and women tremble. The first piece I myself edited (Eleanor would have removed that "myself") was the first piece Caroline Alexander wrote for us. She was an American classicist now at Oxford, in her early twenties, who, with her sister and a friend, somehow got backing to go on an expedition to northern Borneo to investigate the infected insects that were destroying plants there. What she wrote was not only revelatory (about virus-infected insects *and* Borneo plantations) but fluent and charming. And utterly unexpected. This piece, by a writer new to the magazine, was my baptism of fire both with a Gould proof and with the lengths to which *New Yorker* checkers would go to confirm details: Martin Baron tracked down a British plantation owner in Sabah to discuss (among other things) how he and Caroline could have seen the moon over the waters from his veranda on a given evening.

As for the Gould proof, I had never seen anything like it—the tiny handwriting, the long lines and arrows snaking around every page, filling every margin, and not just asking questions of grammar but raising issues of logic, sense, and indirection. It paralyzed me. And when I finally got to work on it, I could absorb only two galleys a day. Most of Miss Gould's emendations were frighteningly on target, and as I slogged through them, I accepted most of her proposed changes, dismissing only a few that seemed exaggerated or misguided. Over time, I learned how to read the Gould proof—always with respect but less slavishly. *She* didn't care: She had done her job, now it was up to the rest of us to take it or leave it.

Susan Sontag left it—and then took it. She and I were working in my office on one of the few pieces she wrote for the magazine. She knew all about the Gould proof and demanded to see it. At first she was furious—who was this person whose pencil had marched all over her prose? Then, suddenly, she saw the light. "Wait a minute," she said. "This woman is a genius! What a mind! I have to meet her and thank her!" I explained that Eleanor had recently turned deaf, but nothing daunted Susan, so I walked her over to Eleanor's office and wrote a note explaining who this was. Susan then wrote an effusive note of thanks and compliments. Eleanor seemed to be pleased. On our way back to my office, Susan said, "If only I could have Miss Gould do a reading on everything I write!" I'm surprised she didn't make it happen—what Susan wanted, Susan got. Only recently did I realize who it was that she had always reminded me of: Kate Hepburn. The same ruthless determination, the same sense of privilege, the same get-out-of-my-way stride. And the same charm.

There was nothing daunting about Eleanor in person. Immediately she had me calling her by her first name—at first I was too respectful to address her as anything but Miss Gould. Eventually she was able to confide in me about a family problem, and I was able to be helpful, or at least comforting. And then disaster struck: One day she suddenly became totally deaf. In my awful handwriting I told her we would have a car and driver carry her to and from work every day. "Of course not," she said. "No reason I can't take the bus." And she took it, until she suffered a stroke (at her desk, of course) when she was eighty-two.

Eleanor went into attack mode when she first encountered the work of Diane Ackerman, whose riveting piece on bats I ran in 1988—a piece that had a radical influence on the way bats were perceived and treated in America. But Diane wrote in a somewhat flowery style, and Eleanor *hated* it, although she admired what Diane had to say. Diane was partly toned down, Eleanor was partly finessed, and we went on to publish other fascinating Ackerman takes on nature—one on sexing crocodiles (it began with Diane and a bunch of scientists groping inside the cloacae of sedated crocodiles, because—who knew?—you can't determine their gender from the outside). More tug-of-war over the Gould proof. And then, in the margin of a piece about penguins in the Antarctic, Eleanor marked a page of her proof with a big star and wrote, "The writing in this paragraph justifies this entire piece!" And as evidence that she had been hooked, she took her daughter on an Antarctic cruise.

Caroline Alexander wrote several other superb pieces for us before going on to write her bestseller, *The Endurance*, about Shackleton's ill-fated Antarctic expedition. Diane Ackerman also became a much-admired and bestselling writer (*A Natural History of the Senses*). But their careers at the magazine—and those of other excellent nonfiction writers, like Sue Hubbell, whose great subject was bees—more or less ended after I left, since their subjects weren't of much interest to Tina. But then *my* predecessor, Mr. Shawn, wouldn't have been as interested in cafeterias or Scottie conventions as I was.

It seems odd to me now that going to *The New Yorker* intensified my interest in America's "fly-over country." I was a born-and-bred New Yorker, who had turned eastward—that is, to England—for a second lodestar. It was those Middle America flea-market trips with Martha that began to open up our country to me—certainly, I came to like the Midwest, and to admire many of the people we casually encountered there. If you eat in enough diners you begin to get a sense of the way the locals live, and who they are. Traveling with Jane and Michael Stern gave us some specific goals: checking out a crab-cake joint in Maryland, or that fried-chicken Mecca in Nebraska City, Nebraska. We had also been with the Sterns, whose book *Elvis World* we were then publishing, at Graceland, for the tenth anniversary of Elvis's death, zipping up and down the lawns on golf carts while mourners stared from behind the famous gates ornamented with musical clefs. Many, many years later I was sent an item from a Minnesota newspaper revealing that Elvis was alive and well, and hanging out in my house in Miami Beach. If only!

As I've reported, I was collecting Scottie artifacts in those days—maybe the less pretentious "amassing" would be the more *juste* word—and, learning from the Scottie collectors' newsletter of a convention just for them, I invited Jane and Michael to cover it for the magazine, which they did briskly, amusingly but not condescendingly, and accurately. (This event is still held annually—in Cincinnati, in case you're interested.) This was my first editorial foray into something that more elegant types saw as kitsch but I saw as an odd and touching phenomenon. There were those at the magazine who were not charmed, but that was their problem, not mine. And then the Sterns wrote a first-rate two-part piece about cafeterias in the Midwest and the South—together, we had carried our trays, blue Jell-o and all, to our tables in many of them. Why not report from the Midwest and Georgia as well as from London, Paris, and Miami? No one, after all, reproached us for publishing Calvin (Bud) Trillin's beloved pieces about the food in his hometown, Kansas City, and all the rest of his celebrated work about down-home and eccentric America.

I also got some flak over a few "outrageous" covers I ran. But the cover art needed shaking up, and so to some extent did the cartoons. To be in charge of *The New Yorker*'s cartoons was an extraordinary turn of events for someone who had been dazzled by them since childhood; and fortunately for me, our art director, Lee Lorenz, himself a prolific cartoonist, was both a good administrator and a good-natured collaborator. As he and Shawn had done, we met once a week for Lee to show me sketches and notions submitted by the regulars, which I would encourage or nix, and then to consider the finished art for cartoons previously okayed. Art directors are a funny breed—often defensive in relation to "word" people, who they suspect look down on them a little, but well disposed if they come to respect your eye. I have absolutely no visual imagination—I simply can't visualize—but I'm strong at layout and at improving visual material I can actually see. (After all, I oversaw literally thousands of book jackets over a twenty-five-year stretch.) After a while, Lee grew more cheerful listening to me on matters of sizing, cropping, adjusting. And he certainly agreed that we needed to cut down on the old standard subjects—two people stranded on a desert island, the couple in bed (not always married, at least to each other), the king addressing his disaffected subjects. (Some of these old friends are still with us.) Cartoonists, like most humorists, are sensitive plants, and Lee had to juggle their needs and feelings in tandem with mine. As with our writers, I felt an obligation to keep the older ones in business as well as to attract the new.

Among Lee's (and Shawn's) major finds had been Roz Chast, Ed Koren, Sempé, and Bruce McCall, whose *Zany Afternoons*, which we had published at Knopf, was just about the funniest book I ever had anything to do with. I was grateful for all of them. As time went by I encouraged the farther-out work of Danny Shanahan, John O'Brien, and the demented, surreal Glen Baxter, both a great cult and popular success in Britain, whose humor was not exactly up *The New Yorker*'s old alley. But it was up mine, and Lee nervously accommodated himself to the Mad Colonel, and I think, or at least hope, came to appreciate him. A typical Baxter caption, though not one that necessarily appeared in the magazine: "As a way of filling brooks with guacamole, it was clearly in a class of its own." Or try, "I was dealing with a dangerous man who might at any moment burst into a selection from 'The Paul McCartney Songbook.'" If they don't make you laugh, probably Lee Lorenz would agree with you.

I simply fell in love with the magazine's processes, not only the meetings with Lee but the daily interactions with the checkers and copy editors. Book publishing doesn't allow for much checking, and although at Knopf we had excellent copy editors and proofreaders, there was never time for the kind of intense perusal of text that *The New Yorker* not only indulged in but demanded. I had always done a great deal of line editing, but this was on a new level, and I relished it, happily turning in proofs on every piece of fiction and nonfiction that we ran. (Ross and Shawn, I'm sure, had done the same.) Just in case all this wasn't keeping me busy enough, I was also still editing certain Knopf authors—Barbara Tuchman, Bob Caro, and others. And I was indulging my determination to get back to writers at the latest on the day after I received a piece from them, and often the same day or evening. Why wait? And more to the point, why make *them* wait?

One of the questions I've been asked most frequently was whether I found the pace of a weekly magazine more difficult to keep up with than what I was used to in book publishing, where everything takes an eternity to happen. But the reality was that once I knew what I was doing, it proved to be far easier and less stressful than what I'd been used to. If I did my basic job—keeping the supply of good material steady—each issue fell into place almost automatically. Only "Talk" and "Comment" could be last-minute crises. Yes, certain writers, particularly among the critics, could be late with their copy, but delinquencies of that kind were hardly crises. Most of the time everything flowed naturally, because the individual departments were so strong, so experienced, and so dedicated. And as for my reading, gulping down even the longest piece was nothing after a lifetime of gulping down seven-hundred-page novels or biographies.

Equally surprising was that, in essence, putting out one issue was more or less like putting out another: The content changed, of course, but the form and structure of the magazine remained the same. And you only had to do it fifty-two times a year. Whereas in book publishing, you were more or less re-inventing the wheel for almost every book—perhaps 150 times a year. Every book had its own needs, its own specificities, its own problems: an angry author, a difficulty with the title, the jacket design, the jacket copy, the binding, the copyediting, the pricing. There were countless steps along the way to a finished book and any one of them could go wrong—and all too often did. If you were the editor of a book, there could be textual difficulties and tensions with the author. If you were the publisher, your energy went into lighting fires to ignite interest in every book while putting out fires that flared up during the process. And then there was the emotional stress of a nasty review, a dissatisfied author (and complaining agent), a writer abandoning ship, an ugly contract negotiation. Or, alas, an out-and-out blatant failure. Since I myself edited twenty to thirty books a year, and published the entire list, I lived in constant turmoil. (Not that I disliked it—until I did.) So in a way *The New Yorker* was a rest cure.

What did disconcert me, though, was my changed relationship to writers. In book publishing, it's the writer who has the final authority, and properly so: It's his or her book, not yours. But if it's the writer's book, it's the editor's magazine. As I was to discover at *The New Yorker*, it's the editor who's in charge, and the writer who's there at the editor's pleasure. In other words, writers had to please me, not the other way around, which is what I was used to. I found this not only disconcerting but disturbing—it was against the natural order of things. I was perfectly comfortable being the boss of a staff, but I didn't enjoy being the boss of writers.

There were times when having that much authority over a writer carried with it unenviable responsibility. When someone was in trouble, it became a family affair, and the Editor was the head of the family. So it rightly was I who had the responsibility of coping with the harrowing collapse of Penelope Gilliatt into desperate alcoholism, and into distressing behavior that affected everyone around her. Like all our staff writers who worked in New York, she had an office of her own, which over a period of time became a pigsty, and one that smelled. She would make scenes, sleep overnight in the office—it was a condition that had been worsening for years, and had got to a point where something had to be done, both to help her and to help calm the disturbances she caused others, particularly her neighbors.

With her flaming red hair, Penelope had been a golden girl—ravishingly beautiful and sexy; famous for her difficult marriage to the playwright John Osborne, known for her relationships with Mike Nichols and Edmund Wilson, among others, and now together with the *New York Times* movie critic Vincent Canby (an extremely nice guy, two of whose novels I had worked on at Knopf). She was also a highly talented writer, who wrote for the magazine in many capacities. For a long time she (uncomfortably) shared the job of film critic with Pauline, each of them covering six months of the year; she wrote profiles (of John Cleese and Jonathan Miller, among others); she produced excellent short stories. She had also written well-received novels as well as the screenplay for *Sunday Bloody Sunday.* In other words, she was a valuable and valued writer for us, even surviving the scandal of having been found guilty of plagiarism in a piece she wrote about Graham Greene.

What to do? I had heard of "interventions" and, after discussions with our admirable Human Resources (née Personnel) director, Ruth Diem, decided to hold one. It took place in Chip's office, and when I asked Penelope to join me there, she encountered not only Chip, myself, Martha, Ruth, Vincent, and an intervention expert, but her sister, whom we had flown in from England. It was dire. She went through what I had learned were all the classic stages: confusion, outrage, denial, fury, wracking sobs, and the refusal to take any kind of action. Which left me with the only weapon I had at my disposal, telling her forcefully that unless she accepted our plan for her, her days not only in her office but at *The New Yorker* were over. Ruth had already explored the possibilities for a case like Penelope's and had identified one of the finest cure institutions in the east, and made the necessary arrangements. We, of course, would pay for everything.

It was horrible having to employ a threat this way, but it was effective—with Penelope, as with so many others, her life at the magazine was to a large degree her identity, and she couldn't bear to lose it. Martha and Ruth saw her off to the designated place in Connecticut, she spent six weeks there drying out, and then they put her on a plane to Minnesota, since the next stage in her recovery was to take place at a clinic there. She got off the plane, went into an airport bar, got drunk, and never turned up at the clinic, nor did she ever return to *The New Yorker.* And she died a year or so later. The intervention had come too late—probably decades too late—and her brain had essentially been destroyed by the alcohol she had consumed.

But this painful episode was unique, and on the whole there was very little tension for me in the relatively calm waters of *The New Yorker.* The magazine could fail or disappoint in the long run, but there were no direct consequences from issue to issue. There was, of course, always the looming question of profitability. Despite Si's unstinting support of the magazine, it was no fun for me to preside over a ship that was leaking money. And who knew how long Si's tolerance, and that of his associates, would last? I wished I could help, but though I knew how to sell books, I didn't know how to sell ads. And given the famous, and basic, separation of Church and State—of Editorial and Business—even if I'd known how, I wouldn't have got involved. The few times I came close, I regretted it keenly.

During these *New Yorker* years I was still going occasionally to

Europe, but twice I went in the opposite direction: to Japan, both times with my great friend Ingrid Sischy, who had come into our lives a few years earlier when Janet Malcolm wrote an extended profile of her for the magazine: "A Girl of the Zeitgeist." (Ingrid was then the editor of *Artforum.*) Author and subject became friends, and through Janet, Ingrid and I did too, and eventually I brought her to the magazine, partly to write, partly to help redesign "Goings On About Town."

Ingrid was well-connected in Japan's art and architecture worlds, and in 1990, after she had become the editor of Andy Warhol's *Interview* magazine—talk about Girl of the Zeitgeist!—we went to Japan together for the first time: me to be a judge for a new translation award being given by Japan's largest publishing house, Kodansha (it owned one hundred magazines). The judges' panel included Donald Keene, the dean of American Japanese studies, and the not-yet Nobel Prize winner Kenzaburō Ōe. The high point of the evening on which the adjudication took place came after dinner as we were all being ushered into our separate limousines and the owner of the restaurant presented each of us with a farewell gift as he bowed us out: a pair of Christian Dior black socks. Why? Being mere Westerners, we'll never know.

Ingrid was in Tokyo to see Japanese fashion people, the most important being Rei Kawakubo of Comme des Garçons, and she begged me to go with her to have lunch with Rei—the only person I ever knew confident Ingrid to be nervous of. And how not! Rei was impenetrable in her severe all-black look (those inky-black glasses!) and her *dédaigneuse* manner. But since I didn't really know who she was, I plunged right in, asking her personal questions and teasing her. Her PR person and Ingrid were clearly in terror, but soon the dark glasses were off and we were giggling.

Two unlikely sequels. She, who never gave interviews, agreed to be interviewed for *Interview* if I would do the interviewing, and even changed her New York dates until I would be available. Even more unlikely was her asking me first in Tokyo, and later through her PR person in New York, to appear as a model on the runway for her Paris collection for men—surely the ultimate in living camp. I had to find a tactful way of saying no, much as I was tempted by the sheer lunacy of the idea, and at her third request, sent her a message saying I was sure that she, being so fanatic about her privacy, would understand the reticence of someone who was equally private. She did understand, and to prove it, sent me as a gift a black Comme des Garçons jacket. You can imagine what I looked like in it.

Two years later, Ingrid and I went back to Japan, me for the second Kodansha prize. But this time we shared a journalistic goal: exploring for a long piece Ingrid would write for the magazine the all-girl, all-singing, all-dancing Takarazuka theater troupe, three hundred strong, which had fascinated me both when it appeared at Radio City Music Hall and in Tokyo, where I had seen it several times on my previous trip. (On one occasion, I was one of only three men in the vast auditorium—the other two were embarrassed fathers chaperoning their daughters.)

We went to the town of Takarazuka itself and spent days watching rehearsals and performances, observing how the girls were trained, and staying in the Takarazuka Hotel, all the other guests middle-aged well-to-do women revisiting, or reliving, the passion they had felt as girls for the young Takarazuka women who took the male roles, some of them giving the girls presents and even money. (When Ingrid's piece reporting this eventually ran, in my final issue of the magazine, the Takarazuka officials were not amused.) Among the set-piece narratives I was able to see were their greatest hit, *The Rose of Versailles* (Marie-Antoinette), *As You Like It*, and several dramas depicting famous moments in Japanese history. Alas, I missed their other greatest success, *Gone with the Wind*, although I do have on tape their *Great Gatsby*.

For the first three years or so of my stay at the magazine, Si was demonstratively pleased with what I was doing—particularly with the redesign of the "Goings On About Town" section at the front of the book, which had been dismally lifeless, and which, with Ingrid's help, I was able to re-invigorate. He read every issue cover to cover, and with insight, but he never made a single editorial suggestion; that would have been totally contrary to what he felt the owner's role should be. In his mind, editors were sacred—until they were history. In fact, he had an almost romantic notion of the editor's role. A number of times he said to me wistfully that the two jobs he would most have liked to have had were directing movies and editing a magazine.

He had, indeed, a compelling interest in magazines as such—he saw them as vital phenomena, as pots that had to be kept at a boil, or at least a simmer. I, on the other hand, had no interest in magazines beyond the quality of their content. For me, the essential thing about *The New Yorker* had always been the consistency of its quality punctuated by the editorial surprises it sprung; I had always considered it on a week-by-week basis, and I suppose I curated it as if it were a weekly anthology rather than concerning myself with its overall editorial development.

But Si lived on change—he needed to make things happen; it wasn't good enough to be good, he liked shake-up for its own sake. And he also shot from the hip. Once he saw a deficiency, it had to be cured instantly. That he accepted Shawn's continuing editorship when he so disapproved of it was evidence of a level of self-control I never would have thought him capable of. So that once I began to sense that he was growing dissatisfied with what I was (or wasn't) doing, I understood that sooner or later he would decide to replace me.

Our monthly lunches (sandwiches in his office—my choice), showed him increasingly restless. He couldn't articulate what it was he wanted, but he wanted something. I inferred from things he said that he was under family pressure. His closest colleague and lifelong best friend was his brother, Donald, who oversaw the newspaper and broadcast arms of what was in essence a family business, and Donald wasn't particularly interested in *The New Yorker.* There were uncles, sons, nephews, none of whom shared Si's feeling for it and to whom, I could sense, his indulgence of it was an increasing irritation—it was hardly a secret that he had overpaid to acquire it. Si was a hardheaded businessman, but he was also a believer, and a secret romantic. That was not the case with the rest of the clan, as I came to know them.

Even so, my head was partly in the sand until we got together in Florida one winter weekend. Si's mother-in-law, Victoria's mother, lived in Palm Beach, and the Newhouses regularly visited her there. They had once driven down to see my place in Miami Beach, and on this occasion I had driven up to spend a day or two with them. Si and I went for a long walk on the beach, and he more or less told me that he felt he had to do something radical about the magazine, since I either couldn't or wouldn't. (It was both.) I wouldn't even agree to reduce the number of issues we put out every year from fifty-two to fifty or forty-eight: I believed we had an obligation to show up on our readers' doorsteps every week of the year. We were a *weekly*. This, remember, was back in 1992—a different world. Who could imagine the direction in which print journalism was heading?

Only a few months later, when I went to Si's office for lunch, he said, "I want to tell you this right away. I've decided to replace you." And before I could respond, he went on to say how upset he was—in fact, that he hadn't been able to sleep the night before. He immediately wanted to outline his financial plans for me, but I interrupted him to say that, first, I needed to know what he would do to protect Martha and Chip, my closest colleagues, and when he asked what I proposed, he instantly agreed to what I came up with. Then he told me what he was doing for me, which was in essence to make me financially secure (and beyond secure) for the rest of my life, and the same for Maria if I predeceased her. Was that okay?

I suggested two minor tweaks to the plan, which he accepted without hesitation—I had the sense that he was so upset, he would have agreed to just about anything. In fact, he was far more upset than I was. I remember saying to him that he had no reason to feel bad about any of this; that he had kept all his promises to me, had been amazingly generous, and that his firing me was not going to affect our friendship. I also told him I had no intention of going back into publishing to run a rival house to Knopf; in fact, that I didn't want to be a publisher at all any longer. What I thought I'd do was go back to Knopf simply as an editor—work with some of my old authors and maybe acquire a few new ones—with no managerial duties and at no salary: I was going to be paid a lot of money by him and would feel better actually earning some of it. So, without any forethought, I settled my fate in a moment. This entire conversation lasted under fifteen minutes.

The only outstanding issue was our timetable. Si hadn't yet, he said, settled on my successor, although he must already have had Tina Brown under consideration: She had done a bang-up job for him at *Vanity Fair.* Or perhaps they had agreed to agree but hadn't concluded their deal—somehow I suspect that *those* negotiations took longer than fifteen minutes. In any case, there would be time to prepare for the changeover. As it happened, I was leaving shortly for my second trip to Japan with Ingrid, and there was no reason for me not to go.

Meanwhile, I needed time to internalize the change all this was going to make in my life. And to deal with the chagrin that anyone must feel on being fired (it had never happened to me before), and in what would inevitably be so public a way. I bolstered my bruised amour propre the way I imagine all people do who've been fired: by telling myself that I'd done a good job, or at least the job I had set out to do. Certainly the magazine was stronger editorially than it had been when I took over, and the staff and writers had easily survived the trauma of Shawn's departure. Also, as much as I had enjoyed the work, and the people, I suspected that I wasn't really going to miss the somewhat mechanical and predictable nature of the job. It would be back to reinventing the wheel with every new book I got involved with.

It took me a few days to tell the very few people who had to know before I left for Japan—Maria and Lizzie, of course, and Martha and Chip, whose lives were also going to be disrupted. And as we got on our plane, I told Ingrid, since I could hardly keep a secret like this from someone I was going to be spending every day with for several weeks. It was while I was in Japan that Si called me to say that he had settled on Tina, and that the announcement was going to be made the following day. Also to ask what he termed a favor: Since she needed some kind of break between jobs, and then would need time at the magazine to get her team (and herself) ready to take over, would I agree to stay on for nine weeks?

I saw it as a favor to me—the opportunity to run pieces I was afraid might not survive a new regime, and also to help make the transition easier for everyone, including myself. During those nine weeks, for instance, I was able to print the last of John McPhee's admirable extended reports on geological phenomena, which I suspected might not engage Tina.

As soon as Si told me that we were going public, I aborted the Japan junket and headed for New York, to take charge of the transition and to relieve Maria, at home, and Martha, in the office, who had been coping with the scores of calls that were pouring in, mostly of condolence. (They had always liked each other, but now they came to understand and respect each other's steel.) But I didn't see why condolences were appropriate. No one had died, no one was in danger—unless you felt that the magazine was in danger, and I didn't, though it would certainly experience culture shock. Tina's taste was not popular at *The New Yorker*, and for most of the staff and writers it really did seem like a case of the barbarian at the gates. No doubt they had forgotten that the last barbarian at the gates had been me, and that I had turned out okay.

My chief responsibilities in the upcoming nine weeks, as I saw them, were to get the magazine out smoothly, clear the decks for Tina and help ease her into the job, and—most important—help keep colleagues calm, sensible, and positive. That was the hard part. Once Tina was on the premises, she and her staff setting up camp on another floor from mine, I showed her what ropes she wanted to be shown. For instance, it didn't make sense for me to be commissioning cartoons that she might not find funny when they came in finished, so I invited her to join my weekly art meetings with Lee Lorenz and to speak up. She hardly did, although once she looked at a finished piece of art and asked, "Is it funny?" She wasn't being sarcastic, she just wanted to know.

Tina was of necessity talking to our writers about what they were doing and wanted to do, as well as to new writers in whom she was interested. Martha was leaving with me, to become a literary agent, but Tina was welcoming both to Chip and to my terrific and beloved assistant, Chris Knutsen, who stayed on to become managing editor before making a foray into book publishing, then back into magazines, always remaining a close friend of mine and of Lizzie's as well—today, their kids are good friends too. There was absolutely no unpleasantness in any aspect of the transition—Tina behaved impeccably and I did too. And why not? I certainly had no quarrel with her—in fact, I had never met her. And although I wasn't sympathetic to her editorial impulses, that wasn't her fault. She had obviously been hired to do what she had done at *Vanity Fair*: make the magazine "hot, hot, hot" (to use a favorite phrase of hers), which I couldn't have done and wouldn't have done even if I could.

In the event, the biggest change that took place wasn't her determination to have everything hot, or her introducing more photography and color into the magazine, but the shift of *The New Yorker* from being about writers to being about subjects. And although as a reader I deplored the change, I kept my mouth shut, despite endless provocation from others who felt the way I did and wanted me to join in their highly vociferous condemnation.

Besides, Tina herself—although, like Si, she thrived on excitement—was good to people and identified and rewarded ability. For instance, she detected the talent in Nancy Franklin, then an editor and occasional "Talk" writer, and gave her the opportunity to shine as the magazine's television critic, and she spotted David Remnick's capacities apart from his talents as a reporter, and deployed them so fruitfully that Si had someone to turn to five years later, when his and Tina's professional romance had petered out.

The hardest aspect of my remaining time at the magazine was trying to soothe the anxieties of those who were unhappy and confused. Should they stay? Should they leave? My advice was the same for everyone: Try it for a while to see how you feel, then go elsewhere if you're really miserable or remain if all is more or less well, which it's likely to be; just don't stay on if you're bitter. People did stay on and many flourished; others drifted away after a while. (Chip, for instance, left to become editor of *The New York Times Book Review*.) Today, twenty-four years later, many of my old colleagues are still contentedly working away at the magazine, having survived my arrival and departure, Tina's arrival and departure, David's long reign, the Condé Nast takeover of many of the magazine's functions, the move of the office down to the World Trade Center, and the digital revolution. Luckily for people like us, the world may have changed but our actual work remains more or less the same.

My departure was punctuated by a big party, for which my author and friend the great choreographer Paul Taylor offered me the use of his house and garden. It was the opposite of a wake, unless wakes are jolly and fond; best of all, as I remember it, there were no speeches. Or maybe I've just blanked them out. The farewell I most cherished came on my last day in the office, a Friday. Chip was away, so I was closing "The Talk of the Town" alone with Eleanor Gould, who was far from being a sentimentalist, and who was still stone deaf. As she was going out the door she turned and, screeching the way some deaf people do, said, "We're going to miss you!" I grabbed a piece of paper and wrote, "I'm going to miss you, too, Eleanor, and thank you for everything." Then she said, and she was really shouting now, "Before you came, we were all afraid you wouldn't respect our way of doing things. But from the moment I saw your first proof, I knew you were a *kindred spirit*!" I thought then, and think now, that this was the greatest compliment I've ever received.

WORKING

Knopf Redux

GOING BACK TO KNOPF, in 1992, seemed completely natural to me—probably because I'd never totally left. Throughout my stint at *The New Yorker* I was working on Knopf books, which meant I was working with all my old colleagues and friends. In fact, many of them are still at Knopf as I write, in 2016: One of the firm's greatest strengths has been the continuity of its staff, which Sonny Mehta not only encouraged but relished. As for Sonny himself, we had always been on good terms, and by this time he was so firmly, and successfully, in charge that my glancing presence could hardly ruffle him, and indeed he welcomed me back warmly.

Even so, I went to extreme lengths to be invisible, which was easy to do since I hadn't the slightest interest in any aspect of the operation other than editing "my" books and seeing them through the publishing process. Apparently I had exhausted my need to run things—I was into my sixties and had been a boss for twenty-five or so years. Not only did I make sure that my modest office was not on the editorial/publishing floor—I shuffled around between the production department and my favorite place, the sales department—but for an entire year I never once set foot on editorial or publishing turf. Finally a day came when I had to escort a writer up to the publicity department, and I broke the ice. No one, of course, had taken notice of my self-conscious non-presence.

To my surprise, almost immediately there was plenty for me to do. Apart from going on with writers I'd edited for years—Chaim Potok, Mordecai Richler, Toni Morrison—I found myself back with John le Carré. Our extremely successful relationship had extended itself with *The Russia House* when I was at *The New Yorker*, but I could tell that he was restless, and when he dedicated it to me I sensed it was a gesture meant to smooth the way for him to move on—David rarely did things without a complicated reason; overthinking was his habit of mind. But in this case he was right: he needed to be directly connected to the heart of his American publishing house, and when he wrote me a charming letter of regret explaining this, I instantly assured him that all was well between us. As it was.

His next book was *The Secret Pilgrim*, and when I read it I was relieved that this cup had passed my lip, since I found it the weakest of all his novels and could think of nothing I might have suggested to salvage it. Meanwhile his new editorial arrangement at Knopf had foundered, so when I returned to the fold we got remarried. The book was *The Night Manager*, and things went well, but inevitably drift set in. I had a hand in *Our Game*, and finally in *The Tailor of Panama*, something of a return to form for him. This was a last-minute business: The book was only a few days from going to press when he asked me to take a look. Of the various changes I suggested, one was highly charged. At some point he described a couple in a restaurant as Jewish-looking and I pointed out that Jews didn't have a "look"—a hook nose? a swarthy complexion?—and that this locution would offend. I knew with absolute certainty that David was not anti-Semitic, far from it, but he had already been unjustly accused of anti-Semitism in relation to *The Little Drummer Girl*, and was extremely sensitive on the subject. No matter how I expostulated with him, though, he didn't grasp that Jews don't see themselves as particularly Jewish-looking. We went back and forth over this point with increasing tension—it was the closest we ever got to a serious quarrel—and he finally, grudgingly, agreed to a tiny adjustment that erased the problem. I'm sure David thought that as a Jew, I was particularly thin-skinned here—and maybe worried about a negative sales impact—whereas I was trying to protect *him*.

This, however, wasn't the reason he soon afterward left Knopf: He felt, I think, that the company was taking him for granted, and that a change of scene would re-energize his career. The reality, as I saw it, was that for a long while every new le Carré novel had been greeted as an Event, but there had been no recent single book strong enough to re-ignite that kind of excitement, and the inevitable law of diminishing returns had set in. No matter. Although such publishing divorces are never pleasant, this one was completely civilized.

I was regretful when David did leave us, because I was proud of what we had done for him (and he for us), but I would have had a problem as his later books grew more and more virulently anti-American. In John le Carré's world there were heroes—usually innocents—and bad guys. In the Cold War days the baddies were unscrupulous agents, either Soviet or Western. Now the Soviets were gone, and that left a different kind of villain, often an oligarch of whatever stripe, often American—and *because* American. Much as I've missed working with David, and David himself, I don't miss the struggles we would have had in this area. As it is, he's written to me about our years together having been a golden time, and they were that for me. For no real reason, not only haven't we worked together since he left Knopf but we haven't seen each other, though in 2001 I was one of the few people apart from his family whom he invited to a seventieth-birthday celebration he was throwing for himself in a beautiful Italian hill town. I wasn't able to go, but I was inordinately pleased to have been asked.

Only a few weeks after I returned to Knopf I had a phone call from Katharine Graham. I had absolutely no connections with Washington or with the higher reaches of American journalism, but we had met years earlier at an author party in New York and immediately hit it off. The party was held in an elaborate duplex apartment, and I remember sitting with Kay for half an hour on the stairs between its two floors, jabbering away. The only link between us—but it was a strong one—was my old friend Meg Greenfield, who, as I've already reported, had become her closest friend and most trusted colleague at *The Washington Post* and *Newsweek*. I was charmed by Kay and urged her to write a book that I could publish. She agreed on the spot, and we drew up a contract.

She didn't sign it, though, telling Sonny after my departure that she simply wasn't ready to go forward. Instead, she plunged into five years of research, interviewing just about everyone she'd ever known, since she didn't trust her memory. And along the way she *did* sign a contract with Knopf. Her editor was to be the illustrious Elisabeth Sifton, who had joined the company after I left, but now Elisabeth had left too. On the phone Kay asked if I would do her a favor and read what she'd written, the first seventy-five pages or so; she wanted to know whether she needed a collaborator, a "ghost," and indeed whether the book was worth pursuing or should be scrapped, and she hadn't had helpful feedback from Elisabeth.

The next morning I went over to see her—she had a pied-à-terre in the United Nations Plaza complex overlooking the East River, about three blocks from my house on Forty-eighth Street. I told her that what she'd written was exactly what it should be. It had, as I've said before, what a good memoir can't do without, something that can't be inserted by a hired hand: a strong, appealing, and totally convincing voice. I believed every word she had written. I also believed that a collaborator would be a disaster, and that all she had to do was keep going. She found this hard to accept—she had no faith whatsoever in her abilities as a writer; I've rarely worked with someone so unsure of herself. When she asked me whether she had to follow Elisabeth to her new publishing situation, and whether I would consider being her editor, I told her no, she didn't, and yes, I would. And so began one of the most agreeable and satisfying associations of my working life.

Since I knew very little about Washington, I felt no awe of Kay, "the most powerful woman in America." Far from being grand or self-important, she was all too ready to denigrate her abilities and to follow my suggestions blindly—not a healthy dynamic. I kept hoping she'd tell me to buzz off, but it never happened. Nor did she think that anyone would want to read her book. "Do you really think it can do as well as Ben's?" she asked me plaintively a couple of times. (Her beloved Ben

Bradlee had just published a fairly successful memoir.) It was the first indication I had of her competitive nature.

Her life, as I was to discover, had reflected her powerful impulse to be passive in relation to strong men: her father, Eugene Meyer; her husband, Philip Graham; Ben; Adlai Stevenson; Warren Buffett; and to a very minor extent, me. Yet when Phil Graham died, she stepped forward and assumed control of the *Post*—hardly the act of a shrinking violet. I came to believe that she was frightened either of behaving like her dominating, aggressive, and cold mother, Agnes Meyer (intimate of such luminaries as Rodin, Mann, Einstein, Brancusi), or of competing with her.

But if she had a withholding mother, she had a supportive father. He obviously recognized the steel in her, and he made her his confidante. Even so, it didn't seem to occur to her to resent having been overlooked when Mr. Meyer handed over the reins of the *Post* to her brilliant, charismatic husband. She adored Phil as only a young woman without much faith in her looks and her intelligence can adore such a man, and she suffered silently through his philanderings and mental collapses, ignoring the way he publicly put her down, defining herself as wife and mother, until his terrifying suicide by shotgun while she was upstairs in their house. That's when the steel took over.

By the time I knew her, decades later, she was an empress, fully aware of her position and power, yet still modest—even humble—about her abilities as a writer, and deferential to authority. She could also be funny and witty, and amazingly outspoken about Phil, her children (whom she saw all too clearly), herself. I was occasionally startled and embarrassed at her casual confidences. One reason her book was so successful was that she didn't shield herself from the realities of her history—she told it the way she remembered it, and was always willing to dive in further and elaborate or expand. Naturally I was anxious about how she would react to having to set down the ugly details of the later years of her marriage, and the awfulness of Phil's ultimate breakdown and death, but I needn't have worried. Kay was first and foremost a reporter—in her early years after college she had worked as one, successfully, in San Francisco, particularly engaged with and sympathetic to the labor movement—and she approached her life story as a reporter would: digging for the facts, and revealing them, at whatever personal cost.

After we reconnected, in 1992, she spent four years writing and rewriting. Someone she trusted—I think it was Bob Woodward—had advised her to open the book with a dramatic story (Watergate, perhaps, or Phil's suicide) and then flash back. I was able to convince her that given how her life was rooted in her relationship with her parents, she should start with them: There was no understanding her life without understanding the Meyers. Every four or five months, as I remember it, I would go down to Washington to read what she'd been writing and discuss where she was going. I would always stay with her in her grand Georgetown house, which meant that over the years we established an easygoing routine—breakfast, for instance, in slippers and dressing gowns at side-by-side tables in the library, with the *Post* waiting for her and the *Times* waiting for me. I would also stay with her when I was in Washington for ballet performances at the Kennedy Center, which meant that we would go our separate ways in the evenings and had to develop a routine for letting ourselves in late at night. Whichever of us got home first would leave a note by the front door, so that the other could do the final lock-up before heading for bed. In other words, it became a surprisingly domestic relationship.

I also had the great luck of working with Kay's editorial assistant, Evelyn Small, who had been at the *Post* for years, knew her boss intimately, was devoted to her yet could see her dispassionately, and who was as calmly efficient as I prided myself on being. We were friends from the first—sometimes a support team, sometimes an attack team, and always an affectionate team. And for outside support (it wasn't needed often) there was Meg, with her occasional no-bullshit interventions. The one time that Kay tried to rescue some material I thought needed serious cutting had to do with a European Commission she had been invited to join. She was especially proud of this venture because it hadn't anything to do with journalism or the *Post* but reflected a growing perception of her as a major player in the business world. (After all, she was the first woman CEO to be named to the annual

Design by Paul Bacon

Design by Janet Halverson

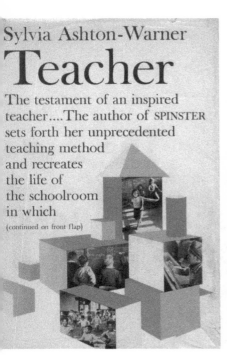

Design by Janet Halverson

Photograph by Philippe Halsman

Design by Paul Bacon

Design by R. D. Scudellari

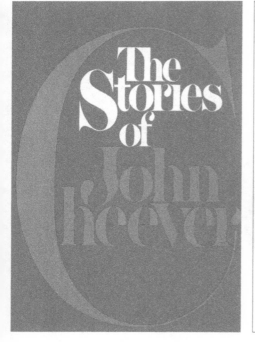

Design by R. D. Scudellari

Design by Paul Bacon

Design by Paul Bacon

Design by Lidia Ferrara

Design by Miss Piggy (who else?)

Photograph by Victor Skrebneski

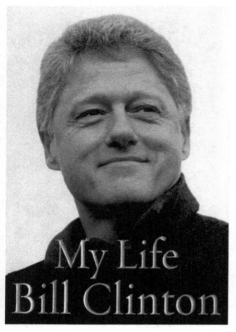

Design by Carol Devine Carson

Design by Abby Weintraub

Photograph of Lizzie Gottlieb by
Dorothy Gelatt; design by Lidia Ferrara

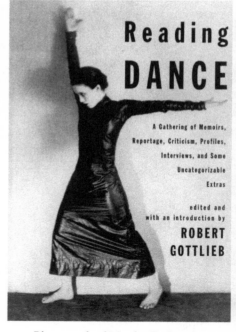

Photograph of Martha Graham by
Soichi Sunami; design by Black Kat Design

Fortune 500 list.) I was gently shaving away at her four or five dull pages on this dull topic, trying to be tactful. Meg, reading along, just crossed it all out and wrote in the margin, "This is all horribly boring. Reduce to one paragraph." There wasn't even a whimper from Kay when I crossed out just about all of it.

In June 1997 Kay threw herself a birthday bash at her home. It was her eightieth, and it was the year of her book's publication. Why not celebrate? I had two memorable encounters that night. The first was with Princess Di at the entrance to Kay's house, she alighting from a limo, me on foot. As I've described this historic encounter elsewhere: "Kay introduced us, Diana smiled her smile and offered her (gloved) hand, and I covered myself with glory by coming up with the following Wildean remark: 'It's a pleasure to meet you.'" This, as it happens, was only a few months before Diana's terrible death.

The second encounter was with Justice Sandra Day O'Connor, whom I was seated next to at dinner, a completely appealing woman— straightforward, warm, honest. We quickly established that we were only a year apart in age, and had a good time remarking that whereas I grew up in a liberal New York family to whom FDR was a living god, she grew up on a Southwestern ranch where his name was anathema. Then we got onto the (senior) Bushes—good friends of hers. I expressed my doubts. "Oh no," she said, "you'd love George and Barbara, they're so much fun!" This was my opportunity. "Well," I said to her, "I'm going to say something utterly inappropriate, so I apologize in advance, and I certainly don't expect you to respond. But whatever the president's other virtues or failings, the one thing I can never forgive is his appointing Clarence Thomas to the Supreme Court." And we sailed on to some other subject. But I don't think I was fantasizing when I thought I detected a twinkle of satisfaction in her eye.

Everything about the publishing of Kay's book went right—there wasn't a stumble along the way. The reviews were ecstatic (Nora Ephron's thoughtful rave on the front cover of *The New York Times Book Review* set the tone). It immediately became, and stayed for months, the number-one nonfiction bestseller—we sold about three hundred thousand hardcover copies. And to crown it all, it won the 1998 Pulitzer

Prize for biography or autobiography—for Kay, first and foremost a journalist, an almost unimaginable honor. I think she felt that this, more than any of her other achievements, was the ultimate answer to her mother's dismissal of her, and the ultimate return she could make to her father for his faith in her. (Typical of Kay: She was the only one of my many Pulitzer Prize authors to invite me to the ceremony. And Ev Small too.)

What was it about *Personal History* that appealed so strongly to readers, apart from the assurance and integrity of Kay's voice? For many years there was a publishing joke: To guarantee bestsellerdom, call a book *Lincoln's Doctor's Dog*—three non-fail subjects with the reading public. Kay's book hit a comparable range of targets. It was essential for journalists: The story of Kay, Ben, Watergate, and the Pentagon Papers was the great journalism story of the second half of the twentieth century. It was a powerful human drama, and a dynastic saga. It was an inside story of Washington, by a quintessential insider. But perhaps most important, *Personal History* became a touchstone for women of all ages, as I discovered when I suggested to Lizzie that she read it. In her mid-twenties—as innocent as I was about Washington and journalism; she lived in the theater world—Lizzie found it not only compelling reading but personally resonant, even though she had perhaps the most supportive mother in the Western world and a father who took for granted that she could do anything and everything she chose to attempt. Nora had put it this way: "Katharine Graham turns out to have had not two lives but four, and the story of her journey from daughter to wife to widow to woman parallels to a surprising degree the history of women in this century." Her story, although she would have shied from anything this pretentious, turned out to be a recasting of one of popular culture's favorite plots: the ultimate triumph of the ugly duckling or the poor little rich girl. It was not only that she took charge of *The Washington Post*, it was that she took charge of her life. She had become a feminist icon.

Nora, too, had become one in the decades following *Heartburn*. By the mid-nineties she was more famous as a movie scriptwriter and director than as a journalist. Her roots were in Hollywood, her parents the screenwriters Henry and Phoebe Ephron, and she soon established herself there as a major player—in the big leagues, along with her friends and colleagues Mike Nichols, Tom Hanks, Meryl Streep, Meg Ryan, et al. Yet she remained a quintessential New Yorker and Hamptonite.

In 2006, when we published her first book in more than twenty years, *I Feel Bad About My Neck*—a collection of funny, pointed, and poignant pieces, mostly about being a woman of a certain age—it had an astonishing and gratifying success. When we were assembling the table of contents we figured the book would do well—Nora's guess was a sale of seventy-five thousand. Our first printing was forty thousand. But a lifetime of publishing or being published is no guarantee that you know what you're doing. Yes, the book was terrific. Yes, it was delectable-looking. And yes, Nora was a fabulous promoter. But those things don't add up to sales of a million. What she had to say, and what she represented, had made her a voice for an entire generation of women. She reminded them of what they already knew about themselves (including their obsession with their necks) while preparing them for what was to come.

Our work together on this book, and on its follow-up four years later—*I Remember Nothing*, which sold a mere half million copies—was as it had been from our start together more than thirty years earlier: problem-free and lighthearted. Our friendship had never faltered. Since she knew I didn't like cocktail parties or dinner parties, when she was in town she and her husband, Nick Pileggi, author of *Wiseguy* (film: *Goodfellas*) and one of nature's noblemen, and Maria and I would go to some restaurant she had heard about, where she would order with a specificity and authority that were awe-inspiring, though as a non-foodie, I just couldn't get very excited about salad dressing.

To me, needless to say, she wasn't "iconic," she was a friend you had a great time with, whom you went to for help or who came to you for the same. The most valuable thing I ever did for her took place in one of those small screening rooms with insanely comfortable lounging chairs but not enough of them. As the room filled up, it was obvious that there weren't going to be enough seats, and harried ushers were hauling in folding chairs. Nora was there with Maria and me, and when she observed the confusion she stood up and started to straighten everyone out. "Sit down, Nora," I said. "You can't be in charge of everything!" It was, she later wrote, a revelation that changed her life (at least temporarily). Assuming that she *was* in charge of everything was part of the fabric of her being—a quality I recognized since, alas, I share it.

At lunch one day in the mid-2000s Nora confided to Maria that she was suffering from a mortal disease and had begun a course of blood transfusions. A few weeks later, she talked to me about it too—forthrightly, calmly, sensibly. No one was to know just how serious things were: Apart from her Nick, perhaps half a dozen people were told, including her sister Delia, her close friend Richard Cohen, and her loving assistant, J. J. Sacha. For a long time she held her own medically, but when things started to get really bad she confirmed the news to her boys, who had known she was ill but not how direly, and a few others. On reflection, I think that she had felt able to tell Maria and me not because we were closer to her than her most intimate friends, like her agent, Binky Urban—that wasn't the case—but because our friendship existed outside their world. Why the prolonged secrecy? She didn't want to go through what was left of her life being an object of pity. And since she was still making movies, secrecy was essential: No studio would hire a director under a death sentence. Janet Malcolm was one of those few who knew what was happening, since her husband, Gardner Botsford, had died of the same disease and Janet could discuss it with Nora with knowledge as well as sympathy. It was during this period that Nora made her final movie, *Julie & Julia*.

When after five or six years her remission ran out, her death came quickly. And to the scores of people close to her, the fact that she had been hiding her condition from the world (and from them) for so long made the awful reality even more painful—and unbelievable. In character to the last, she took charge of her death and her post-death, down to the superbly organized "gathering" at Lincoln Center to celebrate her life, suggesting a list of speakers, specifying the drinks to be served (pink champagne), and—most important—choosing the hors d'oeuvres.

It was the near-universal reaction to her death that made me grasp just how significant she had become in her final decades to hundreds of thousands of women who never knew her yet to a certain extent had come to live *by* her, and maybe even through her. I received phone calls and letters from people who needed to condole with someone, and I was the only someone they knew. I was lucky, though—there was something practical I could do with my feelings. Nora and I had been talking about, and had begun to plan, a giant anthology of her work—*The Most of Nora Ephron.* After she died I spent six months putting it together, and as I wrote in the introduction, working on it gave me the perfect excuse to reread everything she ever wrote. No editorial job I've ever done has been so much fun.

I'm still working for Knopf. I have an office I'm rarely in, an assistant I infrequently deploy, expenses I never put in for, and a computer I've never opened. But, given the Web, one is never out of touch. Editorial work is simpler, now that you can intervene with text electronically, although I still read manuscript, not screens, and always with pencil in hand. One day a dozen years ago I was working in the office with Bob Caro and we went down to Kathy Hourigan's office so that her new young assistant could make a copy of some pages we were laboring over. He was bemused at encountering people who actually worked by making marks with a pencil on what we thought was paper but he identified as "hard copy."

Technologies change, and we adjust as best we can. The basic process remains the same, though: Writer and editor have to find a way to work together, and then they write and edit. Sometimes the process takes time, sometimes there's no time to take: You jump in and assume all will be well. That's what happened between Bill Clinton and me. I was in my place in Miami Beach when Sonny Mehta called to ask me whether I'd consider working with Clinton. There had been sharp public criticism when Hillary Clinton had sold her memoir in an auction for a very large advance, and Sonny shrewdly guessed that Mr. Clinton would want to avoid the same kind of criticism about the book he was planning to write, so he proposed to Clinton's lawyer that we just buy it outright. Clinton had been impressed by Kay Graham's book and what he knew (probably from her) of my role in it, so my potential participation was offered as a point in Knopf's favor. I guess you could say that I was the bait—me and a record-size advance.

This was in 2001; I was just seventy and not at all sure I wanted to dive into so public an arena. On the other hand, it was a flattering proposal, and likely to be a revelation. I told Sonny I was interested but that Clinton and I had to meet—if we didn't get along, it would be a disaster. As it happened, at that moment Clinton was staying at a golfing resort in Miami, so Sonny flew down with Ash Green, and the three of us proceeded to a morning (pre-golf) meeting at Clinton's hotel. Since I'd never met a president, or an ex-president—or, for that matter, a politician—I had no preconceptions, except that I thought Clinton had been a good president and that he was an appealing presence and a smart guy.

We were ushered into the Clintonian suite, where Mr. President (as he was always called) was sitting in jacket and tie (this was Miami, and hot) surrounded by a bunch of aides and Secret Service agents. This was not going to be a tête-à-tête. I was in my usual Miami getup: white sneakers, white T-shirt, chinos. If he took offense, I figured, the relationship was not going to work out. We got through this stilted meeting with nothing of consequence being said, but I must have passed muster, because he signed on with us.

It turned out to be big news. Not only stories everywhere, but at least half a dozen long interviews with me in *The New York Times*, *The Boston Globe*, the Toronto *Globe and Mail*, and so on about my background, track record, marital status—everything but my waistline. Naïvely, I suppose, I had assumed a paragraph in *Publishers Weekly*. This was my first, but not last, exposure to the determination of the press to blow up anything and everything about the Clintons into earthshaking importance. I mean, who outside publishing could really care what editor would be working with an ex-president on his memoirs? For me it meant an interesting adventure and a lot of work, but it was hardly a story. How could I know that down the road it would be revealed, in the pages of *New York*, that when I had overnights at the Clintons' house in Chappaqua I went to bed in my blue pajamas!

Some time after the Coral Gables summit, Clinton came to

Knopf to meet the publishing gang. The corridors were filled with people eager to shake his hand, my first experience of his passion for making direct contact with the public—it was no hardship for him to meet and greet, it was a balm and a blessing. Which is why people who encountered him were utterly smitten: They sensed that he was smitten with them. When all the hands had been shaken, he and I retired into a small office and talked a little turkey: what was the status of the manuscript (it was hardly begun), how would we operate, the timetable, the contents. I felt I had to state the obvious: that he would have to be completely aboveboard about his womanizing, and in particular about the Lewinsky scandal. He told me, and I didn't doubt him, that he was completely prepared to do that. This was not an exchange I had looked forward to, but I was reassured: not only about his willingness to tackle the least palatable part of his history but by his obvious resolve to reveal his life to the best of his ability. A big relief—I wouldn't have to cajole him to open up. (Getting him to shut down would occasionally be a problem.)

The excellent advice he gave me was that if I wanted to understand him, I should read his mother's book, *Leading with My Heart*. I hadn't even known she'd written one—I knew nothing about her at all—but I dug right into it, and was both tickled and moved. What a gal! No punches were pulled about her (four) husbands, (two) sons, and daunting daughter-in-law-to-be, with her thick glasses and flat hair—she was used to Bill's blond bimbos (her phrase)—to whom, as she said, she eventually came around. Virginia Kelley was a fun-lover, a people-lover, and a tough cookie. The apple didn't fall far from the tree.

I was impressed and touched that Clinton was proud of her book—it was hardly a campaign document—and proud of *her*. A long time after his own book was published, I happened to be speaking to James Morgan, Mrs. Kelley's collaborator, on an entirely different subject. When I asked him about her (he adored her), he told me that when she died, just as he was finishing up the manuscript, he had to submit it to President Clinton (this was 1994), since he was his mother's literary executor. Needless to say, Morgan was concerned that the president would be unhappy with certain, shall we say, tactless moments in the text. Within two days after the manuscript went off to the White House, his phone rang and it was Clinton, saying that he loved it just as it was and had no changes at all to suggest: This is my mother's book, not mine, and she should be able to say anything she felt like saying. No spin, just pleasure in his mother's accomplishment. Alas, Virginia Kelley's death precluded any personal promotion for *Leading with My Heart*. If she had been on hand to sell it, without question it would have been a big hit.

I had read it before my next so-called editorial session with Bill. (I called him Bill from the start, since I couldn't envisage myself saying things like "I think we need a semicolon here, Mr. President." Also, he was a lot younger than I was. Moreover, he wasn't, in fact, "Mr. President" any longer.) This meeting took place in his capacious offices on 125th Street in Harlem, and after taking the subway uptown and walking across 125th, I was (eventually) ushered first into his private office and then into a conference room. It was startling to be expected to discuss editorial matters with half a dozen or more aides sitting around—startling and impossible. More generalities were uttered. Then, eager to show me that he was looking forward to our collaboration, he said something like "We're going to have a good time. Ask anyone here. You'll find that I'm very easy to work for." That, for me, was the moment of truth. "Actually," I said, "I have to point out that in this instance I'm not working for you, you're working for me." It was cheeky, and it was deliberate. If he didn't understand that in an editorial relationship there had to be an equality, or at least a balance, it was going to fail: Editors can't do their work properly if they're hired hands. I could tell from the frozen expressions of the people sitting around the big table that I had committed lèse-majesté—or something. But Bill himself didn't miss a beat, and on we went. Not that anything substantial could be accomplished under such circumstances, but we had reached an understanding.

By 2003 he was writing away—very fast and with great assurance. Occasionally I would see some pages and was always reassured both that he knew what he was doing and that he was doing it. What made the process possible was Clinton's very young assistant Justin Cooper, who in his teens had started in the White House as an intern, and was now, in his mid-twenties, indispensable. First of all, he could read his boss's handwriting, something I never learned to do. Left-handed Clinton scrawled on big yellow legal pads, his left arm curved up and around and then down to the page—painful to watch, and more painful to try to decipher. Justin would transcribe it all onto his computer, but also feed notes, quotes, data, to Mr. President, all of which Clinton absorbed in an instant and transformed into his fluent prose. I never encountered a mind that grasped things more rapidly—which was fortunate, since there wasn't a lot of time. The plan was to publish by the beginning of summer 2004, since after that the conventions and then the election would be upon us, claiming Clinton's attention, and the world's.

It was the early sections of the book that had worried me, since I could only assume that everyone else's interest in Arkansas, and particularly Arkansas politics, would be as minimal as mine. But that's not the way it turned out. The story of Bill's home life was engrossing—the struggles his mother went through to provide for him and his younger half-brother, Roger; his abusive but loved stepfather; his escape from Hope to the highest reaches of our educational system: a trajectory of constant success and accomplishment—Georgetown, a Rhodes scholarship to Oxford, Yale Law School. He told it all with vigor and appropriate modesty. My first radical intervention, once I started editing, was to chop away at the tales of his European travels. We all think our stories of youthful excursions to Paris, Rome, wherever, are of consuming interest because *we* were so interested in what we were experiencing—it's the way new parents can't believe you're not as entranced by pictures of Baby as they are. Bill was abashed but good-natured as I slashed and burned, although he fought back and even won some clashes. By this time I had realized that he was a complete professional—that neither ego nor sloth would get in the way of his making his book as good as it could be. I could see that he was enjoying going back over his early life. He was having a good time.

When he wrote about beginning his career in local politics—moonlighting from his teaching job at the University of Arkansas Law

School to make his first (failed) run for the Arkansas legislature—I found myself, against expectation, absorbed. Who could have guessed? I had grasped Texas political life through Bob Caro, but Lyndon Johnson had been a pro from the moment he was born, while Clinton had to learn on the job. He had no money, he had no team, he just had ambition—and brains.

My favorite story of this part of his life was of his driving three hours, alone, from his teaching job in Fayetteville to the northeast of the state to campaign—he was running for state attorney general— then back late at night to get to class the next day. At one point he stopped, in exhaustion, at an all-night bar and grill in a town called Joiner to grab something to eat and fill up on coffee, and started chatting up a few regulars, looking for their votes. "Kid," said one of them, "we're going to kill you up here. You know that, don't you? . . . You're a long-haired hippie professor from the university. For all we know, you're a Communist. But I'll tell you something. Anybody who would campaign at a beer joint in Joiner at midnight on Saturday night deserves to carry one box. So you hide and watch. You'll win here. But it'll be the only damn place you win in this county." And, Clinton goes on to tell us, "He was as good as his word. On election night, I was crushed in the other voting precincts controlled by the big farmers, but I got 76 votes in Joiner and my two opponents got 49." This story made such an impression on me that I put it in the jacket copy, because I had come to realize that this kind of one-on-one interaction wasn't a tactic, it was the man.

I observed the phenomenon up close one day when he and his entourage—in three vehicles—came to pick me up at the Chappaqua train station. As we walked to his station wagon a woman who was waiting in her car for someone else on the train waved from her window and shouted, "Bill! We all wish you were back in the White House where you belong!" He darted across to her, leaned in, gave her a hug—all to the horror of the attending Secret Service men. At that moment he loved her as much as she loved him. He just basked in the warmth of people's response to him. A reflex from his difficult childhood? Or simply a born and completely natural politician being himself? It was charming and bemusing to watch him electioneering when there was no election. Once in a while, I asked myself whether he was deliberately charming *me* and concluded that it didn't matter. I liked him a lot and was comfortable with him, which is what counted. I guess I agreed with the guy in Joiner: Anyone who worked as hard as he did had my vote.

As the book got longer and the time got shorter the pressure built. Bill would write (and rewrite and re-rewrite), Justin would pull things together and bring me a batch of pages—this was before we (or I) edited on the computer. I would perform minor, and occasionally major, surgery, scrawl my comments in the margins, and the pages would be chauffeured back to Chappaqua. We'd go over things on the phone, always late at night: Fortunately we were both night birds. It was an easy process, because we were both fast and focused. A story he repeated a lot when he was promoting the book: I had written in one margin, "This is the single most boring page I've ever read," and he sent it back, scribbling under my note, "No, page 511 is even more boring!" We did a good deal of back-and-forthing about the multitude of names of people that swarmed through the text—names of cousins of someone he once knew who turned up momentarily in his later life. "You're not running for anything!" I kept saying. But I came to realize he was always running for something. Looking back at the book now, I see that despite my efforts, all too many cousins and campaign workers and high-school pals crept past my guard.

I had made the decision to get everything up to the presidency more or less wrapped up in January in order to make a clear run at the rest, so we were processing the first half of the book while he was still writing the second half. Always Justin was standing by, keeping us on the straight and narrow. As Bill wrote in his acknowledgments, Justin "never lost his patience, his energy never flagged, and by the time we got to the last lap, he sometimes seemed to know me and what I wanted to say better than I did." Meanwhile, throughout the entire process I had my own secret weapon—once again, Kathy Hourigan (a fanatic Clinton-lover), who flung herself into the book both editorially and managerially, making the insane schedule pan out. The four of us were a perfect team: four workaholics acting in total harmony. A dozen years later, Justin, Kathy, and I get together regularly, not merely out of nostalgia but out of affection. Undoubtedly we could rope Mr. President into joining us—he loves reunions—but my view is that he has more important ways to spend his time.

As for my forays to Chappaqua, they were comfortable and pleasant. When Hillary was there she was a friendly presence, and it was interesting—and touching—to see how much he valued her opinions and responded to her reactions. The household was relaxed—a modestly large establishment that you might have seen in a thirties movie as the home of a well-to-do banker or broker, casually but carefully decorated. You managed to forget that it was walled in, with Secret Service men outside on constant watch, though I did find it a little surreal to be out on the lawn throwing the ball for Buddy as they looked down on us from the guardhouse. Whereas raiding the icebox with Bill and Justin for ice cream at one in the morning seemed totally natural.

The only tension between Mr. President and me was over the title and the dust jacket. I was absolutely certain that the book should be called *My Life*, since I was certain that that's what Americans would want from him—not an official chronicle of his presidency but a personal account of the life of a man they took personally. As for the dust jacket, early on I had seen a photograph of him that was exactly right— the man people cared for, spontaneous, honest, down-to-earth, responsible. I knew right away that this was the image we wanted—no Oval Office, no American flag. There were doubters, however—Hillary? Chelsea? I never knew—who felt he didn't look properly Presidential. (No. He looked human.) A couple of other pictures were proposed— correct and boring: not *My Life* but *The President's Life*. He hesitated. Clearly he was under pressure.

I asked our art department to mock up and print three different jackets—the two from Chappaqua and the one everyone at Knopf preferred. Then I called Bill and in my most portentous manner—a manner that doesn't come easily to me—said I wanted to come up to Chappaqua to discuss something important. When I got there I asked him to wait in another room while I located three of his books that were the right shape and heft, and wrapped the three jackets around them. Then I stood them up on a table next to each other and asked him to come in and see what I had wrought. "Okay," I said. "Which of these books would *you* want to read?" That, as they say, was that. I didn't feel I'd won, I just felt we'd come out at the right place. Although I have to admit that I had been irked.

The final weeks were harrowing. Chapters would come in, be edited overnight, be copyedited in a day, set in proofs, proofread—and then back for further reading and editing by Bill, myself, Justin, and Kathy. It was an assembly line. At one point we had an entire group of specialists—proofreaders, fact-checkers—brought into the office for days (and sometimes nights) of frantic activity. Our stalwart head of production, Andy Hughes, would be at the printer's—again, often at night—hounding the people manning the presses. Miracles were accomplished, made possible by the devotion of everyone at Knopf to making them happen—for the sake of the company, but also for Bill Clinton. It was scary, it was exhausting, but it was exhilarating. We sent the final text file—of just about a thousand pages—to the printer on May 24, 2004, and on June 7 we shipped the first five hundred thousand copies of the finished book.

Clinton's first book-signing took place at the flagship Barnes & Noble store on Fifth Avenue and Forty-eighth Street. I decided to walk over from my house to see how it was going. A line stretched around the corner, then west down the long block to Sixth Avenue, up Sixth to Forty-ninth Street, all the way back to Fifth, and picked up on the other side of the avenue. I'd never seen anything like it. Apparently, people had started lining up the night before, some of them in wheelchairs. It was raining on and off. No one was deterred. Inside, Bill was signing, signing, signing while aides handed him books open to the right page. But he wasn't just signing, he was also shaking hands, saying hello, beaming at this demonstration of what he meant to people. I think we sold two thousand copies that day. And within months we had sold two million. At one point during those months Bill said to me, "You know, I finally get it about cutting!" He almost always had accepted my cuts even when he wasn't thrilled by them, but even if he'd grasped the concept more vigorously early on, we would have run out of time. I was very content with the book we published, but I would have been still more content if I'd had another few weeks in which to cut, sift, trim, prune, snip, crop, pare, and polish. It's hard to let go.

About a year after *My Life* was published, Clinton asked me how the experience of working on it, and its spectacular success, had affected me. I told him that apart from my professional and personal gratification at what had been accomplished, I thought there would be two practical consequences for me. "When I die," I said, "the obituaries will refer to me as Bill Clinton's editor, not as the editor of *Catch-22*." He liked that. "And?" "And if I were ever to do something as vulgar as write my memoirs, I'd get a larger advance." "Go for it!" he urged. "Go for it!" (I didn't.)

Before, during, and after the Clinton extravaganza there were other authors, other books. When I first got back to Knopf I wasn't interested in taking on a lot of new writers—I just planned to be available if and when needed. Since I had made it clear that I didn't want to be paid, I was under no obligation to pay my way. But books and writers happen. For instance: My lifelong involvement with music had been limited to classical and pop. I had stayed away from jazz, or it from me. Then one Saturday, between two City Ballet performances at Lincoln Center, Arlene Croce and I wandered into a record store and she began browsing the jazz racks. Following behind and heeding her reactions, I casually picked up a few CDs of the jazz singers Lee Wiley and Mel Tormé. Within weeks I was caught up in madness—completely addicted. Singing was always the music closest to my heart, and within months I had acquired and was listening to hundreds and hundreds of albums. (Apart from everything else, this mania gave me something new to collect.) And since for me nothing is real until I read about it, I was going through book after book to give me context and point of view—until I found *the* book. Will Friedwald's *Jazz Singing*, published by Scribner's in 1990, was comprehensive, smart, trustworthy. Since I had no one to talk about jazz with, I thought I might get hold of him and have him bend my ear.

One Saturday I was in an obscure secondhand jazz store on the eighth floor of a dingy building in the West Twenties and I asked the somewhat grouchy owner if he happened to know how I could get hold of this Friedwald. "Yeah," he said, "but"—pointing at the elderly man sitting talking to him at the counter—"you'd be better off asking this gentleman here. He's Will's father." When I asked the elder Friedwald for his son's phone number he grew wary and suggested that I give him my name and number and tell him what I wanted Will for, and he'd pass my message on. A few minutes after I got home, there was Will on the phone, over-excited because the editor of *The New Yorker* was looking for him. I told him right away that I wasn't reaching out to him for the magazine—we had the justly famous Whitney Balliett as our jazz writer—but was calling as a fan.

From the first, we had a great time. Will was a husky guy, full of enthusiasm, and to my eyes, almost pathologically naïve—particularly about his eternal search for the perfect mate. (I've seen him through two divorces.) He was just finishing his book *Sinatra! The Song Is You*, an incisive examination of Sinatra's art seen through the arrangers he had worked with, but he was more or less without an editor at Scribner's. I volunteered to edit it for him, which I did twice—once in manuscript, once in galleys. It made no sense after that for us not to work together officially, so his next books came to Knopf: First, *Stardust Melodies*, the recording history of twelve iconic songs; then his *Biographical Guide to the Great Jazz and Pop Singers*, a monumental tome (more than eight hundred tightly packed, double-column pages) that took him eight years to complete, with me riding herd like a sadistic cowboy. As I write, we're hard at work on a book about iconic vocal albums—from *Ella in Berlin* to Chet Baker's *Let's Get Lost* to *Judy at Carnegie Hall*. Chapters whip back and forth, the book accretes, and it's pure pleasure—at least for me.

I've had an even more collaborative relationship with the distinguished Jeanine Basinger, head of the Wesleyan film department and film archive, scholar, expert, and always a joy to be with. The laughs! I've published her totally satisfying book on *It's a Wonderful Life* (her Wesleyan archive holds all the Frank Capra material); *A Woman's View*— today a touchstone for studies of the "woman's film"; *Silent Stars*—those like Mary Pickford and Valentino who are misunderstood, or those like the Talmadge sisters and Pola Negri who are essentially forgotten. My major contribution to *Silent Stars* was suggesting we include Rin-Tin-Tin, "the dog who saved Warner Bros." (Watching a bunch of Rinty movies with Jeanine confirmed that he deserved his stardom. What a performer!) Then came *The Star Machine*, an examination of how golden-age Hollywood succeeded (and sometimes failed) in creating stars. And most recently *I Do and I Don't*, the marriage film—except that it turned out there's no such thing as the marriage film. Now Jeanine's at work on Hollywood musicals.

Before hitherto obscure movies became available on disc, we had to go wherever they *were* available—to the Library of Congress, to the University of Wisconsin, and many times to Eastman House, in Rochester, New York, the third-largest depository of old films in America. Beginning when my great friend Paolo Cherchi Usai became head of its film department, and now that he's back there, the Rochester trips have been complete pleasure. Jeanine and I can gab away for hours, and we do, not only about movies but about family, diners, detective stories. She grew up in South Dakota and spent her formative years as an usher in the local film palace, seeing everything—and remembering everything. Hollywood has few surprises for her.

Another extraordinary writer on movies with whom I worked was the formidable David Thomson, whose dazzling, idiosyncratic, highly personal, and immensely influential *Biographical Dictionary of Film* we were lucky enough to take over. Since by this time I had my own library of old-movie tapes snatched by me or Ron Haver from TV, I knew something about David's subject. It was serendipitous that my particular passions were somewhat different from his, so I was able to goad him into writing about people, especially stars, from the thirties who held no real interest for him, and when he passed on them, I'd write about them for him. This was also true of some silent-screen actors, and—most important to me—stars of the classic period of Japanese film, with which I have been more or less obsessed for forty years.

I must have written forty or so entries, including, as I remember it, Sonja Henie, Ann Sothern, George Brent, Ann Harding, and the great

Hideko Takamine. I'm not, by the way, giving away privileged information. When we were working on the second Knopf edition of the *Dictionary*, David was determined to credit me in the book with these pieces, but I absolutely refused: It would have muddied the waters for critics and readers, trying to figure out who had written what. Part of the pleasure of it was having my author edit my bits of his book. As I confirmed for myself years later when I became more of a writer in my own right, it's just as satisfying being edited as being the editor—it's the process that's interesting, whichever role you're playing.

These excursions into popular culture reflected my personal interests, just as the many books I've edited on dance reflect my lifelong love for that seductive art—two among them Julie Kavanagh's definitive biographies of Frederick Ashton and Rudolf Nureyev, work made especially enjoyable since I shared it with my colleague Shelley Wanger. I continue to be more and more invested in biographies—not only Flora Fraser's, but those of the clever and stimulating Carolyn Burke, whose subjects have ranged from the beautiful model-turned-war-photographer Lee Miller, to Edith Piaf (anything to justify extended stays in Paris), and now a group biography of that famous quartet of Modernist artists and intimates, Georgia O'Keeffe, Alfred Stieglitz, Paul Strand, and his wife, Rebecca.

I've worked with my great friend Alma Guillermoprieto on three superb books about Latin America—*The Heart That Bleeds*, *Looking for History*, and *Dancing with Cuba*—and am always hoping for another. And I've had an intense and rewarding time working on three books with that heroine of NPR, Diane Rehm, most recently *On My Own*, her moving account of her husband's death and her passionate advocacy of the right-to-die movement. We never disagree—except when I have to rein her in on the subject of her little dog, Maxie. (I think she thinks I'm jealous of him.) Diane is yet another compulsive worker and a perfectionist—about her job, about her (gorgeous) hair. Most impressive, beneath her exquisite manner and manners lies a ruthless bullshit detector: I know at first hand how good she is at her job, having been a guest on her show four or five times. A lot of fun always, but I watch my step.

As for fiction, I decided fifteen years ago that it wasn't fair to young novelists to take them on when I couldn't assume I'd be able to be with them in the long (or even medium) run. So the only novelist I now work with is Toni Morrison. Since we're exactly the same age, the actuarial gods are neutral. I want her to live forever, and I want to edit her forever. We'll see.

And even as the chariot of time hustles me along, I never forget that Bob Caro is coming up from behind with volume five of LBJ. I hope he makes it. I hope I make it. What better cause in which to finally put down my yellow number 2 pencil?

DANCING

WHEN I WAS A KID my radio was never off, and I would dance around my room to whatever music was playing—not, I imagine, an edifying sight, but there was no one there to see. At that time I hadn't seen any real dancing except in a few movies (Shirley Temple and Bill "Bojangles" Robinson, no doubt), and so what called to me was tap. However, although I liked to move to music, and was small, quick, and agile, it would never have occurred to me to ask to take tap lessons (or to my parents to propose them)—nice Jewish boys took piano. And in fact most dancing, certainly ballet, would have been impossible for me, since my feet are as flat as feet can be.

Around 1942, my mother, as always leading me to culture, took me to Ballet Theatre (now ABT) at the old Met to see *Giselle*, with Alicia Markova and Anton Dolin, the most famous partnership of their era. We sat way upstairs, and I was utterly bewildered—why were all those girls in white with little wings at the back jumping up and down? But I retained a distinct impression of Markova and her famous ethereal lightness. (It was a long time before I learned that she owed her lightness to the exertions of her long-suffering partners.) The following year my gallant mother took me to *Giselle* again (*she* loved it), with the same results.

Then, in 1944, Ballet Theatre staged Jerome Robbins's *Fancy Free*, his first ballet and a gigantic hit, and soon afterward the company scheduled a Saturday matinee targeted for boys—*Fancy Free, Billy the Kid*, and *Rodeo*—and my mother hoped it might do the trick. But no, sailors and cowboys jumping around made no more sense to me than *Giselle*'s Wilis had. And so it went until that day in 1948 when my teacher Kay Muhs took me to the City Center to see Ballet Society. One of the works on the program, as I've written above, was the new Balanchine-Stravinsky ballet, *Orpheus*, and it changed my life.

It also changed the life of Balanchine's enterprise. Morton Baum, whose work for the city included overseeing the City Center, was so overwhelmed by *Orpheus* that he offered to take Ballet Society under his wing, change its name to New York City Ballet, and give it a permanent residency. I had sensed at once that Balanchine, about whom I had known almost nothing, was a genius, and by the time I had seen *Symphony in C* and *Concerto Barocco*, which with *Orpheus* made up City Ballet's first program in October 1948, I was certain of it—and had fallen in love not only with him but with the company and with ballet.

My fate was sealed. Through my four years of college I was at the City Center whenever I could afford to go, and that was a lot of times, since the cheapest seats, way upstairs, cost $1.20. Then, at the first intermission, like a lot of others I would creep down into the orchestra, which was more or less empty—City Ballet was far from what the New York ballet audience was used to: too modern, too spare, too intellectual. Not a Wili in sight. The ushers were fully complicit, since the dancers were much happier when there was a discernible audience.

These were the years of the company's growing pains: the entry into the repertory of earlier Balanchine masterpieces (*Apollo, The Four Temperaments, Serenade, The Prodigal Son*) and new ones (his *Firebird*, with the Chagall sets and Maria Tallchief's blazing performance, *Swan Lake Act II, La Valse*). It was revelation after revelation, and the small but ardent audience understood that it was present at the creation of something astounding—there was a strong sense of "we happy few." It was one of the great pieces of luck in my life to have been in New York through those years, and available to Balanchine's genius. Night after night I would come out of the theater with my friends, dazed and filled with joy, jetéing (sort of) up the street to the subway and Morningside Heights. This exposure to Balanchine's art was my great education, and being so young, I took it all for granted, the way Elizabethan audiences probably did with Shakespeare.

In October 1949 a major event took place that changed the course of ballet in America, and confirmed my passion for it: the triumphant first American season of Britain's Sadler's Wells company (later, the Royal Ballet). I read the full-page ad announcing the opening of the box office and dashed downtown to the Met with what cash I had to stand in a long, long line to buy as many tickets as I could possibly afford. But how to choose? The only name I recognized was Moira Shearer, because like everyone else I had fallen for her in the movie *The Red Shoes*. To my confusion, though, it was another ballerina who was again and again first-cast—someone I'd never heard of called Margot Fonteyn. She was completely unknown in America, but not for long. My first view of her, in her tremendous success as Aurora in *The Sleeping Beauty*, was a revelation of a different kind from anything I'd experienced before: For the first time in my life I was in utter submission to a dancer. I simply had never seen dancing on this level before, *and* she was so beautiful, so charming, so radiant! As Lincoln Kirstein one day put it to me, she had the art of pleasing more than any other dancer of the century. She was also my first Odette-Odile in my first full-length *Swan Lake*, another revelation. For the only time in my life I stood outside a stage door waiting to see a performer emerge.

That was the closest I got to anyone in the ballet world until about ten years later, when up in the country at the Provensens' house I met their friend and neighbor Janet Reed, who had been a leading dancer with both Ballet Theatre and City Ballet and whom I'd been captivated by in the original cast of *Fancy Free*, as the soubrette in *Cakewalk*, in the bouncy third movement of *Symphony in C*. She was as startled to find in Clinton Corners an obsessed young ballet lover who knew her work as I was to find there a ballerina I loved.

But that was an accident. I had no interest in meeting dancers or in penetrating the world of ballet, I was just grateful for it. In fact, I never did want to get to know dancers, actors, writers—artists or celebrities of any kind. What would have been the point? It was what they *did* that mattered to me. Besides, what could one say to a Balanchine or a Fonteyn—"I love your work"? Dancers in particular seemed to me creatures from another star, to be worshipped (or not) from afar.

Early in the 1970s, Martha Swope, the official photographer of City Ballet, whom Maria and I knew slightly because she had photographed several plays Maria had appeared in, approached me about publishing an outsize book about the company. It would include an extensive running text in the form of a journal by Lincoln Kirstein and photos by herself and, for the early years, the remarkable George Platt Lynes. I was beyond excited by the possibility, and she and Lincoln came to Knopf to discuss it with me. I had often seen Lincoln in the theater— he would have been hard to miss, this colossal figure, his grim face burning with intensity—but since I knew no one at all connected to the company, I had never met him.

His brilliance was indisputable, his accomplishments legendary (even apart from his persuading George Balanchine, in 1933, to come to America to create a classical ballet company), his personal force almost overwhelming. He was a superb writer, an indefatigable collector of art, a formidable intellectual and artistic entrepreneur, a propagandist, and—alas—he was bipolar, having several times been institutionalized. He was also seductively charming and a supreme gossip, and I came to venerate him, even love him, although loving Lincoln was a dangerous thing to do, because when his paranoia was asserting itself he inevitably turned on people who cared for him. He also was relentless about identifying people he thought might be useful to the company and, in a more disinterested spirit, identifying talent of any kind and helping it on its way.

An example close to home: After I'd known him for some years, he casually asked me one night at the State Theater what Maria was doing at the moment. When I remarked that I hadn't known he was aware of her, he said, "Oh yes, years ago I saw her as Cassandra in *The Trojan Women*, called up the American Shakespeare Festival [in Stratford, Connecticut; he had been instrumental in launching it], and told them I had found their Juliet for the upcoming season." A family mystery solved! Maria, who had simply been offered the part without meetings or auditions, had never understood why.

This invisible orchestrating of events was typical of Lincoln's aversion to receiving credit—he made things happen and was quietly and anonymously pleased if and when they worked out. If they didn't, he never regretted the effort he had made. In other words, he wasn't looking for a return on his investment. This was a lesson I tried to take to heart, but a very hard one for someone like me who is preoccupied with results. (And had to be, professionally.)

Years later, I learned another crucial lesson from him. It was just after Balanchine's favorite ballerina, Suzanne Farrell, returned to the company after a dramatic and traumatic five-year absence. (Delia Peters, the company wit, remarked, "Suzanne's coming back is the best thing that's happened to us since her going.") I was sitting with Lincoln at her return performance, and she was magnificent—it was clear that her dancing had deepened and that she would be reclaiming her dominance of the repertory. I was in tears, but Lincoln had sat stony-faced through the performance. When the lights went on, I turned to him and said, "Wasn't she great? Isn't it wonderful that she's back?" All he said was, "It means the next few years are secure." I was shocked at what seemed to me a cynical response to a historic and thrilling moment. But some time later, reflecting on what I was feeling at Knopf, I remembered what he had said. I had reached a point of taking it for granted that, short of catastrophe, we would continue to prosper. Individual successes had lost the excitement and savor for me they once had had; now I tended to register them with relief, and move on. They meant, in fact, that the next few years were secure.

After the City Ballet book, I worked with Lincoln on his superb *Nijinsky Dancing*, the most elegant book I was ever involved with—the sublime Baron de Meyer photographs, Lincoln's magisterial text, the design, the paper, the printing! Such a book, with a limited audience and a high price, couldn't possibly justify itself financially, but because there was no one looking over my shoulder, it didn't need to be justified. My view remained that as long as we were so profitable, it was no one's business how we were doing on a book-to-book basis.

Lincoln was so pleased with the Nijinsky book, and I suppose so pleased by my passion for City Ballet and Balanchine, that when he decided to detach the company legally from the City Center board of directors and create a new board for the ballet alone, he invited me to become a charter member. I remember telling him that although there was nothing I wouldn't do for the company, I didn't see myself as a board member: I simply was incapable of raising money. "I don't need you to raise money," he said. "I need someone on the board who when the crucial moment comes will make sure the company gets what it needs." He didn't have to spell it out—he was talking about the moment when Balanchine died or couldn't go on. And when I agreed to join up, and the newly constituted board came together, I saw his point. It was a very small group of old supporters and friends, all of whom meant well but who with a few exceptions were far from knowledgeable. They were completely in awe of Balanchine (as who was not?), and they felt as Lincoln did that the board was there only to make possible anything he chose to do. There was no reason, however, to believe that with Balanchine gone, the company would stay on the right path: An injudicious or misguided board could destroy everything Balanchine and Kirstein had accomplished, and they were both getting on in years. Balanchine had put it in a nutshell: "*Après moi le board.*"

By the mid-seventies, New York City Ballet was at a crossroads. It was no longer the elitist underdog of the New York dance world but a major, internationally acclaimed company. It had settled into the grand State Theater in Lincoln Center, had stabilized its finances, and was at its artistic peak. But backstage it was still operating like the mom-and-pop store it had always been. Lincoln was increasingly isolated, and mostly absorbed by the School of American Ballet. Balanchine's health was not going to hold up forever. The board was essentially irrelevant. And the loyal cadre who had administered the company for decades was losing its energies. The strong-minded and extremely capable company manager, Betty Cage, was exhausted from having time and again pulled the company back from the brink, and from worrying about Lincoln's state of mind and state of health—she had always been intensely devoted to him. The situation was not unlike the one I had found at Knopf: a kind of institutional desuetude—except for Balanchine himself, who was still producing masterpieces, and training (and inspiring) his dancers.

Soon after the new board was constituted, Lincoln introduced me to Balanchine, to whom I had nothing whatsoever to say. Since everyone called Lincoln "Lincoln," I assumed that everyone called Balanchine "George," so I did, too. By the time I realized that he was "Mr. B" to just about everyone, I was too embarrassed to switch gears, so for years I never addressed him by name. Not, I'm sure, that he noticed or cared.

One of the things Betty Cage did for Lincoln was to make dinner every Monday night for his intimates, or for people he was wooing—like Mac Lowry, who controlled the money from the Ford Foundation. (City Ballet and the School of American Ballet—SAB—had received by far the largest grant Ford had ever given to a performing-arts organization, to the outrage of other dance companies everywhere.) I was often there at these dinners, and at one of them Lincoln and Betty were complaining about the lack of family audiences at weekend matinees. "Do you really think that parents are going to bring their kids to see *Bugaku?*" I asked, *Bugaku* being the most explicitly erotic ballet in the repertory. Lincoln swung around and stared at me. "You're interested in programming? Help Betty!" Betty, who had been doing it for decades, was no longer interested in programming—in fact, she no longer attended performances. For a while I observed how she went about it, and then, to her relief, started doing it on my own.

Box office income depended on a complicated system of sixteen subscription series, and you couldn't offer subscribers the same ballet more often than once in several years. There were the stringent requirements of the ballet mistress, the music director, and the stage manager. And the ballets had to be scheduled in relation to the needs and capacities of the dancers. It was a fiendishly complex exercise. And beyond the technicalities, each individual program had to make artistic sense, had to provide a balance, a flow.

I knew the repertory intimately. I knew the dancers. And I was a lifelong puzzle solver. This was a job I knew I was born for, and quickly it *was* my job, and remained so for the next dozen or so years. Twice a year I would meet with Balanchine and Jerry Robbins to find out what new works they were planning. How else to map out a season? It would usually take me most of a weekend to concoct a first draft, which would then circulate to Betty, George, Jerry, Lincoln, Robert Irving (the music director), Rosemary Dunleavy (the ballet mistress), and Ronnie Bates (the stage manager). Responses would drift in, and I'd begin the first round of adjustments.

George couldn't have cared less what was being performed. Jerry was obsessed—but only about how his own ballets were being scheduled: There was no pleasing him. It was Dunleavy and Bates who had the most complicated problems, which slowly I began to understand and anticipate. After Balanchine's death, in 1983—in fact, beginning during his final illness—I worked with Peter Martins, his designated successor. In late 1981 or thereabouts Lincoln had said to me, "It's going to be Peter. I want you to get to know him and try to help him—I'm too old." So I did, and we developed a solid bond, at first determined by our mutual intense belief in the enterprise, which gradually mutated into some kind of friendship, even affection—at least on my part.

When I traveled with the company (to London and Copenhagen, or to Saratoga, its summer residence), Peter and I spent many long evenings over pasta and wine together with Heather Watts, the clever and outspoken dancer with whom Peter lived for ten years. There was only one subject: the company—typical of the ballet world, which is so isolated and self-referential. But all I *wanted* to talk about was the company; I certainly didn't want to talk about publishing. There were moments, as more and more red wine was consumed, when the Heather-Peter dynamic took on Strindbergian overtones, but overriding everything was their dedication to their work and to Balanchine. Heather, unlike most dancers, was a serious reader. I remember a moment in London when, after a performance to which I'd brought Doris Lessing, we all happened to end up in the same little Italian restaurant, and Heather's awe at meeting the author of *The Golden Notebook* was matched only by Doris's awe at meeting the dancer she'd just been vigorously applauding inside Covent Garden.

While Balanchine was in the hospital through his long, final illness, Peter was essentially in charge of the company, though with no official position. And when Balanchine died, there were several people who felt they had a right to be considered his heir. But George on two occasions had told me directly that Peter was his choice. One was a casual remark, in passing. But the other was highly specific and clearly deliberate. We were standing alone together in the wings watching Peter partnering Suzanne. Without turning to me he said, "It has to be Peter. He understands what a ballerina needs." Was he referring to Peter's genius as a partner? Who knows? Balanchine, at least with me, came forth with utterances rather than taking part in conversations. Was he making sure that a member of the board could bear witness to his decision? Again, who knows? Whatever was in his mind, I took his statement as a royal command.

My personal relationship with George remained completely impersonal. He was always courteous, always ready to answer questions and discuss company problems, but I suspected he wasn't really certain why I was so deeply involved in his company's affairs. Finally I asked his peerless assistant, Barbara Horgan (she was later the executrix of his will and the head of the Balanchine Trust), with whom I had, and have, a warm friendship, why he trusted the head of a publishing house with the responsibilities I had assumed—I was by this time in charge of the company's marketing as well as its programming. "That's easy to explain," she said. "It's your name. Gottlieb [love of God] is the German equivalent of Amadeus. It's the Mozart connection."

Mozart or not, whenever he said something to me I felt that it had just happened to occur to him while I happened to be standing next to him, not, in most cases, that he was addressing it to me specifically. A bizarre example of this phenomenon took place in Saratoga. We were staying in the same house, and one beautiful morning when he wasn't well enough to go to the theater for rehearsal, we found ourselves on deck chairs out on the lawn, drinking coffee. Suddenly he said, "You know, dear"—everyone was "dear"—"Suzanne has a bad taste." To that there was no conceivable reply. Pause. "Yes, Suzanne has a very bad taste." Pause. Then, "A very bad taste in tutus." I was too flustered to ask him to explain.

When there was something practical to be discussed or decided, he was not only quick, sharp, and decisive, he was obviously in his element. Several times when I nervously called him at home about some crisis, he was far from irritated. He welcomed problems, I concluded, so that he could have the satisfaction of dealing with them. And no task was too small for him to deal with. In 1976 the orchestra rejected our contract offer and threatened to strike. I was one of the five negotiators, along with Betty and Barbara, representing the company. The discussions went on for months, and each time we met with the orchestra's committee the session lasted for hours—many hours. We would make an offer and then wait. The talks were ugly—no surprise to Betty, who, like Lincoln, loathed the musicians: His view was that they were all disappointed artists who had thought they were going to be Heifetz or Casals and were bitterly spending their lives invisible in the pit while the audience was cheering a bunch of twenty-year-olds up on the stage. The orchestra committee—you could see them as firebrands or malcontents—was certainly bitter about something.

The meetings had moved to the World Trade Center. Every scheduled morning we would turn up, read the papers, do the crossword, drink coffee, and call our respective offices. And then one day we ran out of dimes to feed the pay phone down the hall. (No cell phones in those prehistoric times.) In this emergency we decided to leave a message for George Michelmore, the orchestra manager, asking him to bring us a sack of dimes—we were afraid to go out in case the musicians finished caucusing and required our immediate presence. Half an hour later a worried Balanchine burst into the room, bearing dimes. "Am I in time?" he asked. They had given the message to the wrong George. He was so grateful to have been given something useful to do that no one had the heart to tell him that the dimes had nothing to do with the negotiations. We just thanked him profusely and sent him home.

By this time, Lincoln's mental condition was fragile, climaxing in a breakdown in which he turned up at a performance at the State Theater with his head shaved and in an outsize Army uniform, and shouting. He had to be restrained and escorted from the theater by guards. This was before lithium had been prescribed for him and his bipolarism brought under control. It was horrible to watch his psyche fraying, his moods swinging from euphoria to rage. To me, the saddest aspect of his condition was his insistence on believing that Balanchine had no use for him, no longer cared for his ideas or counted on his support. One awful day when we needed to schedule a meeting to deal with some strategic issue, Balanchine suggested to me that we get together at Lincoln's house, and asked me, in my accustomed role as Messenger of the Gods, to arrange this with Lincoln. When I tried to, Lincoln turned on me in fury, roaring, "George didn't suggest that! It was *your* idea, to make me feel George is still thinking about me. George doesn't want any part of me!" I managed to convince him that this wasn't the case, but I was shaken and dismayed that the grand partnership between these two great men had come to this.

But George never faltered in his behavior to Lincoln, consulting him when necessary (and often when not), paying attention to his ideas, visiting him in the institution he had been installed in, honoring him. I had assumed that the two of them had always been close, but it certainly wasn't a close friendship as I understand friendship. They rarely if ever saw each other socially, except at formal occasions. Their interests diverged—George always thinking musically, Lincoln's focus on the visual; George invested in food and drink, himself a cook, Lincoln barely noticing what he ate, even unaware of it: impossible to forget the dry, stale sandwiches his unsympathetic housekeeper would leave out for him and for whatever guests he might bring home after a performance. The two men had been crucial to each other's lives (and to ours), but they were not attuned to each other.

I never stopped feeling in awe of Lincoln, but I was always aware of how precarious my relationship with him was. He was a volcano, and when he erupted it was not pleasant being around him. (He did it to me once, so I know.) Of everyone I've ever known, he was the person I learned the most from and looked up to the most, yet although I was so fond of him, I never felt a true personal bond, despite the amount of time we spent together over the years at countless lunches and performances. I had an insight into the effect he had on me when one day I was walking back to my office from a meeting at the theater at which Lincoln had been his usual forceful and perverse self. Once in a while I find that I'm humming something that's clearly sending me a message from myself. This time I heard myself humming the Scarecrow's famous song from *The Wizard of Oz*: "In my head I was thinkin' / I could be another Lincoln / If I only had a brain." So speaks the subconscious, particularly ironic in relation to Lincoln, who very aggressively denied that the subconscious existed.

When the succession crunch came, Lincoln had his way. His goal was to preserve and safeguard Balanchine's glorious achievements, and to accomplish this he had to protect the institutions he and Balanchine had built—you couldn't have continuity of Balanchine ballets without a major company and school. Besides, Lincoln was a profound believer in institutions themselves, as his history of having been instrumental in the creation of the Museum of Modern Art (especially its film and photographic departments), the dance library at Lincoln Center, and indeed Lincoln Center itself attests. He was not prepared to see New York City Ballet and the School of American Ballet go down the drain, and he felt that Peter was his best hope of preserving them. Also, Peter was a capable choreographer, whom Balanchine had encouraged.

My own connection to the company didn't change for the first half dozen years or so after Peter took charge. But some time after 1987, when I moved from Knopf to *The New Yorker*, it changed dramatically. For years I had been close to Arlene Croce, universally recognized (and by some resented) as the greatest of all dance critics. We had often traveled together—to dance events in Paris, London, Montreal, Washington—and had been together at countless performances in New York. I knew her family, she was welcomed by mine.

As time passed, Arlene—and many other lovers of City Ballet who, like her, had ardently welcomed Peter's accession—grew more and more distressed at what she perceived to be deterioration in the level of the company's performance, and she pulled no punches in her attacks on him in *The New Yorker*. A year or so after I turned up at the magazine, I got a furious call from Peter at work, demanding that I get off the board immediately: "It's not just that you edit her and publish her," he said, "it's that you *agree* with her." It was the only time in my years with Peter that I ever heard his voice charged with emotion. There was nothing I could say: I *did* agree with her. I wasn't wise enough to understand that I had hurt him. All I could say was that I would certainly remove myself from the board, but not at that moment—why have a fuss? My term was coming to a close in a few months, and I just wouldn't stand for re-election.

So ended what I came to think of as the great adventure of my life—my association with Lincoln and George's great enterprise. New York City Ballet, as Arlene once said, was our civilization, and I felt myself supremely fortunate to have been in a position to be useful to it and to observe it from the inside.

There is a postscript to my relationship with Peter Martins. In 1998, *Vanity Fair* invited me to write a long article celebrating the fiftieth anniversary of City Ballet. I was filled with trepidation, but was also drawn to the opportunity to focus my ideas about the company and my relationship to it—they wanted a piece that was both historical and personal. Because there was ongoing dispute in the dance world about Peter's performance, a dispute I couldn't ignore in my article, I felt he should have the chance to state his view of things, and I called his office to see if he would meet with me. The message came back that he saw no reason to participate in what he was certain would be a negative approach to the company and to him personally. I made it clear that that was far from what I had in mind, and guaranteed him complete control not only of all his quotes but of the context in which I used them, and on that basis he agreed to proceed.

We were to meet in his office up on the fourth floor of the State Theater late one afternoon. There was no one around. I walked down the long, dark corridor high above the stage and found him in his office waiting for me with a bottle of red wine and two glasses. We had had no contact with each other for about a decade, apart from unavoidable stiff acknowledgments as we passed each other in the theater. At first, things were tense, to say the least, but quickly that passed, and we found ourselves blabbing away about everything the way we always had. I was startled at how open, even indiscreet, he was—about the company, its problems, *his* problems, his view of his dancers, Balanchine, Robbins, Lincoln, and inevitably our relationship.

What was supposed to have been a half-hour formal interview stretched into a two-hour nostalgic conversation. Peter was the most unguarded I had ever known him, and all my former fondness for him rose up—and, I felt, his for me. It was like a classic family reunion, with everyone falling back into his accustomed role, the old dynamic instantly restored. The most emotional passage in our exchange came when not once but twice he said, "Isn't it ironic? If you hadn't gone to *The New Yorker* you would be here now, running it with me." And it was true. Yes, he said this in an impulsive moment in a highly charged atmosphere, but I preferred to believe, and do believe, that he meant it.

But my joining him at the company would have been a disaster, since I couldn't pretend I was at ease with the path it had taken; we would have been in constant disagreement. I became all too aware of that home truth when, a year later, in 1999, I began as the dance critic for *The New York Observer,* and as bad luck would have it, my first review was of Peter's new version of *Swan Lake.* There was no way I could pretend to like it, and that was the end of any possible rapprochement between us. He had, however, generously okayed the way I presented him and his views in *Vanity Fair,* and I'm grateful that my last extended contact with him was a healing rather than contentious one.

During my City Ballet years I was publishing a wide range of books on dance that carried me further into the ballet world. Most exciting to me was Margot Fonteyn's *Autobiography*—I had never ceased revering her. The manuscript was already far advanced when I acquired it from its British publisher, but there was time for some modest work, and when I first met her I was not only undone by her extraordinary charm and beauty but struck by her total professionalism. Whatever was needed she supplied—except answers to questions she didn't want to consider. I knew she disliked talking about her roles, but I pressed her anyway. "When you were standing behind the cottage door waiting for your first entrance in *Giselle*, how were you preparing yourself?" "Well, you know, Bob, I would be listening to the music and when I heard my cue I would just open the door and start dancing." Very instructive—as were her replies to other no doubt equally fatuous questions I posed. This was my first exposure to the famous Fonteyn stubbornness.

She tried to be cooperative about photos, but as we sat on the floor of the sitting room in her London flat, going through stacks of them, she rejected one after another—she hated her smile, she wasn't turned out, her costume didn't fit correctly, her hair was a mess, she disliked herself in this role, she couldn't expose the deficiency in her partner's line. In other words, no, no, no. It was a long tussle before we exhausted ourselves into a compromise selection. You couldn't push her, but you could appeal to her common sense and her desire to make things work.

When I asked her how many weeks she could give us to promote the book, she asked how many weeks I wanted. When I floated the idea of at least two, she immediately agreed and asked whether three would be more helpful. Yes it would, and that's what she signed on for. (When I announced this at our sales conference, even the more hardened reps applauded.) Months later when the book was published and she was fulfilling a punishing schedule around the country, meeting every obligation and never complaining or demanding special treatment, I called her in her hotel room in San Francisco to ask how she was holding up. "I'm fine," she said. When I asked how she *could* be fine spending day after day trying to answer the same uninformed questions to interviewers whose knowledge of ballet was limited to the names Pavlova, *Swan Lake*, and Nureyev, her answer was "Yes, it's all true, but you see, darling Bob, it's all so much easier than dancing."

The book itself omitted a great deal—her sense of privacy was unassailable—but what it told was told frankly, modestly, and convincingly: It represented fairly the woman and artist we all knew her to be. Her evident strength of purpose, humor, and lack of pretention or self-regard won over reviewers and readers, and made her book a bestseller. Of course, her three weeks of promoting didn't hurt.

In the late 1970s Margot embarked on a highly complicated project—a six-part television series she had dreamed up for the BBC called *The Magic of Dance*. It was agreed that Knopf (me) would edit and design the elaborate accompanying book. The ideas were Margot's, the writing was Margot's, the TV presenter was Margot, and I swept up behind her. What made the whole rushed endeavor possible was the presence throughout of a young woman the BBC had supplied to do the picture research, Catherine Ashmore—as devoted, ingenious, lighthearted, and modest a colleague and friend as one could dream of. (She would become Britain's finest performance photographer.)

We pulled it off, but barely. By this time—it was our third book together—Margot and I had come to know each other quite well. A good deal of our time had been spent in teasing about the comparative merits of Balanchine and her own choreographic god, Frederick Ashton. Over the years I had taken her to a number of City Ballet performances, which she admired, but although she revered Balanchine, its ways were not her ways. A typical Margot tease: She was writing some of the text in our offices, much the way Betty Bacall had done, and again on long yellow pads which I would read at the end of the day before having them typed up overnight. One day she referred to Ashton as "The greatest choreographer of the 20th century." That was a clear provocation, but by then I knew whom I was dealing with. She would have fought me tooth and nail if I had objected, but I kept my mouth shut. The following day, when I saw her revisions, the sentence had been altered. It now referred to Ashton as "With George Balanchine, one of the two greatest choreographers of the 20th century." We had had our fun.

George and Margot had worked together on one memorable occasion, when in 1950 Sadler's Wells invited him to mount *Ballet Imperial* on the company. This sublime but ultra-demanding ballet is notorious for its extended opening passage for the ballerina, coming after a long, breathtaking section for a second ballerina. The role, with its supreme technical demands, was not natural territory for Fonteyn, and I was curious to know how she felt about having done it. (As the company's prima ballerina, she was first-cast in the role; Moira Shearer, who passionately admired Balanchine, and later wrote a book about him, was second-cast.) When I asked Margot about the experience, she was, as always, frank and self-deprecating. "Well, I would stand in the wings through that long introductory section and think, 'If I can get through that first awful passage I'll be all right. But you know, Bob, I never could!'" Years later I asked George about it. "Nice girl, Margot," he said. "Once or twice I take to movies—no hanky-panky, nothing like that, but nice girl. Good dancer. But in *Ballet Imperial,* other one better!" I didn't ask whether there had been hanky-panky with Moira Shearer.

I was able to do one last thing for Margot. In 2004 I mounted an exhibition called *Margot Fonteyn in America: A Celebration* at the dance library at Lincoln Center, a project I had thought up years before. Everyone had been for it but no one focused until—a miracle—a new head of the Library for the Performing Arts was appointed: a dynamo named Jackie Davis (sorry: *Jacqueline*). The first time I spoke to her on the phone I knew we were on our way—I heard clarity, firmness, energy, and high spirits. She felt the same way I did: We were made for each other. And she let me do things my way. (Not all her colleagues were amused.) I inspired the Rudolf Nureyev Foundation to come up with the necessary funding, and I swanned around being a curator. But what really pleased me was to be able to remind the New York dance world of how great a dancer Margot had been, and in particular of what an immense impact she had had on America and our city.

My relations with two other transcendent dancers were more purely professional: Mikhail Baryshnikov and Natalia Makarova. *Baryshnikov at Work* was brought to fruition by the knowledgeable, clever, difficult, and ultimately self-destructing Charles France. Charles's deep knowledge of dance, plus what he had learned while performing the various functions he fulfilled at ABT while acting as second-in-command of the company when Misha was running it, qualified him to extract a mine of information, commentary, and understanding from his boss. And the learned and highly cultivated Russian émigré scholar and writer Gennady Smakov—author of the seminal *Great Russian Dancers,* which I also published at Knopf—was able to do the same for Natasha's *A Dance Autobiography.* Both were books about *work,* each organized around the ballets the dancers had performed, yet each involving personal material as well.

I was never sure how important his book was to Misha. He certainly worked hard on it, and cooperated in every possible way, but it was essentially Charles's project. To me it was a thrilling one, since I felt then, and still feel, that Baryshnikov was the greatest ballet dancer I had ever seen, and probably the greatest the world had ever seen. My most unforgettable memory of him came during the "Kingdom of the Shades" act of *La Bayadère*. There was a leap into the wings beyond anything I had ever encountered. And the audience responded in a way I've never witnessed before or since: not with a roar of applause and bravos but with a gigantic collective intake of breath, a communal gasp of disbelief. Charles told me years later that the not particularly generous choreographer Antony Tudor went backstage that night and told Misha that this had been the single greatest moment he had ever experienced at the ballet.

Misha, famously, had moods. Natasha had temperament—it fueled her performances yet never got in the way of her art. You never knew where her feelings might carry her, whereas Misha seemed always in control. This made things interesting when they danced together. Natasha was very much invested in her book, and was proud of it. I was determined to give her a beautiful object, and I think I succeeded—the layout, the paper, the printing, the cover, had a glamour that reflected her true ballerinadom. She was also funny, and of course a fanatical worker.

And she was quintessentially Russian. One Sunday night she came over to our house to deal with photographs—there were a lot of them! Maria was making pasta, Lizzie and Nicky, who was about two, were very present. It was family supper. So what did Natasha bring to the house? A bottle of wine—predictable; a pretty rattle that her Andrei, a year older than Nicky, had outgrown—charming; and—perhaps less predictable but equally charming—a big box of Pampers. As she told Maria, she hadn't forgotten what it was like on a Sunday night when you ran out of them and all the stores were closed. That wasn't a Russian ballerina, that was a Russian mother.

In my view, the two finest memoirs by dancers of the day were those by Paul Taylor and Allegra Kent, and I got to work on both of them. I was an immense admirer of Paul's work (and of his dancing, having first seen him when he was with Martha Graham), and he was, and is, Maria's favorite choreographer. We had never met, but one day he came to see me. He was going to write a book, he said, and would I publish it? He did, and I did.

Like his dances, his book was filled with surprises, perversities, hilarities, evasions, high dramas, and deep truths. That could all have been anticipated. What couldn't have been was his passion for writing—he loved doing it, was always gleeful at being pressed for more, eager to rethink and rewrite. I recently asked him what he remembered of our work together back in the eighties, and first and foremost he remembered the fun we had doing it. And then he dug up from his basement thick folders of our back-and-forth letters, notes, jottings. Sometimes they were three words long, some took up pages. He was always gnawing away at his worries about how much to tell, how much to reveal of his inner life, how to be candid about people without making them (too) uncomfortable. I was always urging him to dig deeper, he was always trying. New pages would arrive with little notes attached. 1982: "Dear Bob, Before I have second thoughts, better send these 3 pages. Anybody who thinks they were quick and easy is wacko. Fond thoughts, Paul." 1984: "Dear Great Blue Pencil—Is this an ending? I hope. Will call on Monday to ask what's next. If it's time, am dying to know what axing and rewriting lies ahead. Hot diggity!!!!!—Paul." On we went, from 1981 through 1986. The dynamic remained the same, though our salutations to each other got more and more lunatic, until we settled down to Paulsie and Bobbsy, which they remain.

The book's voice was utterly singular, and if certain facts were playfully tweaked, the man himself was there, both his wry take on life and his bleak take on life fully on display. I loved *Private Domain*, and I loved the man who wrote it. Our warm relationship has lasted thirty-five years—less, perhaps, a friendship than that rarer thing, an undeclared closeness.

Allegra's book, too, was a perfect expression of who she was—heartfelt, perceptive, whimsical, evasive, immensely intelligent; all the things Balanchine (and the rest of us) loved her for in her thirty years of dancing for City Ballet. She, like Paul, is a born writer, with a unique and convincing voice. I was not her publisher, but her devoted official editor, alas, had no real dance background. One day Allegra called me to say she was nervous. First of all, her editor wanted her to come down to the office and read the manuscript aloud to her. Huh? And, more serious, the editor had suggested that she rewrite the entire book in the manner of John Dos Passos. Would I read it and advise—to begin with, about whether what she was doing had any validity? That one was easy to answer. I offered to do some editing and help in other ways if that was okay with her publisher, who generously gave me a free hand. I did the usual, and a little more than the usual, coping with the text, the pictures, the dust jacket, the jacket copy, the press list, coming up with the title (*Once a Dancer...*)—all standard stuff—but also coping with Allegra's ex-husband, Bert Stern, the famous photographer and pal of Marilyn Monroe. We needed his pictures, but Allegra didn't feel comfortable dealing with him directly, and of course there were potential legal issues. I was the go-between.

Bert was totally cooperative—wished the project well, gave Allegra the use of any and all photos, was ready to read the proofs and sign off on the legal issues, if any. We had toned down the Bert story as well as we could and stay honest—apart from anything else, they shared three children. At the appointed hour I turned up in Bert's studio to hear his verdict on the text. He had no complaints, which was something of a surprise, since the story of his drug abuse, his unfaithfulness, his violence, his arrest, his involvement with the notorious "Dr. Feelgood," who supplied trendy New York with what turned out to be amphetamines, was not exactly an attractive one. None of that bothered Bert in the least. But he insisted on one change. Allegra had written that on the morning after their wedding night he had asked her to bring him a glass of milk in bed, and when she did, he complained that it wasn't cold enough. At which she flung the milk in his face. "It wasn't milk," Bert insisted. "It was orange juice!" I assured him that

Allegra would make the correction. As I like to say, being an editor is a full-service job.

In this case it led to the strengthening of a long friendship. I had worshipped Allegra as a dancer, but I had thought of her as a goddess; it never occurred to me in my twenties that I was six years older than she was, and that since she is a compulsive and penetrating reader, she might possibly have found me interesting . . .

There were many other dance books, including the memoirs of the beautiful, exotic Japanese-American Sono Osato, who went from the Ballets Russes to Broadway—I had seen her as "Miss Subways" in the original cast of *On the Town.*

There was *Chance and Circumstance*, the revealing and perceptive memoirs of Carolyn Brown, Merce Cunningham's most important female dancer. It was thirty years between the day she signed her contract and the day the book was published, but it was worth waiting for.

There was a splendidly luxe and comprehensive book about Anna Pavlova, by Margot's great friend and photographer Keith Money— we spent a number of contented years obsessing over it. There were the three volumes of Arlene Croce's nonpareil dance criticism. There was David Vaughan's definitive chronicle of Frederick Ashton's work. And there was the elaborate, equally definitive *Suki Schorer on Balanchine Technique.* Suki had been a charming and popular City Ballet dancer, but her fame and influence stem from her magnificent work as a teacher at SAB, and she was able to codify her knowledge and experience for the benefit of all Balanchine teachers to come.

A particularly challenging project had been creating for ABT a book with the scope and luster of Lincoln's *New York City Ballet.* When the company approached me about it, I was dubious, explaining that whereas I understood City Ballet from the bottom up, I had been watching Ballet Theater on and off forever and had no real sense of what it really was. They gave me seats for every performance of their upcoming season, and by the time it was over, I had figured it out: I hadn't grasped the company's basic aesthetic because it didn't have one. It had good ballets and bad ballets, great dancers and not-so-great dancers; beginning with noble intentions, it had become primarily a series of vehicles for stars, with the exception of some notable pieces by Tudor, Robbins, Agnes de Mille, and a few others (including Balanchine's *Theme and Variations* and Twyla Tharp's *Push Comes to Shove*). Now the job was easy: construct a physically alluring book geared to reflect that reality.

Yes, Twyla Tharp—as though there were a lot of Twylas. But it's not her name that makes her unique. I can't remember when or how we first met, but we saw eye to eye right from the start. One night when we were having dinner together she mentioned that she had taken her ballets off the market. I told her she was nuts—even though she had them all preserved on tape, they would die if they weren't performed. Besides, I said, let's face it, you're always on the lookout for money, and you're turning away big bucks. The next morning she instructed her agent to make her ballets available again. I hadn't lived in vain.

We never worked together, but we became colleagues of a sort after I had been associated with Eddie Villella's Miami City Ballet for a few years. (He was Edward in Miami but will always be Eddie in New York.) I very much hoped that the company would start dancing Twyla—the only current choreographer whose work was deeply embedded in the repertory was Paul Taylor—and I was sure Eddie and Twyla would be a great match if they could be brought together. I wanted us to begin with *Nine Sinatra Songs*, perfect for our dancers and perfect for our audience. With some prodding, everyone agreed to agree. Twyla had been wary—she didn't know Eddie or the company. Eddie was wary—he didn't know Twyla, except he knew she was a scrapper. Well, what did this ex-boxer think *he* was?

Rehearsals began. Twyla had insisted on seeing daily rushes of them, and she was so pleased that she flew down to Miami to work with the dancers herself—*and on her own nickel*! And when she came she was fantastic. First of all, she loved Eddie's class: "He knows what he's doing," she muttered to me on the first morning. Unprecedented high praise. And then the company, once it got over its terror, began to realize two crucial things about Twyla. One: She really loves dancers, understands them, and is always in their court. Two: She works harder than just about anyone I've ever known. It's not a conscious work ethic, it's who and what she is. And you'd have to be perverse not to give her back everything she's giving you.

Over the years Miami added more and more of her repertory to its own, including *Push Comes to Shove* and *In the Upper Room*, with its fiendishly demanding energy level. It was the closing ballet at the company's first New York City season (at the City Center), and as the dancers were rushing for their bus to the airport, Twyla and I had dinner. She had been rapturously received by the audience when she took a bow. Now she volunteered that this had been the best performance of *In the Upper Room* she had ever seen.

A few years later, when she was creating a new piece for us in Miami, she asked if she could move into my house for a week—she hated her hotel. It worked out perfectly. She was at the studio and going through her exercise regimen long before I was up, and she was getting home just in time for a six p.m. supper (late for her) before going to bed. We barely saw each other. But these meals were made particularly jolly by our ice cream fights. At first we spooned out the Häagen-Dazs carefully, to be certain no one was cheating. Then things got rougher: one carton, two spoons, two pigs, and no holds barred. The greedy child in her had called out to the greedy child in me. We still perform this sacred ritual whenever we eat at her place in New York.

But the child in her never interferes with her supreme professionalism. She's good at everything she does, except relaxing. Which helps to explain why some people resist her: Not everyone demands and expects perfection. But she never expects more than she provides.

My connection with Miami City Ballet began a short time after I bought a house in Miami Beach, twenty-odd years ago. I was walking on Lincoln Road, not yet re-gentrified, and there was Linda Villella, Eddie's wife, whom I had known slightly in New York and liked a lot. As for Eddie, he was rightly known as Balanchine's—and America's— greatest male ballet dancer. Eddie was as pleased to see me as I was to see him, because, let's face it, there weren't many people in Miami whom one could talk to about ballet. And in our very different ways, we were both part of the Balanchine experience. Put any two Balanchine people in a room together, and five hours later they're still talking.

In 2000, the city of Miami Beach built a magnificent studio for MCB, fortuitously a ten-minute walk from my house. Soon I was spending my days there, observing, butting in, and ridiculously content in the three-way dynamic that emerged among Eddie, me, and his second-in-command, Pam Gardiner, a lawyer who was now the company's executive director. She and I loved each other from the first, sharing a passion for supporting Eddie in the face of the less-than-ardent local population and the horrifying financial abyss that opened up almost automatically every year. It was always touch and go, but under his direction the company never stopped growing and improving.

Perhaps the situation would have been easier if not for Eddie's determination to keep the company Balanchine-oriented, not just in its choice of repertory but in the way he taught and coached his dancers. They were Balanchine dancers—fast, energetic, dynamic—in a town whose idea of ballet (if it had one) was *Swan Lake* and *Giselle*. When I was down in Miami, usually for five or six weeks at a stretch, the three of us were together almost every day, planning and plotting to ward off disaster. Soon I was into everything—encouraged by Eddie and embraced by Pam, I was helping on repertory; working on budgets (after all, I had behind me twenty years' experience running a profitable publishing house); helping with marketing: all those years at City Ballet and a lifetime of selling books. When we decided to put on the full-evening *Don Quixote*—by then, Eddie's plan to introduce the classics to the repertory had taken root—I acted as dramaturg. (I'd seen it a million times.) Etc., etc., etc. My greatest contribution, though, may have been getting the handyman to readjust the door of the company refrigerator so that we could get to the milk more readily. *That* took genius. What I wouldn't do was go on the board of directors, despite Pam and Eddie pushing me to. There was a limit.

During the dozen or so years I was joined at the hip with Eddie and Pam, the company was barely managing to survive financially from month to month. Sometimes it was week to week. Our reputation was much greater around the dance world than it was in south Florida, whose mind was on higher things, like sports and karaoke. (Eddie often said he had come to the wrong city.) The crises were recurrent, relentless, and emotionally draining, particularly for Eddie. Even so, there were two great highs. In 2009 we had a triumphant week at the City Center, the theater where Eddie had grown up on the stage and I had grown up in the audience. And our Paris adventure of 2011 was even more extraordinary—a three-week season at the Châtelet. Paris knew nothing about the company until our spectacular opening night. Typical of the response: Elisabeth Platel, the head of the Paris Opera Ballet School, said to me at the dinner that followed, "We've never seen anything like it! The attack, the joy in movement, and the way they all dance as a *company*, with the same approach and intensity, and with such a sense of community!" (Anyone who knows the very different tone of the Paris Opera Ballet will know what she meant.)

When the curtain came down on *Ballet Imperial* on closing night— after seventeen different programs of fourteen different ballets, my greatest challenge as a programmer—the audience (the *French* audience) roared and cheered and bravoed and stomped for ten full minutes. After the first five minutes everyone connected to the company was out on the stage, beaming, crying, clapping. Eddie was beyond happy: This level of acclaim on the stage where *Petrouchka* had had its premiere exactly a hundred years earlier was beyond what he could have dreamed of. At the reception held for the company a few minutes later, he made an emotional speech, saying, "I will be seventy-five on October first. This is the most incredible night of my entire seventy-five years!"

It seemed as if we had conquered the world. But, back in Miami, it was as if it had never happened. In the three weeks we had been away, the financial situation had worsened, going from dire to desperate. There was no new support, no acknowledgment that the company had pulled off a miracle. After twenty-five years of struggle, Eddie's back was once more to the wall, and it seemed to me that he was falling into a serious depression. His relations with the board, always stressful, got to a point where there was no communication between him and it.

And then he was told that unless he agreed to be replaced, there would be no funds forthcoming. Which meant the end.

My view was simple if brutal: Much as I cared for Eddie personally, my first priority was to try to help save the company. Not because I feel that institutions are more important than people, but because I couldn't bear the idea that dancing Balanchine the way MCB did might vanish. I did my best to help broker a plausible controlled exit plan that would do the least amount of damage to everyone concerned, but too much pain and anger had been unleashed, and the arrangement that was glued together didn't have a chance. Within months Eddie would be gone from the company he single-handedly had created and still inspired.

Who, then, to replace him? As a dance critic, and given my connections with the large world of ballet, I was the logical person to lead the search. A committee of eleven—including board members, friends of the company, and representatives of the dancers, but not me— would make the final choice, but it became my sole responsibility to put before them a slate of candidates. (I liked to call myself the Search Committee of One—the only kind of committee I feel comfortable being on.) I warned the board leadership that Balanchine people who were top-notch and who were actually available were never going to number more than three or four—if we were lucky.

Immediately I got in touch with Lourdes Lopez for consultation. I'd known her forever, had in fact seen her first public performance— in *Stars and Stripes* at the School of American Ballet's annual graduation exercises, in 1973, when she was fifteen—and we had the kind of extended family relationship that everyone in the Balanchine world has with everyone else. But I didn't start getting to know her well until, after twenty-four years dancing for City Ballet, and now head of the George Balanchine Foundation, she organized and led a group to Saint Petersburg to participate in a Balanchine symposium there. I was powerfully struck by the smooth, easy way she managed things, surrounded by people with complicated egos and agendas in a country not easy to negotiate. It was a bravura performance—and an invisible one; *her* ego was not on display.

Together now we went over dozens, scores, of names, very few of which were plausible. Naturally, a number of people, some of them delusional, put their names forward, but only a few of them could be taken seriously. There were perhaps half a dozen potential candidates of the right age who had Balanchine backgrounds, executive experience, and solid temperaments, and almost all of these were settled in important jobs. Even so, I tapped them all for advice. Eventually, I met or spoke with about thirty people, growing more and more disheartened—there was just no substantial slate of appropriate candidates.

Months went by, time was running out, and I called Lourdes again, insisting that she meet me right away for lunch at my favorite diner. Once more we went over the lists. And yet again. And then, in the middle of a sentence, I broke off. "Actually," I said, "I *have* a candidate. You." It had never occurred to me, it had never occurred to her—she was too modest, I was too slow-witted. But she was the perfect choice, and I hadn't even known she had been raised in the Cuban community of Miami and had lived there until she came to New York to go to SAB. Beautiful, appealing, ultra-capable, bilingual (a great plus in Miami), deep in the Balanchine world and tradition, she was now running the company called Morphoses that she and the choreographer Christopher Wheeldon had founded a few years earlier. So why hadn't I pounced on Lourdes at the start? Because I thought of her as embedded in New York: Morphoses active there, her husband working there, her younger daughter at school there. Her *life* there.

She was dumbstruck, scared, elated. The obstacles fell away as her family rallied. And after a short period of suspense (after I'd produced a five-page report detailing the search process), the eleven-member committee elected her by a lopsided majority. No one has regretted it since.

The transition was not pretty. The staff was traumatized, and the stress of his lame-duck situation had led Eddie to an abrupt departure, months before he was expected to go. One Thursday in September 2012 Lourdes was summoned by the board to get down to Miami over the weekend, since she was now in charge of the company. She had already been running the school (mostly from afar) for a few months, since Linda Villella, whose idea it had been and who had run it from the beginning, had resigned during the summer.

Lourdes miraculously calmed the waters. Immediately people began to grasp her artistic integrity, her executive abilities, and her generosity of spirit. What's more, she began attracting new money to the organization and new national attention to the company. The dancers responded as dancers always will when they sense that their leader is on their side. Today, the financial situation has vastly improved, and we're no longer living month to month and hand-to-mouth—only season to season.

Eddie saw my behavior as a betrayal. Naturally I didn't, but my admiration and concern for him have never abated, nor my gratitude to him for giving me a dozen years of excitement and pleasure participating so fully in the life of his company. Pam hung on, proving to Lourdes and the board how valuable she was. And with Lourdes I have the most loving of partnerships, if that's not too presumptuous a word. For her I made the supreme sacrifice. Having steered her into the perpetually fraught job of artistic director, I felt I should be there to back her up if we once again wandered into troubled waters: I joined the board.

Over the past seventy years, my involvement with dance has found me as audience, publisher, critic, and management, and it's never lost its fascination for me. As with most things I'm drawn to, I professionalized my love for it, but as I've become more and more knowledgeable, I've found it harder and harder to rediscover my first simple rapture. And then . . . a superb new ballet, a glorious performance, and I stop seeing things professionally and my wide-eyed faith and joy are restored.

One reason living in the dance world gives me so much pleasure is that there's very little bullshit connected with it (as opposed to the theater world). Dancers know the score. They watch themselves every day in the studio mirrors, not from narcissism but to identify flaws and weaknesses. They know better than you do if a given performance is deficient. And they know when their technique begins to falter after an extended layoff or even a few days without taking class. No amount of flattery can obscure these realities.

Another satisfaction I get from my life in/with dance is the (sometime) camaradarie of the dance critic's life. You see the same people night after night, you share an intense interest in your subject, you help each other out when you can. Which doesn't mean there aren't rivalries, resentments, dislikes, but for the most part, dance critics are generous with each other. Apart from my years of closeness with Arlene, I've enjoyed years of satisfying interaction with Joan Acocella (*The New Yorker*), Robert Greskovic (*The Wall Street Journal*), Mindy Aloff, Nancy Dalva, Deborah Jowitt, Gia Kourlas, Brian Seibert, Marina Harss, and Alastair Macaulay. He and I first met (at Covent Garden) when he was in his early twenties, almost forty years ago, and our paths have never ceased connecting. Twice I brought him to America to write for *The New Yorker* when Arlene was on sabbatical. He's stayed at our house, we've traveled together—to Amsterdam, twice to the Edinburgh Festival—and I was involved in his eventual move to New York and the *Times*. We may sometimes drive each other crazy, but no permanent damage has been done. We're connected.

The question I can never really answer is why for almost all my life, dance has affected me so deeply. After all, from my early childhood, words were the things most precious to me, and there are no words in ballet. I had never wanted to dance, I had no background in dance, it simply transported me, like love at first sight. Perhaps the very absence of words was instrumental: When I see a play or a movie or an opera, its words pass through my brain as if they're unreeling on a tape—it's hard for me to get past them to the basic experience of absorbing what I'm watching. Dance liberated me from the bondage of language, and balanced my life.

WRITING

WRITING HAPPENED TO ME. It sneaked up on me. Unlike many editors, never in my life did I have the slightest interest in writing, or even worse, in being a Writer. I'm a talking animal, not a typing one, although I always typed my own letters—dictating to a secretary seemed pretentious as well as impersonal, and handwriting was out of the question since my penmanship is illegible, even to me.

When I did have to write—papers in college, for instance—the results were cogent and sometimes even pleasing but everything was done at the last possible moment and with resentment. Writing was just too *hard*—conveying what you meant (assuming you meant anything at all) was too demanding. Like studying piano or being in psychoanalysis, it was a painful search for truth. My father, during the seventh-grade year I spent in Tucson, wrote me a letter that turned up half a century later. Commenting on my (rare) letters to him, he informed me that some people wrote to convey serious matters, to tell truths and share ideas; others used language glibly, to charm and avoid. "You are the latter kind of writer," he pronounced, and I accepted the verdict. On the other hand, glibness wasn't the worst quality to command when you were writing the reams of jacket copy and ads a career in publishing demands. Only Nina turned copy into art.

Through the years, I turned out an occasional piece, the only one of consequence a long essay for *The New Republic* on the publication, in 1963, of the twenty volumes of Dr. Leavis's magazine *Scrutiny*, which had been my bible in my college years. I spent an entire summer digesting those twenty (fat) books and thinking about them. But it wasn't the debt I owed *Scrutiny* that spurred me to this punishing task, and it wasn't intellectual curiosity; it was that I couldn't possibly afford the hundred-dollar price tag, and I had to own them. It would be thirty-five years before I exposed myself again to the anxiety involved in this performance.

And then it was a subject of consummate importance to my life that hooked me: New York City Ballet. Nothing could have been more challenging for me, because the stakes were so high, than to accept Graydon Carter's invitation to write an extensive piece for *Vanity Fair* not only about the history of NYCB's fifty years but about my own involvement with it, since I went back all the way. To get it right seemed unlikely, yet I had to acknowledge that there was no one I could think of who had had my double experience as both audience for half a century and total insider: I had lived for many years inside the yolk of the Balanchine-Kirstein egg.

The organization of the piece came to my structural mind instantly. The interviewing, the reading, the terror, followed swiftly. It got done, all fifteen—twenty?—thousand words of it, and nothing was cut; Doug Stumpf's editing was of a supreme delicacy; I was warmly welcomed into the illustration process—crucial for a piece on ballet; and the City Ballet community seemed pleased with the result. But I had hated doing it. The most horrible part was an almost unyielding resistance to sitting down at my typewriter—I could spend days avoiding it, while beating myself up for my recalcitrance. My only satisfaction was in having completed a difficult job. And, yes, the compliments one extracts from one's friends.

At some point during the many months of toiling on the City Ballet project, I was approached by *The New York Observer* to write book reviews for what was then the lively and interesting book section of the paper, edited by Adam Begley. In fact, it was Adam who approached me (we met for the first time in Paris, at a dinner party given by my close friend Diane Johnson), and he was speaking as an emissary from the paper's highly original and eccentric editor, Peter Kaplan. For whatever reasons, Kaplan just wanted me in his paper. We had never met. (And we never did meet; Adam explained, years later, that Peter was afraid that if he and I got to know each other I might "take over his brain." Maybe he knew what he was talking about, but I certainly didn't: Taking over brains was never one of my specialties.)

Given the stress of the *Vanity Fair* experience, I was going to say no, until it turned out that the book Adam wanted me to review was Michael Korda's publishing memoir, *Another Life*. Again irresistible, since, as I've written, it was greatly about our early days at Simon and Schuster. The pressure seemed less this time around because the *Observer*, with its notorious pink paper and irreverent manner, was not high on my radar screen. But one thing led to another, and soon I was writing piece after piece, and since I could more or less choose my shots, I was able to pursue subjects that beckoned to me. One example: I had noticed that three books in a row on the Scott Peterson murder case had reached the top of the nonfiction bestseller list. But why? I knew absolutely nothing about the case—I didn't even know whether Peterson was the killer or the killed—but I bought all the books and soon found out. (He was the killer, in case you don't know.) It was an awful story, but he was a riveting phenomenon—a complete, unmediated narcissist, uninteresting in himself, like most narcissists, but a compelling echo of, yet in profound contrast to, Clyde Griffiths, the tragic murderer of Dreiser's *An American Tragedy*, a book I unreservedly admire and still shudder at. That gave me something to think about—and write about.

Another plus about writing for the *Observer* then was that there was any amount of space available. If I wanted three or four thousand words to talk about Renata Adler and *The New Yorker* (and me), or Diana Vreeland, or the Windsors, or the cruel family dynamic of Francine du Plessix Gray and her unspeakably selfish parents, the space was ready and willing. It was a far cry from the battle for space that today almost every writer has to fight at almost every venue.

But the real pleasure for me at the *Observer* was working with Adam.

There was no push and pull, only give and take; we responded to language the same way. In due course (and none too soon: his was the kind of job you can do for only so long before losing your mind), he quit the paper to go on to higher things—like his superb biography of John Updike. But we were having too much fun together to quit cold turkey, or any other way. Today he and I soldier on together unofficially, casting cool affectionate eyes on all each other's stuff, including my dance reviews, his book reviews, my book reviews, his books, my books. And casting warm affectionate eyes on each other's lives—wives, families, homes. (He and his extraordinarily sympathetic—and good-looking—wife, Anne, live in a Hobbity town in England, but they're frequently here in un-Hobbity New York.)

After a while Adam told me that Peter Kaplan hoped I would write a regular column for him—I could pick my own subject. My first idea was shopping, something I love doing. (Shopping, not buying.) But my saner self prevailed. At that time, the paper had no dance coverage, which I thought a mistake: It was a New York paper, and New York was, after all, the "dance capital of the world." So I offered to write half a dozen times a year, when I felt something important was taking place that our readers should know about. Once I began, however, I quickly grasped that you can't cover sporadically an art form you care about. Soon I was writing twenty to thirty columns a year.

Writing about dance was and is hard for me—I have poor visual memory, no training in ballet vocabulary, and little ability for reproducing verbally exactly what's happening onstage. On the other hand, I have strengths. One is context: I've been watching dance for more than seventy years and have seen a lot and retained a lot. I also have—call it arrogance, call it healthy self-confidence—a solid trust in my judgment of dances and dancers, not unlike the security I felt from the start about my judgment of writing and writers. Finally, I can be funny—not the quality dance writers are best known for. So, despite the feelings of inadequacy that all serious dance critics admit to themselves in the light of Arlene Croce's magisterial work, I manage to forgive myself, or at least excuse myself, for being more of a canny reviewer than an authoritative thinker about this art I love.

As it happens, dance was also responsible for my beginning to write for *The New York Times Book Review*. When Chip McGrath left *The New Yorker* early in 1997 to become the *Book Review*'s editor, I was able to steer him in some right directions and deflect him from some wrong ones. One day early in his reign he called to ask me whether I thought he should consider reviewing the memoirs of Maria Tallchief— he himself wasn't a dance person. I read the galleys and told him that not only did he have to review it but that I was the one who should write the review; Tallchief was the mainstay of City Ballet during my first love affair with the company, and I understood her history, her work, and her central position as muse (and wife) in the Balanchine cosmography. I got the job.

I wrote a score or so of articles for Chip, and because I wasn't writing about books that demanded immediate attention, we could wait to run my stuff until there was room in an issue for the mostly lengthy pieces I was giving him. And because I wasn't financially dependent on my fees, I could afford to spend months reading and digesting just about everything available about a subject I was engaged with: four months, for instance, on Isadora Duncan; and almost as long on "Max and Marjorie: An Editorial Love Story," about the moving relationship between the author of *The Yearling*, Marjorie Kinnan Rawlings, and America's most famous book editor, Maxwell Perkins. The great satisfaction for me in working this way is the luxury of doing all that reading, and having time to ruminate. The great satisfaction for Chip, as he so flatteringly pointed out, hadn't to do with the quality of my work but with the fact that I delivered on schedule, to the agreed-upon length, and with no editorial work required. Anyone who has run a magazine will understand.

Knopf was now distributing the newly revived and handsomely packaged Everyman's Library, and I suggested that I put together for it a big new collection of Kipling's stories—their old volume was skimpy and not very satisfactory, at least to this Kipling lover. The joy was having an excuse to read, in more or less chronological order, the two-hundred-odd stories he had written (luckily, I had a complete Kipling on hand), from his early glittering tales set in India which captivated the world to the painful tragic stories of the Great War, and then to choose among them and try to convey their astonishing variety and depth to new readers; he was, I decided along the way, together with Dickens, one of the two greatest writers of narrative in English fiction. The introduction I wrote to the Everyman Kipling was the closest I've come as a writer to pure literary criticism, and therefore the closest I've come to the path I might have taken if I'd chosen an academic career.

For once I was proud of something I'd written, and sent the book to a dozen or so people I knew. One was Susan Sontag. When soon afterward I ran into her in a bookstore—where else?—she exclaimed, in her customarily flamboyant and less than tactful way, "Bob! I didn't know you could write so well!" Susan was always Susan. (My favorite Susan remark was to a mutual friend who was congratulating her on her novel *The Volcano Lover.* "Yes," she said, "and you'll like it even more the next time you read it.")

Another person I sent the Kipling to was Barbara Epstein, co-founder and co-editor (with Bob Silvers) of *The New York Review of Books*, whom I'd known, though never closely, forever; she and her husband, Jason, had come into publishing at more or less the same time I had. Since the *Review* was the publication I most admired, it was the place I most wanted to write for, if I was going to keep on writing. Fortunately, Barbara was impressed enough to welcome me to the magazine, and when she died, far too young, Bob Silvers kept me on and kept me going. By now twenty-five or thirty of my pieces have appeared there, ranging in subject from Douglas Fairbanks and Ethel Waters to Bruno Bettelheim and Elia Kazan. It's been, for me, a continually rewarding experience, especially since so many of my closest friends—Janet Malcolm, Alma Guillermoprieto, Diane Johnson, Daniel Mendelsohn—write for it too, and just about everyone I know reads it. We contributors know how lucky we are, except when we're bitching about something or other—an activity, I now realize, that's endemic to the freelance life. It makes me squirm to think how *The New Yorker*'s writers must have been griping about me when I was in charge there.

If I was masochistically anxious about everything I wrote for the *Observer* and the *Times Book Review* (and I was), I was still more anxious about appearing in the *Review* and, later, *The New Yorker*. But the dynamic was really the same. For many years I felt I was a fraud or a carpetbagger, to such a degree that I couldn't acknowledge either publicly or to myself that I was "a writer"; I was an editor who wrote, and only the kindness of fellow editors explained my finding myself so frequently in print. To conceive of myself as that sacred thing, "a writer," seemed to me to be on some level an act of assertion, even aggression, for which I was bound to be punished. Since I'm not a delusional person, I did recognize that editors (starting with me) don't do that kind of favor, and during my years in analysis I had begun to understand the level of my aggression and competitiveness—and the extent I went to in order to hide them from myself: Yes, be the boss, but don't act like one; yes, be offered better jobs and more money, but act (to myself) as if they didn't mean anything to me. Well, as editor or publisher I could be more or less invisible, but as a writer I was exposed—*highly* visible and unable to pretend I wasn't asserting myself. I was both appalled and amused at watching myself act out all the neurotic behavior I had been observing in writers for decades.

One day I was complaining (whining?) to Chip about the anxiety I experienced every time I turned in a piece, and he started to laugh. "Come on," I said, "you're a writer too—so you've got to go through the same kind of emotional nuttiness." He assured me that he didn't. "All those years at *The New Yorker*," he said, "I listened to you making fun of the writers who carried on this way, and I internalized the lesson. You didn't."

Things were a little different when I started writing for *The New Yorker*. Yes, I had brought David Remnick in, but as I've said, it was Tina Brown who spotted his larger potential, so that by the time she left, Si Newhouse was easily convinced that he had a more than plausible successor to her. One day at lunch David asked me why, since I was writing for everyone else, I wasn't writing for him. Because I hadn't been asked to, was the obvious answer. So he asked, and I signed on— first, with a long piece on James Thurber. What made this experience particularly agreeable was David's agreeing to let me have Ann Goldstein as my editor, Ann having replaced the great Eleanor Gould as head of the copyediting department, and someone as obsessed as I am with grammar, punctuation, tone. We could talk about a semicolon for five minutes, and go through a series of half a dozen proofs, enjoying ourselves so much that we'd make up excuses to go back to the text yet again. (Ann has become a major presence herself, as the translator of the famous Elena Ferrante Neapolitan novels.) David was a benign overseer, and of course I already knew most of the *New Yorker* cast of characters. Writing for the magazine was like old-home week.

Only one of the pieces I've written for the magazine caused any difficulties—a piece, suggested by me, about a now-forgotten French literary phenomenon of the fifties, a little girl of eight named Minou Drouet who became a bestselling poet and the subject of a torrent of humiliating publicity when half the Paris literary establishment insisted that it was her mother who had actually written her poems while the other half defended her with equal vehemence. (The scandal was covered in both *Time* and *Life*.) David didn't really understand why I wanted to write about her, but I was sure it was a great story and persisted and pursued, and he let me go ahead. When I turned in my copy, he was even more perplexed: He still didn't see the point. However, he gave me an essential bit of advice about restructuring the piece—advice I gratefully took—and then (uncharacteristically) he wavered about whether to print the final version before finally saying that he would, I'm sure as a courtesy to me rather than from conviction. I still believe it's one of the best things I've ever written.

I relate this ordinary incident not for its own sake but because it illustrates the essential change that the magazine had undergone: As I've already said, Tina, following her editorial instincts, had changed it overnight from a magazine about its writers to a magazine about its subjects. And David, with his background as a journalist, has seemed comfortable with that new direction. Minou Drouet wasn't a natural subject for the magazine, and there was no hook. I recounted in my piece how my friend Richard Overstreet and I went to the small town in Brittany where she grew up and still lived. Before making this trip I called her, but she pleasantly yet firmly refused to be interviewed. And who could blame her? During the crisis of her childhood, she had been hounded—persecuted—by reporters. "Our street is vomiting journalists nonstop," she wrote in a letter to her publisher. "It feels like the whole world is after me . . . I wish I were dead."

I certainly respected her need for privacy all these year later, but there was no reason I couldn't go to La Guerche-de-Bretagne and observe how she had lived back then and still lived. And when Richard and I walked past her substantial house on its quiet residential street, we saw a handsome middle-aged woman emerge and go into her garden. Rather than intrude on her privacy, we slunk past. "That's what I don't understand," David said to me later. "You were there. You saw her. Why didn't you knock on her door and talk your way in? That's what reporters do!" "But I'm not a reporter," I said. We were mutually uncomprehending. But that didn't affect our mutual regard.

One of the things I most enjoyed about freelancing was getting to know how different magazines worked. *The New Yorker, The New York Review*, the *Times Book Review, Vanity Fair*, the *Observer*—each has its own methodology, even its own style book. One place was more concerned with fact-checking, another with punctuation. One place did more editing, another place less. Which is why when I was approached by *The Atlantic*, I jumped at the chance. (Also, I jumped at the subject they proposed: Lorenz Hart.) What I discovered was that they had a formidable setup—dedicated copy editors, checkers, even lawyers. Most important: They had a first-rate editor for me to work with, Corby Kummer, whom I had known decades earlier when he was a whippersnapper and whom I had been able to help steer to *The Atlantic* in the first place. Now he had become a seasoned editor, glad to plunge into endless revisions and refinements. What a find! He goes on lending me a hand whenever I need a hand, as service-driven as every good editor has to be, and also endlessly enjoyable and amusing. *The Atlantic* already (2013) was more and more focusing on online journalism and away from what we fondly call print, but that didn't bother me, nor did the fact that although the magazine was solid and successful, no one I knew read it. Corby didn't enjoy my pointing this out.

My favorite kind of literary project was anthologizing, and when in the eighties I suddenly became dementedly interested in jazz, I started to read everything I could find on the subject. (Nothing is real for me until I've read about it.) And to my surprise, I discovered that not only was the literature large, but a considerable part of it was wonderfully written—for whatever reason, many of the jazz greats and not-so-greats had strong, compelling individual voices and terrific lives and stories to recount. I was mentioning all this to Sonny Mehta one day at lunch, and when he told me that he, too, was passionately interested in jazz, I suggested that we find someone to put together a big anthology of the best jazz writing—something the world lacked. "You do it," he said, so I did it.

It took almost ten years to assemble *Reading Jazz*—not ten years of consistent labor but hours snatched now and then from more urgent professional responsibilities. I was starting from scratch, because I didn't have the literature in my head and I had no connections in the jazz world to consult. Nor did we then have the magical Web to dig up material with: It was more a matter of rooting through dusty second-hand bookstores in whatever cities I found myself. The hardest job, as always with anthologies, was clearing permissions—a nightmare. The book itself, published in 1996, came in at something over a thousand pages, and was, and remains, a success—twenty years later I actually receive a couple of hundred dollars a year in royalties. Baby eats tonight!

Reading Jazz, though, was a mere anecdote compared with *Reading Dance*. This one, published in 2008, weighed in at more than thirteen hundred pages—at one point, it was twice that long, but I slashed away at it until it was manageable (sort of). I had a running jump this time—a large dance library of my own, and access to the books of my dance-writer friends as well as to the peerless dance library at Lincoln Center. On the other hand, the literature—going back over centuries—was far more extensive than the literature of jazz; I could still be researching it if I hadn't finally concluded (after eight years) that enough was enough.

Once again, the payoff for me was getting to read so much with the excuse of a discernible professional purpose. But also I relished the challenge of organizing it all—finding a way to help readers through this vast assortment of material. "Assembling an anthology is something like solving a puzzle," I wrote in my introduction to *Reading Dance*, "except that crosswords and jigsaws have predetermined correct solutions. Anthologies can only have ideal solutions, which are impossible to achieve since they depend on so many circumstances, beginning with the taste and judgment of the anthologizer: One man's ideal anthology is another man's mess." The circumstance that made these vast books possible was that I was doing them for Pantheon, part of the Knopf group, and so I was able to fashion my own rules—plus the collaboration of Pantheon's managing editor, Altie Karper, who in her ultra-competent, unfazed, and cheerful way makes all things work.

Another of my anthologies, *Reading Lyrics*, was different in kind from the other two, and was the most fun to assemble. I had been working for years with Bob Kimball on the series of elaborate Complete Lyrics collections we had inaugurated—Cole Porter, Ira Gershwin, etc. Now we decided to collaborate on a one-volume compendium of what we felt were the greatest lyrics of *all* the American and British lyricists, from George M. Cohan to Stephen Sondheim.

Once every week or two, for many months, Bob would come over to my house and we would listen to the countless LPs and CDs I had accumulated, taking notes, comparing, looking for surprises, in some cases taking down the words from recordings when there were no written sources. Even when the songs had been published, we still had to face the unsettling fact that particularly in the early days, printed sheet music was a slapdash affair. No one was taking these songs seriously back then—certainly not the lyricists themselves. A lot of sheet music from the twenties and even later was punctuated by *lack* of punctuation, misspellings, contradictions, confusions. There was no one to consult with, so it was up to us to establish some kind of official text—an unnerving responsibility.

We structured the book around the lyricists in the chronological order of their birth, and I wrote short biographical sketches of all of them—easy when dealing with an Irving Berlin or an Ira Gershwin but nearly impossible for writers who had produced a few first-rate lyrics almost a hundred years earlier and then vanished into obscurity. Yet if you poke around long enough, you come up with something. Poking around also came up with a lot of titles that didn't make it into the book—for instance, Edgar Leslie's "The Police Won't Let Mariuch-a Dance Unless She Move da Feet," "When Ragtime Rosie Ragged the Rosary," and "All the Quakers Are Shoulder Shakers Down in Quaker Town." But there was no doing without his "For Me and My Gal" and the immortal "T'ain't No Sin to Dance Around in Your Bones."

Reading Lyrics appeared in 2000 (containing 1,001 lyrics and forty tightly packed pages of credits) and was greeted as an indispensable reference book—I myself use it all the time, and if you own it, so do you.

And then came actually *writing* books: the final hurdle. Again, I had no desire to write them, but, back as always to Balanchine, it occurred to me that although there were several lengthy and worthy biographies available, there was nothing in the suddenly popular vein of short bios, a couple of hundred pages instead of eight hundred. And that there should be one. James Atlas had launched a series called Eminent Lives, handled and distributed by HarperCollins, and he signed me up to take on a life of Balanchine, which, alas, meant I now had to write it.

A frantic flurry of reading and rereading the entire English-language Balanchine literature; interviewing a universe of Balanchine connections, many of them friends but others previously unknown; looking at Balanchine's ballets even more intensely than I had been doing since I was seventeen. Then the moment came when I had to start typing. And the happier moment when I eventually could stop.

Jim Atlas had more or less retreated from the project, but everyone at Harper's was warmly cooperative—I hope not just because I was so close to Jane Friedman, now head of the company. There was only one drama. First proofs had been sent to a number of dance writers, and late one afternoon I got a call from my old friend Elizabeth Kendall, two of whose books I had edited. She was going to be reviewing the book (favorably), she said, but had come upon two mistakes and hoped it wasn't too late to fix them. And she was right—they were mistakes, and egregious ones. It was four-thirty in the afternoon, and all the Harper's editorial people I knew were gone for the day, but I managed to reach the head of production. "Oh my god," she said, "the book is going on press this afternoon! I'll call you right back if it isn't too late." It wasn't—I had twenty minutes to make my fixes. It took eighteen. She came through, the printers came through, and my reputation was saved, at least in this regard. Such are the perils of writing books, but it certainly helps if you're working with people who are proud of their work and eager to protect writers from their worst selves.

Nothing that followed was of comparable excitement. The book appeared, was well received, the Balanchinists were satisfied, and I was off the hook—a hook I was determined not to get back on.

But then . . .

Yale University Press was starting up its own series of short biographies, Jewish Lives, backed by a startlingly rich businessman named Leon Black, who was putting up a lordly amount of money in order to induce well-known writers to take on important Jewish lives. His editor, Ileene Smith, was not only enchanting, she was canny, and most important, she had a solid background in trade publishing—a crucial stroke of good luck, since as I was to discover, the ways of university presses are not the ways of trade presses. Ileene had read a long piece I had written for *The New York Review* about Sarah Bernhardt, and she was determined that I produce a biography of her for the series. I said no. She came to talk to me, and although she's pretty irresistible, I said no. She flung Mr. Black's money at my feet, and I succumbed—I decided it would be vulgar to resist it. Also I could no longer resist Ileene.

I dove back into the Divine Sarah (far from the only man to dive into her), and was enthralled all over again: You don't get to be the most famous of all Frenchwomen other than Joan of Arc and the most famous French person of the nineteenth century other than Napoleon if you're not a fascination. The literature was staggering—and growing; even while I was at work, two new Bernhardt biographies appeared in France. I read and read and read and read and read. There was a double challenge: to make intelligible to English-speaking readers what her genius as an actor had been to win her acclaim beyond that of any actor before or since; and to trace the extraordinary personal trajectory from her obscure birth and all too sordid (and widely reported) background and youth.

As it came to pass, my *Sarah* became the trailblazer for the Jewish Lives series because I was the first of the commissioned writers to deliver a manuscript. (The early bird . . .) This proved to be a blessing, since I could more or less determine the template for the series. Although Yale thought of itself as virtually a trade house as well as a university press, it just wasn't one. The good news was that the people doing the actual work—the text editor (the Mets maniac Dan Heaton), designers, lawyers—were superb at their jobs and cheerful about working so closely with a writer who, as far as publishing was concerned, knew what he was talking about. My secret satisfaction was that the first volume of the Jewish Lives series was about an illegitimate half-Jew who was brought up a Catholic and baptized one, although she always flaunted and was proud of her Jewish background. It was her courtesan mother who qualified her for the Yale series.

When I could no longer postpone starting to write, I had no idea how to proceed, so I told myself something that through the years I had told many, many blocked writers: "Don't write, type!" I typed: "Sarah Bernhardt was born in July or September or October of 1844. Or was it 1843? Or even 1841? She was born in Paris at 5, rue de L'École de Médecine (that's where the plaque is). Or was it 32 (or 265), rue St. Honoré? Or 22, rue de la Michandière? We'll never know . . ." That gave me the tone the book needed, since, as I went on to say, strict accuracy wasn't Bernhardt's strong point.

For all the fun of reciting Bernhardt's worldwide notoriety, the scandals, the outrageous behavior, what finally called to me most strongly about her was her gradual growth from a byword for frivolity and immorality to a venerated icon of indefatigable spirit and patriotism—a symbol of France. What a subject! I gather that *Sarah* is still the bestselling Jewish Life, but I know perfectly well that whatever success it's had hasn't much to do with me and everything to do with its heroine.

The last of the three biographical books I've written was the only book I was actually excited about writing. For years I'd been thinking about the fraught relationship between Charles Dickens and his ten (!) children—not, for the most part, a success. What happened? And what happened to the children? In the scores of books about Dickens, most of them were mentioned only in passing. They were, to use Diane Johnson's phrase, "lesser lives."

Tracing these lives was in itself gripping, and trying to understand what had gone wrong with so many of them—and why—absorbed me for many months. As always, for me the greatest reward of writing is learning on the job.

Eventually, I came to realize that I had an emotional investment in the Dickens story; that there were reasons I was so powerfully drawn to it. I dedicated *Great Expectations: The Sons and Daughters of Charles Dickens* to "my parents, Charles and Martha Gottlieb, fanatical readers, whose marriage in some ways seems to me to reflect the Dickens marital dynamic. Perhaps my sympathy for the children of Charles Dickens stems from this identification, while being a father allows me to sympathize to a certain extent with his frustrations. Although my children, of course, are perfect."

After Dickens, and having put together a fat collection of my pieces (*Lives and Letters*), I had no other subject for a book in mind, so I started writing this one. For at least twenty years I had resisted the idea of writing a memoir—not only did it seem pretentious, but I couldn't believe the world was waiting for an account of my exploits. Obviously, I changed my mind—partly, as I've said in my note at the front, because there were certain stories I wanted to see recounted accurately, partly because I wanted to put down on paper for anyone who might be interested some of my ideas about editing and publishing, partly because my family wanted me to. All very well, but for me writing has remained drudgery laced with anxiety. (Why do so many people want to do it?) And in this case, I had a subject that just didn't interest me much: myself. What was there for me to learn on *this* job?

The chief thing I've learned from writing in general is that I could actually do it, which I hadn't really believed when I started. The two people who were certain I could, and should, were Maria and my great friend Bob Cornfield, who for years pushed, prodded, nagged, and insisted that I cut the nonsense and get going. (As if that weren't enough, Bob has also been the most devoted, generous friend and guide to Nicky.)

What working on this particular book has done for me is make me look back, something I usually don't spend time doing, and perhaps it's helped clear my head. If it's been amusing or instructive to others, all the better: Writing, too, is a service job.

LIVING

ON JULY 5, 2015, I celebrated (if that's the word) my sixtieth anniversary in publishing. It was exactly sixty years from the day I started work at Simon and Schuster, sitting with Phyllis Levy outside the office of our new boss and waiting to be told what to do. Not that I ever liked being told what to do, but what choice did I have? It turned out that what I was going to do was have a good time, and be paid for having it. My luck was that just about all my work depended on reading, which was the thing I most liked doing, and something I knew I was good at.

But publishing for me turned out to have another great attraction: It was collaborative, and although I had been a loner as a child, I discovered I was much happier as part of a relatively small group of congenial, like-minded people with whom I shared a common goal. In other words, a family. Indeed, Nina and Phyllis and Kay and a number of others turned into the family I never had—a family that kept expanding. The Cattarullas, the Provensens, the Richlers, Janet Malcolm, Deborah Rogers, were not only colleagues and/or friends but in different combinations grew close to each other as well as to me and Maria and our children.

Looking back over what I've written here, I see that I'm constantly talking about friendships and families. I wasn't very good at being a child, and although on the whole I behaved responsibly, I wasn't very good at being a son. Husband? Ask Maria. Father? Yes, at least to Lizzie—somehow I got that right, but then she's easy to get right. Roger? He's as nice a man at sixty-three as he was as a boy of ten, and I'm very fond of him, but our lives rarely converge. Nicky? I've tried my best (not as good as Maria's best), and he's come a long, long way as a buoyant, appealing oddball. Boss? I believe yes. Editor? Presumably yes. Publisher? Yes, because although I realized publishing was a game, it was one I took very seriously. All in all, though, I feel I've been at my best as a friend—it's a natural state of being for me. Total intimacy and grand passion are not my style; shared interests, affections, and concerns are the stuff of my life.

I'm still at it, finding or helping shape families to be part of. My life has taken an odd configuration. Two-thirds of the year I'm in our house in New York, where I both like to be and *have* to be as long as I'm writing my dance column for the *Observer*—which means going to dance performances scores of times a year (most of them disappointing, to put it tactfully). This is not so easy to do as my body starts to let me down, as bodies will. Twice a year, a month or more each time, I'm in my house—the Villa Serena, it's called—in Miami Beach; twice a year, for about the same amount of time, I'm in my apartment in Paris. I guess I'm a real estate collector, though not by design. (Maria collected our house in the country—actually, she built it—but I'm not there very often. It's beautiful, it's beautifully situated, she loves it, but for me it has an inescapable flaw—it's in the middle of Nature.) When I was in my sixties and it turned out that I had more money than I needed to live on, I didn't see the point of squirreling it all away, to increase or decrease with the fluctuations of the market, when I could deploy it in ways that would make all our lives fuller. I bought the Florida house on a whim; the same for the Paris apartment. Each place has given me a new life—and a new family.

In Paris, there's my onetime author Diane Johnson—Dinny—and her husband, John. They live around the corner from me and we're always together. It's like being in junior high with your best friends: There's an assumption that we do things together. Mid-morning Dinny and I are on the phone. Going shopping at the Bon Marché? Let's meet on our corner for coffee at eleven-thirty. Then on to the store. Time for lunch. Home for a nap and some work. Dinner? At their place, maybe, since Dinny loves to gather people around her table. But I don't always like to be gathered, so we agree on leftovers the next day. Dinny, from exotic (to me) Moline, Illinois, is unruffled: no psychic tension, no agenda, just common sense, equanimity, hard (superb) work, and a dead-eye sense of humor that never wounds. We're just totally easy with each other, and John is delighted, since he doesn't have to go shopping with her. On one famous occasion, her son Simon—in from Japan, where he's lived the entire time I've known Dinny—was getting married in Paris at a moment when John had to be in California, so I took over John's role at church and at various celebrations as father of a bridegroom I had never met. *That's* family.

And then there's Richard Overstreet, an American artist who's lived in Paris for fifty-five years—multi-talented, enchanting, loving, game for anything, and a constantly wonderful companion, now that he's accepted the fact that I won't go with him to museums and galleries. (Maria does that with him. The two of them have a lot in common, especially a huge capacity for appreciating things. I struggle to keep both of them from using the word "EXTRAORDINARY!") Richard's wife, Agnès Montenay, is another enchantment—a clever, elegant French one. What a relief when you really enjoy your best friends' spouses, partners, significant others . . . Richard is close to Dinny and John too, so the circle is expanded. And again with our friend Mary Blume, who was for many decades a much-loved columnist for the *International Herald Tribune* and is recently the author of an excellent biography of Balenciaga. Stylish, severe in her judgments (but luckily not of me), yet another obsessed reader, she's a grand companion—she and I and Dinny and John have done a lot of traveling together. And let's throw into the mix Isabelle Boccon-Gibod, ex-wife of Adam Begley, a beauty, a first-rate businesswoman, a writer, a photographer; against the odds, we fell into a true intimacy, despite the forty-odd-year gap in our ages—it's the old story of elective affinity. (Adam marries well.)

My apartment is on the fashionable rue Jacob, though I've never understood why it's so fashionable. This address is the only thing about me that impresses Parisians. The apartment is up three flights of stairs (they didn't make provisions for *ascenseurs* in the eighteenth century), but it's commodious, filled with light, with magnificent floors, and has big closets—not an ordinary amenity in Paris. And it's perfectly located, a few steps from boulevard Saint-Germain, a few steps from the Seine, a few steps from three big movie houses, a few steps from most of my friends. Who knows how much longer I'll be able to handle the steps and the travel, but so far, so better than good.

This Paris life, so pleasantly lived, is more or less without pressure, apart from the pressure of whatever work I've brought with me to do there. Which is mostly reading. For instance, it was there, sitting in the Luxembourg Gardens, that I read my way through the entire body of John Steinbeck's work for a *New York Review* piece. (Whereas it was in Miami that I read the forty-odd books that went into a piece about near-death experiences. To know anything you have to know everything, or so I tell myself—no doubt to justify my gluttonous appetite for books.) And both Paris and Miami are good places to edit—fewer distractions, so sharper concentration.

My life in Miami is centered on Miami City Ballet—watching class and rehearsals, occasionally advising dancers, writing and editing copy, talking budgets, collaborating on programming, making connections, consulting with Lourdes on anything with which I can be helpful—a kind of elder statesman, I suppose. Ballet companies are even more like families than publishing houses are, with gratifications and crises popping up every ten seconds. To be part of such a dynamic— when you believe in the quality and importance of the work that's being done—is pure joy. Dance is the world that today I feel most comfortable in. It excites me in itself, and in Miami it has the added advantage that no one connected with the company really knows of or is interested in the rest of my life—the editing/writing side. A few people were curious about my time with Bill Clinton, but the dance world isn't populated by readers of *The New York Review of Books*, and why should it be? Life there for me is a rest cure. I have one close non-dance friend: Esther Percal ("the queen of Miami Beach real estate"), who sold me the Villa Serena a quarter of a century ago, enthusiastically recommended to Ingrid Sischy and me by her great friend the artist Julian Schnabel. Esther has a big personality, a big wardrobe, and an even bigger heart. She's one of the rare people who have adopted Nicky—not out of do-goodism but because she cares for him. And he for her.

It's also in Miami where I spend the most time with Daniel Mendelsohn, who in recent years I've been as close to as to anyone. When I first met him twenty years ago, Daniel was clambering out of the academic world (having got his PhD in classics at Princeton) and into the world of literary journalism. It didn't take long for him to be recognized as a big talent, a star at *The New York Review* and *The New Yorker*, writer of esteemed books, and eventually back in the academic world with a chair and tenure at Bard. Which, since our house in the country is close by, means that he's constantly with Maria too. When we're together in Miami he works, I work, we watch TV serials (*Scandal*, season four, a recent excitement), and talk and talk and talk about books. We're some thirty years apart in age, but who cares—or notices? We just fit neatly into each other's lives and minds. And, crucially, he's my tech guru, available for consultation wherever in the world he may be when something goes wrong with my computer—which is all the time. Like Janet Malcolm and Claudia Roth Pierpont, he's at our house for Christmas every year—same cast of characters, same Moroccan pigeon pie. And always ready, wherever we may be, with the cocktail shaker—bartending was one of the ways he put himself through college. He's a full-service friend, and I try to be the same for him.

Although I've never stopped working on books for Knopf, once Random House was acquired by Bertelsmann and moved across town from my house, I started spending less and less time in the office and, given computers, more and more time working at home. But it's the same old work, the work that's been the basic fabric of my life. Indeed, when I divide up my adult life it's almost always in terms of what I was working at and where. Work is my natural state of being . . . working, and reading. As I've said already, my greatest piece of luck was stumbling into the right occupation at the right moment. And in the right places, so that none of my energy was ever deflected from the work itself into politicking or rivalries. Or maybe it was having enjoyed miraculously good health through most of my life—Nina once said I was psychosomatically healthy. Or maybe my *greatest* piece of luck was the boundless energy I seemed always to have at my disposal.

But what was all that energy about? Why did I cram my life with projects and obsessive interests that had nothing to do with my official work and then professionalize them? Yes, I fell in love with those 1950s plastic handbags that I came upon by accident and began collecting before I even realized what they were. But then I organized much of my spare time into a relentless search for them in flea markets, junk stores, wherever, long before there was such a thing as eBay. And then I researched and wrote a book about them. Why in the sixties, given that I'm a relatively unpolitical person, did I turn my belief in the cause of civil rights into semi-professional engagement with SNCC? Why, at Cambridge, did I have to organize and direct play after play? Why, for that matter, given my enormous workload as an editor and publisher, did I transform my love for dance into a second lifelong and consuming occupation?

Why, also, considering that my personality is so relentlessly ebullient, have I since childhood felt so melancholic, perhaps even depressive? I suspect that I've summoned up my hyper-energy to keep running fast enough to ward off that depressive tendency—the few times I brushed against the real thing were so distressing that it's no wonder I've done everything possible to avoid it. Besides, I've always believed that if energy doesn't find wholesome outlets, it quickly curdles. Which is why it's so important that children—who have more energy than anyone—be constantly active, even if their activity consists of something as passive-seeming as reading. Or daydreaming. Or solitaire. Or even computer games.

An example for me has been the life of Dickens—the raging energy and the ways he spent it are object lessons. To read the biographies, to study his letters, to consider the trajectory of his life, is to encounter a man on the run, masking the anger and despair of his childhood in almost frenzied activity. Not even the immense achievement of his writings, his hands-on editing of the tremendously successful magazines he founded and ran, the exhausting public readings of his work, the private theatricals he directed and performed in, the countless speeches, the thousands of (handwritten) letters, the immense load of charity work, the perpetual close engagement with his children, the passionate friendships, the elaborate domestic entertainments he presided over—not even all this could use up his amazing energy. To do that he needed to tramp through the streets of London night after night—ten, fifteen, even twenty miles at a go. And even so, he couldn't escape his demons, as the emotional and moral breakdown of his middle years— his "midlife crisis," as we (unfortunately) say today—goes to show. Alas, his genius, which allowed him to observe so penetratingly and report to the world the realities of so many other lives, gave him little insight into his own, and his damaged psyche caught up with him. Naturally, I don't compare myself to Charles Dickens—only an idiot would—but I do see a faint reflection of my own contradictions in his glorious yet ultimately sad life.

Is this kind of energy hereditary? Not in the case of Dickens: His father was more or less a washout, and his mother capable but hardly exceptional. As for me, I had a father with great drive and ambition, who pulled himself (and my mother and me) up by his bootstraps, making the transition from poor slum boy to successful upper-middle-class professional on his own, with no help from anyone. And from what little I know of *his* mother, this drive was genetic.

She grew up in the shtetl of a small town pronounced "Vashkivits" on the Prut River in the province of Bukovina, in what was then Austria-Hungary and since then has been Hungary, Romania, the Soviet Union, Ukraine, Moldavia. She married the local Talmudic scholar—a great honor, but not a practical move. Soon she had five babies, all of whom quickly died, at which point they realized that something was wrong with her milk. She then had five more babies, all of whom survived with the help of a wet nurse. When her oldest daughter, Fanny, was fifteen and my father, Charles, her youngest, was four, she decided to immigrate to America. She took those two with her across Europe by cattle car, then on to New York by steerage, finding jobs in the garment district for herself and Fanny, while my father grew up in the streets of the Lower East Side. She saved her money and eventually was able to send for her husband and the other three children. Her husband never learned English and never worked—studying the Talmud was the most important work a man could do. She never stopped working. Along the way she established a society to bring other Jews from Vashkivits to America. Then she died, surely of exhaustion. I like to think I would have liked her—my father did, and hated his Orthodox father.

My mother's background was equally unusual. Her father—Gramps—was born in the Latvian port city of Libau. He had a conspicuous talent for drawing that came to the attention of the local countess, and she and her husband sent him to study in the Academy of Fine Arts in Vienna. He then went to America, returned home to Libau to see his family and marry my grandmother, then brought her home to Boston, where their two daughters lived as children.

My mother, Martha, was gentle, kind, cultured; her jolly side, as I've written, was suppressed by my father, who was many admirable things, but jolly wasn't one of them. It was her sister, Dorothy, who had the energy in that family, which lived in very modest comfort, supported by my working grandmother. Aunt Dorothy's life was even more unlikely than those of my various grandparents: After the Russian Revolution she became a fierce Communist and married a man supposedly from Finland named Arthur Adams. My father intensely disliked Dorothy—he didn't appreciate feisty women—but he immensely admired Arthur, hence my middle name: I'm Robert Adams Gottlieb. In the 1920s, Dorothy and Arthur moved to the new Soviet Union, but came back to America every few years, purportedly to see her father, who lived with us.

Once I was five or six I started receiving amazing presents from Russia—a thrilling group of stamps for my collection; a wonderful set of wooden architectural building blocks. Then, once the war began, silence. Needless to say, my mother was frantic with worry about her sister. And then when the war ended, more silence, although an old friend of Dorothy's reported that she had caught sight of Arthur on a street in Manhattan. Which was on the one hand impossible and on the other deeply hurtful.

In 1948, my father was summoned to Washington to testify in secret before the House Un-American Activities Committee. Arthur Adams, it emerged, had for years been the chief Soviet spy in America—successfully collecting top-secret information about the Manhattan Project during the war and nuclear information from Oak Ridge later on. The FBI had caught up with him, but given post-war tensions with Russia, our recent ally, the government decided not to arrest him. He managed to escape the country in late 1946.

By the time my father was questioned, the country was in the grip of growing paranoia about Russia, and although he had been treated civilly by the Committee, he was naturally unsettled. (There was never any follow-up from Washington; my father was rather conservative in his politics, with no connection whatever to any left-wing organization.) At least we now understood that Arthur had stayed away from us to protect us.

Even so, my father, confirmed in his lifelong anger at Dorothy, felt badly betrayed by this man, one of the few people he had really liked. My mother simply wanted to hear how her sister had survived the war—if she had. When the political situation eased, and Americans were able to visit the Soviet Union, several friends of Dorothy's youth managed to see her in Moscow. Arthur was dead, but he had been anointed a national hero and she was living in comfort. Not long before my mother died, a telephone call was arranged—the first time they had spoken in more than twenty years. What was there to say? It was snowing in Moscow; Bobby (me) was blooming.

At some point after my mother's death—I must have been about thirty-five—a letter from Dorothy made its way to me. It was plaintive, it was touching, but I was indifferent. And my father was enraged: He would consider my responding to her another act of betrayal. And I didn't have much inclination to do so—I had last seen her when I was seven years old, and she wasn't real to me. Even so, this disregard for an old woman living without family in isolation is one of the episodes in my life about which I'm least proud.

My relationship with my father had been difficult from the start. He clearly loved me, and although I was at first frightened of him and later angry at him, I loved him too. Your father is your father. I think he was afraid that I would inherit or absorb my mother's timidity or what he saw as her father's fecklessness, and he disapproved of the literary bent my life was taking as I proceeded through college: I lived in an ivory tower instead of engaging in the "real world" of potential doctors, scientists, businessmen . . . lawyers. And yet mine was the life I'm certain he would have preferred to lead.

Once we were reconciled after the break over my marriage to Muriel, he tried hard if only occasionally to be good to Roger, and when I married Maria he was unfailingly courteous to her—he couldn't know that his not very well disguised bitterness and anger distressed her. We saw each other rarely—being with him wasn't easy for me. I still felt emanating from him a strong suppressive impulse toward me, and I would over-react.

But perhaps it wasn't over-reaction. He was very aware of my growing success and I knew that he boasted of it to others, but here is a typical statement of his, made when I was already editor-in-chief of S & S and earning about the same amount of money he was: "You know, Bobby, I've always disliked the theater world that Harold [his partner] often works in"—Bette Davis was a client—"but I've encouraged him to maintain his connection to it so that if you should lose your job, you'll have something to fall back on." You didn't need years of analysis to detect the aggression beneath that remark. I would flare up at such moments, violently pointing out the obvious. But time passed, I must have been quietly evolving, and the last time he said such a thing, I heard myself replying, "Thank you very much!"—and meaning it. I don't know which of us was more surprised. But that was the end of it—even with destructive dynamics, it takes two to tango.

Even more remarkable is that in his final year, when he was sixty-nine, he began to demonstrate an unheard-of vulnerability. "I hope Maria likes me," he said to me one evening over dinner; "I know this is my last chance." I almost burst into tears. This was the first vulnerability he had ever manifested in my presence—I was close to forty—and I didn't know what to do with it; I could deal with the King Lear of the first four acts of Shakespeare's supreme masterpiece, but I didn't know how to deal with the Lear of act V. In retrospect, though, I'm grateful that he was able to reach this level of self-understanding before he died, suddenly, of a heart attack on vacation in Italy.

I can see that much of my life was spent both fighting my father and struggling not to become him. Yes, I'm aware that many of what strengths I have come directly from him: If we weren't two peas in a pod, we were surely an oak and an acorn. This became dramatically evident to me late one winter evening in the mid-sixties. It was a cold, bleak Sunday and I was working alone in the office, as I often did on weekends. Happening to glance down Fifth Avenue from my corner window on Fiftieth Street, I noticed a single light on in an office building across Fifth and four blocks down. It didn't occur to me to hesitate: I picked up the phone and dialed my father's number. It had to be him, and of course it was.

I was an only child. Dorothy had no children. On my father's side, I have a single cousin, Nessa, of whom I'm fond but see only rarely. In other words, I'm a man without family, except for my immediate family and those families I've created or helped create. For instance, ever since some time in the early 1980s, a group of close pals at Knopf has gathered together for a Christmas event—maybe ten of us in all: Martha Kaplan, Vicky Wilson, Kathy Hourigan, Nancy Nicholas, the late (and much missed) Nina Bourne and Ash Green, and Alice Quinn, who came to work at Knopf in the early seventies as Nina's assistant and went on to become a superb copywriter and editor before leaving Knopf for *The New Yorker* and slowly becoming a crucial figure in the American poetry establishment: a true pure-of-heart, a force for good, a worshipper of Nina (she too was at her deathbed), and another devoted friend of, and support to, our Nicky.

This party started off casually in Vicky's office, but it too overtly excluded our colleagues, and so it was moved to our house, every year Maria cooking up a storm, with a blizzard of presents, most of them jokey and to the point—we all know each other far too well. Only Vic and Kathy are still at Knopf (and me, sort of). On the other hand, spouses and partners (and Nicky) have thickened the mix. It's been well over thirty years.

In a similar spirit, a small group of ex–*New Yorker* friends—a *New Yorker* diaspora—has a revoltingly huge lunch every December, usually at the over-the-top restaurant Carmine's, Chip McGrath and Chris Knutsen joining me in powerful Manhattans. (Luckily, this happens only once a year.) Martha, Deb Garrison, Alice Truax, Ruth Diem, Nancy Franklin, are more circumspect. Yet another joyous family dynamic. So why don't more *real* families have such joyous dynamics? Maybe because we didn't choose those other families?

Other continuities have persisted. When Knopf's invaluable senior editor Chuck Elliott—he masterminded *Alistair Cooke's America*, for instance—decamped from New York to London in the eighties (where he succeeded in adding P. D. James to the list), I replaced him as one of the jurors of the annual Japanese translation award. An intense interest in Japanese literature had taken hold of me in college, when I devoured Arthur Waley's great rendering of *The Tale of Genji* and came upon that modern classic, Tanizaki's *The Makioka Sisters*, which I've read over and over.

(These Japanese books were not part of Columbia's literature program, which I now realize was fatally circumscribed: "The novel" meant English, American, French, or Russian, plus *Don Quixote*—a highly provincial notion of literature. Over the years I had to discover for myself the greatness of Germany's Fontane, Brazil's Machado de Assis, Spain's Galdós, Portugal's Eça de Queirós, and track down their (and others') work, book by book, not always easy in those pre-Web days. I could read certain major books by Arnold Zweig and Arthur Schnitzler, for instance, only in French translations acquired in Paris.)

Fortunately for me, Knopf published most of the major mid-century Japanese writers (and currently Murakami), so I wasn't completely unanchored when I first began participating in the translation award. After thirty years I still get from a dozen to a score of texts each year, and each year I plunge into them with zeal; in fact, with glee. I don't read Japanese, of course, but I read translatorese, and that's what's called for. Nor has my passion for classic Japanese film abated: Indeed, my favorite of all movies is Ozu's *Tokyo Story*, which overwhelmed me when it first was shown at the New Yorker Theater in the early seventies and which I've watched a dozen or more times. It's a lucky circumstance for me that Japan Society is located two blocks from my house, so that when it used to schedule retrospectives of the great Japanese directors and actors I could be there almost weekly, soaking everything up.

Another annual event in my life is speaking at the Columbia (once Radcliffe) publishing course, where I ramble on to a hundred or so students hoping to have careers in book publishing or journalism. What do I tell them? The basics of editing as I understand them: "Get back to your writers right away." "It's the writer's book, not yours." "Try to help make the book a better version of what it is, not into something that it isn't." "Spend your strength and your ego in the service of the writer, not for their own sake—or yours." And over and over again, "It's a service job." And the basics of publishing as I learned it and tried to practice it: "Publishing is the business of conveying your own honest enthusiasm for a book and a writer to the rest of the world." "If you believe in a book, there are others who will too, because you're not special." "Every book has its own potential readership—figure out what it is and reach for it, don't try to sell every book to everyone." "Take every detail seriously, since we just don't know what makes certain books do better than others. Except, of course, their innate qualities." And, perhaps hardest to accept, "Readers aren't stupid—their instincts may prove to be sounder than yours."

My love affair with readers was ignited and confirmed by the message that Richard L. Simon expressed to the entire staff of Simon and Schuster by means of bronze paperweights on which were etched these words: GIVE THE READER A BREAK. There was one on my desk waiting for me on my first day of work sixty years ago, and it's on my desk as I type today. This succinct philosophy can be adhered to in many ways. For me: Keep the price of a book as low as possible. Make sure the type is legible—when possible, generous; readability is all. Don't talk about an important photograph or portrait and then not show it. Deploy useful running heads—the name of a particular story or essay rather than the name of the author (the reader knows the name of the author). Shun running feet as opposed to running heads—they drag the reader's eye down the page. Don't deploy fancy ornaments or folios on the page that may distract from the text—in other words, don't over-design. Etc., etc. It's easy—just remember the things that irritate you in books you're reading. Do unto others . . .

I've been saying all these things at the course for about thirty years, and naturally as I get older and older and the students get younger and younger, my frame of reference rings fewer bells—most of yesterday's admired and successful books or plays or movies mean nothing to today's twenty-year-olds; names central to me and my coevals are simply unknown to later generations.

It's all in the nature of things: Just about everyone short of Homer, the Greek playwrights, Shakespeare, Dante, Bach, Mozart, Beethoven, Rembrandt, Leonardo, and a few others eventually goes over the cultural cliff. How many people much younger than I am have ever heard of Mary Pickford, who was the most famous woman in the world from 1915, say, to 1930? One well-educated thirty-two-year-old I know had never heard of Greta Garbo, and finally remembered, under prodding, that Judy Garland was that girl in *The Wizard of Oz*. A twenty-six-year-old guy I recently met had never heard of Bing Crosby.

Not his fault. Time marches on. The torch passes. You're young, you're old. Accept it. This was Ozu's message to the world. Yes, it's sad to be out of touch with the moment, but it's sadder to be having to prove to yourself and the world that you're hip to the latest zeitgeist. I realized some time ago that most everything I write about, except dance, is of the past, and even in dance I'm mostly interested in the classics up through Balanchine. Even pop music, which I've loved all my life, has left me behind.

Just as, far worse, the deaths of family, loved friends, and colleagues have. It turns out that people die. Every day I sneak up on the obituary pages of the *Times* in fear of what I'll find. Am I frightened of finding myself in them? Probably, given my lifelong morbidity. At least I lost my fear of flying, once I relinquished the need to control everything—as though one had real control in a train or car. Or walking down a street. I learned *that* lesson one day decades ago when I was crossing Third Avenue at Fiftieth Street and a great steel girder from a construction

site crashed to the ground a dozen feet behind me, just missing cars—
and me.

I attempt not to think about death, but there's no avoiding the fact
that we're all the pre-dead. I try not to brood about my lessening physical forces, and try to avoid what I'm sure is the number-one killer:
stress. Luckily, I don't use up psychic energy living in regret: What's
the point? Or in worrying about the future: Why encourage anxiety?
The present is hard enough.

A premature death that distressed me deeply was Muriel's. Our
marriage had been a disaster, but our divorce had been a success. The
decision to separate was a mutual one, in fact proposed by her: She had
no effective life in New York, no work she enjoyed, and a distant husband. She certainly cared for Roger, but she wasn't particularly maternal and in any case, by the time he was in his teens, he was mostly
away at boarding school. Since we had no property and no money—
this was in 1965—the only dispute we had was over child custody,
which we solved on our own. (The lawyers kept getting in the way.)

Muriel moved to Camden, Maine, and gradually created a good
life for herself there. I went on paying her a modest alimony, and if she
got into financial difficulties—needed a new car, a new roof—would
"lend" her whatever she needed. We'd talk on the phone a couple of
times a year, always stimulated by each other, but saw each other only
once again: at Roger's wedding.

When I was fired from *The New Yorker*, in 1992, she called me to say
that if I was in financial difficulties she'd gladly try to do without her
alimony, at which point I told her that actually I was now in the chips
and had already decided to *increase* her alimony. It was an O. Henry
story with a happy twist. And then when she died, I found to my dismay that although she had left her house in Camden to Roger, she had
left to me whatever modest financial assets she had as repayment for
those old "loans." When I tried to get her lawyer to transfer this inheri-
tance to Roger, it proved to be legally impossible—I had to accept the
legacy and then pass it along to him. Whatever had been wrong with our
marriage had nothing to do with money.

For all the continuities in my life—work, friendships, reading—the most important continuity is the domestic one. Maria and I started living together in 1965; it's now been more than fifty years, and forty-two of them in the same house. Our temperaments are opposite—one cool and puritanical, one effusive and lavish. (Guess which is which.) One is organized and deliberate, the other spontaneous and eruptive. One likes nature, the other cities. One likes it cool, one likes it hot. One expresses feelings she may not even have, the other prefers to believe he doesn't have any. (There! The use of the pronouns gives the game away.) One cooks, one eats. But . . .

We like the same people. Maria is one of the best readers I know, and we tend to like the same books. (What if we didn't?) We have the same sense of humor, and a lot of it—she likes to say she would have walked out decades ago if I didn't always make her laugh. (Do you think she means it?) We have the same approach to money—uninterested when we have it (now), uninterested when we didn't have it (then). I have absolute belief in her acting, and always felt it was more worth paying attention to than my own amusing but, to me, prosaic occupation. I also have faith in her judgment, although she'll often try to hide it rather than appear judgmental—after all, she was brought up by her mother to be devout, not wise. Her intelligence is deep if masked, though it's irksome that Janet Malcolm insists Maria is more intelligent than I am. (I can't believe she really means it.) Her devotion to her children and grandchildren—Lizzie's wonderful twins, Oliver and Jacob—is beyond the call of duty, and sometimes beyond the call of nature, but then I happen to be devoted to them too. And weathering stormy times with Nicky strengthened rather than demoralized us. Lizzie's first documentary film, *Today's Man*, is about him and has become a prime source of knowledge and comfort for people in the Asperger's community. Indeed, Lizzie and her boys are at the center of our lives, and Lizzie's and my relationship has been ideal. (She would say so too.) We think the same way, we react the same way, we even share an unfortunate tendency toward irritability, though rarely at each other. And I'm constantly grateful to her for giving me a perfect son-in-law, Michael Young, and so giving her children a perfect father. When occasionally she tells me she's irritated with him, I remind her that guys stick together, and I'm automatically on his side. But she knows this isn't true; hers is the side I'm on, always.

Maria and I have managed to adapt to each other's schedules. When in rehearsal or doing eight performances a week, or out of town, or when she's in the country, she's a part-time wife, but then, when I'm in Paris or Miami for weeks at a time, I'm a part-time husband. It works—I need aloneness, she needs to surround herself with people. And we have the telephone—the blessed telephone. Besides, her voice is balm, except when she's disagreeing with me. Oh yes, she's also a beautiful woman, but someone in a marriage has to be beautiful, and it was never going to be me. As my mother would say when I was a little boy—and dotingly—"You have a face that only a mother could love." To my astonishment, it turned out not to be true.

I go on working, with less concentration, perhaps, and certainly with less staying power, but I don't sense that my mind is slipping, except for the usual loss of names and, occasionally, words. As far as I know, my health is sound except for something called spinal stenosis, which is a kind of arthritis of the lower spine that makes walking slower and more tippy. (When recently I was being given an MRI, the very nice technician was startled to hear that I had no pain. "That's very rare," he said, and, with a touch of disappointment, "If you were in a lot of pain, we could do something to help you." Here was another man who loved his work.)

I sympathize. What greater fortune than to be fully occupied with what you spend your life doing? I never thought that I had been born with more than a healthy slice of intelligence, but I had that Gottliebian energy, and I had grasp. And luck. What could be sadder than to reach my age and realize that you hadn't made the most of what you'd been given? I never had great expectations for myself, or specific ambitions, except to do things well and make things work. And I was rewarded with an interesting life and far more recognition than was good for my character. But at least I didn't seek it out.

As I began to recede from whatever limelight I had once been in, I was curious to see how I would react to having less authority, less public acknowledgment, hoping that the satisfactions of being published might make up for the dwindling satisfactions of being the publisher. I thought I might feel resentful, even depressed. But it hasn't been like that at all. Recently I came upon these lines from Robert Frost—"No memory of having starred / Atones for later disregard, / Or keeps the end from being hard"—and was surprised to realize that my reactions are opposite to these. I never felt I was a star. I don't now feel disregarded. And, yes, the end may very well be hard, but perhaps fate will be kind, and at least let me keep on reading for a while.

ACKNOWLEDGMENTS

Me and Jonathan Galassi being honored at the 1984 PEN awards

Jon Galassi, head of FSG, persisted through the years in encouraging me to write this book. In other words, it's *that* boy's fault. But the faults of the book itself are not his, only mine. I thank him for his relentless though charming prodding, and his unfailing intelligent support. And for presiding over such a benign and pleasant workplace.

Another incentive for me to proceed was the arrival at FSG of Ileene Smith, with whom I had worked so happily at Yale University Press after she had bribed and bullied me into inaugurating their Jewish Lives series with a biography of Sarah Bernhardt. We had so much fun together that the opportunity to have more of it with this account of my so much less colorful Jewish Life was irresistible. She understands when to push, when to pull, and when to leave me to get on with it.

Everyone who knows FSG knows how great the contribution of Jeff

Seroy is to its flourishing condition. Friend, enthusiast, clever strategist, toiler in the fields, hearty laugher—who could ask for anything more? If only I'd been clever enough a million years ago when he was a young slave at Knopf to grasp his potential, he might be there still. So I'm happy that I wasn't!

Yet again I had the pleasure of working with Abby Kagan, who designed this book. Not every book designer is so sensitive to the wishes (whims?) of a writer, and certainly not every designer is so open to collaboration. Fortunately, Abby and I see things the same way, so we move gleefully to the same ends—adjusting, readjusting, fiddling, tweaking, until we're both content, only disappointed when the process is over: no more fun until the next book. And then there's her boundless supply of M&M's . . .

As for Scott Auerbach, my production editor, his obsessive determination to get things right is a happy complement to my own. Check, check, and check again—whether it's about facts, punctuation, usage, tone, the impulse is the same. No doubt errors have crept in, because not even the most compulsive vigilance can catch them all, but Scott did as much as—did more than—can properly be expected of anyone in his situation. And, more astounding, his cheerfulness never falters. I had a terrific time working with him and hope he did with me.

FSG's executive managing editor, Debra Helfand, also worked at Knopf at one time, so she's used to me, and she presided over the process with not only her great competence but with extreme forbearance for my sometimes wayward attitude toward rules and schedules. Her iron fist never came into play, but I was always aware that it was there, beneath her unruffled niceness.

I was beyond lucky to have three vastly experienced outside professional readers, who patiently trekked through the manuscript, giving unstinting time and attention to my work: Adam Begley, for years my editor at the *Observer*, but more important a close and loving friend; Corby Kummer, of *The Atlantic*, whom I first knew as an eager pup and who's developed into a sage and scrupulous hands-on editor—and generous (and amusing) friend; and my intimate friend Bob Cornfield, who knows me (and mine) very, very well, and who is the person who first forced me to start writing. He's a remarkable editor, at once sympathetic and tough-minded—the kind of conscience every writer should have. And the kind of friend *everyone* should have.

My other devoted readers have been, as always, my wife, Maria, and my daughter, Lizzie. They wanted me to write this book, and so here it is, with love.

Others have been generous with their support. Andy Hughes, head of design and production at the Knopf Doubleday Publishing Group, old friend and colleague, but first and foremost, to those who know him, a truly noble character. His help has been essential, and given quietly and profusely. At Photofest, Howard and Ron Mandelbaum and their colleagues acted, as they always do, not just with unwavering efficiency but with warmth and generosity. They're a pleasure to do business with. To the photographers who contributed pictures, including my beloved friend Richard Overstreet, heartfelt thanks. (Jill Krementz, in particular, had to put up with my constantly changing requests and requirements.)

Thanks, too, to Bruce Diones at *The New Yorker,* Jonathan Karp at Simon and Schuster, and Chip McGrath; to Justin Cooper for sternly vetting my Clinton memories; to Kathy Hourigan for a lifetime of practical support and unswerving affection; and to a few of the many people close to both Deborah Rogers and me: her protégé and colleague David Miller; her partner and dear friend (and mine) Pat White; her husband, Michael Berkeley; and Sue Rogers Bond, her sister and my great pal.

And my gratitude to all those friends, colleagues, and acquaintances, too many to single out, who listened, answered questions, and buoyed my confidence.

INDEX

CPSIA information can be obtained
at www.ICGtesting.com
Printed in the USA
BVHW041052100723
666910BV00011B/53